DAILY
Register,

By His Majesty's Patent.

[Price Two-pence Halfpenny.

THE TIMES

NO. 56,621
PRICE 9D.
ROYAL EDITION

THE   TIMES

OR·DAILY·UNIVERSAL·REGISTER

PRINTED   LOGOGRAPHICALLY

SATURDAY, JANUARY 19, 1788.

PRICE ( ) 4d.

TIMES

LONDON MONDAY OCTOBER 3 1932   PRICE ( ) 4d

THE STORY
of
THE TIMES

THE STORY
OF
THE TIMES

OLIVER WOODS

and

JAMES BISHOP

LONDON
MICHAEL JOSEPH

First published in Great Britain by
MICHAEL JOSEPH LIMITED
44 Bedford Square
London WC1
1983

ISBN 0 7181 1462 0

Printed in Great Britain by New Western Printing Ltd
and bound by Dorstel Press, Harlow

CONTENTS

ILLUSTRATIONS

Erratum

The caption to the photo of Denis Hamilton in
the section following page 288 should have read:
Sir Denis Hamilton, Editor-in-Chief of
Times Newspapers, 1967-81

PREFACE

Oliver Woods began preparing this book in 1970, when he retired after thirty-six years on the editorial staff of *The Times*. He was for many years the paper's Colonial Editor and Deputy Foreign Editor, and in 1961 took over responsibility for the paper's home news as an Assistant Editor. Throughout his career he was a dedicated *Times* man, sharing those ideals for the paper which, as will I hope become apparent from this book, have been held by many of the men and women who have worked for *The Times* and have, over nearly two hundred years, established its unique character and reputation. Oliver died suddenly in 1972 before he finished the book, but with the exception of the final chapters he had virtually completed a draft, and *The Story of The Times* remains very much his book. After his death his widow Joan and many friends and former colleagues worked on the book in the hope of completing it for publication.

For a variety of reasons the possibility of publication did not arise for some years, until the project was revived some eighteen months ago. I was asked to edit the book and add a couple of chapters to bring the story up to date. For a number of years I had worked closely with Oliver, serving as his assistant in the foreign department of *The Times*. A young journalist could not have had a more sympathetic mentor, and I hope that, in completing his book, I have in some measure repaid the debt I owe him.

Although the book was originally commissioned by Sir Denis Hamilton when he was Editor-in-Chief and Chief Executive of *The Times* it is not an official history, and *The Times* is not to be held responsible for the interpretations of its history that appear in these pages. There is a four-volume official history already in existence, covering the paper's history up to the Second World War and this, together with *The Times* archives which were made available up to this period, has been a prime source, although new material has been unearthed, some errors of omission and commission rectified, and not all the judgments of the official work have been accepted. For the later period the main sources have been the memories and accounts of many of those who took part in the events described, though only I can be held responsible for what has been written.

Among those consulted and who have helped at one stage or another in the completion of the manuscript were Lord Astor of Hever, Hugh Astor, David Ayerst, Asa Briggs, Arthur Cook, David Daiches, Reginald Easthope, Jack Fletcher, Roger Fulford, E. C. Hodgkin, Owen Hickey, Jacqueline Hope-Wallace, Derek Hudson, Duke Hussey, Enid Knowles, Sir Alan Lascelles, Jack Lonsdale, Iverach McDonald, W. Macleod, Michael Mander, J. S. Maywood, Barbara Miller, Pamela Nichols, Gerald Norman, Gordon Phillips, Anne Piggott, Lord Redcliffe-Maud, Sir William Rees-Mogg, Josanna Robson, A. P. Ryan, Sir Campbell Stuart, Anthony Thorlby, C. V. Wedgwood, Sir Dick White, Colin Wilson, Douglas Woodruff. There may be others whom Oliver consulted; if there were, I hope they will forgive my ignorance and thus my failure to acknowledge their contribution. To the names listed I must, add those of Michael Joseph Ltd, who saw the book through to publication, of Denis Hamilton, for his inspiration, and of Joan Woods, for her unfailing kindness, support, and determination. It is to Joan that this book is dedicated.

James Bishop
London, April 1983

1 THE FOUNDING OF *THE TIMES*

(i) Mr Walter's New Plan

In March 1784 Mr John Walter, founder of *The Times*, took possession of the old King's Printing House in Blackfriars, situated between St Paul's and the River Thames.

The house purchased by Mr Walter was a two-storied, redbrick building standing in a small court then called Printing House Yard, a name which John Walter soon altered to the more fashionable 'Square'. Over the main door, facing south, was a pediment bearing the Royal Arms, still quartering the arms of France and Hanover, which were later to be used in the masthead of *The Times* newspaper. The printing house had replaced the earlier one destroyed by fire in 1737, and was empty at the time of purchase. Parts of it were still standing in 1960. They were demolished, together with the nineteenth-century offices of *The Times*, to make way for the present modern block which covers the Printing House Square site.

John Walter was a man of courage and enterprise who had his ups and downs in life. Starting out in the coal trade, he switched to underwriting colliers, and later to general shipping. 'The coal trade,' remarked Mr Micawber to David Copperfield, 'may require talent, it certainly requires capital. Talent Mr Micawber has, capital Mr Micawber has not.' John Walter had some talent and some capital, but by 1784 his venture into the insurance world had rendered him bankrupt. 'I was twelve years an underwriter in Lloyd's Coffee House, and subscribed my name to six millions of property,' he wrote to Lord Kenyon in 1799, 'but was weighed down, in common with above half those who were engaged in the protection of property, by the host of foes this nation had to combat in the American wars.' He was referring of course to the destruction of shipping by privateers. 'Judge what must be my sensations on this trying occasion,' wrote the founding father of *The Times*. 'Twenty-six years in the prime of life passed away, all the fortune I had acquired by a studious attention to business sunk by hasty strides, and the world to begin afresh, with the daily introduction to my view of a wife and six children, unprovided for and depending on me for support.'

Yet he was evidently liked and respected by his creditors, for they did not press him hard. Nor did they regret their leniency, for at last John Walter's enterprise stood him in good stead. He became interested in a new method of printing, logography, and with what he saved from the wreckage, and with the help of others, he was able by 1790 to clear most of his liabilities. A portrait of John Walter I, painted at the turning-point of his life when he started in the printing industry, shows a face judgmatical, philosophical and courageous, without a trace of bitterness or defeat, despite the catastrophe which had overtaken him in middle age. There is no evidence of any special motive, other than economic necessity and chance, that directed Walter's interest into the printing industry.

There was, and is, no craft more conservative than printing. The techniques available in John Walter's day differed little from those invented by Gutenberg in 1440 and introduced by Caxton to England thirty-six years later. Type could only be set by the printer picking individual letters out of a box and setting them in line. By the late eighteenth century the needs of commerce were demanding faster processes. To meet them, a printer called Henry Johnson had invented a system of setting groups of figures in one block which he called logography and used for the printing of lottery numbers. This invention it was that Walter purchased and converted to the use of letters, setting whole words and syllables in blocks together so that they could be more rapidly assembled for printing than by the old-fashioned method of picking out each letter separately. Although logography was to prove inadequate for the printing of a daily newspaper, it was from this early experiment that the Walters were to develop into the greatest innovators in printing since Gutenberg.

John Walter started by publishing books and pamphlets, and was given encouragement by Benjamin Franklin, at that time American Minister in Paris, who kept a private printing press at Passy. To Walter he wrote of a '*Nouveau Système typographique, ou moyen de diminuer de moitié . . . le travail et les Frais de composition et correction et de distribution,*' which had been discovered in France ten years before. In 1785 Franklin lent his name to the list of original subscribers to the Logographic Press. This patronage may account for the refusal of that of royalty, which is hardly to be wondered at considering that one of Franklin's duties in Paris had been to commission those very privateers which had been the cause of Walter's original bankruptcy. It was to Benjamin Franklin that Walter wrote, in May 1784, 'I am going to publish a newspaper by my Plan'. On 1 January 1785, the first copy of the *Daily Universal Register* appeared. Three years later Walter abbreviated the name to *The Times*.

Although he did not know it, John Walter had chosen a most propitious time to start a newspaper. Towards the end of the eighteenth century all the factors necessary for the development of modern journalism were beginning to emerge and conjoin.

The great development of commerce, particularly in the City and Port of London, had established a larger pool of wealth from which both readership and advertising revenue could be drawn. Improvement in communications facilitated distribution, and an important contributing factor to the success of *The Times* was the advent of John Palmer to the Post Office as Controller-General in 1786. He had already done much to speed up the mails through a plan submitted four years earlier which had been backed by Pitt.

The Post Office was directly concerned in newspaper distribution. The press and the postmasters had been closely associated since the early seventeenth century not only in England, but on the Continent too. In the eighteenth century the Post Office undertook bulk distribution of newspapers outside London. After leaving the printing office, they were delivered to the six 'Clerks of the Roads' who sorted out the mails and dispatched them along the six main arteries leading out of the City.

John Palmer started life as a theatre manager in Bath. It is noteworthy that he was one of the original subscribers to the Logographic Press and that he received steady editorial support from Walter's *Daily Universal Register*. Like all reformers he needed it, for he faced much opposition from Post Office officials and from the Postmaster-General who resented his intrusions.

At this time the mails were carried by post-boys on poor quality nags, and the rate of loss by highway robbery was steadily mounting. Palmer transferred them to fast mail coaches and saw that these were armed. The mail coaches were punctual and virtually inviolable. Palmer saw that as the Post Office received a fat revenue from the Stamp Duty on newspapers it paid them to co-operate with publishers in increasing their circulations. That he was successful is suggested by these figures: in 1764, under the old system, the number of newspapers sent through the post was only 3,160; by 1790, after Palmer's reforms and just five years after Walter had started his newspaper, circulation in the provinces had climbed to 12,600.

Walter and Palmer had their quarrels. One cause was the persistent late arrival of newspapers at the Post Office, which delayed the departure of coaches. Another was that the bundles arrived 'in so wet a state as to deface the directions of many of the letters which went in the same bags'. To obviate this, Palmer in 1787 set up a separate newspaper office to handle this side of the Post Office business. The Post Office, in effect, took over the whole of what would now be described as the wholesale and retail distribution of newspapers in the countryside.

Within London, newspapers in the eighteenth century were distributed by hawkers. These had recognized 'beats', as is shown by advertisements, such as this in *The Times* of 15 April 1792:

An old established NEWS WALK to be disposed of that brings
in £1 12s per week clear profit; situate in the best part of London, and capable, with care and assiduity, of great improvement:
such an opportunity seldom offers for an industrious person.
Enquire tomorrow at No. 14 Portugal Street, Lincoln's-Inn-
Fields.

The hawkers not only sold papers on the 'walk'. They carried them
round in bundles to booksellers, coffee houses, and the Post Office.

Wars have generally been great promoters of newspaper sales. The
early history of *The Times* provides another example of this rule. Had
Walter not started his paper at a time when a great Continental war
was about to break out, it is possible that he might not have succeeded
in establishing it as he did. By the end of the century, from small beginnings, *The Times* had achieved circulations of 4,800 at peak. This
was in large part due to public eagerness for war news.

In all this tally of developments which favoured Walter's enterprise
nothing has been said of improvements in printing. The reason is that
there had been none. It is a curious reflection on the laws of technological progress that, of the two epoch-making technological discoveries
of the Renaissance, the gun and the printing press, their history was so
different. Throughout the sixteenth, seventeenth and eighteenth centuries artillery had constantly improved in accuracy, mobility, and in
methods of mass production, but printing had remained static. No
doubt soldiers, who paid heavier penalties for professional failure than
printers, were under greater pressure to innovate.

For typography and lay-out, Walter made extensive borrowings from
John Bell, founder of the *Morning Post* and the *World*, who was the
first to adapt types and display to the especial needs of newspapers.
S. H. Steinberg has described Bell as 'the godfather, however unwilling,
of what was to become the greatest newspaper in the world'.* John
Walter was at least a good borrower, for the first number of the *Daily
Universal Register* was a handsome production. But for innovations in
printing, John Walter had to rely on himself and no one else.

(ii) *A Foreign Service*

In its earliest issues *The Times* was probably most appreciated for its
financial and commercial news; but the section of the paper which was
destined first to mark it out from its contemporaries, and make it
almost a necessity for any man in public position to read, was the
foreign news.

Here the Post Office again comes into the picture. The appetite for
'foreign intelligence', especially after the French Revolution, was vora-

* S. H. Steinberg: *Five Hundred Years of Printing*, Penguin, 1955.

cious. The principal means of satisfying it was through the importation
of foreign journals, which were used as a basis for their own news
services by the English papers. In transmitting them, however, the Post
Office was not content with acting merely as a post-box. Their officials
translated them, summarized them, and made excerpts. All this caused
delay. The Post Office was in fact acting as a self-appointed news
agency. The English newspapers were charged at least a hundred
guineas a year each for these services.

The system, of course, gave every sort of opportunity for favouritism,
corruption and for bringing pressure to bear on editors whose writings
displeased Ministers. *The Times* and a thrice-weekly paper, the *Evening Mail*, which Walter was then running as well, were originally given
preferential treatment. But Charles Stuart, who was employed by the
Government as a kind of public relations officer – a 'press engineer', as
he himself described it – advised against this. 'I am afraid,' he wrote,
'that government are proceeding on a wrong plan. They do not consider that by monopolizing Intelligence to a Morning and an Evening
paper, they render the other papers hostile.'

Mr Stuart may not have been entirely disinterested. His brother owned
the *Morning Post*. No doubt his advice was sensible, but in 1792 the
Government interpreted it by transferring their favours to John Heriot,
owner of the *Sun* and the *True Briton*. The reaction from Printing
House Square was instantaneous.

> I have just had a visit [wrote Bland Burges, an Under-Secretary
> at the Foreign Office to Charles Long, Joint Secretary at the
> Treasury] from young Walter, who is furious about the success
> of the *Sun* and came to me, as to an impartial person, to complain of the partiality shown by government and especially by
> Mr Rose [another Joint Secretary at the Treasury] to that paper,
> which he said was very unjust considering his long services and
> the many advantages which government, and especially Rose,
> had derived from *The Times* . . . He was very sulky and impudent.

Later 'young Walter' – in fact John Walter's eldest and rather ineffectual son William – wrote to the Home Secretary:

> It is notorious, and I could prove the fact, that scarce a Dispatch
> comes from the Armies, or is there a Paris Journal forwarded to
> any of the Public Offices, but what is immediately transmitted to
> the *Sun* Office. This system is now become so general, that I
> foresee my property in particular must suffer, if it continues.

Both sides in the conflict between Britain and France understood
only too well the necessity for 'press engineering'. 'The truth is,' wrote

Charles Stuart, 'everything is to be managed, by managing the press. The artillery of the French could not be managed a month without they managed the artillery of the press ... When I hear of the French casting *cannon*, I think nothing of that at all, provided you can only prevent them from casting *types*.' Napoleon put it much the same way. 'Three hostile newspapers are more to be feared than a thousand bayonets.'

Chauvelin, a name familiar to readers of *The Scarlet Pimpernel*, was busy bribing English newspaper owners, though here the hands of the Walters were very clean. Their paymasters then 'were still at least their countrymen'. The newspapers accused, probably with justification, of accepting money from the French were the *Morning Chronicle* and the *Argus*.

The Times won its case against the Post Office and was eventually restored to favour. But John Walter drew the lesson. The incident was one of the considerations which determined him to free *The Times* from dependence on government for foreign news by setting up a foreign news service of his own. In 1792, recognizing that 'continental affairs are so engrossing', *The Times* announced:

> We have established a new correspondence both at Brussels and Paris, which we trust will furnish us with the most regular and early intelligence that can possibly be obtained. Our communications will not be confined to the ordinary conveyance by the Foreign Mails only, as we have taken such measures as will enable us to receive Letters from abroad on those days when the Foreign Mails do not become due.

A foreign sub-editor, or the equivalent, was advertised for to handle the incoming news:

> Wanted immediately, a Gentleman who is capable of translating the French language. In order to prevent trouble, he must be a perfect Master of the English language, have some knowledge of the Political State of Europe and be thoroughly capable of the situation he undertakes. His employment will be permanent and take up a considerable share of his attention; for which a handsome salary will be allowed.

Thus began what was to be, for more than a century, the most famous foreign news service ever organized by an individual newspaper. The new organization soon made its mark. On 3 August 1792 it scooped its competitors over an important anti-revolutionary declaration by the Duke of Brunswick. Letters dispatched from Brussels on the Saturday reached Printing House Square on Monday evening. The service was immensely expensive and subject to every sort of interruption, even with 'Agents at the out-ports to forward our letters'. When Napoleon's blockade was declared *The Times* employed professional smugglers to bring news across the Channel. *The Times* had the satisfaction of so much reversing the situation with the Post Office that twenty years later the Foreign Secretary [Lord Castlereagh] was forced to inquire, 'Will Mr Walter have the goodness to tell him if he has received any Intelligence of the reported defeat of the French near Dresden.'

(iii) Crabb Robinson

The first foreign staff correspondent of *The Times* was not appointed until 1807. He was Henry Crabb Robinson, who has a good claim, also, to have anticipated William Howard Russell by being the first war correspondent ever appointed by a newspaper. 'Old Crabby' was one of those sociable, gossipy, itinerant Englishmen who have done so much to illuminate the history of the period. He was educated at Jena University and had the knack of getting to know most of the important people in any country he happened to be in. A perennial bachelor, Robinson lived to be ninety-one. He had a great influence on the writers of his time, simply as a personality whose opinions they respected. His own description of himself was a 'busy idle man'. In his *Diary, Reminiscences and Correspondence* he has left voluminous evidence of his life, including his experiences as *The Times* correspondent during the Napoleonic Wars.

The first place in which he represented the paper was Altona, the capital of Holstein, on the Danish border. From that distant vantage point (date-lined 'From the banks of the Elbe') he reported the fall of Danzig, the battle of Friedland at which the Russians were defeated at such shocking cost to the French, and the Treaty of Tilsit.

Robinson had plenty of difficulties and adventures. When, in July, Lord Cathcart landed 20,000 men in Zeeland the Bürgermeister of Altona was ordered to arrest all Englishmen. Robinson's friends gave him a quick warning, and persuaded him not to sleep at home that night. He spent the small hours going the rounds to pass the word on to all other Englishmen in the town. The police called at his lodging but found him flown. Next day his protectors hit upon the ingenious plan of smuggling him into Hamburg by boat, in the guise of family tutor. Several of his Holstein acquaintances clubbed together to supply children for the expedition in order to lend verisimilitude to the deception. The ruse was successful. The whole party set off down the river in high spirits, dodging a police boat on the way.

In Hamburg Robinson was not much better off. The French had recently marched in. He had to continue in hiding. One day he was returning from a walk when he luckily spotted two French 'gens-d'armes' lolling by the side of a passage, within sight of his door. 'In an instant

I was off. I ran into a market-place full of people, and was not pursued. If I had been, I have no doubt the populace would have aided my escape.' During this period he was not filing for *The Times*, though he did manage to get a letter through to John Dyas Collier, assistant to John Walter.

Robinson's rooms were broken into by the French, but meanwhile he had escaped, disguised as a clerk, to Dobberan, a watering-place on the Baltic. From there he could see British men-of-war on the horizon – this was before the Battle of Copenhagen. After trying unsuccessfully to pass himself off as a German (his accent was atrocious), Robinson eventually escaped to England by boat via Sweden, and nine months later was sent to Spain by *The Times* to cover Sir John Moore's disastrous Corunna campaign.

Robinson landed at Corunna on 31 July 1808. He put himself 'in immediate connection with the editor of the miserable little daily newspaper, and from him I obtained Madrid papers and pamphlets'. It was his business to send back messages by every ship that left for England, and he did indeed use the date-line 'Shores of the Bay of Biscay'.

From here he was able to report the arrival of the second wave of the British expeditionary force, commanded by Sir David Baird:

'In the morning, when I was over my books, I was startled by the report of cannon, and, running to the ramparts, beheld more than 150 vessels, transports, sailing in a double row before a gentle breeze. It was a striking spectacle, and I felt proud of it.' He reported also the arrival of the Spanish national hero, General Romana: 'On beholding the hero, my enthusiasm subsided. Romana looked, in my eyes, like a Spanish barber.'

Robinson's dispatches faintly prelude those of William Howard Russell in the Crimea half a century later:

> The utter want of all preparations for promoting the march of that army was seen with deep affliction by both British and Spaniards. No man pretends to fix the culpability upon any one; they can only judge of those who are privy to the negotiations which preceded the expedition. The sad effect, however, is very obvious.

He reported great waste and mismanagement, amounting to dishonesty, in the 'economical department of our campaign.' One of the Commissariat came to him 'in great glee' because he had put £50 in his pocket. On Robinson's expressing surprise, he said 'Oh, it is always done in all purchases.'

Robinson gave an off-stage report of the battle which has become famous for the death and burial of the British commander, Sir John

Moore. On 8 January 1809, he wrote from within sound, rather than within sight, of the guns:

'Our streets swarm, as a few weeks since, with English officers; but the gaiety and splendour which graced their first entrance into Spain have given way to a mien and air certainly more congenial with the horrid business of war.' Three days later: 'In the course of this day the whole English army has either entered within, or planted itself before, the walls of this town ... The late arrivals have, of course, made us far better acquainted than we possibly could be before with the circumstances of this laborious and dishonourable campaign, which has had all the suffering, without any of the honours of war.' On the following day: 'An alarming symptom is the extreme scarcity of every kind of provisions. The shops are shut – the markets are abandoned.'

Then, on 15 January:

> The last two days have materially changed the appearance of things. Yesterday evening, the fleet of transports, which had been dispersed in their passage from Vigo, began to enter the harbour, and the hearts of thousands were relieved by the prospect of deliverance. I beheld this evening the beautiful bay covered with our vessels, both armed and mercantile, and I should have thought the noble three-deckers, which stood on the outside of the harbour, a proud spectacle, if I could have forgotten the inglorious service they were called to perform.

On the last evening, he was dining at his hotel, when he suddenly noticed all the officers had left the dining room – 'not a red-coat to be seen'. This was the final battle. Robinson went aboard his vessel. The last sounds he heard were a rattle of musketry. It was the cavalry shooting their horses before embarking. Then the noise of the powder magazine being blown up – 'when the cloud of smoke which had been raised was blown away, there was empty space where there had been a solid building a few moments before: but this was a less exciting noise than when, about one o'clock, we heard a cannonading from the shore at the inland extremity of the bay. It was the French army.'

Thus *The Times* was able to furnish an eye-witness account of an early Dunkirk.

(iv) Budget

John Walter, in the leader appearing on the front page of the first issue of his paper, was frank about its objectives, which were defined as:

> To facilitate the *commercial* intercourse between the different parts of the community, through the channel of *Advertisements*; to record the principal occurrences of the times; and to bridge the account of debates during the sitting of Parliament.

Few newspaper proprietors today would have the effrontery to acknowledge advertising as the principal aim of publishing their paper, and to
italicize it, too.

How successful was Walter, in fact, in making his paper pay? One of
the difficulties in working out a balance sheet is that so little is known
about advertising revenue. *The Times* allotted rather over half of its
four pages to advertising. The front page contained theatre notices and
notices of other entertainments, publishers' announcements, shipping
and commercial advertisements, and government notices, all paid for.
The back page included notices of sales and auctions, property, and
horses and carriages. The theatre 'bills' were soon transferred to the
centre page, because of their late arrival. This page came to be known
as the Bill Page, right up to the time of the transfer of news to the
front page in 1966.

The practice was to fill up space with free advertisements, as an encouragement, if paid ones fell short. Items were sent in either direct,
or to such agents as: 'Mr Searle's No. 55 Oxford Street; Mr Thrale's
opposite the Admiralty; Mr Wilson's No. 45 Lombard Street; Mr Pratt's
No. 84 Wapping; and Mr Sterney's No. 156 opposite St George's
Church, Southwark.'

Advertising rates, whether of *The Times* or of its rivals, are not easy
to determine precisely. The minimum for the *Advertizer* in 1730 was
2s 0d. The *Public Ledger* charged 3s 0d in 1767 for 'every advertisement of a moderate length' – probably eighteen lines. In 1786 they
charged 3s 6d for eighteen lines, with a surcharge of 2s 0d for the front
page. The tax was 2s 6d (3s 0d after 1789) on each advertisement
regardless of length. Of *The Times*, John Walter wrote to an inquirer
in 1792:

> For long advertisements we charge a small matter more than our
> Contemporaries, short ones only the same price, and the good
> sense of those who advertise will readily admit a small advance,
> when *The Times*, we are well assured, is higher in number than
> any other Morning Print.

The Times, in other words, was even then chasing circulation to
attract advertising revenue. The relationship between sales and advertising rates was well understood. 'Some agents,' continued Mr Walter
disapprovingly, 'will resort to Papers low in sale, to get [advertise-
ments] inserted cheaper, but their Principals will best judge whether
their interests are consulted, as the more their intentions are circulated
the better their end is obtained.' On these calculations, gross advertising
revenue before tax may have been about £5,000 a year. As most of
the advertisements were small, the tax on this may have been as much
as half the total.

Revenue from sales is easier to assess. The cover price of *The Times* in the eighteenth century was:

From January 1785 – 2½d
From April 1785 – 3d
1789 – 4d
1794 – 4½d
1797 – 6d

The 1789 and 1797 increases were due to a rise in the stamp duty (from 1½d to 2d and from 2d to 3½d). Th 1794 increase was due to higher wages and other costs.

It has to be remembered that the Post Office carried newspapers free of charge, so that there was some return for the tax. Hawkers received a commission of 1d on each copy and were allowed two papers in every quire – twenty-six for twenty-four.

In December 1792 audited figures were issued for daily sales of *The Times* over a three-week period. They ranged from 2,810 to 3,131 (the latter on a Saturday), and a year later an average circulation of nearly 4,000 was claimed – 'a number which was never before attained by any Morning Paper under any circumstances.' But this was exceptional, and John Walter put the daily average sale for the whole of 1794 at only half that figure.

Sales revenue was a pretty steady item, but less is known about income derived 'under the counter'. The sole exception is the sub-vention from government, which is recorded in the secret service records. About nine papers received regular annual sums – *The Times*, £300. But this was not all profit, since after receiving it Walter complained that he had forfeited in consequence 'all the advertisements and civilities of Opposition'. The subventions to *The Times* ceased suddenly, and without clear explanation, in 1799.

Revenue from theatrical 'puffs' is impossible to estimate. 'There is,' wrote Cobbett, 'and always has been in this country a natural alliance, a sort of family compact between the press and the theatre.' The compact was three-way. The theatre was allowed to insert advertisements at reduced rates, the newspapers actually paying the managements for advance information about forthcoming productions. And dramatic criticism occupied a prominent part in the centre of most newspapers. But it was not unrewarded criticism. The newspapers were paid for 'puffs', though how much, in the case of *The Times* at any rate, is not known.

As for suppression fees, there are no records of prices paid to *The Times*. Mrs Fitzherbert, the Regent's morganatic wife, objected to some paragraphs and sent her brother to threaten Walter. Mrs Sumbel, who relates this story, was the ex-mistress of Captain Topham, who started the *World*, at one time a rival of *The Times*. She claims too that her own husband summoned the then 'Editor' of *The Times*, William Finey, and complained about items relating to herself. 'Will that be enough?' asked Mr Sumbel, pulling some notes out of his *escritoire*. 'Give me a few more,' replied Mr Finey, 'and by St Patrick I will knock out the brains of anyone in our office who dare ever *whisper* your name.'* But she does not say how many notes her husband paid over.

On the expenditure side of the balance sheet, paper probably cost about £1,300 for the year and the wages of the mechanical staff £1,800. Stamp duty, at 2d a copy, would come to over £5,000 a year – the highest single item. There are no means of reckoning how much was spent on editorial or communications, but it is known that, in spite of the struggle, *The Times* in these early years was usually in profit.

(v) *John Walter's Libel Case*

John Walter's relationship with government involved him in one traumatic experience which coloured the last twenty years of his life. It may well have been the memory of his father's experience which later determined his son, John Walter II, to rid himself and *The Times* of government shackles.

The subvention of £300 a year which John Walter received from the Government dated from 1789. He had also secured the appointment of Printer to HM Customs. The services which he was expected to render in return were to give the Government general support in the columns of his paper and, more specifically, to insert certain paragraphs which were supplied to him bearing a distinguishing mark on the paper which indicated their source. In order to understand how it was that John Walter got into trouble it is necessary to take a brief look at the political situation at the time.

When John Walter went into printing and journalism, the Younger Pitt, protégé of George III and ally of the Tories, had recently become Prime Minister, and his position in the country had been strengthened by the general election of April 1784. But his survival in office depended on the health of the King, for it was generally assumed that, should the King's recurrent bouts of insanity make him incapable of ruling, the Prince of Wales would become Regent, dismiss Pitt, and ask Fox to form a Ministry. These were years of great anxiety for the Government, but in February 1789 the King was officially pronounced sane and restored to health. There were public rejoicings.

John Walter inserted in *The Times* of 21 February two paragraphs which had been supplied to him, in accordance with the agreement, by Mr Steele, Secretary of the Treasury. They were 'signed with his private

---

* *Memoirs of the Life of Mrs Sumbel, late Wells*, London, 1811.

Mark'. One of them appears to have been drafted by the same Mr Heriot who was later to become owner of the *Sun* and supplant Mr Walter in government favour.

> The Royal Dukes, and the leaders of opposition in general, affect to join with the friends of our amiable Sovereign, in rejoicing on account of His Majesty's recovery. But the insincerity of their joy is visible. Their late unfeeling conduct will forever tell against them; and contradict the artful professions they may think it prudent to make.
>
> It argues infinite wisdom in certain persons, to have prevented the Duke of York from rushing into the King's apartment on Wednesday. The rashness, the Germanick severity, and the insensibility of this young man, might have proved ruinous to the hopes and joys of a whole nation.

A few days later a similar paragraph was published which criticized the Prince of Wales.

Both Princes proceeded against John Walter, and the case is of some interest to lawyers and journalists because of its bearing on the responsibility for libels in newspapers. Walter was prosecuted in his capacity as a bookseller. He pleaded guilty, but put in a written statement as a plea of extenuation. The plea was that as proprietor he was unable to control every detail that went into his newspaper. The haste inseparable from its production had induced unwitting error. Both Mr Justice Ashurst and Sir Thomas Erskine, the prosecuting counsel, were scathing about this defence, Erskine remarking that 'if he had sworn that he was misled to insert this unprincipled and infamous calumny, the Court must have sent him to Bedlam instead of a prison'.

Walter refused to give away his sources. In this he was establishing a sturdy journalistic tradition, though the effect was somewhat lessened because many people must have guessed what those sources were. Walter also assumed, wrongly, that powerful patrons would help and recompense him.

The sentence was swingeing. On the first libel he was fined £50, sent to Newgate for a year, sentenced to stand in the pillory at Charing Cross for an hour and ordered to give security for good behaviour for seven years. As soon as he had served his term, he started on another twelve-month sentence for the libel on the Prince of Wales.

The pillory was remitted, but for sixteen months Walter was confined in Newgate. His letters to ministers asking them to help him out of the plight they had got him into describe the conditions in gaol:

> Though I am confined to what is called the State side, and, paying for a room, have one to myself, the same entrance leads

likewise to the felons and whenever any are brought into the jail, the outward door is shut and they are fettered in the common passage, so that it discourages my friends from access – such is the audacity of the turnkeys that they will frequently keep them and those who bring my provisions an hour at the door, even when they are lolling in their chairs in an adjoining room . . .

Representations were made to the Prince of Wales on Walter's behalf by his family and friends, drawing attention to the ignominy of his position, the financial straits to which he was reduced and his physical ill health; it was finally through the intercession of the Prince, not the Government, that he was released. The latter gave him £250 as compensation for his sufferings on their behalf.

Considerable controversy exists over who actually edited *The Times* in these early days. Walter was known according to contemporary custom as the Conductor. This appointment corresponds with the present American appellation of Publisher. William Finey, already described in the incident over Mrs Sumbel, was Editor in 1797. He may have held that appointment since 1788, when the *Daily Universal Register* changed its title. In the earliest years, Walter probably edited the paper himself in conjunction with a Dr John Trusler, described in the *Dictionary of National Biography* as 'an eccentric divine', and William Combe.

William Combe is a shadowy figure who flits in and out of Printing House Square throughout most of this period. He was a seedy Etonian, whose career is hard to authenticate because he was such a congenital liar. He was an acquaintance, if not a friend, of that same John Palmer, the Controller-General of the Post Office, who did so much to facilitate the distribution of newspapers when the *Daily Universal Register* was starting. The acquaintanceship, characteristically in Combe's case, was founded on the relationship of creditor and debtor. Palmer had him imprisoned for debt and subsequently arranged his release.

Professor Harlan W. Hamilton expresses the belief in his book *Dr Syntax* that it was Palmer who first introduced William Combe to Walter and that the whole transaction was prompted by Palmer's need to secure editorial backing for his reforms, when they were being obstructed by officials within the Post Office. Combe, who is best known as the collaborator with Rowlandson in *The Tours of Doctor Syntax*, was an acquisition to Walter. He was the best hack journalist of his day. If he was not officially styled Editor he was certainly the *de facto* Managing Editor in the early years of the nineteenth century when John Walter's son was actually controlling the paper.

Crabb Robinson, who was officially nominated Editor in 1808–9, wrote of him in retrospect:

It was on my first acquaintance with Walter that I used to notice in his parlour a remarkably fine old gentleman. He was tall with a stately figure and handsome face. He did not appear to work much with the pen but was chiefly a consulting man. When Walter was away he used to be more at the office and to decide in the *dernier ressort*.*

The probability is, therefore, that Combe was the dominating member of the editorial staff under the Walters in the decade ending in 1807. Combe conducted his business for most of this time under a somewhat disconcerting handicap. In 1799, not for the first time, he was arrested for debt, and spent the rest of his life either in prison or 'within the rules' of the King's Bench, a condition which, however, did not prevent his working for *The Times*. 'Living within the rules' allowed him to reside, nominally, in a lodging house in Lambeth, near the prison. The prisoners were supposed to be confined to a given area, but the tipstaffs were lax and it was comparatively easy to leave this area, especially at night. This suited Combe, since his work at Printing House Square was conducted during the night hours.

He also managed regularly to visit a young girl at Camberwell, to whom he wrote letters which were published after his death. To her he describes his return to Lambeth from work at Printing House Square. 'I repassed the bridge this morning as St Paul's struck three; and in all my pilgrimages over those arches I never experienced such an inhospitable passage – rain, storm, and cold! The very lamps were generally extinguished, and I had no light either from heaven or earth.' In this passage he speaks for generations of journalists making their way home after the 'late turn' in Printing House Square.

Eventually the tipstaffs caught up with him. His violations of the rules were too blatant. He was clapped back into the King's Bench Prison and had to resign from *The Times*.

My dear Sir [he wrote to John Walter from King's Bench], it will astonish you for I am sure it has astonished myself that I am at this moment an Inhabitant of this place and that instead of the pleasure of attending you last night, I had the very great displeasure of being conducted here. I was liable to it, but having escaped for five years I thought myself safe from any inconvenience . . . I need not add that it will be necessary for us to meet.

Dishonest, pretentious, pathetic, Combe was nonetheless a dedicated journalist. It is comforting to think that while in prison, and getting on

* *Diary, Reminiscences and Correspondence of Henry Crabb Robinson*, edited by Thomas Sadler, 1869.

for seventy, he was working on *The Tour of Doctor Syntax in Search of the Picturesque*, which was to give him a posthumous immortality.

By the end of the eighteenth century *The Times* was at a low ebb. The Conductor had been in prison and barely escaped the pillory. The Managing Editor, such as he was, lived as a prisoner on parole. Under the management of John Walter's elder son, William, the profits were shrinking. Yet the foundations of a good newspaper were being laid, and if the prospects from Printing House Square looked gloomy, the days of achievement were about to begin.

2 THE FORMATIVE YEARS

(i) A Paper for 'The Middle Orders'
The years 1800 to 1840 were the great formative years of *The Times* and for the achievements of these years, as in all success stories, due credit should be accorded to the man at the top.

John Walter II, the second son of John Walter I, was born in 1776 and at the age of twenty-one became an equal partner with his father in 'the Trade, Art, Mystery or Business of Printers'. In January 1803, when it had become plain to all that his elder brother William was not suited to be either the editor or the manager of a newspaper, he was given sole charge of all activities at Printing House Square. The paper for which he thus became responsible was in a sorry state. Circulation had sunk well below the 2,000 mark, and *The Times* might easily have vanished from the scene. Instead, John Walter II was to promote the paper from the position of *primus inter pares* to that of *facile princeps*.

The second Walter was as different from his father as was nineteenth-century man from eighteenth-century man. Each was typical of his age. John Walter I was staunch, buoyant, enterprising, and a fair example of the rising commercial classes of the period. Although his business standards were sound, he shared its easy-going concepts of probity. Nevertheless, he and his like laid the trail for the economic expansion of the nineteenth century.

John Walter II was modest, a hard worker, and hard on those who worked for him. Integrity, respectability, gentility – these were the guiding lights of his life, as they were of so many of his generation and class. Father and son, for all their differences of temperament and thought, seem to have worked reasonably well together until a year or two before the father's death in 1812. But the son's friends did not mince matters in discussing 'the old man'. 'As dishonest – worthless a man as I have ever known,' declared Crabb Robinson, while William Combe accused him of making his money through extortion and calumny.

Whatever the reason may have been, John Walter I left a will which at the time was considered unfair to his successor, and which – far more serious – contained seeds of discord which a hundred years later were to threaten the survival of *The Times*. The newspaper and the printing business had already been separated. John Walter I made over to his son in his lifetime the printing business, with which went the freehold of Printing House Square absolutely, but he left his son in a strange position over the newspaper. He was responsible for its management and was to be paid £1,000 a year on a sliding scale so long as it was profitable. If it were not, his salary was to be reduced proportionately. But he only had three-sixteenths of the share interest, with the prospect of acquiring three more sixteenths by purchase and reversion. He and his successors were therefore liable to be faced with a 'palace revolution' of the other shareholders if these did not agree with their policies.

Although John Walter I did have trouble with individual shareholders, who were mostly members of the Walter family and their in-laws, he never suffered serious opposition. In a way he aggravated the situation for his descendants by reducing his own holdings voluntarily. Decades later there was to be a serious revolt by the shareholders which led to the sale of the paper, an event which could not have happened had John Walter I left *The Times* as a straight bequest to John Walter II.

John Walter II and Lord Northcliffe were the two greatest proprietors *The Times* ever had. They resembled each other only in their ability to manage newspapers, and in their odd hankering to transmit their success in this field into political influence exerted through conventional means. John Walter II had none of the theatrical panache of Northcliffe – the Napoleonic mien, the hanging forelock, the dark glasses. Walter sounds a rather dull grey man. His portraits show him as trim, with a straight eye and a slightly beaky nose. The epithet 'genius', so freely lavished on Northcliffe, would never have been applied to Walter. Yet the achievement of the two men was comparable. And Walter did not, like Northcliffe, go mad.

The first half of the nineteenth century, during which John Walter II's paper grew from a struggling subsidized agglomeration of news and advertisements to the most influential print the world had known, was a time of unparalleled political turbulence and social change. The population doubled. The new centres of industrial wealth in the Midlands and the north of England continued to expand. The country was criss-crossed by a network of macadamized roads, canals and, eventually, railways. The established Church embarked on a vast programme of church building, while the different nonconformist sects were even more zealous in erecting their own chapels and meeting-houses. Sunday schools taught letters as well as godliness to thousands of poor children, and the mechanics' institutes from the mid-1820s onwards satisfied the growing thirst for knowledge among industrious artisans.

It is always rash to generalize about public opinion, but clearly the England of Peterloo and the great Reform Bill, of Chartism and the

Anti-Corn Law League, was a country which, if never actually poised on the brink of violence and revolution, was inhabited by men and women capable of feeling and giving vent to strong political passions. *The Times* was a child of this new age, and the mouthpiece of many of the new interests trying to express themselves.

Its audience was what in modern advertising terms would be known as the A B readership, the upper and upper-middle classes, though it also touched the C1s and C2s, the clerical workers and the skilled artisans. The 1851 census numbered the professional classes at 357,000, but it was not just numbers that affected the fortunes of *The Times*. The new middle classes were becoming avid for material to read. The upper-middle classes included many evangelicals and nonconformists, and Protestantism, particularly of the dissenting order, has always been a promoter of reading and literacy. Women were becoming voracious readers, too. With the increasing army of domestic servants time could hang heavy on their hands. By the 1820s advertisements for 'ladies' academies' provided one of the major items in *The Times* advertisement columns. At home, the family reading circle was an established institution.

The evangelical middle classes, moreover, were chary of indulging in outside amusements. Most of those open to them at the time, such as the theatre, were not considered respectable. Even the opera was only rendered so by the advent of Jenny Lind, a woman of profound religious dedication. Nor had sport yet made itself felt as a major interest in the daily life of all classes. Cards, hunting and the prize ring were all forbidden to strict evangelicals.

The development of railways in the 1830s and 1840s helped distribution and readership. As Richard Altick has written in *The English Common Reader*, 'A railway trip meant an hour or a day of enforced leisure . . . It is by no means accidental that from the 1850s onward a whole class of cheap books was known as "railway literature" and that a large portion of the retail book and periodical trade of England was conducted at railway terminals.'

From 1815 to 1836 the cover price of *The Times* was 7d, due to the stamp duty, which had gone up to 4d in 1815. This was bound to channel it into the hands of the wealthy, but it was also read lower down the social scale, because the habit of multiple readership had increased since the eighteenth century. The newsmen, after delivering copies to subscribers, did a roaring trade in making seventy or eighty separate 'lendings' of *The Times* at a penny an hour. Thereafter these dog-eared copies were posted to country subscribers at the price of 3d each.

Apart from being read in coffee-houses, *The Times* was also circulated in news rooms, where it could be read by the better-educated mechanics and artisans. In 1833, for instance, John Doherty, a trade-union leader, opened such a room in Manchester, and it took ninety-six publications, including *The Times*. Charges ranged from 1d (reading only) to 6d (pot of tea, sugar and cream included). 'Eggs, One Penny each, Muffins, Crumpets, &c.'

Such were the public and such the readers whom *The Times* was to win to itself during these fifty years. How far was the strategy deliberate? We do not know for certain, but there is a strong presumption that the men who made it knew what they were about. Barnes, who became Editor in 1817, was always preoccupied with the role of the 'middle orders'. He first became acquainted with Walter in 1809. We know that in those days much consultation used to go on in Walter's 'parlour' in Printing House Square. That such ideas were put forward and discussed would be a reasonable assumption.

At least with hindsight we can trace the strategy evolving. The first stage was to free the paper from the jobbery, the chicanery, and the bribery which John Walter I had acceded to in the eighteenth century, and to make it truly independent. Stage two was to break away from the Caxtonian printing techniques and devise methods which would make mass production and mass readership possible. Stage three was to raise the quality of the staff from the Grub Street level typified by Combe and Finey, and, above all, to find a worthy Editor.

In each of these tasks John Walter II had been completely successful by 1820. At the same time he had achieved this success by converting a marginal business into a highly profitable one.

(ii) The Principles of Independence

In the early part of his management John Walter II had brushes with the Post Office, arising from his aim of freeing *The Times* from government control. The days of direct bribery were over, but the governments were ever seeking means of indirect control of the press. One means was to withhold news or delay mails, and this is where the Post Office was important. Another means was by the placing or withholding of advertisements. In this, many government departments were concerned, and the practice was much harder to combat. A third means was by the granting of government printing contracts. *The Times* had held the contract for HM Customs since its inception, but in 1805 Pitt's administration, piqued by the newspaper's support of the Addingtons, cancelled the contract. By then, however, Walter was building up enough independent news services of his own, and enough commercial advertising too, to scorn such pressures. *The Times* was becoming independent of government.

Walter next turned his attention to freeing it from another kind of pressure, that deriving from the acceptance of money or favours for 'puffs' of theatrical performances. This was to involve him in some unpopularity. 'Puffing and plenty of tickets were the system of the day', wrote Leigh Hunt in the *Examiner* in 1805. He was then the only editor who could lay claim to publishing unbiased theatrical criticisms. In the same year Walter made a new appointment which was to prove crucial in more than one respect. He recruited to *The Times* as his dramatic critic a young man aged twenty called Barron Field, and it was Field who introduced to *The Times* his friend Thomas Barnes, who was to succeed him as dramatic critic in 1810. The immediate effect was to introduce candid theatrical notices in *The Times*. The reaction was hostile, typified by such articles as that in a contemporary:

> The writer who furnishes *The Times* with theatrical criticisms (if that which is exhibited in utter contempt of critical principles can properly be termed criticism at all) is evidently a gentleman of much light reading. And, indeed, he attacks every individual who comes within his reach, with so sharp a superfluity of quotation that his writings make us shift as furiously as a schoolboy does who has been cheated with mustard on his bread.*

Walter came into conflict with Sheridan, the most famous theatrical manager of his day. The custom had been for *The Times* to accept theatrical advertisements at cost, i.e. at the price of the advertising duty only. In pursuance of his policy of independence Walter insisted the advertisers pay the full rate. He insisted, too, that his critics pay for their tickets, which had hitherto been issued free. Sheridan resented the new type of critique:

'Addressing you, not as an Editor, but, on the footing of the fair and friendly intercourse, which, as a private man, I have always met you and your Father, I must regret, that you could have permitted the publications of such libels.'

Some ten years later Hazlitt, one of the greatest theatre critics, contrasted out of his own experience the difference between Walter's and other editors' methods. By Perry of the *Morning Chronicle*, for whom he worked at one time, he was, he complained, 'generally sent out of the way when any debutant had a friend at court . . . Poor Perry! What bitter complaints he used to make, that by running-amuck at lords and Scotchmen I should not leave him a place to dine out at!'

Of *The Times*, on the contrary, with which he worked for six months in 1817, Hazlitt had this to say: 'I would advise any one who has an ambition to write, and to write his best, in the periodical press, to get if possible, a situation in *The Times* newspaper, the Editor of which is a man of business, and not of letters. He may write them as long and

* *Le Beau Monde* magazine.

as good articles as he can, without being turned out of it.' Hazlitt was a man of high standards and harsh judgments, and his testimony is therefore the more to be valued. He shows that Walter, by sticking to his guns against the theatrical managers, had established *The Times* as an independent journal in the cultural sphere.

Dramatic criticism may seem to the modern reader a small corner of the paper. But the theatre was so important an element in early newspapers that unless he had firmly established his claim to independence there Walter would have been unable to maintain it in politics or in any other field. Hazlitt's statement is a remarkable early definition, if couched in rather loose terms, of what has come to be regarded as the proper relationship between management and editorial staff. He shows too that this relationship was not general to the press of the time. *The Times* led the way in working out the constitution of an independent newspaper.

(iii) *Speeding Up the Presses*

By his sturdy assertion of the principles of independence, John Walter II had earned a claim to moral leadership of the daily press. He was now to assert undisputed claim to technical leadership as well. The first and greatest, though by no means the sole, technical achievement for which he was responsible, was the introduction of the first working steam press in Britain for the printing of newspapers. This he introduced for *The Times* in 1814, just five months after Stephenson produced the first steam railway engine.

To grasp the implications of this development, it is necessary to recall the process invented in 1440 by Gutenberg. He had used his goldsmith's experience to find a means of casting individual metal letters. These letters it was possible to assemble in lines and columns and, by placing the columns alongside each other, to make up whole pages in metal. The pages were next placed within a wooden frame which was tightened up by wedges to prevent any letters slipping out of place. The metal page was then smeared with ink by a hand roller, and a sheet of paper placed over it. The whole was then pushed under a hand-operated press, which applied the correct pressure to produce a good printed page. The process was a slow one, and even by John Walter II's days could only be relied on to produce 250 copies an hour. By 1800 a number of people were seeking methods of speeding it up.

That this process had lasted for some 350 years without improvement was probably due to psychological factors. Masters and workers in the printing trade were intensely conservative. The masters regarded printing as an art. They were suspicious of 'improvement' which might sacrifice quality to speed or gain. 'What can reasonably be expected but disorder and confusion,' wrote one of their number in 1824, 'when each master is endeavouring to supplant his neighbour, not as to excellence, but as to cheapness; this they endeavour to do by means of the new-fangled articles which have been produced.' The writer, John Johnson, was referring to Walter's steam press.*

The printers' trade unions were also strong and ahead of their time in organization, largely because printers had been better educated than most other craftsmen. As early as 1587 restrictive practices were in operation – 'ffyrst that no formes of letters be kept standing to the prejudice of Woorkemen at any tyme'. This meant that, with certain specified exceptions, such as grammars and catechism, the assembled metal letters had to be broken up after 1,500 sheets had been printed from them. The first agreement on wage scales ever made between proprietors and unions in England was completed in the printing trade in 1785, the same year that John Walter I was starting the Logographic Press.

For anyone trying to speed up the processes of printing, there were three points at which he could start. He could try, first, to speed up composing – that is, the assembling of individual letters, which had always been done by picking them out of a wooden case by hand. This is what John Walter I was trying to do with logography. One of the reasons he had to abandon the experiment was that the compositors' organization opposed it. 'I perceived,' he wrote to W. Larman, secretary of the typographic delegates, 'that the minds of the men employed in my Printing House had been poisoned – and that they threw every obstacle that they could in my way.' As a matter of fact, the problem of mechanizing composing proved the hardest of all and had to wait for solution until the 1870s, when *The Times* once more was in the lead.

The second point of the printing process to attract the attention of innovators was after the type had been locked into its formes. Here some progress had been made in the eighteenth century. Instead of the metal having paper directly impressed on it, a plaster of Paris cast was moulded from it, into which liquid metal was poured. The result was a solid metal printing plate onto which the paper sheets could be imposed. This metal plate, unlike the forme, could be preserved for an indefinite period. It is hardly necessary to add that both masters and compositors fought hard against the introduction of this process. By doing away with the necessity of re-setting books for subsequent editions, it threatened to deprive the latter of work.

Stereotyping of this kind was not crucial to newspapers, though it became so when, instead of using plaster of Paris, a material was discovered which could be bent. This happened in 1824 with the use of *papier mâché*. By producing a curved mould, it eventually became

* John Johnson, Printer, *Typographia*, London, 1824.

possible to produce semi-circular metal stereotyped plates, which in turn could be fixed to a rotary cylinder. *The Times*, again, was to be first in the field with the installation of rotary presses in the mid-nineteenth century.

This, however, is anticipating. The end at which John Walter II tackled his problem was the final stage of the printing process, the actual press which imposed the paper on the forme. The hand press used a screw or lever to press down the paper. The steam press shuttled the forme to and fro mechanically beneath a cylinder, and rollers, which inked it and pressed the paper down on it. For practical purposes it meant that Walter could print 1,100 sheets an hour, instead of only 250. By 1820 this figure was raised to 2,000. At this stage, however, composing was still done by hand, and the printing was flat, not rotary.

The inventor of the steam press was a Saxon, Friedrich Koenig, who had been unable to interest his own countrymen, even more conservative than British printers, in the project. With him was associated another German, Andreas Bauer. So it was the countrymen of Gutenberg after all who could claim another 'first' in printing invention. At least two Englishmen, including Thomas Martyn, a *Times* man, were working on similar projects. Walter encouraged Martyn, but in the end backed Koenig and Bauer. They in turn had tried to interest others, including that same Mr Perry of the *Morning Chronicle* who had been so upset at Hazlitt criticizing the friends of the great in his theatre reviews. Perry 'did not consider a newspaper worth so many years purchase as would equal the cost of the machine' and declined an invitation to see a demonstration of its working. But the advantage of the new process was economy as well as speed. When on the hand presses circulation rose above a certain point, it became necessary to set up duplicate pages. This additional composing cost was now eliminated.

Walter concluded a contract with Koenig and his associates which allowed him to continue experiments in mechanical printing. With the help of two Englishmen, Applegath and Cowper, he produced in 1828 a printing press capable of turning out 4,000 copies an hour. In view of past history, John Walter II was not unnaturally anxious about the printers' reaction to his innovation and took precautions accordingly. He had had one unhappy experience with his workers in 1810, when they had struck for a wage increase which had been put forward by the printers' unions. Walter prosecuted twenty-one of his men for conspiracy, of whom nineteen were sentenced at the Old Bailey, and although, taking a leaf out of his father's book, he subsequently petitioned the Regent for the exercise of clemency, one of the men had died in prison. *The Times*, in modern terminology, was 'blacked' as a result and afterwards employed non-union labour until the twentieth century. *The Times* workers formed groups of their own called 'companionships'. Later the trade-union movement came to accept that *The Times* was a law unto itself as regards industrial relations. The Walters were the largest employers in the trade, and good ones at that. This independence of *The Times* workers and their confidence in the Walter family enabled further mechanical advances to be introduced during the nineteenth century, which would have been resisted in other 'houses', and thereby contributed to the continued prosperity of the paper.

In 1814, then, when the great day for steam printing arrived, John Walter was taking no risks. Piece by piece he had smuggled the machinery of Koenig's press into a secret room in Printing House Square. 'D' Day, 28 November, arrived. In order to prevent interference, Walter had a cover plan: he kept the printers and compositors on an emergency standby till 6 am waiting for a bogus foreign news story. By this time he had run off the whole of the issue of 29 November on the new machine. Dramatically he entered the press room and announced '*The Times* is already printed – by steam'. He promised his astonished employees that there would be no redundancies in consequence and that any necessary staff reductions would be effected by normal wastage. He also added a warning of firm action against any Luddite manifestations.

John Johnson, who objected to 'new-fangled articles', was forced into reluctant admiration:

> At length this machine, which had been made in obscurity, was brought forth [in 1813–14] to astonish the world by its wonderful action, in receiving and delivering an almost incredible number of sheets per hour; the place selected for this experiment was the Office of *The Times* Newspaper, where the very extraordinary impression that is daily taken of this 'leading Journal' was struck off in a very short space of time compared with what would have been necessary by manual labour at the presses, which required such great exertion . . . For the sake of humanity, there is no one, we believe, that would object to the adoption of these machines for Newspapers of an extensive circulation.

(iv) *The Appointment of Barnes*
After providing the technical means for printing larger issues of *The Times* more speedily, Walter turned his attention to providing the paper with more effective editorial control. He was also engaged in improving staff standards by bringing in university men. As the result of an advertisement the Rev. Lovett Fraser, a Cambridge don, was brought on to the staff in 1807, though he was loath to accept heavy administrative responsibilities as he wished to continue living in Cambridge. This was about the same time that Henry Crabb Robinson was taken on. It was between his Danish and Spanish reporting experiences that

Robinson, back in London, found himself briefly invested with the title of 'editor'. From Robinson's own description of his duties they were more like those of a modern night editor or chief sub-editor:

> After a time I had the name of editor and as such opened all letters. It was my office to cut out odd articles and paragraphs from other papers, decide on the admission of correspondence etc, but there was always a higher power behind. While I was in my room, Mr Walter was in his, and there the great leader, the article that was talked about, was written. Nor did I ever write an article on party politics during my continuance in that post.

Much of the work was done over Walter's dining table in the private apartment in Printing House Square. Later, in 1813, Walter appointed Dr Stoddart, an Oxford don, and Hazlitt's brother-in-law, as Editor. Stoddart was a fanatical anti-Bonapartist, and while his immoderate style of article went down well enough during the war, he became an embarrassment after peace was declared. He was apostrophized by contemporaries as 'Dr Slop', the blimpish character from *Tristram Shandy*.

His leaders had become so unbridled that Walter asked Thomas Barnes, who was now working on *The Times* as parliamentary reporter as well as dramatic critic, to edit them. After a quarrel, Stoddart left to start a rival (and unsuccessful) right-wing paper, the *New Times*. This happened in 1816, and Walter was again left with sole responsibility (which he had not coveted) for the conduct of the paper.

The Proprietor had long realized that the business of editing and managing *The Times*, managing and improving the printing press, and acting as chief executive of the whole Printing House Square complex, including a thrice-weekly evening paper, was too much for one man. The days when he was content to live 'over the shop' were passing. He had just married for the second time and was beginning to raise a family. He built, at Bear Wood in Berkshire, a country house where he had ambitions to live the life of a country gentleman. Later he was to be elected to Parliament. All these activities were good reasons for a shake-out in managerial structure. The solution at which he was to arrive was of historical importance in setting a workable pattern for the relationship between Proprietor, Editor, and Manager of an independent daily newspaper.

That John Walter adopted this pattern as part of a carefully thought-out plan is unlikely. He hit upon it to suit his own convenience, and, in the English way, by trial and error and luck. The luck was that he had in the office, in Barnes, the ideal person to exercise the function of an independent but loyal and responsible editor. Before coming to the final decision of appointing him – the hesitation was probably due to Barnes's radical political views – Walter made one more attempt to find an editor from outside. He authorized Crabb Robinson to approach the Poet Laureate, Robert Southey, who was a freelance journalist, of right-wing if unorthodox views. The details of the offer are not clear. Southey turned it down; and so Thomas Barnes became Editor of *The Times*.

Barnes was one of the founding fathers of nineteenth-century England. His influence was comparable to that of Nelson on the Navy, Peel on the Police and Arnold on the Public Schools. He created the nineteenth-century English newspaper.

The first editor to understand and practise consistently the use of a newspaper to influence opinion, he achieved his objects at a crucial point in British history, thereby greatly aiding the country's peaceable development. Moreover, since nineteenth-century England provided the models on which a large part of the world tended to fashion its institutions, *The Times* in due course became the ideal towards which newspapers in many other countries strove. Barnes's influence was universal.

To reclaim from the past the personality of a character who so consciously wreathed himself in anonymity as did Barnes is not easy. Brief references by diarists, and articles inferentially attributable to him, are the main sources. Barnes, said Tom Moore the poet, delighted in mystification. That Barnes made a fetish of anonymity for the fun of it is most improbable. Pseudonym and anonym had been traditional in the best eighteenth-century journalism since Junius. Barnes's friends and contemporaries, such as Leigh Hunt in the *Examiner* and Charles Lamb in the *Essays of Elia*, still adhered to the practice. For *The Times* it was a matter of policy, but in his own case Barnes pushed it to an extreme. The only reference to him ever to be printed in the paper he edited was his death notice: 'On the 7th inst., at his house in Soho-square, Thomas Barnes, Esq., in the 56th year of his age.'

Barnes was born in 1785 – a coeval of the newspaper he was to edit. He was the son of a country solicitor, but his family came from the London middle classes, 'citizens and clothworkers'. He was a product therefore of the class which was to lead the world, and which he himself could claim to lead. To arouse 'the public-spirited exertions of the middle-orders' was his self-appointed destiny.

Barnes was of medium height, and the adjective 'robust' was frequently applied to him, both of body and of mind. In youth he was athletic, and excelled in swimming and boxing, though like many athletes he ran to fat in middle age. He was a handsome man – candour looks out of his eyes and intelligence is stamped on his brow. His portrait shows a strong jaw and rather untidy fair curly hair. He appears in every sense a well-rounded man. He was no self-made lone wolf.

He had the good fortune to have had the best education to be obtained in his day and to have spent his youth in one of the most remarkable milieux that have ever graced England – the circle of Lamb and Leigh Hunt. All three were schooled at Christ's Hospital. In influence on British history they and their coterie may be compared to Ascham and the Cambridge group who played such a part in the shaping of Elizabethan England.

The ramifications of Leigh Hunt's circle permeated the literary, artistic and to a great extent the political and radical life of England during the early part of the nineteenth century. They had close contacts with the Lake poets at one end of the scale and with middle-class politicians and civil servants at the other. Like Ascham's group, they flourished at a time when England was on the brink of a great expansion and flowering, and they were an element in guiding it on progressive and relatively beneficent paths.

Barnes never forgot his Blue Coat connexion. 'The Christ's Hospital boy's friends at school are commonly his intimates through life,' wrote Lamb. When Leigh Hunt was in prison Barnes was one of his regular visitors. But although loyal to his old school fellow Barnes had loyalties which were not of the unreasoning, sentimental kind. Typically, he criticized the traditional uniform of his old school. He thought it absurd and unhealthy, and later published a letter in *The Times* advocating that the boys should wear something more sensible. Nor, should it be added, did personal loyalties obtrude into his political judgments. He was the man to visit a friend in gaol but not to stick through thick and thin to a political associate when he thought he was wrong. Of this there were to be some notable examples.

Barnes is more easily understood by what he wrote than by what people wrote about him. In an age when religion was the concern of a large section of the middle classes, he does not appear as a religious man. He supported the Established Church as a political policy, but he was tolerant – one of his first great fights was for Catholic Emancipation. In personal conviction he was probably an eighteenth-century sceptic. In private life he has been variously described as Bohemian, 'a complete voluptuary', and 'one of the style of Epicure'. Some caution should be applied to acceptance at their face value of such epithets when they emanate from the prim lips of nineteenth-century civil servants. As a young man, he used to get drunk. Derek Hudson, in his biography of Barnes,* quotes Horace Smith reminiscing on an evening spent at Sydenham with the Hunts, Barron Field and others in 1811. Barnes had left the dinner table, but failed to arrive at the inn where he was putting up:

* Derek Hudson & Harold Child: *Thomas Barnes of The Times*, Cambridge University Press, 1944.

Our kind-hearted host and his servant, each provided with a
lantern, immediately sallied forth in search of our missing friend,
and were fortunately enabled to track his footsteps past the inn,
to a drift beneath a bush upon the open common, where they
found him lying down, endeavouring to pull the snow over his
body, and indistinctly muttering, 'I can't get the counterpane
over me! – I can't get the counterpane over me!' . . . A frightful
attack of rheumatism crippled him for several months.

Barnes may have been thinking of this incident when he wrote, with
characteristic pawky wit, in an essay on Tom Moore:

Dante, the Petrarch, and Tasso, never confounded with the
restless gloating of lasciviousness, that devotedness of heart which
breathes but for one object, and grows greater and better by
the perpetual contemplation of it. They do not invite a lady
to a bed of roses sprinkled with dew – (a most uncomfortable
bed by the way, and especially to be dreaded by all persons
subject to rheumatism).

Barnes would have been in his mid-twenties when he was picked up
in the snow. In later life he was acknowledged to keep a good table
and a fine cellar, but there are no records of excesses nor could he
well have kept the working hours that he did had he continued to
indulge in them.

What really worried the Victorians about Barnes was the status of
Mrs Barnes. In common with his contemporaries, the Prince Regent and
leading Radicals such as 'Orator' Hunt, Barnes lived with a lady whose
marital status was ill-defined. In fact, unlike Mrs Fitzherbert, Mrs
Barnes was not married – at least, not to Barnes. Her former husband
refused to divorce her. The situation was a constant worry to John
Walter, who was well aware of the facts and anticipated the pruderies of
the coming age. Mrs Barnes was seven years younger than Barnes, and
was generally described as vulgar. This she may well have been; but
she was evidently cosy. She gave Barnes a comfortable home, and it
would seem from his letters that he loved her. In the political society
into which Barnes's duties occasionally led him she was the subject
of slighting remarks. Disraeli, whose own wife was frequently sneered
at, wrote waspishly, 'Mrs Barnes looked like a lady in a pantomime,
very funny, surrounded by dukes and privy councillors.' But she got
on with the wives of her husband's friends, when they came to know
her, and even with the blue-stockings such as Mary Russell Mitford.

There is no doubt from his writings that Barnes as a younger man
took an interest in women. But in some ways he too was prudish. He
disapproved of the Restoration Dramatists, and could refer to 'the
abominable indecencies and blasphemies' of Vanbrugh's *Relapse*. He

was, incidentally, a feminist. He felt a strong sense of outrage at the treatment of women in his age:

> The condition of women is, in all branches of society, sufficiently pitiable, educated as they are solely for pleasure, and contemptuously nourished with flattery instead of truth . . . We not only look upon women as decidedly the most loveable part of creation, but we are perfectly assured that in the daily duties of social life they display qualities more useful and more estimable than those of the best men.*

Barnes was often accused of being cynical. If the scepticism induced by a lifetime of dealing with early-nineteenth-century politicians can be described as cynicism, the charge is true. He was a practical idealist. In any given situation he always chose the humane and the enlightened course. He battled doggedly for political reform and consistently supported the under-dogs of his age – the Catholics, the Dissenters, the new industrial working class, the poor, even the unappetizing Queen Caroline. Yet he was a reformer, not a revolutionary; a builder, not a destroyer; and in some ways a conservative. He resolutely supported radical causes but opposed seditious methods. His idealism was tempered by his only too penetrative understanding of the egotism, the baseness, and sometimes the evil by which so many of the people with whom he had to deal were motivated.

There was nothing either doctrinaire or woolly about his particular brand of idealism, and his methods of pursuing it often came as a shock to the ambitious statesmen whom he used, and who tried to use him. When he abandoned those people, they were wont to charge him with inconsistency. 'He was,' says *The History of The Times*, 'consistent in his vocation to the apostolate of Politics in the Concrete.'

Lest Barnes should seem too much of a paragon, his weaknesses should also be reported. He was little interested in finance and economics. He was not totally reliable in preserving the confidence of his informants. In public he was so – but certainly on one occasion he betrayed a confidence to Brougham, the Lord Chancellor, thereby delivering his informant into Brougham's hands politically. He does not appear to have taken much interest in the lay-out and make-up of the paper. While John Walter was still in personal charge there was continuous experiment and development, including the use of wood blocks for illustration. When Barnes took control *The Times* went through a static period in its visual make-up; illustrations ceased, not to be revived again, except in advertisements, until the arrival of Lord Northcliffe in the twentieth century.

There were in truth paradoxes, though not inconsistencies, in Barnes's

* The *Examiner*, 18 December 1814.

character. He lived in an age of transition. John Walter I, as has been remarked, was part and parcel of the eighteenth century. John Walter II was a seal-pattern early Victorian. Barnes partook of the ethos of both centuries. His education and background inclined him to the manners of the eighteenth century and the Age of Enlightenment. His creative vision and his instincts were deployed ahead of them in a world which men could not know by experience but could only descry through the exercise of their imagination – a world of steam, of machines, of vast migrations of peoples, of democracies and of empires.

3 PETERLOO: *THE TIMES* COMES OF AGE

The Times by 1817 was well recognized as the leading source of intelligence on foreign affairs. But it was on the home front that Barnes was first to establish it as the 'leading journal' during the next fifteen years.

For a newspaper to be successful it is necessary for it to have something more than an efficient news service, or even than clear, well-informed comment. It must have a consistent, forceful and constructive editorial policy, combined with an individual tone and style.

Barnes was in some ways lucky. He came to the Chair at a critical point in British history, when all the institutions which seemed so firmly based and eternal later in the century – monarchy, parliament, freedom of speech, trial by jury – were in danger. The nation was divided into mutually incomprehending and intolerant groupings – manufacturers and landowners, north and south, churchmen and dissenters, magistrates and paupers. 'It seemed as if English politics would henceforth conform to the continental pattern, and that for the future there would exist in England, instead of the historic parties, only these two – the party of revolution and the party of counter-revolution,' wrote the French historian of Britain, Elie Halévy.

There were many forces which helped to avert this disaster. Not the least of these was that those who governed Britain had to take account of the marshalling by Barnes and *The Times* of the powerful but largely unorganized middle opinion of the emergent classes which was, broadly speaking, in favour of reform but opposed to violence. By turning to these classes the Editor at the same time did an inestimable service to his paper. The country might have survived without a strong, liberal newspaper: but it is doubtful whether *The Times* would have flourished without a strong, liberal cause – a cause which triumphed, which in historical retrospect proved self-evidently right, and of which *The Times* not only was the leading independent advocate, but was seen by all to be so. The phrase 'Thundering for Reform' well expresses the keynote of this period.

Barnes found his task congenial. By his intellectual background he was influenced to favour reform. Very likely his known views on the subject were the cause of Walter hesitating before appointing him Editor. At the same time Barnes was a man of strong, pragmatic commonsense, well conditioned by eighteenth-century humanism and scepticism, and unlikely to go off at a tangent after Jacobin solutions. Almost immediately on his coming to the Chair a singular opportunity occurred of marking out the ground which *The Times* was to occupy.

In the north of England conditions bore many of the hallmarks of a classical revolutionary situation. For over two decades large sections of the rural population had been migrating into towns to work in the new textile factories. In becoming part of an industrial labour force, they severed their connexions with their traditional social and political background, and a local government whose backbone was the squirearchy and the Church. They had become 'de-tribalized'.

In the early days the change-over to industry promoted prosperity. But the conditions of war, and its aftermath, brought a slump and much unemployment. The Corn Laws of 1815 increased the price of food just at the time when wages were falling. The people were uprooted, discontented and, as *The Times* itself reported, 'half starved'. In July 1818 the Lancashire cotton spinners went on strike, to be followed a month later by the weavers. In September a large Manchester mill was attacked by thousands of workmen, and one of the attackers was shot dead. As the new year began mass meetings were held in many Lancashire towns at which political as well as economic demands were raised in favour of parliamentary reform as well as repeal of the Corn Laws.

Lord Liverpool's Government was worried. The Home Secretary, Lord Sidmouth (Addington), whom *The Times* had first supported and then quarrelled with, was obtuse and reactionary. In July 1819 he instructed the Lords-Lieutenant to take all measures they thought necessary for the preservation of order, and to keep the yeomanry ready. But this partially trained yeomanry was as ill fitted an instrument for dealing with civil disorder as the American National Guard.

The danger threatened to come to a head at a gigantic meeting which was to be held in Manchester in August 1819. The meeting was to be in support of parliamentary reform. Henry Hunt, one of the foremost and most extreme radical leaders, was to chair it. The venue chosen was an open space in the centre of Manchester called St Peter's Field. (The name Peterloo was coined subsequently.) Both the Home Office and the local authorities were apprehensive, and most uncertain how to act.

'Orator' Hunt, the chairman-designate, was in many ways an unlikely man to be an early radical leader. He was not a working man, nor a philosopher, nor a minister – indeed he actively resisted family proposals to send him into the Church. He was a Wiltshire farmer, a keen but insubordinate yeomanry officer who had once challenged his colonel to a duel, and an unsuccessful brewer in Bristol. A tall man, with a stentorian voice, Greville described him as 'like a country gentleman of the old school, a sort of rural dignity about it'. His gimmick was to wear a white hat, to symbolize radical purity: but – like the then Editor of *The Times* – he lived in lifelong concubinage with somebody else's wife. Hunt's radical colleagues were less tolerant than Barnes's. 'He rides the country with a whore,' grumbled Cobbett.

Hunt could be a rabble-rouser, but he was no candidate for martyrdom. All the indications are that he was as nervous as the magistrates about the outcome of the Manchester meeting. The wording of his proclamation is revealing: 'Come,' he urged, 'armed with no other weapon but that of a self-approving conscience.'

The Times at this period ranked as an anti-Jacobin, if not anti-Radical, paper. Its editorials constantly denounced the activities of 'Orator' Hunt and his associates. They opposed the calling of the Manchester meeting, but were equally hostile to the Home Secretary. *The Times* thought he was a bad minister, and that his department was incompetent.

The Manchester meeting was originally billed for 9 August. The magistrates banned it on a technicality. The wording of the agenda suggested that besides advocating parliamentary reform the intention was to elect an alternative or 'shadow' MP for the unrepresented people of Manchester. This was held to be subversive. Hunt did not disagree. He called another meeting on 16 August, removing the offending paragraph.

This time the magistrates acquiesced. They took the precaution of placing themselves in a house overlooking the meeting-place, and called on the military for assistance. A brigade group of horse, foot, and guns was dispersed in adjacent side streets. A large part of the mounted component was volunteer yeomanry cavalry.

Barnes determined to send a staff reporter from London to cover the meeting. He was the only editor of a national newspaper who had the perspicacity, the news sense, and in all probability the resources to do so. In 1819 it took four days to get a message back and forth between London and Manchester. His decision proved more than justified. Peterloo was a turning-point for *The Times*, as it was for the country.

John William Tyas, the reporter whom Barnes selected for the assignment, had been with *The Times* about two years. He was to remain on the staff for over four decades. The paper described him, after the incident, as 'a gentleman of talent and education'. Robert Walmsley, in his recent exhaustive study, *Peterloo: The Case Reopened*, while exposing much Peterloo mythology, leaves the reputation of *The Times* reporter intact: 'The most perspicacious observer on that day was not a local reporter but John Tyas, the writer for *The Times* who had been sent to "cover" the meeting.'

Early, like a good reporter, John Tyas took up his station at 10.30 in the morning, when St Peter's Field was still empty except for a few loafers. An hour later, according to his report in *The Times*:

> The first body of reformers arrived on the ground, bearing two banners, each of which was surmounted by a cap of liberty. The first bore upon a white ground the inscription of 'Annual Parliaments, and Universal Suffrage'; on the reverse side: 'No Corn Laws'. The other bore upon a blue ground the same inscription, with the addition of 'Vote by Ballot' . . . shortly afterwards a dung-cart was brought, into which the standard bearers were ordered to mount, and from which all the standards arriving afterwards were most appropriately displayed.

Tyas duly notes the presence of many women among the marchers:

> A club of Female Reformers, amounting in numbers, according to our calculation, to 150, came from Oldham; and another, not quite so numerous, from Royton . . . The latter bore two red flags, the one inscribed *Let us die like men, and not be sold like slaves*; the other *Annual Parliaments and Universal Suffrage*.

While waiting for Hunt, the crowd were kept in play by minor speakers. Tyas tried to estimate their number. Anyone who has ever tried to count a crowd at a political meeting will sympathize with him. He gave the figure as 80,000; the Reformers claimed more. Later a figure of 50,000 was generally accepted, which was no mean size by any standards – the organizers claimed it as the largest meeting ever held in England. The magistrates' concern is understandable.

Tyas describes the arrival of the Law:

> The Reformers who had up to this time arrived in the field demeaned themselves becomingly, though a posse of 300 or 400 constables, with the Boroughreeve at their head, had marched in a body into the field about 12 o'clock, unsupported by any military body to all outward appearance. Not the slightest insult was offered to them . . . the people . . . crying 'Let us keep peace and order'.

Meanwhile, though Tyas did not know it, the magistrates and constables in the house overlooking the field had received depositions by respectable citizens expressing their apprehension of riot. The magistrates subsequently claimed that the Riot Act was then read out of a window. This is one of the key facts about Peterloo which remain to this day disputed. If it was, few heard it. Tyas did not report it.

By one o'clock Hunt had still not arrived and Tyas was getting bored. He went to look for him, and met him at the Exchange. Hunt was travelling in an open landau with the other leaders. Seated on the 'dicky' was a female Reformer carrying Hunt's flag and cap of liberty. The cortège was accompanied by a cheering crowd. Tyas realized that his only chance of getting back to a place of vantage was to secure a place on the hustings. A man of resource, he went up to Hunt, whom he had never met before, and asked to be accommodated. 'Mr Hunt, on this individual's asking to be admitted, immediately acceded to his request.' This was to have unforeseen consequences for Tyas.

Hunt mounted the hustings, followed by Tyas and the rest, and had some difficulty in obtaining silence before he began to speak. Meanwhile, within the house the magistrates, again unknown to Tyas, had decided to arrest Hunt and his associates. The constables told them they dare not do it without military assistance. Joseph Nadin, their leader, gave as one reason that he had been attacked with paving stones when trying to serve a warrant three nights before.

What happened next happened suddenly, and has been told by many. No two accounts agree. Tyas, perhaps the only observer who was both impartial and trained, reported as follows:

At this stage of the business the Yeomanry Cavalry were seen advancing in a rapid trot to the area . . . their ranks were in disorder, and arriving within it, they halted to breathe their horses, and to recover their ranks. A panic seemed to strike the persons at the outskirts of the meeting, who immediately began to scamper in every direction. After a moment's pause, the cavalry drew their swords, and brandished them fiercely in the air; upon which Hunt and Johnson desired the multitude to give three cheers, to show the military that they were not to be daunted in the discharge of their duty by their unwelcome presence. This they did, upon which Mr Hunt again proceeded. This was a mere trick to interrupt the proceedings of the meetings; but he trusted that they would all stand firm. He had scarcely said these words before the Manchester Yeomanry cavalry rode into the mob which gave way before them, and directed their course to the cart from which Hunt was speaking. Not a brickbat was thrown at them – not a pistol was fired during this period: all was quiet and orderly, as if the cavalry had been the friends of the multitude, and had marched as such into the midst of them. A bugle-man went at their head, then an officer, and then the whole troop. They wheeled round the waggons till they came in front of them, the people drawing back in every direction on their approach . . .

After they had surrounded them in such a manner as to prevent all escape, the *officer* who commanded the detachment went up to Mr Hunt, and said, brandishing his sword, 'Sir, I have a warrant against you, and arrest you as my prisoner'. Hunt after exhorting the people to tranquillity in a few words, turned round to the officer, and said, 'I willingly surrender myself to any civil officer who will show me his warrant.'

Hunt and Johnson then surrendered to Nadin. Some of the others escaped.

As soon as Hunt and Johnson had jumped from the waggon, a cry was made by the cavalry. 'Have at their flags'. In consequence, they immediately dashed not only at the flags which were in the waggon, but those which were posted among the crowd, cutting most indiscriminately to the right and to the left in order to get at them. This set the people running in all directions, and it was not until this act had been committed that any brickbats were hurled at the military. From that moment the Manchester Yeomanry cavalry lost all command of temper... a man within five yards of us in another direction had his nose completely taken off by a blow of a sabre.

In the confusion, Tyas allowed himself to be arrested with the rest. The result was he did not see the second phase of the action, when the regular cavalry (15th Hussars) came on the scene. They were generally credited by eye-witnesses with having done something to restrain the Yeomanry, though such hospital statistics as exist show more casualties caused by the regulars.

Tyas's report was both of prime immediate and long-term historical importance because it constitutes the only independent witness that it was the Yeomanry, and not the crowd, who first resorted to violence.

Like so many events which have changed the course of history Peterloo was over in a flash. Packed though St Peter's Field was, it took the cavalry but ten minutes to clear it. Hence much of the conflicting evidence. Casualties were about a dozen killed and 420 wounded. More may have been concealed.

But the situation, so far as *The Times* was concerned, was ironic. Here was their special reporter, unable either to see the end of the affair or to get his message away. 'It is only justice to the man who apprehended us' – and here Tyas is using the editorial 'we' – 'to state, that he did everything in his power to protect us from ill-usage, and showed us every civility consistent with his duty.' But he saw the constables beating up Hunt with their staves. Tyas spent the night in prison, completing his report, and was released next day.

Meanwhile two local Manchester reporters, John Edward Taylor and Archibald Prentice, had realized the situation. Taylor was the future

founder of the *Manchester Guardian*, Prentice the future historian of
the Anti-Corn Law League. Neither, according to their own accounts,
had actually been present at the time the Yeomanry entered the Field.
But they sat down and wrote two reports which they sent off to two
London papers that night. One – we do not know which – went to *The
Times*. This was something more than a classic case of one reporter
helping out another. They wanted the news in the paper to anticipate
the magistrates' official report.

Next morning, Tuesday the 17th, Tyas was released and dispatched
his own account.

The confusion in Printing House Square must have been considerable.
On the morning of Wednesday, the 18th, *The Times* carried the first
reference to the disaster in a brief leading article. Acting on imperfect
information, the leader writer commented:

> We kept the press open until a late hour this morning in the
> hope of receiving minute accounts ... The Riot Act was read ...
> Hunt himself was taken prisoner – and we add, with unfeigned
> sorrow, that several lives were lost ... the local troops, it is said,
> behaved with great alacrity ... The prancing of the cavalry and
> the active use of the sabre . . . created a dreadful scene of con-
> fusion, and we may add of carnage . . . killed eight; wounded
> eighty to a hundred . . . such is the brief or general outline . . .
> what menaces were uttered . . . which induced the Magistrates
> . . . to disperse the meeting by force of arms we cannot possibly
> state.

This was an understatement of the facts, but the best Barnes could
do in the circumstances.

The following morning, Thursday the 19th, *The Times* devoted seven
out of twelve columns to Peterloo. These included a leader, eleven
reports from other papers and correspondents, including the one from
Taylor or Prentice, and Tyas's own report, which arrived after the
others. 'Express from Manchester. Just as our paper was going to press,
we received from the gentleman deputed by us to report the proceedings at Manchester, the following account . . .'

The irony was that Tyas's report was more favourable to the
Yeomanry than the one sent by the two Manchester journalists. This
described the Yeomanry as 'hacking their way up to the hustings'
which Tyas expressly had not said. However, the magistrates had only
themselves to blame if the first impressions received in Printing House
Square were even worse than those of the paper's own reporter.

The paper, after once again censuring Hunt for calling a meeting in
such circumstances, commented on 'the dreadful fact, that nearly a
hundred of the King's unarmed subjects have been sabred by a body of

cavalry in the streets of a town of which most of them were inhabitants, and in the presence of those Magistrates whose sworn duty it is to protect and preserve the life of the meanest Englishman.'

Objection has been taken to Barnes's having based his leader on the Manchester reporter's account rather than on Tyas's. However Tyas was clear on the main issue, that the Yeomanry struck the first blow.

The Times leaders and reports raised a storm throughout the nation. 'Middle opinion' was horror-struck. Protest meetings were held and subscription lists opened for the victims. Overnight the cause of parliamentary reform became respectable. The Government, it would appear from private memoranda, realized the magistrates' mistake. But they were compelled to maintain the sense of authority and stuck out against an inquiry. But the trials and inquests dragged on for years. The newspapers would not leave it alone.

Peterloo may have had some deterrent effect. The rising tide of radical violence in the North gradually died away. And the Government clamped down on political meetings and newspapers by passing the repressive Six Acts. But *The Times*, previously regarded as a Tory paper, was now firmly committed to Reform.

Hitherto Barnes was little known in the world of affairs. Barely a week after Peterloo, he received a summons which showed that he now had to be reckoned with as a power in the land.

On the morning of 25 August *The Times* published an open letter to his constituents from the radical MP for Westminster, Sir Francis Burdett. He invited them to a protest meeting over Peterloo. The Government determined to prosecute. On the day that *The Times* published this letter, Barnes, who liked to get out of the office and see things for himself, attended a meeting at Smithfield where several radical leaders spoke on the 'Manchester massacre'. The speakers were fully reported in *The Times* next morning. When Barnes returned to Printing House Square he found waiting for him a letter asking him to come to the Home Office. He ordered a 'hackney-coach' – evidently there were no 'staff coaches' in those days – and went down to Whitehall. On sending up his card, he was ushered in to what he described, in a letter to Walter, as the 'great divan'. He was placed in a chair, with the Cabinet seated round him in a semicircle. Barnes, who was shortsighted, was not quite certain who they all were, but he picked out the Prime Minister, Sidmouth, Wellington, Castlereagh – some of the great names of British political history.

Barnes was unperturbed. 'Being conscious that they could have no matter against me, which I need be alarmed at, I was, notwithstanding a slight hurry of spirits, perfectly firm.' Indeed almost everybody in the room had more reason for perturbation than Barnes.

Sidmouth was the spokesman. His first question conveys the mystery which still surrounded the identity of the Editor of *The Times*. 'What is your name, sir?' 'Barnes.' 'In the absence of Mr Walter you have the management of the Paper?' 'I certainly consider myself responsible.' Sidmouth then told him the purpose of the meeting. He wanted to confirm that the letter published in *The Times* on 25 August really came from Burdett. Barnes gave a straightforward answer, and Sidmouth wound up by deprecating, in the most marked manner 'any idea of personal hostility to the paper.'

'Nothing,' concluded Barnes, 'could exceed the courtesy of their behaviour.' Barring a word from Liverpool, and a nod from Castlereagh, no one else seems to have spoken during the session. On the face of it, it all seemed a great to-do about nothing. But no doubt the real reason for the summons was to warn Barnes to mind his step. The incident is a clear indication that the Government recognized the influence that *The Times* now wielded in the country. Walter's paper had come of age.

4 THUNDERING FOR REFORM

(i) Partnership with Brougham

The next twelve years of Barnes's life were spent in advocating all those reform measures which culminated in the great Reform Bill of 1832. Sir Robert Peel, speaking in the House of Commons, summed up the record of *The Times* during this period in these words: 'The great, principal, and powerful advocate of Reform – *The Times* newspaper.'

It was during this period that *The Times* earned the nickname of *The Thunderer*. On 29 January 1831 *The Times* published a leader in which it said: 'Unless the people – the people everywhere – come forward and petition, ay, thunder for reform, it is they who abandon an honest Minister, – it is *not* the Minister who betrays the people.' 'Thundering for Reform' thereafter became a common phrase about *The Times*.

The actual phrase 'thundering' had however been used a year before. Lord Graves, who was a courtier, committed suicide. He was separated from his wife and scandal had linked her name with the detested Duke of Cumberland. The coroner's inquest was held early in the morning following Lord Graves's death and the haste of this inquest was most severely handled by *The Times* with many innuendoes about the Duke of Cumberland. Subsequently the coroner wrote a letter of explanation to *The Times*, and the Editor withdrew his implications, coupling this on 11 February 1830 with an article by way of exculpation stating: 'When the Coroner's inquest, which should have elicited the truth was curtailed of its fair proportions – then we thundered out that article in Tuesday's paper which caused so great a sensation.'

Cobbett, a Radical in the fullest sense, and at times a fomenter of violence, gave Barnes an impeccable certificate of respectability among the middle classes by abusing him. In his *Political Register* he constantly lavished on *The Times* such epithets as 'cunning old trout', 'ranting, canting, trimming old *Times*', 'brazen old slut', and 'the bloody and stupid old *Times*'. As a writing journalist Cobbett was Barnes's only rival, but he lacked his editorial and managerial skills.

The first issue after Peterloo which gave Barnes the opportunity of defining *The Times*'s new political orientation was the trial of Queen Caroline in 1820. Why this sluttish woman should have engaged the support of the London mob, the Radicals, *The Times* and ultimately the official Whigs may today seem difficult to comprehend. But support for the Queen was not positive support: it was an 'agin' movement, springing from dislike of George IV and affording an outlet for more general frustrations and discontents. Barnes reported the trial himself. His face can be seen in the painting by Sir George Hayter which still hangs in the National Portrait Gallery. He sits, notebook in hand, behind Copley, the Solicitor-General, who later as Lord Lyndhurst was to play a major role in the history of *The Times*.

The trial of Queen Caroline, which was sensational and salacious, provides an early testimony of the principle that news makes circulation. The sale of *The Times* doubled to 15,000. However, the real significance of the trial to Barnes was not that it sold more copies of his paper but that it brought him into daily contact with a man soon to become one of the most powerful politicians in Britain and the Editor's own closest political confidant. This was the principal counsel for Queen Caroline, her Attorney-General, Henry Brougham – that brilliant but erratic polymath.

Brougham was a strange man and like Barnes he had a wild youth. One night in Edinburgh, in 1799, four men set out from a late drinking session to steal the head of Galen from above a chemist's shop. The party included Sydney Smith and a young physics student and barrister – Henry Brougham. He it was who egged them on to their enterprise by brewing a particularly lethal rum punch. When the others had mounted on each others' shoulders to steal the head, they noticed Brougham was missing. At that moment, the watch appeared. Those narrowly escaping arrest included a clergyman (Sydney Smith), a professor, and the Clerk of Sessions. Accompanying the watch was the informant, Brougham, who had also been the instigator of the plan.

Later in life Henry Brougham was to be a spearhead of the Reform movement in Parliament; to recast a great part of our legal system; to be the first to introduce a measure of state education; and with others to found London University. But the trick he played on his friends in Edinburgh as a student was typical of his later conduct in politics.

Long trials are fertile seedbeds for the formation of friendships between journalists and lawyers. Barnes must have had some acquaintance with Brougham before the royal trial, since it was Brougham who had defended his friend Leigh Hunt when he was prosecuted for libel. But during the trial of the Queen, Brougham and Barnes got to know each other very much better, and Brougham slipped Barnes an important document – the Queen's letter of protest to the King. This was published exclusively in *The Times*, and was the first fruit of their long partnership.

In temperament and character the two men were extreme opposites. Where Barnes was self-effacing, Brougham was an exhibitionist. Where Barnes was reliable, Brougham was unpredictable. Where Barnes was sane and of sound sense. Brougham was what would now be termed pathological in his behaviour. Yet these two had enough community of interest to work together for some fourteen years before they began to quarrel. Barnes broadly supported Brougham's policies. Brougham, as *a de facto* leader of the opposition and later as a Minister, supplied Barnes with many of the classic 'scoops' which built up his paper's reputation for omniscience and infallibility. Editors of *The Times* have had a tendency to acquire advisers on whom they have relied for ideas. Henry Brougham was the nearest to an *éminence grise* that Barnes ever had.

The other steady supplier of information – though not of ideas – over this period was Charles Greville, the diarist, who from 1821 till 1859 was Clerk to the Privy Council. He was about the best-informed source in the kingdom. No wonder *The Times* flourished.

Following the trial of Queen Caroline, the next fight of the Liberals was for Catholic Emancipation. This was to bring together for the first time those two great forces in the nation, *The Thunderer* and the Iron Duke. Their interaction provides a fascinating insight into the relations between *The Times* and government.

Wellington's general opinion of the press was low. He accepted the conventional attitude of his class on this subject. *The Times* had aroused his especial ire in a personal matter. Nothing was calculated to get the Duke on the raw more than criticism of his long-standing friend Mrs Arbuthnot, the wife of a Treasury official. In May 1826 *The Times* reported Wellington as taking Mrs Arbuthnot to a fancy dress ball dressed as a man. Mrs Arbuthnot claimed she was dressed as Mary Queen of Scots. Her escort's anger at the error would, in normal circumstances, seem disproportionate. He seriously contemplated prosecution and it was on this occasion that he referred to Barnes as an 'insolent, vulgar fellow'.

The Duke, however, was not the man to let a private grievance stand in the way of public policy. Catholic Emancipation, like parliamentary reform, had been a lively issue in British politics for more than a generation, at the core of the 'Irish Question'. Pitt, in the 1780s, might have settled Ireland, relieved the Catholics of their disabilities, and reformed Parliament, had he had a more sympathetic monarch and had the Napoleonic Wars not intervened. But the chance was missed.

The Duke of Wellington, Irish born and bred, had thought much about Emancipation before becoming Prime Minister (January 1828). He was not opposed to it in principle, though he feared it might weaken the Union. George IV, on the other hand, had even more scruples on the subject than his father, and threatened abdication. What brought matters to a head was the announcement by Daniel O'Connell, head of the Catholic Association, that he was putting himself forward as candidate at an election in County Clare. It was true that Catholics could not sit in Parliament, but there was no law to stop them from standing for it. O'Connell was elected by a large majority. What was to be done next? The Duke's practical mind opted for conciliation.

For a government bent on Catholic Emancipation the backing of *The Times* would be essential in order to ensure that 'middle opinion' supported it. The Duke was prepared to get that backing. 'I hate meddling with the Press,' he wrote to Croker, 'but I am afraid we do meddle, that is to say the Secretary of the Treasury does; but he does not attend to it; nor does he meddle with that degree of intelligence which might be expected from him. I must put this to rights.' Barnes, a convinced advocate of Catholic Emancipation, had already met the Duke halfway in leading articles. He had prepared himself for the occasion by a visit to Ireland, to study conditions on the spot.

An intermediary, Digby Wrangham of the Foreign Office, was entrusted with the delicate assignment of ensuring that Barnes received advance intimation of all government moves. The meetings were held in their private houses. The information was strictly 'off the record,' but *The Times* was allowed to publish it and so be easily ahead of all rivals in accuracy of forecast.

Wrangham defined the status of these exchanges as follows (10 February 1829):

> I ought perhaps to apologize for the appearance of reserve towards you indicated in my so frequently accompanying the information I give, with a request that you will not make use of it for the purpose of confirming any statement you make, as if it came from authority...the reason for thus qualifying my information must be obvious to you as well as the advantage which results from it both to you & the Govt. – To You, by avoiding the appearance of too intimate a connection with the Govt., and thus preserving your character for independence quite beyond suspicion – And to them, on the other hand, by having the benefit of that independent support, which is of course much more valuable than it could be, if any intercourse & understanding was supposed to exist between the parties.

The principle on which the relationship was founded could scarcely be more candidly expressed. As for Barnes, he was merely collecting a bonus for supporting a cause which he believed in, though the Duke's decision to make his job easier for him was intelligent. The Bill emancipating the Catholics was strenuously opposed by many Tories but it received a reluctant royal assent on 13 April 1829.

With Catholic Emancipation out of the way it was now time, in

Barnes's view, for the next step – parliamentary reform. Barnes did not believe that the Duke of Wellington would repeat his performance over Catholic Emancipation and introduce a Reform Bill, and accordingly he withdrew his support from Wellington's Government. This was the kind of action which drew on *The Thunderer* accusations of inconsistency, and earned it the alternative nickname of *The Turnabout*. Those who thought this way failed to understand the position. Barnes supported policies, not parties or personalities. This, to him, was the meaning of independence. The Duke bore no grudge. He was to turn to Barnes again later.

Meanwhile it was left to the Whigs, returned to power in 1830, led by Grey and with Brougham as Lord Chancellor, to push the Bill through. The final stages of the legislation were marked by unparalleled excitement and disorder in the country.

In October 1831 the Bill, which had passed the Commons, was thrown out by the Tory majority in the Lords. Barnes was afraid that the Bill would be watered down. His reactions to suggestions that there might be a compromise can be found in *The Greville Memoirs*. (Barnes did not know at that time that it was Greville who was supplying him with information that came to him through Henry de Ros, his close friend and a man of fashion – it was de Ros who reported Barnes's reactions to Greville.)

> His rage and fury exceeded all bounds. He swore Brougham and Grey (particularly the former) were the greatest of villains. After a long discussion he agreed to try and persuade his colleagues to adopt a moderate tone, and not to begin at once to *jeter feu et flamme*. Henry's object was to persuade him, if possible, that the interest of the paper will be in the long run better consulted by leaning towards the side of order and quiet than by continuing to exasperate and inflame. He seemed to a certain degree moved by this argument, though he is evidently a desperate Radical . . . There is an article in the 'Times' this morning of half-menacing import, sulkily and gloomily written, but not ferocious, and leaving it open to them to take what line they think fit.*

The above passage is interesting as showing that Barnes was always ready to listen to argument. The phrase 'persuade his colleagues' is a nice example of the way in which he could retire behind a smoke screen when convenient. Such are the advantages of the convention of anonymity.

The passage of the Reform Bill in 1832 marked the beginning of the end of Barnes's comradeship with Brougham. Was it that the apprentice

* *The Greville Memoirs*, London 1875.

was growing too big for the sorcerer? Brougham, always strange, showed symptoms of growing manic. But it was not on grounds of personal conduct that they parted. As always with Barnes, it was on policy.

The Reform Bill could be thought of as a station on the route to democracy. The Whig Cabinet responsible for its enactment alighted there and waited on the platform. Barnes went puffing on to the next station. Some of the Whig Government's measures were ameliorative – for example, the Factories Act and the Abolition of Slavery Act. Two, in Barnes's view, were not. These were the repressive Irish Coercion Bill which Barnes prophesied would make Ireland the permanent enemy of England, and the Poor Law Bill which he believed would permanently divide the upper and the working classes.

Barnes, like Walter, considered the Poor Law Bill heartless. For him the exclusion of outdoor relief was the sticking point:

> Our principal objection [he wrote to Brougham's secretary, Le Marchant], is to one branch of the measure — a very important branch certainly — the refusal of relief except in workhouses: a system in my opinion enormously expensive, degrading to the honest pauper and ruinous to fathers of families who will not any more receive that temporary relief which might set them on their feet again without being torn from their wives and children who will all be pauperized and imprisoned under the new system because the parent requires 20 or 30 shillings to set his loom or stocking frame a-going.

Barnes attacked Althorp, the responsible Minister, mercilessly. He was sure of his ground. His local reporters everywhere informed him that the county justices, who knew what they were talking about, agreed with him. The Bill, in his view, was the work of theoretical economists totally out of touch with the people. As for Lord Althorp, 'such was his Lordship's mind that he did not understand his own Bill'.

The Government decided on revenge. But their efforts were fumbling. They misunderstood the nature of newspaper finances and, to make things worse, they started off with a major gaffe. Lord Althorp sent a note to Brougham: 'The subject I want to talk to you about is the State of the Press, & whether we should declare open war with *The Times* or attempt to make peace.' Brougham, who received the note in the Court of Chancery, tore it up and threw it into his wastepaper basket. Somebody picked it up, stuck it together again, and sent it to Barnes. The fragments still survive in Printing House Square, with a pencilled scrawl 'Picked up by a Friend & sent thinking it may be of service as a private principle of action.' Barnes immediately bearded Le Marchant with this indiscretion:

Show this to the Lord Chancellor.

June 11th, 1834.

My dear Sir,

I told you I would always treat you frankly: and in that spirit I think it right to say that I am aware of Lord Althorp's application to the Chancellor for his opinion whether 'the Govt. should declare open war with the *Times* or attempt to make peace.' What does the Gaby mean?

Yours ever,

T. Barnes.

After all [Barnes wrote later with amiable hauteur], our support is in a great measure indeed I may say altogether a matter depending on yourselves.

If you bring forward beneficial measures and urge them on with the same persevering firmness with which you passed such unpopular measures as the Coercion Bill last Session and the Poor Bill now, we *must* support you.

The Whigs tried to rejuvenate *The Times*'s old rival *The Morning Chronicle* – nicknamed by Barnes *The Grunticle* – by pumping money into it. Brougham, who had as yet not finally parted company with Barnes, was suspected of writing for it under the pseudonym of Vindex. On one occasion he was accused of attacking in *The Grunticle* an article he had himself written anonymously in *The Thunderer*. If true, the story would be well in character.

But the Government's secret weapon, from which the most lethal effects on *The Times* were confidently expected, was the lowering of the stamp duty. This was achieved in 1836 by Spring Rice, the Liberal Whig from Limerick, who succeeded Althorp as Chancellor of the Exchequer. The stamp duty had long been denounced by liberal opinion as a 'tax on knowledge'. Its abolition or reduction was therefore a morally elevating measure for a reforming cabinet to adopt. Properly handled, they reckoned it could kill *The Times*. Cheaper papers, with inferior resources, would be able to compete. The idea was sound, but the execution was bungled.

In order effectively to injure *The Times* it was necessary to weight the tax against papers of a certain size. Barnes and Walter, supported by other newspapermen, argued Spring Rice out of this part of the deal. The stamp duty was merely reduced from 4d to 1d, involving a reduction in the cost of *The Times* from 7d to 5d.

The result was hardly what the Government had hoped for. *The Times* had been jogging along for a decade with a circulation around the 10,000 mark. The graph now began to climb steeply and uninterruptedly until by 1855 it had all but reached 60,000. Most of its 1836 contemporaries had by then ceased publication.

Barnes's long support of Brougham had by now turned to all-out attack. No epithets were too bad for his former friend. Brougham was a trickster and a mountebank, drunken and near mad. 'For some months past the Lord Brougham has been under a morbid excitement seldom evinced by those of HM's subjects who are suffered to remain masters of their own actions.' The switch is not flattering to Barnes as a private individual. Some believe that personal feelings too were involved, and that a reckless statement of Brougham's at Brooks's Club was overheard by Barnes.

Meanwhile Brougham grew odder and odder, and after the fall of the Grey Government in November 1834 he was never to hold political office again. In 1839 he actually spread a report that he had been killed in a carriage accident, so that he could catch out the newspapers and see what kind of obituaries they would publish. Barnes was the only editor not to fall into the trap by reporting Brougham's death. On the contrary, he published a short denial of the report.

Old 'Wicked-Shifts', as Creevey used to call him, faded out of politics. He was accused, almost certainly unjustly, of giving Barnes a final scoop over the dismissal of Lord Melbourne's Government by the King in 1834. When Melbourne returned to power, he left him out of the Government. He died at the age of ninety in Cannes, a small fishing village which he had developed into a flourishing resort.

This was the man of whom Samuel Rogers wrote when he was at the height of his powers: 'This morning, Solon, Lycurgus, Demosthenes, Archimedes, Sir Isaac Newton, Lord Chesterfield, and a great many more went away in the same post-chaise.'

(ii) 'The most powerful man in the country'

Barnes in the 1830s was at the zenith of his power, but at one turn of the political wheel he contrived to exert this power in a new and potentially dangerous way. In the normal course of events *The Times* used its influence straightforwardly and directly. Greville, who accurately divined Barnes's policy as revealed in retrospect to Le Marchant, put the case thus (the passage refers to the Irish Coercion Bill):

> Yesterday there appeared an article in the '*Times*' in a style of lofty reproof and severe admonition, which was no doubt as appalling as it was meant to be. This article made what is called a great sensation; always struggling, as this paper does, to take the lead of public opinion and watching all its turns and shifts with perpetual anxiety, it is at once regarded as undoubted

evidence of its direction and dreaded for the influence which its powerful writing and extensive sale have placed in its hands.

Barnes's strategy consisted in recommending or opposing specific policies on their merits. In the interests of his paper, he cultivated close contacts with the principal actors on the political stage, but not – save in one case, that of Brougham – so close as to make disengagement awkward when their policies had to be withstood.

In the episode now to be related Barnes, without abandoning his role as critic and advocate, became to some degree a participant in the formulation of a party's policy. The change set a dangerous precedent, posing questions of the proper role of a newspaper editor in public events. In Barnes's case the step was not to be repeated.

In November 1834 William IV dismissed Melbourne and the Whigs and called on Wellington and Peel to form an administration. In so doing he was exercising a royal prerogative which had not been used since the eighteenth century and which was never to be used again. But, though fully aware of the dangers, the Duke accepted the mandate, only insisting that Peel, and not he, should be the Prime Minister. Unfortunately Peel was on holiday in Italy, and until he could be found and brought back the Duke was obliged to carry on more or less single-handed, personally holding five major and three minor offices. Weak in the Commons and far from popular in the country the Tories desperately needed the support of public opinion. This meant *The Times*.

Two persons – Sir James Scarlett, *The Times*'s legal adviser and a former Attorney-General, and Charles Greville, its crypto-communicant – advised the Duke to secure the newspaper's co-operation. Greville told him that there appeared in *The Times* 'a considerable disposition to support the new Government'. The Duke replied that he would be glad of such support, but he did not think *The Times* could be influenced. Further, in his position, he did not like personally to interfere, or to place himself in the paper's power. 'I hear they call me a Reformer,' he said, laughingly.

The Duke was probably more conscious of the dangers than his advisers. Politics did not turn on a single straightforward issue, like Catholic Emancipation. Rather, the Tories were faced with the necessity of presenting to the post-Reform electorate new policies and a new style and with very little time in which to do it. Was it wise to associate a newspaper in this process? For this is what Wellington was being asked to do.

The decision was made to contact Barnes. Lord Lyndhurst, the Lord Chancellor designate, was deputed to act on behalf of the Government. As Sir John Copley, he had prosecuted Queen Caroline. Now he was about to replace his old opponent, Brougham, on the Woolsack. His

mind must have gone back to those days, nearly fifteen years ago, when
he, Brougham and Barnes had spent those long hours together at the
Queen's trial, listening to the picaresque evidence of her Latin hangers-
on.

Barnes put on paper the terms on which he was prepared to support
the Government. They were: no mutilation of the Reform Bill; the
adoption of those measures of reform which had already been sanctioned by Parliament during the last session in regard to the Church and
the municipalities; no change in foreign policy. This virtually meant
a bi-partisan programme. After much to-ing and fro-ing, papers by the
Duke and Lyndhurst were read to Barnes which satisfied him. There
is no trace of these in writing, but their content can be surmised from
what was to follow. 'Why,' commented Lyndhurst, 'Barnes is the most
powerful man in the country.'

Meanwhile Sir Robert Peel was posting back to London from Italy.
He landed at Dover on 8 December 1834, and immediately accepted
the task of forming a government. Two days after his arrival John
Walter weighed in with a suggestion of his own. As MP for Berkshire
he found the liberal wing of the Conservative Party suspicious of the
new government, particularly of the Duke of Wellington who, as he
said, was regarded with 'unreasonably angry hostility'. This hostility
was not extended to Peel. If, as seemed inevitable, there was to be a
general election, and if the Tories were to increase their slender strength
in the Commons, positive action would be needed. Walter proposed
that Peel should put out a 'popular declaration' with the aim of 'cor-
recting wrong opinions and inculcating right ones'.

Peel was receiving similar advice from other quarters, and although
there was no precedent for a pre-election policy statement of this sort
the Cabinet liked the idea. The only question was the form it should
take. Eventually Peel decided that, since he would have to face an
election whatever happened (ministers in those days had to resign their
seats on taking office), he would issue it as an address to his constituents. Thus was born the Tamworth Manifesto, often regarded as the
charter of modern conservatism.

But before the document was finally issued for publication to three
selected newspapers (*The Times*, the *Morning Herald*, and the *Morning
Post*) in the early hours of 18 December drafts of it had been seen by
many people. One of these was Barnes, for Scarlett, still acting as intermediary, wrote to Peel: 'I now send you the proposed address as altered
by Mr B. He will be ready to adopt any other alterations that may be
suggested in the language.'

Some of the phrases in the Manifesto betray Barnes's style. After
pledging that the Reform Bill was a 'final and irrevocable settlement
of a great constitutional question,' the Manifesto denied 'that we are

to live in a perpetual vortex of agitation'. Certainly *The Times* seems
to have been as much involved as many members of the Government
in drawing up the document.

In 1840 Barnes's health began to fail. This time it was something more
than corpulence due to good living and a sedentary life. There was talk
of an internal tumour and of stone. On 2 May 1841 he wrote that he
was extremely unwell and could not attend to any kind of business.
Although he had been in the Chair for twenty-four years, he was still
only fifty-five. The life span of editors of *The Times* – or managers for
that matter – has not generally been long. Barnes underwent an operation on 7 May, in the early morning, and later saw Thomas Alsager,
who had set up the paper's city office, but he died before the day was
out. There was no obituary, only the routine death notice already
recorded. Though *The Times* was silent, other papers were not: 'Of the
great talent and energy of Mr Barnes the newspaper which he conducted
for upwards of twenty years is the best evidence,' wrote the *Examiner*,
which his old friend Leigh Hunt had founded. His will, signed the day
before he died, consists of a few lines. In it he leaves all his property
'unto my dear wife or reputed wife DINAH MARY MONDET'.

Much of the aura surrounding *The Times* is founded upon the
achievement of Barnes. Already, during his lifetime *The Times* in
countries like France was looked upon as the organ of the British
Government – an assumption founded on continental practices at that
time. It was of course incorrect, for though the paper was closely
embroiled with government, it had succeeded in evading the bear's hug.

The success of *The Times* was not achieved by Barnes's editorial
efforts alone. There were others in England who could write as stylishly,
comment as intelligently, and support causes as vigorously as he. They
lacked, it is true, his statesmanlike judgment and vision, but they lacked
also something else – a management. This John Walter supplied. He
it was who had put into Barnes's hand the weapon which he flourished
with such deadly efficacity. Walter was fortunate too in having, in the
Leigh Hunt circle, a brilliant set of men from whom he could recruit.
Both Barnes and Alsager came from it and it also included Haydon,
whose well-known picture 'Waiting for *The Times*' provided a superb
piece of gratuitous promotional advertising.

The progress made in the managerial advancement of *The Times* is
also illustrated by a system of extraordinary expresses introduced in
1834, which entailed changing both horses and carriage instead of only
the horses at the staging points. The reporters were trained to write out
their copy *en route*. 'It is certainly not very agreeable but it is by no
means impossible to write in a post-chaise whirled along at the rate of
more than 13 miles an hour,' wrote one of them.

In 1835 Charles Dickens, reporting for the *Chronicle*, and a Mr Denison, for *The Times*, raced each other from Exeter, carrying the report of a speech by Lord John Russell: 'On our first stages we had very poor horses,' wrote Dickens in a letter to a colleague on the *Chronicle*. 'At the continuation of the second, *The Times* and I changed horses together; they had the start two or three minutes, I bribed the post-boys tremendously and we came in literally neck and neck – the most beautiful sight I ever saw.'

Equally spirited efforts were made to speed up the overseas services. Dispatches from Paris to London were delivered in 1840 in less than twenty-two hours.

A gale of wind . . . rendered it necessary that the Britannia steamer, which was engaged to carry our despatches, should go out of Boulogne harbour on Thursday night, and lie off in the roadstead till she was wanted on Friday morning. On the arrival of the courier at Boulogne the sea ran so high that it was not an easy task to convey our despatches on board the Britannia, but when that was accomplished Captain Bushill soon placed his vessel in a position to receive all the aid that could be derived from both wind and steam.

The Times had a special arrangement with Waghorn's agency in Egypt by which it sent correspondents' dispatches from the Far East overland to Cairo, whence they were forwarded by sea to Marseilles and rushed through France to the Channel ports. This service outstripped the regular mail. Messages posted from Bombay on 1 October 1840, from Singapore on 13 August and from China on 3 July reached *The Times* by this route on 11 November. They arrived in Printing House Square at three o'clock in the morning and that day's paper carried eight columns.

This was the quality of the service built up by Walter, Barnes and Alsager, between them. 'What is more difficult to understand,' wrote A. P. Wadsworth (editor of the *Manchester Guardian* from 1944 to 1956) in his study *Newspaper Circulations 1800–1954*, 'is why, between 1820 and 1855, one paper should have come to dominate the field. The rise of *The Times* under Barnes and Delane is extraordinary even by the eccentric standards of our own day.' The answer in part lies in the meticulous organization and dauntless enterprise of the men who served the paper.

5 DELANE TAKES OVER

(i) Walter's Young Friend

The new Editor of *The Times* was a young man of remarkable self-confidence. 'By Jove, John,' he said, bursting into the room of his friend Blackwood, the publisher, 'What do you think has happened? I am editor of *The Times!*'

Delane was twenty-three years old when he succeeded Barnes in the summer of 1841 and had had one year's experience on the paper. But so far as is known he was Walter's first, only, and unhesitating choice. Walter had certainly had plenty of opportunity to judge him: his father was a manager of *The Times* and lived close to Walter's Berkshire home.

How, it may be asked, was a man of twenty-three, with only one year's service on *The Times*, able to take over this great organization without making fatal misjudgments in the early stages, before he had time to acquire the necessary experience? The question certainly needs an answer. Such an appointment would scarcely be credible today, and when John Walter III tried to repeat the performance later in the century there was to be disaster.

The answer lies primarily in the innate qualities of Delane himself, 'including his assiduity and tact', as a colleague put it. But he started off with certain other advantages. His apprenticeship had been short, but of the right kind. He had been brought up in the atmosphere of Printing House Square and Bear Wood, and must as a boy have absorbed much newspaper lore through listening to the talk of his elders. He had done casual journalism at Oxford, served a spell in the parliamentary gallery, read a little law, and above all been trained under the Master – Barnes. In Henry Reeve, who had recently succeeded Edward Sterling as principal leader writer, he had a highly competent and well-informed lieutenant. He inherited, too, some notable contacts.

> The friendly relations which had for some time subsisted between Mr Greville and Mr Barnes [wrote Reeve], were strengthened and consolidated under the administration of his successor. Mr Delane was well aware that he could nowhere meet with a more sagacious adviser or a more valuable ally. He owed to Mr

Greville his first introduction to political society, of which he made so excellent a use.

The testimony of Reeve is confirmed by Greville who explained that he became more intimate with Delane than he had ever been with Barnes. But whatever introduction to society Delane may have had from others, he remained in that society because of his position as Editor of the paper.

Most important of all, Delane could count during the early years on the guiding hand of the proprietor. John Walter II adopted the same policy with Delane as he had with Barnes in 1817. Only gradually did he transfer complete control to the new Editor. Walter, now sixty-five, stumped up to London and took his seat once again at the desk in Printing House Square. 'Short conversation after dinner,' notes an aspirant journalist, 'then the subject was announced, and I was left alone till tea-time, when Mr Walter appeared, read aloud what I had done, with criticisms, and after correction carried off the copy to the printer.' The picture, corroborated from other sources, is of a Chief Proprietor exercising at this time complete executive control of the paper. To a 'newsy' young journalist like Delane this régime may at times have appeared irksome.

> In consequence of my conversation with you this morning [wrote Walter to a Conservative party manager], I made an immediate visit to my young friend [Delane] at Blackfriars. I there imparted to him, in a great degree, what had passed between us – that I thought it ought to be satisfactory to him, as I am sure it would have been to me in early days, that the Government communications should be made impartially – equally, fairly, & impartially – to all the Government Journals, without any reference to their several sales, or their presumed influence upon that ground . . . *The Times* & the *Standard*, the *Post* & the *Herald*, should be upon the same footing.

One wonders how his 'young friend' reacted to the visit. No doubt he said 'yes' but meant 'no'. In the coming years he was not to show much reverence for such sentiments.

Walter had good reason for preferring not to be associated too openly or closely with editorship of *The Times* from 1841, since he was still actively engaged in politics. He had petitioned against his defeat in the June election at Nottingham, and the process went through some complicated procedures before he was finally unseated. Delane's tutelage ended in 1847 with Walter's death. From then on the roles were reversed. Delane repaid the debt to his sponsor by putting an arm round the shoulder of his son and successor, John Walter III.

(ii) The Cabinet's Secret

The pinnacle of Barnes's power had been reached at the time of the Tamworth Manifesto, when he helped to put a new government in. The pinnacle of Delane's was to come in the Crimean War, when he was largely instrumental in putting a government out. But before this John Walter's 'young friend' was responsible for one of the most spectacular journalistic coups of history.

Shortly after Barnes's death in 1841, Sir Robert Peel had become Prime Minister again. Four years later Peel, who had come in as head of a strong government, became convinced of the necessity to repeal the Corn Laws, although most of his supporters were protectionists. The subject was every bit as emotive as Catholic Emancipation or the Reform Bill. The conflicting interests of town and country, landowners and commercial classes, Whigs and Tories were involved, backed by rival economic philosophies and deep-seated traditional prejudices. The Duke of Wellington, who was in the Cabinet, would once more be asked to do an 'about-turn'.

On 4 December a startled country awoke to read in its morning Times the following paragraph:

> The decision of the Cabinet is no longer a secret. Parliament, it is confidently reported, is to be summoned for the first week in January; and the Royal speech will, it is added, recommend an immediate consideration of the Corn Laws, preparatory to their total repeal. Sir Robert Peel, in one house, and the Duke of Wellington in the other, will, we are told, be prepared to give immediate effect to the recommendation thus conveyed.

That morning, in the words of Greville, 'the whole town had been electrified'. Peel's Government in those days included a Minister, Lord Wharncliffe, who was responsible for press relations. He was Greville's chief, so Greville was in a good position to know what was going on. Wharncliffe immediately sent for Reeve, and denied the truth of The Times report. But he refused to be quoted in print. This was not good enough for Delane and Reeve. They stuck to their story.

The Tory press described it as an 'atrocious fabrication'. But again Delane noticed that the description was 'non-attributable'. The Government still shrank from authenticating a denial. Delane stuck his neck out. He republished the story, with a slight amendment. The revised version substituted the words 'heads of the government' for 'Cabinet' as being the parties who had agreed to repeal. Delane knew by now that there were minor dissidents in the Cabinet. What Delane did not know was that, during the interval between the publication of the two articles, the whole situation had changed completely. On the day when he published the first article he was right. But next day the opposition of the anti-Repealers proved so boisterous that the Government resigned. Wharncliffe, of course, as a member of the Cabinet, knew about this but could not say. Once more he warned Greville and Reeve 'neither you nor Reeve know anything of what is going on'. Reeve got cold feet, but Delane was not to be shaken. 'Dear Reeve,' he wrote, 'we are quite safe – plenty of Cabinet opposition but we are sure to be proved right by facts.'

So he was. The opposition soon failed to form a government. Peel's Government returned and duly repealed the Corn Laws. Once more *The Times* proved omniscient and its rivals looked silly.

Delane's informant was Lord Aberdeen, the Foreign Secretary, with whom he had quickly established cordial relations. This is why Delane was so sure he was right. But Aberdeen only told him half the truth. He never warned him about the Government's resignation on the following day. When Delane found this out on 1 December, he must have gone through some anxious days. Only on 21 December did Peel resume office.

Delane may be considered lucky, or superhumanly prophetic, according to one's outlook. He himself said 'that the whole thing turned on the Duke of Wellington'. Did he know that the Duke had agreed? Aberdeen did not tell him in so many words; but he may have said enough for Delane to have inferred it. Or is it possible that Delane learnt it in some other way which he never revealed?

It is not unknown, of course, for politicians and journalists to conspire together to produce an effect. Both Aberdeen and Delane believed strongly that the Corn Laws ought to be repealed. Aberdeen knew that most of the key figures in government were in favour. Delane knew the middle classes, i.e. 'public opinion', were in favour, and that only the squires opposed repeal. They may have decided between them to force the pace. In the long run Delane could hardly have been wrong. The incident is a classic example of his method, and a tribute to his steady nerve.

The story had a curious aftermath which has passed into literature. Rumour had it that Delane acquired his information from a more romantic source than Lord Aberdeen. Sidney Herbert, the young Secretary at War, was said to have leaked the information to a famous beauty, Sheridan's granddaughter Caroline Norton. Mrs Norton, who was an occasional contributor to *The Times*, hastened with her news to Printing House Square, where she obtained admittance to the Editor in his 'dark, dark den'. To him she sold her information for £500, being at the time in need of ready cash.

The story died hard. Delane never denied it. George Meredith picked it up and wove it, with melodramatic embellishments, into his novel

Diana of the Crossways. In later editions he was persuaded to add – no doubt by his publishers' lawyers – that the incident must be read as fictional. It is a case where fiction, if not stranger, was certainly more enduring than the truth.

(iii) Preparing for War

Disraeli many years later was to call the Crimea 'a just but unnecessary war' – thus prefiguring almost the exact words another leader of the Conservative Party, Winston Churchill, was to use about the war which broke out in 1939. A series of blunders, misunderstandings, and miscalculations by all those concerned caused this explosion of the perennial Eastern Question.

Public opinion in Britain shared few of the Aberdeen Government's reservations. For a generation anti-Russian feeling had been strong. It was now whipped up to a fury. 'The violence and scurrility of the press,' Greville wrote in his diary for 26 September, 'exceeds all belief. Day after day the Radical and Tory papers, animated by very different motives, pour forth the most virulent abuse of the Emperor of Russia, of Austria, and of this Government, especially of Aberdeen.'

On 30 November a Turkish squadron was annihilated by the Russian Black Sea fleet in the harbour of Sinope. As hostilities between the two countries had broken out some weeks earlier there was no reason why this should not happen, but the British public worked itself into a state of hysteria over the 'massacre of Sinope'. Already the ways of the Government and *The Times* had diverged and a breach been effected in the personal relations between Aberdeen and Delane, but Sinope was the open breaking-point. A leading article in *The Times* of 13 December called for Britain to declare war on Russia, though it was to be over three months before this actually happened.

The run-up to the Crimean War was not *The Times*'s most glorious hour. If ever there were times when it reflected, rather than led, public opinion, this was one. Privately John Walter admitted that the paper had been 'browbeaten into support of the war'. For *The Times*, the nation, and the other countries involved, it was a case of the old Homeric saying – 'For the iron itself draws a man on.'

Now there was to be a war Delane's business was to see that *The Times* was best equipped to cover and comment upon it. The first need was to appoint correspondents who were to follow events in the theatre of operations. The next was to arrange a visit for himself to the Crimea, in order that as Editor he should have first-hand knowledge when handling news and planning leaders in London. But before all this happened, *The Times* pulled off another of its journalistic coups.

The ultimatum offering peace or war to the Russians was sent via Paris and took some days to reach St Petersburg. Delane got hold of this fact, and of the gist of the terms, and published them before the courier arrived.

The leading article of 28 February 1854 declared that:

> The Governments of England and France have resolved to address to the Emperor of Russia a formal summons calling upon him to give within six days from the receipt of that communication a solemn promise and engagement that he will cause his troops to evacuate the principalities of the Danube on or before the 30th of April. The couriers who are the bearers of this despatch from London to Paris started on their journey yesterday morning. The refusal on the part of Russia to comply with this just demand will be regarded by the Powers as a declaration of war.

So the Tsar first read the ultimatum in *The Times*. Both government and opposition were incensed. Lord Derby, the opposition leader, had already attacked Delane for publishing a secret proposal by the Tsar to partition Turkey. Now he accused Aberdeen of leaking. This was ironical. Since Delane had gone over to the war party, they had been scarcely on speaking terms.

The Government were almost certainly falsely accused. In all probability the information came from Sir Charles Napier, who had been given command of the naval force which was to attack the Russians in the Baltic. He owed his appointment in part to Delane, was a regular informant, and had been dining with the Editor.

The Times felt called upon to make a declaration of policy and did so in terms which have since served as a credo for all independent journalists:

> We hold ourselves responsible not to Lord Derby or the House of Lords, but to the people of England, for the accuracy and fitness of that which we think proper to publish. Whatever we conceive to be injurious to the public interests, it is our duty to withhold; but we ourselves and the public at large are quite as good judges on that point as the leader of the Opposition, whose object is not to serve the State, but to embarrass the Ministry.

The phrases are justificatory and sonorous. They carried the war into the enemy's camp. One can well imagine the smile on the face of the writer. *The Times* had been through a bad year. The staff needed a morale-booster before starting on the next phase. Now they had it.

The posting of staff to the scene of war fell properly within the responsibility of Mowbray Morris, the new Manager. Morris, a man in his thirties, with cultural interests, resembled more the past school of Barnes and Alsager than did Delane.

The most critical choice, that of the correspondent with the main British force, appears to have been Delane's. On a February evening William Howard Russell, who had been recruited in 1844 by Delane to report on Irish affairs, was summoned by the Editor and told that he was to proceed with the Guards to Malta. Russell, who had now moved to London as a part-time employee of *The Times*, had shown abilities as a war correspondent in the short Schleswig-Holstein campaign of 1850. He had become a popular figure in London literary society, and several fellow members of the Garrick, including Dickens and Thackeray, clubbed together to give him a farewell dinner.

Next, a stringer had to be found to cover the operations of the Turks on the Danube. Mowbray Morris heard of a young officer, Charles Nasmyth, on sick leave from the Bengal Artillery. Nasmyth proved a useful correspondent and a magnificent *condottiere*. In March 1854 he took charge of the Turkish defence of Silistria as a result of which the Turks beat off the Russians. His enthusiasm for fighting sometimes caused him to neglect to file, and drew hasteners from Mowbray Morris. But the kudos which he collected over the successful defence of Silistria certainly added lustre to the paper that employed him.

Into Constantinople, as anchor man and to cover the diplomatic side, Morris put Thomas Chenery, a brilliant linguist and a future editor of *The Times*. The paper also needed a rover, someone to go to unexpected emergencies, relieve a colleague in sickness, or help one who was over-strained. For this role they selected General Eber, a Hungarian freedom fighter. Ferdinand Eber was another inveterate *condottiere*. If offered a brigade of any nationality to take into battle he could never resist accepting.

Morris's policy was that no two correspondents should ever be in one place at the same time but it took more than this to keep Eber away from the scene of action. It was to Eber that Russell exclaimed after Inkerman 'God! Wasn't it an awful day!!!' 'Awful?' replied Eber, looking up from his supper which was spread on an old newspaper, 'No, a most bewdiful day: fine baddle as ever vos. No men ever fide bedder! . . . De Generals should all be shot.' Such were the men who represented Printing House Square in the first systematic attempt by a newspaper to give comprehensive coverage to a major war. They did not fail her.

Delane's own trip to the scene of action was soon arranged. His travelling companions were Alexander Kinglake, who later wrote the history of the war, and Sir Henry Layard, a diplomat and archaeologist. Armed with letters of introduction from the Secretary of War, the Duke of Newcastle, they were accorded the status of 'TG's', or Travelling Gentlemen, and suffered none of the inconveniences which were to afflict Russell. The party journeyed via Vienna and Athens to Constantinople, where Delane dined with the Ambassador, Lord Stratford de Redcliffe, and recorded that he was 'disgusted at the tone of the whole Embassy'. He then went on to the Crimea, where he witnessed the landings, saw the principal commanders, and had consultations with Russell. 'In every regiment,' he noted, 'there are sad traces of cholera and fever in the pale faces, lank forms, and tottering steps of the men. The Guards are by far the worst.' In early October he was back at his desk. He had profited much by the meetings and the first-hand impressions he had gained. But he missed the Alma, when these fever-stricken regiments, with the Guards in the forefront, hurled from the heights an army in position and in immensely superior force.

6 CRIMEA: THE MELANCHOLY CATASTROPHE

(i) The Influence of 'a Mr Russell'

When Russell set out in February 1854 to accompany the Guards Brigade to the Mediterranean, war had not yet been declared. He duly presented himself at Southampton, where the troops were embarking, but here he encountered a setback – the first of many. His official permit had not arrived. The Guards would not let him on board. Russell was compelled to make his own way to the next staging point, Malta; there the Greenjackets gave him onward passage to Gallipoli. They sailed on 31 March, three days after the declaration of war. Russell left at one hour's notice. His Maltese servant had absconded with his kit, after being given an advance of wages to leave 'with his wife and three small children'.

The Allies' campaign was conducted in two parts. The first was the landing of a force to support the Turks in their resistance to the Russians on the Danube. The actual expedition to the Crimea – what would now be spoken of as a large-scale combined-operations raid – was an afterthought.

Russell's transport discharged its burden at Gallipoli on 5 April, and from here we get the first of his warning dispatches. Russell reports the daily arrival of the French:

> The admirable completeness of all their arrangements in every detail – hospitals for the sick, bread and biscuit bakeries, wagon trains for carrying stores and baggage – every necessary and every comfort, indeed, at hand the moment the ships come in.

With the British, the state of affairs was far different:

> With the augmentation of the allied forces, the privations to which the men were at first exposed became greater, the inefficiency of our arrangements more evident... Amid the multitude of complaints which met the ear from every side, the most prominent were charges against the commissariat ... Early and late these officers might be seen toiling amid a set of apathetic Turks and stupid araba drivers, trying in vain to make bargains and give orders in the language of signs ...

The men suffered badly from the cold. They only had a single blanket, and some had no beds to lie on. 'The worst thing was the continued want of comforts for the sick. Many of the men labouring under diseases contracted at Malta were obliged to stay in camp in the cold.' This was a mild foretaste of horrors to come.

Russell inveighed particularly against the wearing of the stock. The men, he wrote, were 'red in the face as bakery cooks,' and gasping for breath, for 'a rigid band of leather is fixed tightly round their throats'. Their coats were buttoned up so as 'to aid the work of suffocation'. Largely due to Russell's dispatches, wearing of the stock was soon made optional. The Guards set the trend. Some months later Sidney Herbert, the Secretary at War, abolished it.

That Russell's strictures were not just the carpings of a barrack-room lawyer is proved by the voluminous corroborating evidence contained in private correspondence. Raglan's officers were great letter-writers; and in those days there was no censorship. Delane, like Barnes, believed in checking on public opinion. These letters home, after reaching the families of men in power, had a cumulative effect; no doubt many reached Printing House Square.

The higher command, who naturally did not like Russell's criticisms, took minor reprisals. They forbade him to bivouac within army lines, and on at least one occasion his tent was thrown down. Yet neither his writings nor his personality were unpopular at lower levels, particularly among the junior officers. George Lawson, a young surgeon who had volunteered for the campaign, belonged to a service singled out for particular criticism by Russell.

> I read in *The Times* Newspaper [Lawson wrote], which came out here a capital account of Gallipoli, headed 'from our correspondent'. He is a Mr Russell, an exceedingly amusing man, a general favourite out here.
>
> He remained at our quarters for some time, and would write his letters for *The Times* when the room was full of men and all talking. His account of Gallipoli is perfectly true and not the least exaggerated. What astonished us most was the cool manner in which the Duke of Newcastle contradicts his statements and makes out that the arrangements out here are admirable.*

Newcastle was by no means so unshaken by Russell's dispatches as he appeared to be publicly. Behind the scenes, the Secretary for War was already nagging the Commander-in-Chief.

> During the few days I remained at Scutari [wrote Sir George Brown, Commander of the Light Division, in disgust], instead

---

* George Lawson: *Surgeon in the Crimea.* Edited by Victor Bonham-Carter, Constable, 1968.

of having leisure to look about me or time to attend to necessary business, I was most unprofitably occupied in entering into explanations as regards to charges of neglect preferred in Mr Russell's gossiping letters from Gallipoli, which the Duke of Newcastle had considered of sufficient importance to cause to be cut from *The Times* newspaper, and referred to Lord Raglan!

Raglan was aware that things were wrong. He was simply too old, and too polite, to fight the home authorities on behalf of his army as his old chief the Duke had done in Peninsular days.

(ii) The Landing

The decision to land in the Crimea and to capture the Russian naval base and fortress of Sebastopol was taken on 28 June. According to Kinglake, Newcastle read to a somnolent Cabinet his dispatch to Raglan pressing for an invasion. By this time the army round Varna had little left to do. The Russian withdrawal from Silistria – for which *The Times* stringer's military initiative was so largely responsible – had removed the immediate threat to Turkey. The Austrians, too, had intervened. But public opinion in Britain wanted an identifiable victory.

On 15 June, about two weeks before the decision was taken, *The Times* wrote in a leader:

> The grand political and military objects of the war cannot . . . be attained as long as Sebastopol and the Russian fleet are in existence . . . we hold, therefore, that the taking of Sebastopol and the occupation of the Crimea are objects which would repay all the costs of the present war, and would permanently settle in our favour the principal questions now in dispute.

The timing of this leader has led some to credit Delane with the whole scheme. This is going too far. Delane, as usual, was crystallizing public opinion. No doubt he was in communication with those who knew about the plan. On the morning that the leader appeared, Palmerston made a similar recommendation in Cabinet. The coincidence suggests at least some communication, but there is no proof.

When Raglan received Newcastle's dispatch at Varna, he sent for his old Peninsular contemporary, Sir George Brown. Pushing the paper across the desk to him, he went on with his work. When Brown had had time to digest it, Raglan asked for his opinion. Brown asked what information he had about the strength of the Russians at Sebastopol, and Raglan told him none.

> You and I [observed Sir George Brown], are accustomed, when in any difficulty . . . to ask ourselves how the Great Duke would

have acted . . . Now, I tell your Lordship that, without more certain information . . . that great man would not have accepted the responsibility of undertaking such an enterprise as that which is now proposed to you. But notwithstanding that consideration, I am of the opinion that you had better accede to the proposal . . . it is clear to me . . . that they have made up their minds to it at home, and that if you decline to accept the responsibility, they will send someone else out to command the army, who will be less scrupulous.

Thus was the plan decided upon. For Russell, the problem was how he should accompany the seaborne landing. Delane had been promised at the War Office that his correspondent should be allowed to accompany the army and to draw rations. So far the higher command had shown no signs of honouring the charge – were, indeed, positively hostile.

Writing to Delane – 'there is no beef for the men for three days, only mutton which gives them dysentery; the sappers do their surveys in full dress, as their undress clothes were not ready when they left' – Russell lets out a *cri de coeur*: 'Am I to tell these things or hold my tongue?'

For Russell's passage to the Crimea, help came from an unexpected source. The commander of the 2nd Division was Lieutenant-General Sir George De Lacy Evans. Sir George was a hatchet-faced man with frizzy hair who had more experience of command in war than any other British general in the Crimea. He had served in India, in the Peninsula, at Baltimore (two horses shot from under him) and at Waterloo (two more); later he had commanded the British legion in the Carlist Wars in Spain. In between he represented Rye in the House of Commons as a Radical. He was also an Irishman. The Irish general took pity on the Irish scribbler. He gave him a berth in his own transport. Later, he took to scribbling himself – to the Editor of *The Times*, without the knowledge of the Commander-in-Chief.

At dawn on 12 September Russell and a group of officers were on deck. On the port side they could see a dark line. As the sun got up, they could identify it as land. The curiosity and trepidation at the first view of an invasion beach infected all those aboard. Russell, peering through his glass, was beginning to pick out the landmarks:

The impression as we drew near was that the coast presented a remarkable resemblance to the dunes of La Belle France. The country was flat, but numerous herds of cattle were to be seen in the plains and salt marshes and the farmhouses became more frequent as we proceeded.

The solid stone houses close by the sea coast were so increased by refraction that they looked like forts. Towards the south side were innumerable windmills, and several bathing boxes gaily painted along the beach gave an air of civilization to the place.

Russell had plenty of time for such observations. The landfall was followed by no flurry of landing-craft leaving the transports. The actual landing beach had not been decided upon at Varna: it was selected by Raglan after local reconnaissance. The sailing transports carrying the French were some way behind the steamers, and were still awaited. The fleet cruised around off Eupatoria and Kalamita Bay for two days. Luckily for the Allies the Russians were just as lackadaisical. Except for a Cossack officer making sketches from the back of his horse, there were few signs of hostile movement.

On 14 September Russell landed with one of the first waves. He was dressed in the borrowed motley which was to become the distinguishing mark of *The Times* Crimea correspondent – a commissariat officer's gold-rimmed cap, a rifleman's dark patrol jacket, and light breeches stuffed into black butcher boots.

In his eagerness to get ashore, Russell had not made good his lines of retreat. He shared the wretched, sodden first night with the troops. Like his enemy, Sir George Brown, he crept under a cart to sleep. Of the senior generals only that old campaigner Sir George De Lacy Evans thought to bring a tent ashore. It was one praiseworthy point about the Crimean commanders that, old as they were, most of them shared their discomforts with their men – always, of course, excepting Lord Cardigan. To him this 'organized discomfort' made no appeal.

(iii) *March to Sebastopol*

A few days later, on 19 September, the army set off for Sebastopol, marching across the plains in their scarlet tunics with bands playing and colours cased. 'The effect' observed Russell in his dispatches, 'of these grand masses of soldiery descending the ridges of the hills, rank after rank, with the sun playing over forests of glittering steel, can never be forgotten by those who witnessed it.' As they approached the heights beyond the river Alma, they encountered the Russian army in position.

Russell's problem – and it was to be that of many of his successors in later wars – was to find the best position from which to report the battle. In making his choice he had the advantages neither of well-tried experience, nor of headquarters' briefings. Having transported him to the scene of action De Lacy Evans made it clear that *The Times* correspondent could now fend for himself. General Pennyfeather, whom Russell encountered that morning, did not help either. The correspondent, riding past the general's headquarters, was summoned to his presence by an ADC and asked his business.

'By God, Sir,' exclaimed the General, when Russell told him, 'I had as soon see the devil! What do you know about this kind of work, and what will you do when we get into action?'

'Well, sir,' answered Russell, 'it is quite true I have very little acquaintance with the business, but I suspect there are a great many here with no greater knowledge than myself.'

Pennyfeather laughed. 'Begad, you're right. You're an Irishman, I'll be bound, and what's your name, sir?' Russell told him. 'Are you from Limerick?' 'No, sir; but my family are.' 'Well, good-bye; go to the rear, I tell you now. There will be wigs on the green today.'

Later, as round-shot crashed about them, he met Sir George Brown. 'I could not help thinking there was a little pleasant malice in his salutation to me. As he rode past, he said in a very jaunty, Hyde Park manner, "It's a very fine day, Mr Russell".'

After the victory, Russell spent a melancholy day among the wounded. The British, he noted, were sent to the sea in jolting native carts or litters. The French, in contrast, were transported in well-appointed hospital vans drawn by mules. What Russell could not yet know was that this journey was only the beginning of a long and painful pilgrimage, in ships with no medical facilities of any kind, to crowded and under-staffed base hospitals in which a large proportion of those who ever reached them would die.

The army marched on, and past Sebastopol. Raglan was, it is generally believed, in favour of assaulting there and then. Had he done so the fortress would have fallen. But the French opposed him. St Arnaud, their Commander-in-Chief, preferred to wait for the siege train. If Raglan had backed his own judgment the campaign would have been over. Instead the armies had to endure the fearful winter in the trenches while the Russians, under the direction of the great military engineer Todleben, strengthened their defences.

At this time, a false report circulated that Sebastopol had actually been taken. Injudiciously, *The Times* published it. The report did not originate from Russell.

After the Alma the army settled down around the British base at Balaclava, and Russell shared the life of the camp. His dispatches continued to be well respected in the regiments. 'I find *The Times* correspondent's letters very interesting,' wrote Captain Sir George Ashley Maude, the Commander of 'I' Troop, Royal Horse Artillery, 'as they tell us of things we did not know of, not having happened to be with that particular part of the army.'

(iv) Balaclava

On 25 October Russell had the privilege of reporting one of the most famous battles in British history. This time he had no need to worry about choosing a vantage point. From the heights above Balaclava he could see the contending forces laid out as if in the display case of a military museum.

The battle was divided into three acts: the attack of the Russian cavalry on the 93rd Highlanders – later the Argylls; the charge of the Heavy Brigade; and the charge of the Light Brigade up the 'valley of death'. Never before or since has so famous a battle been so fully reported by so distinguished a war correspondent.

In Act One of the battle, masses of Russian cavalry, after clearing the Turks out of a series of gun redoubts, swept down on Balaclava harbour. All that stood between them and the British base were Sir Colin Campbell and the 93rd, drawn up in line, two-deep.

The silence [wrote Russell] is oppressive; between the cannon bursts one can hear the champing of bits and the clink of sabres in the valley below. The Russians on their left drew breath for a moment, and then in one grand line dashed at the Highlanders. The ground flies beneath their horses' feet; gathering speed at every stride, they dash on towards that thin red streak topped with a line of steel . . .

With breathless suspense everyone awaits the bursting of the wave upon the line of Gaelic rock; but ere they come within 150 yards another deadly volley flashes from the levelled rifle and carries death and terror into the Russians. They wheel about, open files right and left and fly back faster than they came. 'Bravo, Highlanders! Well done!' shout the excited spectators.

All this took place on the right of the British position. Meanwhile, nearer the centre, another vast mass of Russian cavalry, 3,000 to 4,000-strong, was advancing towards Balaclava. Brigadier-General Scarlett's Heavy Brigade, about 500-strong, waiting concealed behind a fold in the ground, charged the Russians.

As lightning flashes through a cloud [wrote Russell] the Greys and Enniskilliners pierced through the dark masses of Russians. The shock was but for a moment. There was a clash of steel and a light play of sword blades in the air, and then the Grays and the redcoats disappear in the midst of the shaken and quivering columns. In another moment we see them emerging and dashing on with diminished number, and in broken order, against the second line . . . Already gray horses and redcoats had appeared right at the rear of the second mass, when, with irresistible force, like one bolt from a bow, the 1st Royals, the 4th Dragoon Guards and the 5th Dragoon Guards rushed at the remnants of the first line of the enemy, went through it as though it were made of pasteboard, and . . . put them to utter rout.

Russell reports that the British casualties were light. Apart from losses by artillery fire, 'there were not more than four or five men killed outright'. The Russian cavalry was now in full retreat, but unpursued. There was an interval of about forty-five minutes before the curtain went up on the Third Act – which Russell describes as 'the melancholy catastrophe which fills us all with sorrow' – the charge of the Light Brigade.

From his vantage point on the heights, Russell saw one of the ADCs, a brilliant and dashing hussar officer called Nolan, plunge down to the cavalry bearing Raglan's order for the charge. The speed and *élan* with which he descended into the valley excited the admiration of the watchers. Raglan's order, as scrawled by his quartermaster-general at a vantage point whence both could survey the whole battlefield, seemed to them clear. It read: 'Lord Raglan wishes the cavalry to advance rapidly to the front – follow the enemy and try to prevent the enemy carrying away the guns – Troop horse artillery may accompany. French Cavalry is on your left.' In those days the numbers of guns taken in battle were a measure of the victory gained. The guns in the redoubts to the British right could be seen from GHQ plainly, with the Russians preparing to tow them away to the rear.

The horse artillery troop referred to was Captain Maude's. 'I' Troop had been busy shelling the Russian cavalry in the early stages, but by now had lost most of its horses and guns. Its gallant commander was on the way to Balaclava, having lost a leg, an eye, and an arm. 'It has pleased God that I should be wounded this time,' he wrote to his wife. 'A large shell burst along side my poor old mare, and killed her.'

The French cavalry were the Chasseurs d'Afrique, who later delivered a smashing diversionary charge into the Russian artillery who were enfilading the Light Brigade from the left.

Clear as all this was to Raglan, it was Chinese to Lucan, the divisional commander, down in the smoke and confusion of the valley. He could not see what was happening up on the redoubts, the horse artillery was no longer mobile, and he had no contact with the French.

Nolan, who was required to interpret the order, was not a trained staff officer in the modern sense. He was an outstanding horseman who introduced into the British Army novel methods of training cavalry horses. But his behaviour that day showed that he had no conception of the proper functions of a liaison officer in querying and explaining orders. Whether he understood, or even thought he understood, Raglan's order remains to this day an unsolved mystery. When questioned by Lucan. he behaved in an excited manner and waved his arm – always a fatal gesture in a battle – towards the guns with the main Russian forces at the head of the valley.

Lord Lucan [wrote Russell], with reluctance, gave the order to Lord Cardigan to advance upon the guns, conceiving that his orders compelled him to do so. The noble Earl, though he did not shrink, also saw the fearful odds against him . . . The whole brigade scarcely made one effective regiment, according to the numbers of continental armies . . . As they passed towards the front, the Russians opened on them from the guns in the redoubt on the right, with volleys of musketry and rifles. They swept proudly past, glittering in the morning sun in all the pride and splendour of war. We could scarcely believe the evidence of our senses! Surely that handful of men are not going to charge an army in position? Alas! it was too true – their desperate valour knew no bounds, and far indeed was it removed from its so-called better part – discretion. They advanced in two lines, quickening their pace as they closed towards the enemy . . . At the distance of 1,200 yards the whole line of the enemy belched forth, from 30 iron mouths, a flood of smoke and flame, through which hissed the deadly balls. Their flight was marked by instant gaps in our ranks, by dead men and horses, by steeds flying wounded or riderless across the plain. The first line is broken, it is joined by the second, they never halt or check their speed an instant; with diminished ranks, thinned by those 30 guns, which the Russians had laid with the most deadly accuracy, with a halo of flashing steel above their heads, and with a cheer which was many a noble fellow's death-cry, they flew into the smoke of the batteries . . . We saw them riding through the guns . . . to our delight we saw them returning . . . When the flank fire of the battery on the hill swept them down, scattered and broken as they were. Wounded men and dismounted troopers flying towards us told the sad tale – demi-gods could not have done what we had failed to do . . . At 11.35 not a British soldier, except the dead and dying, was left in front of these bloody Muscovite guns.

Russell concluded his dispatch: 'All our operations in the trenches were lost sight of in the interest of this melancholy day, in which our Light Brigade was annihilated by their own rashness, and by the brutality of a ferocious enemy.'

This dispatch certainly ranks as the classic example of the military correspondent's art. Russell himself was not satisfied with it. He issued amended editions in later life, some to correct factual details, some points of style. Chief among these was the alteration to the phrase describing the stand of the Argylls. In later versions 'topped' became 'tipped' and 'thin red streak' became 'thin red line'.

(v) *'What will they say in England?'*

Such battles as Balaclava supplied Russell with the purple patches in his correspondence. The bulk of it was devoted to more mundane matters. All the time he was plugging away describing to *The Times* readers the appalling state of the men's rations, clothing, accommodation, and medical services, and giving warning of what was likely to happen with the onset of winter. 'What will they say in England?' he used to ask himself as he sat scrawling away in his tent. As the winter progressed, his dispatches became more harrowing. Even the generals who had passed their youth in the Peninsula admitted they had never seen anything like it. The officers, like the men, slept in their clothes. 'Many delicately-nurtured youths never changed shirts nor shoes for weeks together.'

On 14 November came a new calamity – the hurricane. 'The air was filled with blankets, hats, greatcoats, little coats, and even tables and chairs . . . Sheets of tent-canvas went whirling like leaves in the gale towards Sebastopol.' Even the highest did not escape. Lord Raglan had his roof blown off. 'Lord Cardigan was sick on board his yacht.' Seven vessels were reported sunk, and more driven ashore, some of them containing much-needed stores for the troops.

On 28 November cholera broke out again. As for Balaclava itself: 'Words could not describe its filth, its horrors, its hospitals, its burials, its dead and dying Turks, its crowded lanes, its noisome sheds, its beastly purlieus, or its decay.'

The hospitals aroused Russell's deepest horror. The commonest accessories were wanting. The stench was appalling. 'The foetid air could barely struggle out to taint the atmosphere, save through chinks in the walls and the roofs.' The men died without the least effort to save them: 'There they laid just as they were gently let down upon the ground by the poor fellows, their comrades, who brought them on their backs from the camp with the greatest tenderness, but who were not allowed to remain with them. The sick appeared to be tended by the sick, and the dying by the dying.'

There was no warm clothing. It was either sunk, or lost, or left in the open to saturate. When supplies did arrive, nobody would take the responsibility of issuing them to the troops.

In January, the men were still in filth. Huts had been sent out, but there was no means of transporting them to the camps. 'Now and then I met a wretched pony, knee-deep in mud, struggling on beneath the weight of two thin deal planks, a small portion of one of these huts, which were most probably turned into firewood.'

As these reports reached England, indignation mounted. They were confirmed by countless private letters reaching private families. The public knew them to be true. Russell had been accused of exaggeration and sensationalism, but the official figures were, if anything, more terrifying than his vivid imagery. Reports showed subsequently that nearly 80 per cent of all deaths during the war were caused by disease, as against 20 per cent by battle. During the medically critical months from October 1854 to April 1855, 35 per cent of the total strength of the army died from cholera, fever, and bowel and lung diseases. 'In the month of January' – so ran the official report – 'the health of the army rapidly deteriorated . . . thus illustrating the terrible, appalling, and almost, if not altogether, unparalleled result of an army *being nearly decimated in a single month.*'

The inefficiency of the authorities was systematically killing off the only army Britain had. Owing to the extremely long term of service for the regulars – enlistment was for life – there were no reserves. The high state of training, the toughness, and the miraculous *esprit de corps* of this army enabled it to perform prodigies. Its fever-stricken infantry could struggle uphill in face of a vastly superior enemy and drive him off the heights; its dragoons could hack their way through ten times their number of Cossacks; surprised in the dark at Inkerman the British regulars could fight off unlimited numbers of attackers without orders or direction from anyone. The replacements, quite naturally, were not of the same quality. This was shown only too clearly in the latter stages of the war, when their performance was not up to that of the French.

Delane had long realized that the source of trouble lay not so much in the failings of individuals as in the diffused responsibility for military affairs. The principle of the system dated from the Restoration, and was devised rather to prevent the King assuming military powers than to produce an efficient expeditionary force.

The Minister principally concerned with waging war was the Secretary of State for War and the Colonies, but he was prevented from devoting his undivided attention to the one, because he was also burdened with the other. But even in the sphere of war his powers were desperately hampered. Another Minister, the Secretary *at* War, was responsible for military finance and administration. The Chancellor of the Exchequer had to provide for the Commissariat, which was still a civilian organization working on contract. Inside the army the confusion was as great. The Commander-in-Chief commanded only home forces, and 'teeth arms' at that. The Master General of the Ordnance held sway over artillery, engineers, fortresses, arms and equipment and stores. The Home Secretary was concerned with the militia.

The system was *ipso facto* self-defeating. Everything was everybody's business, and nothing was one person's sole responsibility. The only reason why, at a later date, Florence Nightingale was able to make head-way in improving the medical services was because she was backed by private funds, her own and those of *The Times*. On one occasion *The Times* clothed a whole regiment, arrived from India in tropical kit, with winter underwear.

Delane had been campaigning all along to streamline the system. In June 1854 the Government took a first step, for which *The Times* claimed credit, by separating the Colonies from the War Ministry. Delane would have liked Palmerston to have had the new Ministry, but the incompetent Duke of Newcastle was left in control. Step by step the rationalization continued. In February 'For War' and 'At War' were merged. Some months later the office of Master General of the Ordnance was vested in the Minister.

(vi) Florence Nightingale

In October Chenery who, it will be recalled, was *The Times* man in Constantinople, intervened with dramatic results. He had been horrified to learn of conditions at the base hospital at Scutari, to which the wounded from the Battle of the Alma had been conveyed. The story was the usual one – lack of accommodation, lack of surgeons or dressers, lack of medical stores. There was less excuse for shortcomings than in the Crimea itself, since this was a hospital outside the battle area, where there had been ample time for preparation.

Chenery wrote a series of dispatches describing these conditions, and Delane capped them with a leader appealing for public benevolence. The response was instantaneous. The leader was published on 12 October, and on the same day Sir Robert Peel, the son of the former Prime Minister, sent *The Times* a cheque for £200 suggesting that it should raise a fund. This letter was published and money began to pour in.

On that day Chenery wrote in the paper that there were no dressers or nurses at Scutari. The French, as usual, had far better medical arrangements. 'They have also the help of the Sisters of Charity, who have accompanied the expedition in incredible numbers.' 'Why have we no Sisters of Charity?' demanded the writer of a letter to *The Times* the next morning.

The same morning, 14 October, Florence Nightingale sat down to write to her friend Mrs Sidney Herbert, wife of the Secretary at War. In her letter Miss Nightingale informed Mrs Herbert that she was going out to Scutari with three nurses paid for by a private benefactress, Lady Maria Forester. 'I do not mean to say that I believe *The Times* accounts, but I do believe that we may be of use to the wounded wretches.' Mrs. Herbert's husband, however, did believe *The Times* accounts. He knew the truth only too well. He was a man of conscience who was suffering from the knowledge that the economies practised by his department were partly responsible for the shortages. He too had been busy letter-writing that morning. The letter he wrote crossed Florence Nightingale's. In it he appealed to her to lead just such a mission with full official backing: 'There is but one person in England that I know of,' he wrote, 'who would be capable of organizing and superintending such a scheme.'

On 21 October Miss Nightingale sailed for Scutari with thirty-eight nurses. John MacDonald, a future manager of *The Times*, sailed with her as almoner to administer *The Times* Fund, now swollen to £7,000. His instructions were to give her all the help in his power. When he was recalled in February 1855, a young man called W. H. Stowe – a brilliant classical scholar, and Fellow of Oriel, who had been a member of the staff since 1852 – was sent out to replace him as administrator of the Fund and to act, when necessary, as correspondent. In May he contracted cholera and, as he was a civilian, was refused admission to the military hospital. He died on 22 June. Comment in the paper was understandably bitter.

So were conjoined the two most dynamic forces which emerged from the Crimean War – *The Times* and Florence Nightingale. The Government reacted with equal meanness and futility. They tried to discredit *The Times* – 'which has done us infinite mischief by descriptions of wounds and sufferings and hospital deficiencies' – and at the same time sent out a commission of inquiry which took four months to substantiate Chenery's reports.

Hitherto *The Times* had confined itself to picking its targets. In December Delane widened his attacks to cover the whole Government, together with Lord Raglan, the Commander-in-Chief. The Government, on its part, tried to belittle *The Times* Fund, which rose from £12,000 to £20,000, and to dissuade Florence Nightingale from making use of it. Miss Nightingale wanted an old burnt-out ward of her hospital repaired in a hurry and, getting no response from the Government, used money from *The Times* Fund and her private means to carry out the necessary work.

'We wipe our hands of the war under the existing management,' wrote *The Times* on 25 January 1855. The same day Lord John Russell resigned from the Government. The Duke of Newcastle attacked *The Times* in the Lords, alleging breaches of security and threatening to stop its correspondents' rations (intermittently issued as they were). In reply *The Times* revealed that it had offered to submit Russell's dispatches to censorship but that Newcastle had turned down the offer. As for the rations:

Let him comfort himself . . . the full value of every ration shall be repaid, and the churls who represent a generous country shall not have one farthing to charge to the historian of the war . . . It was but the other day another representative of *The Times* clothed a regiment which had been sent utterly unprovided by the War Department to rot away in the trenches before Sebastopol.

On 29 January the Government could hold out no longer. A radical MP, J. A. Roebuck, had moved for a Select Committee to inquire into the conduct of the war. The majority against the Government was 157, and there was no option but to resign. The new Prime Minister was Lord Palmerston. In spite of years of antagonism – both political and personal – between *The Times* and Palmerston, in this state of emergency his appointment was heartily welcomed by Delane on whose support the survival of the Government now largely depended. Lord Panmure, known as the 'Bison' because of his large head and shock of hair, became Secretary for (and at) War. Of him Kinglake, the historian of the Crimean War, wrote: 'He received his marching orders submissively from *The Times*, proceeded at once to obey them, and so trudged doggedly on, without giving other vent to his savageness than a comfortable oath and a growl.'

Lord Raglan soldiered on till 29 June, when he retired on grounds of health. The news of his death followed the announcement of his retirement by one day. Sebastopol fell in September. The French by now, because of conscription, vastly outnumbered the British, who at the storming of the Redan failed signally to live up to their past reputation. Some of the new recruits did not know how to fire a musket.

The Times as might have been expected, was the first to learn and to publish the news of the Russian acceptance of peace terms in Vienna. The members of the British Government read it in a special edition which was on sale by 11 o'clock on the morning of 17 January 1856, the message having been dispatched from Vienna at 10 o'clock the previous evening.

(vii) *The Organization of Opinion*

Wars, as has been noted, have been a principal stimulant of newspapers. The Crimean War was no exception. As a result of it *The Times* grew in stature. Barnes 'thundering for reform' had made the paper a domestic power; Delane, by his influence on international politics and strategy, and by publishing Russell's reports, had made it a European one.

Prince Gortschakoff, the Russian Commander in Sebastopol, later told Russell that his cousin in Warsaw used to forward him copies of *The Times*. It is a touching spectacle. There were the two Commanders-in-Chief, Raglan sitting in the sun in his white hat, and Gortschakoff down in the citadel behind the bastion; both poring over their morning *Times*. One would be interested to know who got his copy first – Gortschakoff overland from Warsaw or Raglan by sea from Constantinople. The story nonetheless has point in illustrating the extraordinary ubiquity of *The Times* in the places of power.

The war exposed new problems in the relationship between press and government. The first of these was censorship. Lord Raglan was constantly complaining that *The Times* was guilty of breaches of security and such breaches there undoubtedly were. No matter that Prince Gortschakoff later testified that he learnt nothing from *The Times* that he did not know already – he well might have done. Russell advanced as an argument in his defence the time-lag, but the time-lag was steadily being reduced. The Crimean War saw the laying of the submarine cable from Varna to Balaclava, linking London almost directly with the Crimea.

But over security the Government was equally to blame. *The Times* had offered to subject itself to voluntary censorship and had been rebuffed. The Government saw only too clearly the criticisms they would be exposed to if they once undertook this prickly responsibility, yet at the same time they dared not exclude *The Times* correspondent from the war area. Neither party had embarked on this war with any proper appreciation of the problems that would be raised by a professional correspondent accompanying the forces.

Among those who landed with reinforcements at Balaclava was a young lieutenant named Garnet Wolseley. Years later he brought out the first handbook designed to prepare soldiers for war and duties in the field. In *The Soldiers Pocket Book* he tackled the status of the press in his usual business-like manner. Under the heading 'Newspaper Correspondents' he wrote: 'Soldiers of course object to their presence in camp upon military grounds, but as long as the British public's craze for sensational news remains as it is now, the English General must accept the position.' So far, Raglan would have agreed. But Wolseley then proceeded to formulate 'Rules for Newspaper Correspondents at the Seat of War':

A Staff Officer will be named to act as Press Censor. He will register licences granted under the authority of the C-in-C at home . . . He will be the channel of communication between the GOC in the field and the correspondents . . . All communications must be sent through him . . . The GOC will through his SO give as much information as he may consider advisable, and consistent with his duty, to correspondents . . . The military Authorities will facilitate, so far as they can, the dispatch of the messages of correspondents.

The Times may have railed at Raglan, but the enlightened spoon-feeding of Sir Garnet would have made Russell's activities wholly impossible.

Security was not the only new aspect of the relationship between press and government raised by *The Times*'s role in the Crimea. Russell did for the Victorian public something of what in modern days television has done, for example, for the Americans over Vietnam. He brought the realities of war for the first time into ordinary homes – not of course visually, but far more swiftly and vividly than anything known to previous generations. And the public thereby reacted the more swiftly and violently upon the Government.

The Times during the Crimean War was described variously as mischievous, infamous, grovelling, and reckless. 'If England is ever to be England again, this vile tyranny of *The Times* must be cut off,' wrote a former Prime Minister, Lord John Russell. More precisely, *The Times* correspondent was accused of exaggeration and sensationalism. Russell was not, it must be admitted, 100 per cent accurate in his facts. In the lone-wolf life that he led, writing on the backs of saddles, by the light of guttering candles, and amid the clatter of the camp, he did very well to be as accurate as he was. His descriptive style was indeed sensational. He wrote to be read. The commanders who let 35 per cent of their army perish through sickness had no right to complain if Russell painted the picture in primary colours. Without Russell and Florence Nightingale, herself an emanation of *The Times*'s journalistic campaign, the figure would have been very much higher. The generals were accepting the conditions of eighteenth-century warfare in the mid-nineteenth century. That they saw themselves as disciples of the Great Duke seems strange; he least of all was given to toleration of sloppy administration.

Delane's conduct towards the Government was more than honourable. He did not confine himself to attacking them in print. He did his best to warn them in private. Russell, like all correspondents, wrote to his Editor private letters not meant for publication. These letters, Delane once wrote to him, 'went the round' of the Cabinet. Delane also saw Newcastle after his own visit to the scene of war and gave him some frank and sound opinions. The relationship between Delane and Ministers remained fairly close until the Editor cleared the decks for all-out war in December 1854.

That such close relations were a desirable part of an Editor's function is indisputable. The Government, when many of its members realized that the main burden of *The Times*'s charges was true, had however no right to complain that the paper had put its own interests before those of the nation. What angered them, no doubt, was the form in which Delane's general attack was launched. Delane, like Barnes, was waging a class war – not a class war in the Marxist sense, but a war of the new middle classes against the old landed aristocracy. Although the Reform Bill had established these classes in politics, large oases of power, of which the army was one, were still left to the aristocracy. In the conduct of the war, the middle classes found themselves largely spectators. Once again, it was the function of *The Times* to organize middle-class opinion, so that it might become an effective participant in government.

7 THE RISE OF THE PENNY PRESS

The situation of *The Times* at the end of the war was dazzling. The paper had wielded some influence in the making of the war, and decisive influence in its conduct. Delane and Russell between them had saved an army and destroyed a government. For promotional effect, the raising of *The Times* Fund and the part played in the Nightingale mission were unexampled in newspaper history. Russell's reportage was studied world-wide: coverage of the war by other papers apart from the work of the war artists of *The Illustrated London News* and the photographs of Roger Fenton, had been negligible.

The managerial basis of the paper was sound. In the first fifteen years of Delane's editorship the average annual circulation had climbed from 20,000 to over 58,000. This was more than three times the aggregate circulation of the whole of the rest of the London daily press. There was a waiting list for advertisements. The handful of shareholders were receiving fat dividends; in a good year a single one of them could get £6,000. Total annual dividends rose from £17,000 to £50,000 in these fifteen years. Nevertheless, in 1855, even before the war had ended, serious threats faced *The Times*. They were both political and financial.

On the political side, the venom with which *The Times* was regarded in some circles was strong. Its critics and enemies were powerful, and included the Crown, sections of the Whigs, the old Tories, and many Radicals. Nor was hostility purely unreasoning. In Britain, if any extra-constitutional body becomes too powerful it tends to provoke a reaction. In 1855 *The Times* provoked the same sort of fears that television and the trade unions provoke today. People might approve of Delane's fight to save the army before Sebastopol, but they questioned the moral justification for his wielding so much power.

The newspaper's 'monopoly' was constantly attacked. *The Times* could reply that it had no monopoly except that derived from the quality of the product. The critics thought differently. They attributed it to unfair advantages due to the 'taxes on knowledge'. *The Times*'s enemies, moreover, were by now much wiser than they had been in 1836, when Spring Rice and Brougham had attempted to undermine the paper's influence by a flat-rate reduction of the stamp duty. They realized that to be effective any further tax reduction must be discriminatory.

In July 1855 the stamp duty was totally repealed, to be replaced by a postage charge based on weight. This was designed to hit *The Times* as the bulkiest paper. A few months later Delane suffered a blow of a different sort in the resignation of his principal leader writer, Henry Reeve.

The criteria by which Delane's leader writers were selected seem astonishing today. Of the principal writers all four were employed in other more or less full-time external jobs. Henry Reeve was Clerk of Appeals to the judicial committee of the Privy Council. Robert Lowe was an active politician. Thomas Mozley was a beneficed country clergyman who had been a Fellow of Oriel. And Henry Annesley Woodham was a resident Fellow of Jesus College, Cambridge. As a means of organizing the leader writing in a great newspaper the system appears bizarre, and with no telephones it must also have been maddening. The railways now made it possible for letters and copy to pass backwards and forwards within the day, but Delane complained that Mozley and Woodham were only available for 'second day subjects'.

Reeve and Lowe, in addition to being leader writers, were important sources of information. Reeve, who worked under Charles Greville, the Clerk to the Council, must have been one of the best-informed men in the country. He regularly used his background knowledge in *The Times*'s interests, and no doubt also passed on hard news which he obtained from his friend Lord Clarendon, the Foreign Secretary. He was a man both of integrity and of pronounced views, whose speciality was foreign affairs. His politics had become progressively out of alignment with Delane's, and he quarrelled with Dasent, Delane's assistant editor. In October 1855 he finally resigned, ultimately to become the first editor of Greville's diaries and an honoured figure in the political society of the West End of London. The estrangement of Reeve, coming at the same time as the discriminatory postal rates, was awkward for Delane. Just when he most needed up-to-date information to deal with new press competitors, he had lost his best news contact.

At an even higher level, Delane's contacts were in need of repair. Palmerston, the new Prime Minister, had been *The Times*'s *bête noire* for over two decades, but he had been helped to his position by Delane's attacks on Aberdeen's Government and he badly needed Delane's continued support if his own Government was to prosper. Delane wanted a new contact at the top. In August there was a meeting between the two, and the alliance was sealed by a curious letter in *The Times* of 10 October signed by 'A Constant Reader'.

> That *The Times* has been converted by Lord Palmerston, no one will maintain . . . That Lord Palmerston was converted by *The Times* might or might not have been true . . . But the final and

most likely alternative – that both arrived more or less independently at the same conclusion, *The Times* by means of its extra-
traordinary information and consummate ability, and Lord
Palmerston in virtue of his own genius and experience as the
master diplomatist of the day, is a likelihood equally flattering
to both parties.

Old Lord Brougham described the whole transaction as 'devil wor-
ship'. Queen Victoria was so disgusted by the Crimean articles and
particularly by an attack on the reigning house of Prussia that she wrote
to Palmerston asking 'whether it is right that the Editor, the Proprietor
and the Writers of such execrable publications ought to be the honoured
and constant guests of the Ministers of the Crown?'

The 'taxes on knowledge' were removed in three stages. The removal
of the advertisement duty seems to have passed without much noticeable
effect on the structure of the press. Advertising rates in those days
were uniform for all papers – 3s 6d in the provinces and 5s 0d in London
for 'small' advertisements, i.e. classified advertisements of a few lines
each. This gave *The Times* an average yield of nearly ten guineas a
column in 1849. There was an average of $19\frac{1}{2}$ columns of classifieds a
day in *The Times* proper, exclusive of supplements.

In 1849, the first year in which accounts were fully recorded, gross
advertising revenue was £107,000 and gross revenue from sales of the
paper was £156,000. From these figures must be deducted £22,000 for
advertisement duty and £60,000 for the stamp tax. It is interesting to
see therefore that the net revenue from advertisements and sales was
about equal. Ten years later, when both taxes had been abolished,
advertising revenue was £225,000 – over double that of 1849 – and sales
revenue £219,000, not quite so large an increase. Although there were
no taxes to pay, there was still £17,000 to be deducted from the sales
revenue for postage.

The newspapers were naturally relieved to be rid of the tax, and
The Times must have benefited more than others since it carried far
more advertisements. Indeed, in 1822, when it first began to print
regular supplements, the motive had been to accommodate extra advertising, and the earlier four-page supplements usually carried nothing
else. *The Times* continued as a matter of policy to charge a low rate
for advertisements, and this remained unchanged between 1820 and
1850. The charges were fixed on a simple principle – 5s 0d for those
under four lines, and 6d for every line extra up to twenty lines. Advertising was not solicited during this period, the paper relying on its
overwhelmingly superior circulation to bring it in. In July 1861 *The
Times* carried 4,000 advertisements, a record for any newspaper.

One of the reasons for keeping the rate low was that the management had a keen appreciation of the importance of advertisements as news. Many readers bought the paper for no other reason than to study them. *The Times* with its unique position in the country was the prime means of supplying commercial information and domestic needs. However, the repeal of the second 'tax on knowledge', the stamp duty, compelled *The Times* to revise its policy of cheap advertising rates, for reasons which will be explained.

In October 1855 the stamp tax was finally and totally abolished. Although by now the tax was only 1d its repeal revolutionized the British press. The abolitionists were inspired by a number of motives. One was sheer malignancy towards *The Times*. Another, more worthy, motive, which had particular appeal to 'Manchester Radicals' such as Cobden and Bright, was encouragement of the provincial press, particularly among poorer readers. A third was that repeal seemed to be the culmination of the liberal policies of the age, the corollary of the repeal of the Corn Laws in 1846.

The abolition of the tax alone would scarcely have produced the desired consequences. But the tax had covered free postage of newspapers, and under the new dispensation postage was to be paid for by weight. *The Times* with its bulky supplements crammed with advertisements was heavier than any of its competitors. The postal charge incurred by the paper would be 1½d as opposed to 1d by other London papers. This meant that *The Times* outside London would cost 1½d more than its competitors in the provinces, and ½d more than other London papers.

So blatant was the malice towards the paper that one of its most hostile critics, Henry Drummond, MP, refused to vote for the Bill. 'They attacked *The Times* – they were afraid of it,' he declared. 'Go where they might, upon what railway they pleased, every man was reading and abusing *The Times*; but, instead of standing up boldly against it they gave it this dirty stab in the dark.'

The results of repeal were probably even more startling than its advocates had expected. *The Times* was now faced with the first real crisis in its career since 1800. The forward trend in its circulation was arrested. Average annual circulation remained in the low fifty thousands from 1857 to 1861, when the price was lowered to 3d. For the next seventeen years it remained close to 60,000, after which it began to fall away.

In 1856, the year following the repeal, 200 new newspapers were started. Some of the provincial press, hitherto mostly confined to weekly or bi-weekly periodicals, often exerting considerable local influence, converted to daily publication. Among famous newspapers which underwent this change were the *Manchester Guardian* and the *Scotsman*.

Among those launched in 1856 were the *Liverpool Post* and the *Sheffield Telegraph*. In subsequent years more titles were added to the roll. To this development *The Times* neither could, nor would, object. But from these years, possibly, dates the paper's tendency to be a metropolitan paper with circulation concentrated in the south-east.

The appearance, however, of a new, popular press, published in London and priced at 2d, which was quickly to drop to 1d, did seriously threaten *The Times*. Chief of these was the *Daily Telegraph*, founded in 1855. Joseph Moses Levy, its printer, who bought the paper a few weeks after a somewhat unsuccessful start, was the first man since John Walter II to make a commercial success out of national newspapers. The circulation reached 30,000 in 1857 and 141,000 by 1861. The latter figure far outstripped that of *The Times*. The *Daily News*, started in 1846 with Charles Dickens as Editor, also had early struggles, but rallied and reached 150,000 by the time of the Franco–Prussian War. Each of these papers found a writer of exceptional quality to further their sales. Archibald Forbes, of the *Daily News*, was acknowledged as the most successful correspondent of the Franco–Prussian War. George Augustus Sala, of the *Daily Telegraph*, was one of the most versatile and colourful journalists who ever bestrode Fleet Street. In 1857, the *Standard*, an evening paper, became a morning paper at 2d. Reduced to 1d in the following year, it helped to dent *The Times*'s circulation.

The Times had been accused of having a monopoly. In defending itself against this accusation on 11 February 1850, it had argued: 'Our monopoly is the monopoly of Barclay and Perkins porter, of Twining's tea, of Mr Cobden's agitation, and of Fortnum and Mason's hams. It is the monopoly of nothing but the first place, won by fair fighting and held against all comers on the same terms.' That monopoly, if such it was, had now ended. The contenders were no longer paper tigers, but efficiently produced newspapers.

In retrospect, it seems strange that the mere abolition of a penny tax should have had such far-reaching effect, when a reduction from 5d to 1d in 1836 had so little, except for accelerating the rise of *The Times*. The explanation lies in the attendant circumstances. The stamp tax repeal in 1855 was certainly a help to other papers, but the signal for, as much as the cause of, newspaper expansion. For by the mid-fifties many new factors were at work. There was a much larger readership ready for a brighter, cheaper type of newspaper. In many ways *The Times* had pointed the way to its rivals. The paper had been the first to use 'the electric telegraph' (1844), to introduce the rotary press (1848), and to show the world during the Crimean War what international newspaper coverage really meant. All these new resources were available for men of enterprise and ability to use, and the rise of the penny press, the provincial press, and the agencies – Reuters started in 1851 and the Press Association in 1865 – was to transform the scene in which *The Times* was to operate.

Thus in 1855 John Walter III, Delane and Mowbray Morris, the Manager, were three proud but perplexed men. They could not foresee the effect of these new developments, but a frank reappraisal of all their commercial assumptions was called for. They rose to the challenge.

Editorially, *The Times* suffered from one weakness which made it vulnerable to competition from a popular press addressed to a larger and less serious-minded readership than *The Times*. In spite of continual technical advances, there were still mechanical limitations on the size of the paper. The first sixteen-page issues were produced in 1851 and papers of this size became normal after 1855, but previously the problem had been to pack as much as possible into twelve pages. This necessity had an impact on the appearance and readability of the paper.

Barnes had tended to ignore problems of make-up. In the eighteenth century, *The Times* had shown a certain elegance of presentation, but early in the 1800s this was sacrificed to competitiveness. More and more small type – minion or 7-point – was used in the paper's columns. In 1816 the introduction of a still smaller type, 6-point, had caused labour unrest owing to the unwillingness of John Walter II to pay more for setting it. Progressively headings became smaller, there was less 'white' in the paper, and 'leading' between lines was reduced. On some occasions the two outer columns of the front page were run right up into the top corners – the 'ears' – on each side of the title. In short the paper was unattractive to look at and difficult to read. Delane was conscious of the problem. He preferred more 'white' on the page, and did keep an eye on the printer. Certainly, from 1840 onwards, the space allowed between lines showed a slight increase. Essentially, however, Delane left the paper much as he found it in appearance.

The whole attitude, no doubt, was typical of the early Victorians. The paper was produced on strictly utilitarian principles. Emphasis was laid on the quality and quantity of the content, not on fripperies. *The Times*'s readers were expected to be of such a calibre that they would be prepared to read their news the hard way.

However, a paper produced on these principles laid itself open to successful competition by a popular press seeking a new popular readership. Whereas the provision of a high-class foreign service was an expensive luxury, the production of a brighter and more attractive paper cost no more and could be used to compensate for lack of news. Here was a dilemma which was to confront *The Times* in different forms many times in its history. John Walter III regarded maintenance or abandonment of the character of the paper as a moral issue; his

rivals regarded the striking of a balance between content and presentation from a more commercial standpoint.

Although advertising, circulation and dividends were sound in 1855,
Walter could not afford to be complacent. In the last year of his father's
life there had indeed been a short, but unpleasant, financial crisis. The
truth of this 'scompiglio', as Charles Greville described it, will probably
never be known. It took place in 1846–7, and it is noteworthy that
The Times accounts start from 1849, suggesting that previous records
had been destroyed. John Walter II had detected irregularities in the
accounts. A fictitious profit was shown by the two devices of carrying
forward the newsprint costs into the subsequent year and including the
reserve set apart for contingencies in the current year. There is no
surviving evidence that this juggling of the accounts was done for
private peculation; its purpose was probably to deceive the Proprietor,
who was dying of cancer. The two persons responsible were Delane
senior and Alsager, who was now joint manager, and John Walter called
for the resignation of both. Alsager, whose wife had lately died, cut his
own throat.

William Delane could be ousted from the managership, but he was
also a shareholder in the printing business. Walter was determined to
oust him from this too. Delane resisted, and as a result the position of
his son as Editor was threatened. John Delane took his father's side
against Walter, and to the end of their days his family and their in-laws,
the Dasents, maintained that the Proprietor had acted meanly to the
men who had built up his fortune. There was widespread concern that
John Delane might fall a victim to his father's obstinacy. Finally, Lionel
Rothschild was called in and persuaded Delane *père* to withdraw, in
order to secure his son's future.

The root of the trouble seems to have lain in the very high costs of
Alsager's communications department. His special expresses involving
the changes of complete carriage and horses at the posting stations, his
dromedaries traversing the Suez isthmus, the pigeon post from Paris to
Boulogne, chartered ships across the English and St George's Channels,
and, later, special trains – all these were an essential part of the build-up
of *The Times*'s unique position as a newspaper, but they were exceed-
ingly expensive. At the time of Alsager's suicide in 1846 they were
running at £10,000 a year – a high cost even by modern standards having regard to the difference in value of money. The advent of the telegraph did not make communications any cheaper – only faster and
more competitive.

Faced with the crisis caused by repeal of the stamp duty, Walter
and Mowbray Morris found one immediate means of cutting costs.
They took the distribution of *The Times* out of the hands of the Post
Office which, as has been seen, was not only the main carrier but

virtually the distributing agent. The railways were prepared to carry newspapers in bulk, at a cost of ½d per copy regardless of weight. In three years' time this competition compelled the Post Office to climb down so far as to carry *The Times* at the same cost as other papers. But not, of course, before the damage to *The Times* had been done, since the new popular and provincial press was by then well established. W. H. Smith, who had inherited a newsagency business from his father and was later to enter politics and become First Lord of the Admiralty, now became *The Times*'s main, and virtually sole, distributor outside London. This efficient and highly organized firm had profited by the abolition of the stamp duty through virtually taking over newspaper distribution from the Post Office. In 1862 it had obtained the exclusive right of selling books and papers on all the important railways of England. The smaller agents in the country obtained their supplies through Smith's national network.

Smith's tended to sell *The Times* at prices above the cover price – i.e. the price fixed by Printing House Square, and displayed on the cover – because of the costs of carriage. The Proprietors of *The Times* disliked this arrangement, by which *The Times* might be on sale in two different places at two different prices, and tried to obviate it by raising their discounts to W. H. Smith. Various agreements were entered into, none of them wholly satisfactory, and the situation became even more difficult when the cover price was lowered from 4d to 3d in 1861. To ease the wholesalers' problems Walter instituted, in 1871, the system of 'sale or return', which later became a recognized practice in the newspaper trade. By this system, Walter agreed to take back 'all copies unsold by Smith at the Railway Stations – such copies not to exceed a certain proportion to be agreed upon'.

Another possibility that Mowbray Morris explored, but without success, was the provision of cheaper newsprint. Several times between 1855 and 1858 he advertised a reward of £1,000 to anyone who would invent a substitute for rags in the manufacture of paper, but had to wait thirteen years before wood pulp met the need. Meanwhile *The Times* was paying around £160,000 a year for paper.

All this time the Walters were searching for faster methods of printing. They needed to succeed, first because of the swelling volume of news and advertisements and the rising circulation: and secondly because of the complaints by subscribers, agents and railways, of late delivery. John Walter III was a perfectionist. He read all the proofs himself. The staff dare not let a paper go out uncorrected even if it meant missing a train.

The primacy of Printing House Square in printing development continued to astonish the world. The Walter family had a natural bent for printing, as well as a financial incentive for putting it to use. They themselves had another explanation for their success – their refusal to employ union labour. The unionized printers working in the other printing houses opposed technological progress; the printers at *The Times* co-operated.

In 1817 Koenig and Bauer had returned to Germany. Their successors at Printing House Square were the engineer Augustus Applegath and his brother-in-law Edward Cowper. Through improvements to the existing presses they stepped up capacity from 1,100 to 2,000 sheets an hour. Meanwhile they were working on a new printing machine of their own. Like its predecessor it was a steam-driven combination of rollers and flat bed, what is technically known as a 'cylinder reciprocating machine'. But it was a more elaborate contrivance than Koenig's and Bauer's invention, twin-decked, with a rather Heath Robinson appearance. The old prints show it being fed by eight mechanics in shell-jackets and white caps, the overseer sporting a frock-coat.

Twenty years later, in 1848, Applegath and Cowper introduced a new press on a totally new principle. This was a vertical rotary machine. The rotary principle was ultimately to solve the problems of high-speed printing, but Applegath's and Cowper's version was of a rudimentary kind. Instead of the cylinders and rollers simply being used to impress paper and ink on a flat metal forme, the actual forme was affixed to rotating cylinders. The inventors of the 1848 version were handicapped becaue they could not yet make a curved stereotype plate. This meant that their cylinder was neither circular nor horizontal: it was octagonal and vertical. *The Times* of the day gives a graphic description of how this strange machine worked:

> Instead of being laid an a table traversing a railroad, the types are now built up, as it were, on the face of a cylinder revolving on a perpendicular axis. This cylinder is a drum of cast iron, about five feet six inches in diameter. The 'formes', or pages of type are made segments of its surface, just as a tower of brick might be faced with stone, or a column inlaid with marble. Eight printing cylinders, forty inches in circumference, are arranged round the drum, and suggest the idea of an orb and its satellites. Eight sheets are now printed in every revolution.

During the following years Printing House Square was experimenting with curved stereotype plates cast from *papier-mâché* moulds. By 1857 *The Times* engineer MacDonald had perfected the process, with the idea of fixing them to the Applegath vertical machine. Meanwhile Walter visited America and found that the American presses were already using a horizontal rotary manufactured by Hoe. In 1858, much to the consternation of his staff, he bought and installed in Printing House Square two ten-cylinder Hoe machines, at a cost of £10,000. Their capacity raised output to 20,000 sheets an hour.

But this was not the end of experiment at *The Times*. In 1866 the Walter press was patented and progressively introduced, which combined both horizontal rotary printing and curved stereotypes, together with a new method of feeding the paper into the presses. Hitherto all printing machines, up to and including the Hoe, had been fed separate sheets. The new machine fed the paper in off reels, or 'webs,' as they were called, a process which Walter had copied from calico printers, just as Gutenberg had copied his first printing press from the wine-makers.

The Walter press was the first to print both sides of the paper at the same time. The webbed sheets were automatically severed after printing and carried down by tapes to a delivery platform. Capacity was 12,000 sheets an hour – printed on both sides. The Walter press was the father of all modern newspaper printing presses up to, and even including, web-offset.

'The Griff', as John Walter III was known to Delane and Dasent, was a very different man from his father. The nickname was short for griffin, defined as 'a grim looking or extremely vigilant guardian'. Like his father and grandfather he reflected much of the age in which he lived. In his youth he had been deeply influenced by the Oxford Movement, and is believed to have contemplated taking Holy Orders. In later life, his attitude to *The Times* was sacerdotal. Also like his father before him, he was at odds with his own father. That old family gossip, Crabb Robinson, visited Bear Wood in 1846 and explained why:

> After dinner I took a walk with [young] John Walter. He is living retired not concealing that he left Printing House Square from dissatisfaction with *The Times*. His Puseyism was offended by the tone of the paper on Church matters. He talked seriously and consistently and is a man of firmness and if the paper were ever under his government it would become a very different thing.

'Crabbie's' diagnosis was prophetic. John Walter III resembled his forebears in his continued concentration on printing development, though in editorial matters he was more intrusive. He irritated Delane by turning up in the Editor's office at night and messing up the proofs or discussing points of principle while the paper was going to press. He worried the Manager, as has been said, by holding up the trains for small corrections. And he mistrusted the Assistant Editor Dasent so much that he would never let Delane go on holiday when he himself was away. He was in short a fussy man.

Delane's relations with his proprietor were, nonetheless, harmonious.

They were founded, no doubt, on mutual respect. Delane trusted Walter's detached judgments on long-term issues, and had a sense of service to the Walter family inherited from his predecessor. Moreover Delane was nothing if not a diplomat. He might have a greater position in political society than his employer, but he knew where he stood inside the office. The combination of the two men worked consummately well for thirty years. After Delane's death, Walter made at least one mistake which was to have very nearly fatal consequences for *The Times.*

At the time of the repeal of the 'taxes on knowledge', Walter's judgment was not found wanting. To the repeal of the stamp tax in 1855 Walter reacted by passing the benefit on to the customer through reduction of the cover cost from 5d to 4d. He then sat back and watched developments, reducing distribution costs in the manner that has been described. Six years later, in 1861, the paper tax was abolished. The overall bill for paper however continued to run at over £150,000 a year until the end of the 1860s. After wood pulp was used for making paper in 1868 it was called newsprint.

Two courses were open to Walter. He could seize the opportunity of the small saving afforded by abolition of the paper tax to reduce the price of *The Times* drastically, entering thereby into competition with the new penny press. Or he could stand his ground and continue to produce a quality paper. In coming to a decision, he had the example of the collapse of many of the older papers after the repeal of the stamp tax. It was not encouraging.

Walter, as might have been expected, was guided by moral considerations as much as by commercial ones. During the forty-seven years of his proprietorship *The Times* learned to think of itself in terms which might have seemed unduly solemn to John Walter II and Barnes, and certainly quite inconceivable to John Walter I and Combe. The paper declared itself to be 'the most signal example of useful enterprise in the Empire', and spoke of its own 'unexampled devotion and unsurpassed independence'. 'We belong', it said, 'to the public, we are proud to think that England is proud of *The Times.*' The conception of *The Times* as an instrument of service towards the community and an object of dedication on the part of its staff derived from John Walter III. In later years it became crystallized in the mind of the nation, which thought of *The Times* as a national institution rather than a commercial undertaking.

John Walter wished to perpetuate this conception, but he wanted also to make sure that he did it by establishing *The Times* on a sound commercial footing. His reckoning was that the price should be reduced to 3d, not less. This would cost £70,000 a year. Part of the loss he hoped would be offset by the saving on newsprint. Another £15,500 would be

I PRESUME to folicit a few Moments of your Attention to a Subject which claims the Patronage of every Friend to Science, and from which the Public will derive very diftinguifhed Advantage.

About four Years fince, I undertook to introduce a Mode of Printing with CEMENTED TYPES, *inftead of fingle Letters; by which Means, a greater Degree of Expedition and Correctnefs was given to that ufeful Art. The Hiftory and Procefs of this fuperior Improvement in the Bufinefs of Printing, with the Difficulties I have experienced, and the Oppofition I have encountered, in bringing this Invention to its prefent State of Perfection, are related and confidered at Large in a Pamphlet which I have written and printed for that Purpofe. Nay, fo far has the Jealoufy arifing from* LOGOGRAPHIC PRINTING *operated againft me, that many of the Trade* HAVE ACTUALLY REFUSED TO SELL ANY BOOKS WHICH PROCEEDED FROM MY PRESS.

To obviate, however, the Inconveniencies to which this new Undertaking has been fubject, from the malicious Apprehenfions of thofe who tremble at the Profpect of my Succefs, I am fitting up the Houfe late Mr. DEBRETT's, *in Piccadilly, oppofite* Old Bond-Street, *which will be opened, immediately after the Chriftmas Recefs of Parliament, as a* BOOKSELLER's *and* STATIONER's SHOP; *where all Publications whatever may be had, and* PRINTING, *in every Branch, executed with the greateft Care and Difpatch.*

A SEPARATE APARTMENT *is alfo arranged for the elegant Accommodation of fuch Gentlemen as chufe to pafs any part of their Mornings in a Circle of literary or political Information.*

Here alfo will be publifhed THE TIMES, *a* MORNING PAPER, *which is very high in the Public Efteem, for its early, accurate, and important Intelligence, and whofe Sale, at prefent, is at leaft on an Equality with the moft refpectable of its Competitors, and* DAILY *continues advancing to a decifive and unqueftionable Superiority.— But thefe are not the only Advantages in its poffeffion:—From the improved Mode of printing* LOGOGRAPHICALLY, *it* ALONE *has the exclufive Ability of uniting Exactitude and Fulnefs in the Report, with fuperior Celerity in the Communication, of all* PARLIAMENTARY INTELLIGENCE;—*a Convenience long-wifhed for in* ALL, *but hitherto unattainable by* ANY OTHER *Daily Publication.*

It is, therefore, with fome Degree of Confidence that I offer my Undertaking to your Protection.—Improvements in Art or Science naturally look to Men of Tafte and Literature for Encouragement and Patronage; and the Favour of yours to the LOGOGRAPHIC ART OF PRINTING, *will be confidered as a very great Honour, and received as a lafting Obligation, by*

YOUR DEVOTED, AND

OBEDIENT HUMBLE SERVANT,

Done at the
Logographic Office,
Printing-Houfe Square,
BLACK-FRIARS,
December, 1785.

JOHN WALTER.

An early example of a publicity leaflet done at the Logographic Office, Printing House Square.

John Walter I

The first Lord Astor of Hever, who as Major Astor, purchased *The Times* after Northcliffe's death.

Sir William Haley 1952–1966

NINE EDITORS

Geoffrey Dawson 1912–1919/1923–1941

Thomas Chenery 1877–1884

W. F. Casey 1948–1952

R. M. Barrington-Ward 1941–1948

H. Wickham Steed 1919–1922

G. E. Buckle 1884–1912

John Thadeus Delane 1841–1877

Thomas Barnes 1817–1841

John Walter's headpieces, including the clock device to which
the scythe was added in 1845.

The Times office *circa* 1850, and 1874

The Private House and Printing House Square, 1931, from a drawing by Sydney Jones.

met by raising advertising rates. The estimated balance of £20,000 would have to be faced, if necessary, in reducing profits and dividends. The paper, the Proprietor believed, could be maintained at 3d on its existing standards. To reduce the price any further would mean excessively cutting editorial costs.

His decision proved right. The paper became established as a high-quality product read by an educated élite. The social structure of Britain proved well able to provide a commercial basis for such a paper for some decades. If anything, the management of *The Times* had over-estimated the threat of the so-called popular press of the 1860s. The *Daily Telegraph* and its contemporaries were a threat to the circulation of the paper, but not to its profitability. That threat was to develop half a century later, with the rise of Northcliffe and the halfpenny press.

The price of *The Times* fixed by Walter at 3d in 1861 was maintained until 1913. The circulation went up immediately by 10,000 and remained at that level for nearly twenty years. The cost of paper remained at its 1861 level until the invention of paper made from wood pulp, when it dropped slightly. Editorial, communications and office costs held fairly steady. They were running at £55,000 a year in 1860, but rose to £67,000 by 1870, not an unreasonable upturn considering the extended services provided by *The Times* in competition with its rivals. Advertising revenue, as has been seen, was more than healthy. So profitable was *The Times* that dividends, standing at £62,000 in 1861, reached £70,000 in the next three years and continued to climb until they reached £89,600 in 1870. John Walter III had indeed achieved 'Philanthropy plus five per cent'.

8 WARS AND PEACE

(i) Relying on Russell

During the 1860s *The Times* continued to rely very largely on Russell for its reputation as a purveyor of foreign news. Russell did not have an easy time for although his personal standing gave him advantages over his rivals he found himself up against new methods and new standards in journalism. Nor did Mowbray Morris, the Manager, who was responsible for administration of the foreign service, recruit first-rate assistants for him. The result was that *The Times* began to be overtaken by such competitors as the *Daily News*.

The arrangement by which the Manager ran the foreign service had ceased to be viable. The job had altered since the days of Barnes and Alsager, and Walter and Morris had far too many other preoccupations, including the installation of new presses and plans for the re-building of Printing House Square. Such operations are distracting for those trying simultaneously to run a daily newspaper. Most of the burden of the printing and rebuilding fell directly upon the shoulders of the Chief Proprietor and his Chief Engineer, MacDonald, but the Manager can scarcely have remained uninvolved. His letters to foreign correspondents occasionally betray the petulance of a harassed man. It was only after many hesitations that he was persuaded in 1858 to make limited use of the new Reuters service as a supplement to *The Times*'s own correspondents.

Mowbray Morris's whole theory of how a newspaper's foreign service should be organized was mistaken. 'Every correspondent except the favoured one at Paris is but a Rover,' he declared. Such a system has advantages from the managerial point of view, since it ensures that a correspondent is at the point of maximum news interest at minimum cost; but for a serious newspaper like *The Times* it is more important to keep at major centres resident correspondents who have acquired, by continuity of service, a thorough insight into the problems of the country in which they are working. The 'fire brigade' system, as reliance on roving correspondents is sometimes known in Fleet Street, can only work if the firemen are of very exceptional quality. William Howard Russell was; but even Russell, as he grew older, could be outpaced by younger men who placed more emphasis on speed than on quality.

The answer to these problems was the appointment of a Foreign Editor; but it took *The Times* many years yet to come to this conclusion and in the meantime its foreign correspondents had to serve two masters: the Editor and the Manager.

Russell's first important assignment after the Crimea was the Indian Mutiny. His instructions were not so much to report a campaign which might well be over by the time he arrived as 'to judge of the truth of the accounts of hideous massacres and outrages which were rousing to fury the people of England'. Russell did not disbelieve the stories, but 'wanted proof, and none was forthcoming',

By this time Russell was famous, and treated everywhere *en prince*. Within a few days of his arrival in Calcutta he had been received by the Governor General, Lord Canning, who gave a promise that his dispatches should be given precedence only second to service messages. When he moved on to Cawnpore it was fortunate for him that the Commander-in-Chief, with his headquarters there, was his old Crimean acquaintance, Sir Colin Campbell.

Campbell greeted him with warmth and with a proposal: 'You shall know everything that is going on. You shall know all my reports and get every information that I have myself, on condition that you do not mention it in camp or let it be known in any way, except in your letters to England.' 'I accept the condition, sir,' Russell replied, 'and I promise you it shall be faithfully observed.' Both men kept their word.

Russell accompanied Campbell on his campaign for the final relief of Lucknow, and on 9 March 1858 was with the Commander-in-Chief at the assault on a prominent section of the defences called the Martiniere.

After Lucknow Russell continued with Campbell in the Rohilkhand campaign. This was at the end of April; they crossed the Ganges at dawn, when Russell, trying to save his horse from some 'uproarious stallions', was severely injured in the stomach and thigh. In great pain, he had to be carried in a litter for days afterwards, in the heat and dust. Although further weakened by a starvation diet, leeches were put on his leg. He was also nearly cut down by mutinous cavalry at the Battle of Bareilly. But he continued to send his dispatches.

Morris complained that Russell's telegraph bill came to £5,000, but Delane rightly felt he had got good value for money. Both Delane and Russell gave their support to the conciliatory policies of Lord Canning – not an easy course when opinion had feasted so deep on horror stories. 'The public feeling has righted itself more promptly than was to be expected,' Delane was able to write as early as April 1858, 'and we had before the recess a debate in which the most humane instead of the most bloodthirsty sentiments were uttered.'

Russell stayed in India till March 1859. He thought deeply about the country and its problems, and as always his comments showed a robust and humane common sense.

> I believe [he wrote to Delane], that some great effort must be made to check the aggressive and antipathetic treatment of the natives . . . Our rule is now more secure in India than it has ever been before, and nothing but extreme oppression and injustice, and the misery and wretchedness and despair which may arise from these, can produce another rising; but, at the same time, there are more doubts as to our intentions, more suspicions of our motives, greater jealousy of our race, than there ever was before; and these feelings are mixed up with the animosities of a defeated nationality, such as it is, and with resentment against those who in their indiscriminate zeal and desire of vengeance punished the innocent with the guilty.

(ii) *Civil War in America*

In 1861 the American Civil War broke out. This was for *The Times* a missed opportunity – an opportunity to report great events and to guide public opinion in the interpretation of them. Many people on both sides of the Atlantic used stronger language. Leslie Stephen, in an anonymous pamphlet published in 1865, went so far as to accuse *The Times* of being 'guilty of a public crime'. It had 'made a gigantic blunder from end to end as to the causes, progress, and consequences of the war'.

How far was this charge justified? *The Times*, like the great mass of the British people, was strongly abolitionist but it did not believe that the conflict was fundamentally about slavery. After all, Lincoln in his inaugural address had said that he did not propose 'to interfere with the institution of slavery in the States where it exists'. *The Times* argued that economic issues were dominant: 'Protection was quite as much a cause of the disruption of the Union as slavery.' The North was protectionist; the South free-trading, and as the huge industry of Lancashire depended on American cotton there were strong British commercial ties with the South. The Northerners had appeared to the British – over both Canada and Ireland – as meddlers; might they not be meddling in the South? Certainly *The Times* could use respectable arguments to justify its policy and there is no need to cite Mowbray Morris's slave-owning West Indian background to explain why the paper hesitated before supporting the cause of the North.

As the struggle developed the fact that the North was fighting to preserve the Union and that its leaders favoured a more democratic society than did the aristocratic leaders of the South, attracted the support of like-minded people in England. The failure of *The Times* to modify its position during the later stages of the war is therefore less understandable, even though it shared that position with William Ewart Gladstone.

The lack of sound and consistent information from America was the main cause of *The Times*'s failure to assess the situation. Although Delane had spent a holiday there in 1857, the journey does not seem to have left any great impression, apart from giving him a poor view of the American press. However, when war seemed imminent he took the right decision – he sent out Russell. Russell arrived in New York on 16 March 1861. Ten days later he was in Washington, and it is a measure of his standing and that of the paper he represented (as well as of the free and open habits of Washington at that time) that the day after he arrived he was received by the new Secretary of State, Mr Seward, who took him straight to the White House to see President Lincoln. It is worth quoting part of Russell's account of his first meeting with the President as a reminder of his powers of descriptive writing:

> Soon afterwards there entered, with a shambling, loose, irregular, almost unsteady gait, a tall, lank, lean man, considerably over six feet in height, with stooping shoulders, long pendulous arms, terminating in hands of extraordinary dimensions, which, however, were far exceeded in proportion by his feet. He was dressed in an ill-fitting, wrinkled suit of black, which put one in mind of an undertaker's uniform at a funeral; round his neck a rope of black silk was knotted in a large bulb, with flying ends projecting beyond the collar of his coat; his turned-down shirt-collar disclosed a sinewy muscular yellow neck, and above that, nestling in a great black mass of hair, bristling and compact like a ruff of mourning pins, rose the strange quaint face and head, covered with its thatch of wild republican hair, of President Lincoln... A person who met Mr Lincoln in the street would not take him to be what – according to the usages of European society – is called a 'gentleman'; ...
>
> Mr Seward then took me by the hand and said – 'Mr President, allow me to present to you Mr Russell, of the London "Times",' On which Mr Lincoln put out his hand in a very friendly manner, and said, 'Mr Russell, I am very glad to make your acquaintance, and to see you in this country. The London "Times" is one of the greatest powers in the world – in fact, I don't know anything which has much more power – except perhaps the Mississippi.'

Two weeks later Russell decided to go to the South and see the other side for himself. He was away for over two months, visiting

Charleston, Savannah, Montgomery, Mobile, New Orleans, and returning by steamer up the Mississippi. He reported on all he saw – on a slave auction, which 'produced in me a feeling of inexpressible loathing and indignation'; on Jefferson Davis: 'Wonderful to relate, he does not chew, and is neat and clean-looking, with hair trimmed, and boots brushed. The expression of his face is anxious, he had a very haggard, care-worn, and pain-drawn look, though no trace of anything but the utmost confidence and the greatest decision could be detected in his conversation.'

All might have gone well had Russell been able to report the whole course of the war. But this was not to be. The trouble started with his report of the Battle of Bull Run – the first major clash between the two armies – which took place on 21 July just outside Washington. The untrained Northern troops were routed, and Russell recorded what he saw:

> The scene on the road now assumed an aspect which has not a parallel in any description I have ever read. Infantry soldiers on mules and draught horses, with the harness clinging to their heels, as much frightened as their riders; negro servants on their masters' chargers; ambulances crowded with unwounded soldiers; waggons swarming with men who threw out the contents in the road to make room, grinding through a shouting, screaming mass of men on foot, who were literally yelling with rage at every halt, and shrieking out, 'Here are the cavalry! Will you get on?'

When, a month later, his messages, sometimes in garbled versions, penetrated back to New York there were howls of execration. Forgetting their own abuse of the army and its commanders at the time, the papers now turned on the foreigner who had dared to criticize. He became known as 'Bull-Run Russell' and was ostracized by military and civilians alike. Anonymous letters threatened his life. A German soldier on guard in Washington thrust a loaded rifle at him, shouting 'Pull-Run Russell! you shall never write Pull Runs again.'

More serious, Russell's application to go south with the Federal army was refused. It was this refusal – ostensibly at least – which determined him to up sticks and come home, but concern for his family was probably a stronger motive. Mrs Russell had now four children and her health was extremely bad (she was to die at the beginning of 1867). Russell felt miserable at having to leave her, sometimes for years at a time and always on missions that bore a high degree of risk. So he booked a passage to England in April 1862 without informing London – indeed, just at the moment when Delane was sending him a letter urging him to 'hold on'.

Once Russell was back there was nothing to do except send out a replacement; it was here that Delane made his worst mistake. A journalist called Charles Mackay, not on the staff of *The Times*, was chosen in spite of the fact that he was known to be a fanatical supporter of the South. Even Mowbray Morris protested: 'I ask myself [as I read your letters] whether any Government or set of men can be so wholly bad that not a single good word can be said for them by an impartial witness.' Of course Mackay made no pretence of being impartial. But it was not until April 1865, when the war was over, that he was sacked. Although some effort was made to strengthen the coverage the fact was that the great battles of the Civil War went unreported in *The Times* from the Northern side. No doubt if Russell had stayed the story would have been different. The Federal authorities made a great mistake – one to which all commands are prone – in not welcoming this fair and sympathetic reporter to stay with their armies. On Delane's behalf it can be said that at the most critical moment of the struggle as far as Anglo-American relations were concerned, when war between Britain and the North threatened over the 'Trent affair' in November 1861, *The Times*, together with the Prince Consort and Lord Lyons, British Minister in Washington, was a force for moderation.

(iii) *Franco-Prussian War*

The Franco-Prussian War of 1870 provided Russell with his last big war assignment. Here, as in its coverage of the Italian liberation war 1859–60, *The Times* found itself outpaced in speed by the popular press. But Russell, who accompanied the German armies, was, as usual, on familiar terms with all and sundry. The Crown Prince gave him an exclusive account of the private talk between the King of Prussia and Napoleon III after his surrender at Sedan. The shock may be imagined when he read a paragraph in the *Standard*, authorized by Bismarck, in which the story was described as being without foundation. Russell at once confronted Bismarck and secured a reluctant recantation. 'When you hear things from that dunderhead the Crown Prince you should know better,' grumbled the Iron Chancellor.

Russell may have been on terms of intimacy with the mighty, but when it came to getting his dispatches to London the great star was liable to be beaten by a younger man, Archibald Forbes of the *Daily News*. 'The express manager of the *Daily News* is evidently more acute,' observed Mowbray Morris in a letter to *The Times* representative. Later Forbes revealed some of his techniques. One of them was to secure advance plans from the Crown Prince of Saxony's staff, and send prefabricated messages to London; he would then instruct his office to hold them for release. This he did with success at the start of the bombardment of Paris. When the first gun went off, he telegraphed 'go ahead'.

Russell, as Matthew Arnold suggested, had become a little too ponderous and grand.

> You know the sort of thing [Arnold wrote satirically], he has described it himself over and over again. Bismarck at his horse's head, the Crown Prince holding his stirrup, and the old King of Prussia hoisting Russell into his saddle. When he was there, the distinguished public servant waved his hand in acknowledgement, and rode slowly down the street, accompanied by the *gamins* of Versailles, who even in their present dejection could not forbear a few involuntary cries of 'quel homme!'*

Forbes, it was generally agreed, carried off the honours as the most successful correspondent of the war, but Russell secured by lucky chance an important exclusive story, that of the opening of negotiations for the capitulation of Paris.

The war also produced one historic stroke for *The Times* in London, which provided a good illustration of the value placed upon its influence by Bismarck. In 1866 the French Government had made a proposal to Germany that, in return for French recognition of a federal union between North and South Germany, the King of Prussia would support France if she invaded Belgium. On the outbreak of war in 1870 Bismarck communicated this document to the British Government, in the hope of discrediting the French. Gladstone decided not to publish it. Bismarck then dispatched a Prussian diplomat to London with a copy of the draft treaty to be handed to Delane. Publication of this shocking French proposal by *The Times* led to the guarantee by Britain of Belgium's neutrality, a guarantee which was eventually to become the chosen issue on which Britain entered the First World War.

(iv) *The Triumphs of Blowitz*
The Franco-Prussian War may have been William Howard Russell's swan-song: but from the ashes of the Paris Commune there arose if not a phoenix, certainly a peacock. This was Henri Stefan Opper de Blowitz. Although in no sense representative of the type of person employed by *The Times* at home or abroad, Blowitz contrived to hang the reputation of *The Times* like a label round his neck. In spite of oddities, and indeed dishonesties, he must take his place without challenge in the first eleven of *Times* foreign correspondents. He was one of the most successful, and easily one of the most flamboyant, the British press has ever known. He was preposterous, vain, brash and

* Matthew Arnold: *Friendship's Garland*, London, 1871.

egotistical, but underneath calculatingly methodical. When Blowitz 'rose up to seek the truth and patiently ensue it', he generally succeeded. Outside his profession he was a dreadful liar, but in substance his news stories generally stand up. There was at least one famous occasion when *The Times* failed to publish one of his stories and lived to regret its caution.

Blowitz was an immigrant to France from Bohemia. He had worked most of his life as a professor of German in French state schools, and was forty-five when he joined *The Times*. In preceding years he had lived in Marseilles, where he married a widow of aristocratic connexions slightly older than himself; she was, it appears, handsome. One of Blowitz's qualities was that he was easy with women. He admired them and they told him things.

The general, though not the exact, details of how Blowitz came to join *The Times*, are clear; he has related them in his *Memoirs* but, as in the case of William Combe, one of the early editors, Blowitz's reminiscences seldom coincide with any surviving documentary evidence. During his time in Marseilles Blowitz, according to his own account, corresponded with Thiers, the historian. On the abdication of Napoleon III Thiers became first President of the Third Republic. At the time of the Paris Commune there was a sympathetic revolutionary outburst in Marseilles. Blowitz, who seems always to have been interested in the techniques of communication, was able to help the local authorities by passing messages when they were cut off from the outside world by the Communards. He was summoned to Paris by Thiers, and for his assistance was subsequently awarded the Legion of Honour.

In Paris he met Laurence Oliphant, *The Times* correspondent, to whom he was able to supply valuable information through his close contact with Thiers. By dint of making himself useful he established himself as an assistant in *The Times* Paris office. Oliphant retired in 1873, and his successor died a year later. Blowitz, by sheer persistence, eased his way into the chair, despite qualms in Printing House Square. He wrote his dispatches in French and they had to be translated, a habit which he retained to the end of his life. He was moreover 'viewy', and careless about descriptive detail.

Into the credit balance he threw qualities which impressed Delane – his photographic memory, his gift for the timely interview with important personages, and his knowledge of modern communications, a field in which *The Times* was conscious of its inferiority. In 1872 (according to Blowitz) after taking Delane to hear Thiers speak in the Assembly, he put him on the train for London. Delane's parting shot was to remark how useful it would be if such a speech could be reported in London next morning. It was. Blowitz went straight to the

Post Office, wrote a fair account of the speech from memory and transmitted it by telegraph. Not only Delane in London, but the whole of Paris read it for the first time next morning either in *The Times* or in telegraphed summaries to Paris. In the same year Blowitz published an exclusive interview with the Comte de Paris, the Bourbon pretender to the French throne. Two years later he installed in the Paris office of *The Times* a special telegraph wire to London.

It was in recognition of all these services that Blowitz finally became confirmed in his appointment as *Times* staff correspondent. His advent undeniably pumped new life into the paper's foreign service, for he did not confine himself to reporting French affairs but became in effect a diplomatic correspondent resident in the French capital – almost, indeed, an expatriate foreign editor.

Blowitz's greatest triumph was his coverage of the Berlin Congress of 1878. His exclusive publication of the treaty, on the morning that it was signed, ranks as one of the most remarkable feats of newsgathering in the history of journalism.

In Printing House Square the most careful thought had been given to the choice of a chief representative to report the Congress. It was MacDonald, the Manager, who decided to send Blowitz. He was given a strong supporting team. Chief among these was that old warrior General Eber, now figuring as Vienna correspondent, who could be counted on to tap Andrassy, the leader of the Austrian delegation. The others were Abel, the Berlin correspondent, and a young Scot, Donald Mackenzie Wallace, later destined to become the first Foreign Editor of *The Times*.

Blowitz started laying his plans well ahead. His first problem was to get into Berlin at all. He was disliked by Bismarck, because of a story he had published in *The Times* in 1875 under the heading 'The French Scare', in which he had reported that the war party in Germany were planning a pre-emptive strike against France. The story had been given to him by the French Foreign Minister, and although Bismarck later admitted that it was in essence correct publication aroused much indignation in Germany. Luckily for Blowitz, one of his cronies – the word is not too strong – was the German Ambassador in Paris, Prince Hohenlohe. The Ambassador smoothed the way with the Iron Chancellor.

His entry into Berlin assured, Blowitz now applied his mind to his next, and most ambitious, aim, which was no less than the securing of an advance copy of the treaty before it was signed. With nothing short of this would he be content. Information would not be easy to obtain; the delegations were pledged to secrecy. 'In Paris,' complained Blowitz. 'the fish talk. In Berlin the parrots are silent.'

From now on, we must follow his own narrative, with all its inconsistencies and *lacunae*, for it is all we have. It is, at its lowest level, a good story – and the outcome is verifiable fact.

In October 1877, according to Blowitz's story, a 'young foreigner' had called on him in Paris in search of a job. For family reasons, he said, he wanted to earn enough money to get away and start life again in the colonies. His visitor cannot have been French or English, or Blowitz would hardly have called him a foreigner; but who the young man was Blowitz never told. *The Times* correspondent now had a brainwave – he himself ascribed it to the intervention of a supreme power.

'As, at the very time that the idea of going to Berlin plunged me in despair, my door opened and I saw my young friend enter, it struck me that he was destined to assist me in the accomplishment of the task devolving on me in Berlin.' He struck a bargain with the young man. The latter was to go, armed with a letter of introduction given to him by Blowitz, to the private secretary of a foreign statesman who was likely to attend the Congress. He was to ask for an appointment as an unpaid attaché in his office; he was then to insinuate himself so that the statesman took him to the Congress on his staff. In return he would supply Blowitz with the articles of the treaty as they were adopted. Blowitz would not publish them at the time, but would hoard them till the end of the Congress and then publish the whole. The reward for Blowitz's informant was to be the money necessary to take him to the colonies.

As to the identity of the foreign statesman to whom Blowitz's protégé was to attach himself, he again 'never told'. Frank Giles, in his biography of Blowitz*, suggests that he was one of the Turkish delegates – these were in fact a Greek and a renegade German – and while there is no circumstantial evidence, Giles, from his long experience of covering international conferences, believes that it was 'in the nature of things'. If Blowitz's 'young foreigner' is an invention – some of the other incidents related in Blowitz's *Memoirs* are certainly fictitious – the likelihood is that Blowitz had steady information through Eber from Count Andrassy, who had been one of the leaders of the Hungarian rising of 1848 in which Eber had fought.

To continue with Blowitz's narrative. Both he and his young friend arrived in Berlin and foregathered in the former's room in the Kaiserhof Hotel. As the young man was being watched, they had to devise a means of communication. The first plan they made did not please them, but they could not think of a better one. Then, relates Blowitz: 'He left the room, but returned almost immediately, saying: "Excuse me – I have taken your hat for mine." An idea struck me. "Shut the door," I said, "and sit down; your method of communication is found."'

* Frank Giles: *A Prince of Journalists*, Faber & Faber, 1962.

That method, which succeeded admirably, was of childish simplicity. 'I was staying at the Kaiserhof. Every day he came there for lunch and dinner. There was a rack where hats were hung up. He placed his communications in the lining of his hat, and we exchanged hats on leaving table.' The scheme worked perfectly well except for one horrible moment when a stranger took the loaded hat in mistake for his own. Luckily it fell down over his nose and he came back and exchanged it for the correct one.

There are only two effective ways of reporting a 'closed' conference. One is to establish a more or less recognized line 'under the counter' with the chairman or a principal delegate. This has the advantage of ensuring a steady supply of news, but the disadvantage of placing the correspondent under the obligation of suppressing what his informant chooses to withhold, which is embarrassing if his rivals happen to stumble upon it through unauthorized means. The other is to stay 'outside the ring', using a low-level contact whose information is necessarily scanty but can be developed by the technique of using it as a basis for cross-questioning others. Blowitz, according to his own account, employed a combination of the two, switching from the latter method to the first towards the conclusion of the conference.

From his 'young friend' Blowitz obtained enough information on the proceedings of the conference to work on. He would then go the round of the diplomatic parties metaphorically slipping ferrets into the delegates' pockets and watching what came out. In this way he was soon able to provide his readers with a steady stream of accurate reporting on the conference. So much so that Bismarck is claimed on one occasion to have lifted up the tablecloth 'to see if Blowitz is not underneath'. But *The Times* correspondent was now to have opened to him the opportunity of receiving information at top level.

On 2 July Blowitz realized an ambition as important to him as the obtaining of the treaty itself. He was granted an interview by Bismarck, the only press correspondent to be so honoured. The interview took place over dinner in the Chancellor's private apartment and lasted five hours. Blowitz described how he was taken to the apartment by Hohenlohe:

> The door of the drawing room . . . opened, and the Chancellor appeared. He was much taller than I had imagined. I had never seen him – except at Madame Tussaud's in London, where there is only a small figure of him – and when I saw this giant in uniform enter the room I was quite taken aback. There was something still more extraordinary about his head. His ears were large, wide open to the hundreds of rumours which came to them from the four corners of the universe. His chin made a

strong foundation for th big jaws, which would certainly never lose anything they held until it was in shreds; whilst his eyes, well set, with their projecting eyelids and well exposed eyebrows, had a far-away look in them, as though they were going out beyond the visible horizon.

The fourth person present was Princess Bismarck. After complimenting Blowitz on his German, she does not seem to have taken any further part in the conversation. Bismarck took Blowitz on a *tour d'horizon* not only of the Congress, but of the world at large. He also questioned Blowitz closely about the views of other delegations. *The Times* correspondent culled enough from that evening to last him in dispatches for many months. In conclusion, the Chancellor spoke of Disraeli:

> Beaconsfield has the most extraordinary presence of mind. He is accommodating and energetic, and never allows himself to be disturbed by anything. He defends his cause admirably, and last Friday, when the negotiations were broken off, he was ready to lead his country courageously to war.

It was getting late, the clock struck eleven, Hohenlohe rose to break up the party. 'Just as I was going out of the room,' writes Blowitz, 'the Chancellor asked me if I would not have another cigar . . . He insisted on lighting it for me himself, and he held the match for about a minute. My cigar was lighted at last, and I went away. The interview – an interview which had lasted five hours – was at an end.' One can almost see the glow of that cigar: it was nothing to the glow in Blowitz's heart as he made his way back to the Kaiserhof. All he wanted now was the treaty.

Next morning, *The Times* correspondent, as might be expected, found the attitude of diplomatists towards him changed. This is a common experience for journalists when they have been suddenly shown favour by the highest. He had no further need to seek information: it just flowed in.

Blowitz suffered one setback as a result of this incident. The glory of it went to the head of his young informant who committed some unnamed indiscretion and had to be dropped. This meant finding some other means of obtaining the treaty.

Blowitz's expertise in communications now came in useful. He realized that should he ever obtain the treaty the Prussian Post Office would almost certainly refuse to telegraph it; he therefore laid plans for an alternative mode of transmission. He called upon the Belgian Minister in Berlin and put to him a proposition. *The Times*, he said, was contemplating organizing a nightly telegraph service between

Brussels and London. He asked the Minister to give him a letter of introduction to the Belgian Director-General of Posts, requesting him to co-operate in what would now be called a 'dummy-run', at short notice. Armed with the Minister's letter Blowitz felt his communications to be assured.

A pantomime now started which was unprecedented in the history of journalism. The day of signing approached. Blowitz had met 'a diplomatist who had always been friendly to him' in the hotel lobby. *The Times* correspondent looked depressed and was reading a letter, which he showed to the diplomatist. The letter referred to the joy with which its writer would see him crown his campaign by being the first to publish the treaty. The diplomatist, moved by Blowitz's dejection, promised to hand him the treaty the day before the Congress ended. Who the diplomatist was, Blowitz never revealed, but *The Times History* remarks in a footnote: 'It is generally assumed to have been one of the French representatives, probably M. Waddington.' The French Government would have had the strongest motives for binding the Paris correspondent of *The Times* to them by an obligation of this kind.

Blowitz then went through the motions of asking Bismarck for the treaty. He was rebuffed. The request was mainly a blocking device, prompted by fear that the Chancellor would give the text to the German press. But once he had refused Blowitz he would be more likely to refuse them too, or so Blowitz argued.

On the great day, Friday, 12 July, the day before the Congress ended, Blowitz called on the unknown diplomatist and collected the treaty – less two clauses and the preamble, which were not ready. To put colleagues off the scent, Blowitz, on returning to his hotel, feigned anger, giving as his reason Bismarck's rebuff. He sent for his bill, booked accommodation on the night train for himself, Mackenzie Wallace and his secretary, and dispatched his luggage to the station. He then called on Count de St Vallier, the French Ambassador, and by showing him that he already had the treaty, secured the preamble. In a spirit of melodrama, Blowitz made the Ambassador read the preamble out to him as a test of his famous memory. In fact, it was very short, and even so is paraphrased in Blowitz's published report.

From then on, everything worked according to plan. Once on board the train, he realized his party was being shadowed, probably by the Prussian police. He dictated the preamble to his secretary, slit open the lining in Mackenzie Wallace's coat, and stitched inside it the treaty, the preamble, and the letter to the Belgian Director-General of Posts. As a precaution, Wallace travelled in a separate compartment and changed at Cologne into a train for Brussels, while Blowitz continued on his way to Paris.

Arriving at 5 am, Wallace was, as expected, turned away by the telegraph clerk, but woke up the unfortunate Director-General to whom he presented the letter from the Belgian Minister. The treaty (actually 57 out of 64 clauses) duly appeared in the later editions of Saturday's *Times*. Telegrams from London relayed it to Berlin just at the time the treaty was being signed. Blowitz's ambition was realized. In his coverage of the conference, the interview with Bismarck, and the 'scooping' of the treaty, he had carried off an historic triple event.

Bismarck was most puzzled about the preamble, because of its late drafting. He accused St Vallier – possibly he was on the drafting committee – of having leaked. The Ambassador did not deny it. 'And what did he say when you told him?' Blowitz asked. 'Excuse me,' said the Count, smiling, 'but he did not tell me to repeat it to you.'

There were aftermaths to the Berlin Congress and the Bismarck interview. Printing House Square held up and published after two months a dispatch on the interview in which Bismarck was reported as attacking Gortschakoff, leader of the Russian delegation. This led to Bismarck in turn attacking *The Times* correspondent in the Reichstag. The attack did Blowitz nothing but good. Then (according to Blowitz) Bismarck sent a beautiful spy to Paris to worm out from him the secret of how he obtained the Berlin Treaty. She was a Princess Kralta. Blowitz related the incident in a chapter of his *Memoirs* headed 'The Revenge of Venus':

> On the day and at the hour indicated I went to the house in the Avenue du Bois. The butler . . . ushered me into the second drawing room, where the Princess was wont to receive her unofficial visitors . . . in the deep silence that reigned I heard that peculiar sound which is made by the soft step of a woman advancing over a heavy carpet, amidst the vague rustle of her silken robes. . . . she invited me to take a seat near her on the sofa, between the high candlesticks and the immense mirror in which the light was reflected.

The Princess then performed the well-known confidence trick of relating to Blowitz the story of a secret mission on which she had been sent by the Kaiser to Bismarck. Blowitz realized what was coming next. 'She is only just back, as it were, from her visit to the Prince [Bismarck] to whom she has promised that she will solve a mystery which has irritated him long enough . . . I accordingly awaited her request, quite prepared to grant it.

'The Princess duly put the question, "How were you able to accomplish a feat until then unique – the publication of a treaty of a congress at the very moment of signature?"'

At this point Blowitz noticed one of the candles flickering. He felt a draught coming from the mirror, and looking at it closely saw that a slight gap had opened between two sections of it – the room was, in a rudimentary fashion, 'bugged'. There was someone waiting behind the mirror to take down his words.

> I perceived at once that I was the victim of treachery [proceeds Blowitz], which is what I hate above all else in the world . . . Rising suddenly, and in a voice which I vainly strove to render calm, I said, pointing first at the flickering flame and then at the cloven mirror – 'Madam, you see that I have understood' . . . Turning away her head, she touched an electric button. The door opened, a servant appeared, and, without looking at me, she stretched out her hand and indicated me the way to the door.

Blowitz continued to work for *The Times* until 1902. But when his former assistant Mackenzie Wallace was appointed to the newly created post of Foreign Editor, Blowitz ceased to have such free range. Mackenzie Wallace, who in his own way was even more of a swell than Blowitz, was unimpressed with his contacts in high society, and did not see why his subordinate should usurp his own functions by acting as an unofficial foreign editor. Dry and paining rebukes from head office became the Paris correspondent's too frequent lot. Finally, he retired with the title of 'honorary correspondent' of *The Times* – a distinction he much coveted. A month later he died.

Blowitz was a bluffer, but by no means a charlatan. He should be judged by his achievements rather than by his methods, or his own account of them. Apart from his journalistic talents, his interest in, and ability to put to best use, modern telegraphic inventions was a great help to *The Times*. He also did much to exploit the favourable position created by Russell in the Crimean War by making *The Times* a truly European journal. In the first half of the century the paper, though widely read in Britain for its foreign news, had found its principal political mission in domestic issues. Blowitz gave *The Times* something of the place in European capitals which Barnes and Delane had given it in London.

9 THE PASSING OF DELANE

In the 1870s the closely knit group which had run *The Times* success-fully for so long broke up. Walter, Delane, Morris and Dasent (the Assistant Editor) were more than a team, they were almost a family; both Morris and Dasent were Delane's brothers-in-law. There were also family worries. Delane's wife was in a home under medical care and Morris's son was in Australia using his father's name to raise loans. Then – as now, and in Barnes's day – the strains on the senior execu-tives of *The Times* were exceptional. They were never really 'off duty', like civil servants. They did not go in and out of office, like politicians; they worked unhealthy hours.

1870 was a particularly bad year for *The Times*. Morris's health broke down and he went into hospital. Later his mind gave way. He resigned and died in 1874 at the age of fifty-six – almost the same age as Barnes at his death. Dasent, who had been told he would never edit *The Times*, became a Civil Service Commissioner: 'Believe me,' he wrote to Delane some years later, 'I look upon my present life as dull and cheerless compared with that when I was with you so many hours every day, and I reproach myself continuously for not seeing more of you to whom I owe almost everything that makes life enjoyable.' Ironically it was at this moment that the Government clamped down on the form of contact which *The Times* had traditionally enjoyed with the Civil Service. A letter from the Lords of the Treasury to Heads of all Departments in June 1873 declared:

> My Lords are of opinion that such breaches of official confidence [giving information to the press] are offences of the very gravest character which a public officer can commit, and they will not hesitate, in any case where they themselves possess the power of dismissal to visit such an offence with this extreme penalty . . .

At Bear Wood, the Walters' family home in Berkshire, a tragedy of a different kind occurred. Young John Walter, whom his father was grooming as heir apparent to *The Times*, had returned from a 'grand tour' abroad and his father gave a round of parties for him. On Christ-mas Eve 1870 the young people were skating on the lake when the ice gave way; young John's two brothers and a cousin fell through and got into difficulties. Without hesitation, young John plunged in to rescue them, but the shock killed him. Thereafter old John Walter, always reserved, turned away from many of his worldly activities, though without surrendering his firm control over the paper's fortunes.

The great Editor, too, was soon to fail. In spite of the hours he kept Delane was a remarkably healthy man; his only complaint was eyestrain, which was hardly surprising, but by 1861 it had become a serious worry, threatening blindness. Palmerston offered him the post of Permanent Under-Secretary of War, in the belief that he might welcome a respite from the burdens of editorship, but Delane made it clear that he had no interest other than the paper.

His good health had been due in large measure to his régime. He countered late hours and a sedentary occupation by some austerity and much exercise. He drank sparingly and did not smoke; in the country he hunted; in London he continued to pay his calls on horseback, accompanied by a groom. The photographs of him in frock-coat show box-spurs discreetly peeping out beneath the trouser-leg. He had suffered two family losses. In February 1869 his mother died. She was his only sheet-anchor outside the office; and in 1874 his wife died. There is deep silence on the subject of Mrs Delane, for a few years after the marriage she was 'placed under medical care'. The Editor himself never spoke of her to his friends.

With the loss of his mother, the loss of Morris, his capable yoke fellow, and the loss of Dasent, his right-hand man, even Delane's magnificent physique began to give way. When he reached the age of fifty-six, he was absent from the office with a serious illness. On his return his colleagues noticed with sorrow how shrunken was his frame, how shaky his handwriting. A spirit of melancholy permeated his communications but still he carried on. 'He is incarnate obstinacy,' remarked his old friend William Howard Russell.

By 1877 Walter had decided that he must intervene. 'Ah me!' wrote Russell, 'how broken he is, to be sure; thin, old, bowed, speaking slowly, with glassy eye.' But Delane was not one to welcome retirement. 'I may or may not live a few months,' he wrote, when Walter first broached the subject, 'but my real life ends here. All that was worth having of it has been devoted to the paper and I do not repine.' He gave his blessing to Walter's choice of a successor and retired on 9 November 1877. He died just over two years later, at the age of sixty-two.

The career of an editor of *The Times* is by its nature nine-tenths hidden and therefore difficult to chronicle. 'Venetian' is the description which another great editor, Garvin of the *Observer*, was to apply to the operations of Printing House Square. Yet the achievements and character of Delane emerge without prompting, from the overt acts of his editorship.

He found *The Times* in a position of unique, but newly-acquired power. There had never been anything like it in the land. One sometimes gets the impression that Barnes and his colleagues were astounded at the power of the instrument which they had created. Delane undertook the task of consolidation, which is sometimes duller and harder than that of original creation. During his first fifteen years as Editor he not only maintained for *The Times* that position of influence which Barnes had won for it at home, but extended it throughout the civilized world. When external circumstances later destroyed *The Times*'s self-generated near-monopoly as purveyor of news and organ of opinion, he had by then so strengthened the paper that he was able to preserve its hegemony against all comers for another twenty-five years.

Delane was never a party man. His politics, however, followed a consistent pattern and have sometimes been expressed by an adaptation of Thiers' phrase 'the heart of France beats left centre'. In domestic affairs he was a supporter of the middle classes against the aristocracy but not of electoral reforms tending to strengthen party politics, which he heartily disliked. In foreign affairs he put British interests first. He was a non-interventionist and, except over the Crimea, opposed to war. Like Barnes, he believed that British public opinion had a life of its own, which would eventually frustrate governments in policies which ignored its existence. Both regarded the business of *The Times* to be the exposition, as much as the leadership, of this opinion.

In the last resort Delane put the interests of the country above those of the paper. This is well illustrated by an incident in his relationship with the Crown. Delane was the foremost critic of Queen Victoria's retirement from public life, and saw it as his duty to warn the Queen at the price of her displeasure. On one occasion the Queen herself replied in a letter to *The Times* explaining her feelings on the matter. The publication of a letter to the Editor written by the Sovereign naturally served to increase the authority of the paper. The Queen's Ministers deplored her action and considered it 'infra dig'. On a later occasion, in 1865, *The Times* printed a small paragraph criticizing the privacy of her official landing at Woolwich. The Court sent an explanation on behalf of the Queen. In advising this time against publication, Delane wrote: 'It is only as a loyal subject, not as a journalist, that I make this suggestion, for of course such a communication would be very acceptable to any newspaper.'

How did Delane manage to perform this monumental task of editing *The Times* successfully for nearly forty years? One answer is, by discriminating organization of his time.

The great secret of the success of *The Times* newspaper [wrote a contemporary] is that its Editor has never delegated to subordinates what an editor should do himself, and that in a spirit of mistaken zeal he has never hastened to overload himself with the thousand small duties which may be safely left to vicarious industry and well-salaried discretion.*

Delane concentrated on policy and news, and on supervision. He never cut himself off from an interest in the commercial efficiency of the paper but he did not on the other hand engage in a power struggle with Mowbray Morris. He was content to let the Manager administer the foreign department, which he had not time to do himself. He only complained when he thought Morris was administering it badly, and then, probably, without mincing his words. According to oral tradition, there were times when he and Morris were not on speaking terms. Delane was fortunate in that he was able largely to delegate the technical side of newspaper production such as lay-out and make-up. That would not be possible for an editor today, when the appearance of a paper constitutes a prime element in attracting readers.

Another question, which is not readily answered, is how Delane, with so little experience of writing, managed to edit a great paper. There are many arguments for editors applying to themselves a self-denying ordinance in regard to the time-consuming occupation of writing their own leaders, but those who have done so have generally been correspondents or leader writers in their youth. Delane was not. He had a good epistolary style, pure, lucid and forceful. But he was primarily a man of action, not a man of letters, and certainly not a scholar. He was an impresario, not a performer.

The official historian of *The Times* observes that there was an element of grimness about Delane. Certainly there is something inhuman in this picture of a man continually going the social rounds, not because he enjoyed it, but because that was where the secrets were; perpetually briefing writers and sub-editing their copy but seldom writing anything himself; with no married home life, only an office life. It suggests coldness – yet that is not the way his contemporaries saw him. Society found him easy and agreeable; his colleagues found him warm-hearted and kind. Leaving aside political abuse and the sneers of the disappointed, it is hard to find anything unpleasant said or written about Delane by his contemporaries either in letters or literature.

The end of an editor's term of office is a good time to look at the balance sheet. Below are comparisons of items taken from the revenue and expenditure accounts of *The Times*:

(a) For 1849, the first year for which complete records are available.
(b) For 1877, the year of Delane's retirement.

* *The World*, 21 July 1875.

	(a) 1849	(b) 1877
Average annual circulation	32,165	62,193
Gross advertising revenue	£107,806	£234,518
Total revenue	£283,611	£406,663
Total expenditure	£261,336	£332,715
Dividends	£21,700	£79,600

The size of *The Times* when Delane took over in the 1840s was generally eight pages, with four-page supplements occurring with greater frequency up to the end of the decade. After the abolition of the newspaper tax in 1855 sixteen-page papers became normal with frequent twenty-page papers after the abolition of the duty on paper in 1861.

The dividends represent roughly the profits. They reached a nineteenth-century peak – £90,000 – in 1875–6. Not all the expenditure went outside the House; in 1877 John Walter was paid £107,000 for printing the paper and £2,000 in rent for Printing House Square. Delane might well feel satisfied with the profits his paper had made for his Proprietor. He had been a good steward.

The annual receipts and expenditure do not of course give the whole picture. In the late 1860s Walter had paid for the installation of the new presses out of his own capital and by 1874 had rehoused *The Times* by the same means. The old King's Printing House built in 1740 had become too small a century later.

> We found ourselves [wrote a member of a conducted tour in 1843] in a small court, dignified with the name of Printing House Square. The first emotion – like that of most foreigners on seeing St James's Palace – is wonder that so great a power should be lodged so meanly . . . The apartments employed in the business of printing are chiefly contained in the building of two stories . . . they are four in all – two upon each floor.

The composing room, housing sixty-two compositors, was upstairs. 'Such cramming, it may be remarked,' continued the description published in Chambers' *Edinburgh Journal*, 'is scarcely known out of London.' They visited the machine room and then the editorial.

> At the earnest solicitation of our party, we were conducted to the part of the establishment where the intellectual operations go on – and here we experienced the same irrational though natural disappointment which the whole establishment is likely to convey. Adjoining to that room on the upper floor where the news matter is set up, is a plain chamber, furnished with a couple of long deal tables, with a range of small black desks along them:

while the walls sustain some shelves loaded with files of the
paper, parliamentary reports, and other volumes of a bulky
description. This is the Reporters' Room. Adjoining, and acces-
sible by passing through it, is another room, of the character of
a plain library, the surrounding shelves being filled with Annual
Registers and others works chiefly of a historical kind. This is
the Editor's room ... There are no other accommodations here
for intellectual labourers ... the laborious duties of a reporter are
rewarded by a salary of five guineas a week.

No doubt the 'intellectual labourers' would have laboured on in these
conditions without complaint, but the advent of the Walter press in the
1860s compelled rebuilding.

John Walter visited America to study the latest examples of newspaper offices. He was his own architect and provided his own bricks
and joinery from Bear Wood. Years later the son of one of the original
labourers told a member of the staff that the new structure was built
like a shell over much of the old building in order that the work of
producing the paper should not be interfered with. An 'observer', writing
to *Notes and Queries*, reported that he had noticed in the course of the
rebuilding that a fragment of a wall and buttress of the old fortress of
Montfichet was still standing as part of Printing House Square. The
new offices were opened in 1874, the front conforming with the façade
of the new Queen Victoria Street, cut through the City by the Corporation. John Walter III's building lasted *The Times* till the 1960s when
it in turn was demolished to make way for the existing block.

Thus *The Times* in the 1870s presented a brave façade to the world
– editorially, mechanically, financially and architecturally. But behind
that façade weaknesses in the structure were beginning to develop
unseen. In 1867 John Walter III made what was perhaps his first major
error of judgment which can be attributed to strong moral principles
taking precedence over common prudence. Over the years he had built
up a contingency fund of £200,000 to meet any emergencies. This he
had done by quietly setting aside a small fraction of the annual profits
throughout the long period of his proprietorship. Now he felt it his
duty to disclose this to the other co-proprietors who held small shares
in *The Times* under the terms of John Walter I's will. To his surprise,
far from approving his foresight, several immediately demanded a share-
out. This demand Walter felt compelled to concede; he was thus
deprived at a stroke of his carefully husbanded reserve at a time when,
had he but known, *The Times* was about to need it most desperately.

Another source of weakness was a human one. In 1870 top management had seemed strong and relatively young but in the next ten years
came the sudden series of deaths, resignations and retirements already

described. Walter was caught unprepared and had difficulty in finding adequate replacements. On the managerial side the intention had been to train his eldest son, John, to succeed first as Manager and then as Proprietor, but on his death nothing had been done to equip the second son, Arthur, for these responsibilities.

For Mowbray Morris an immediate successor was found in MacDonald, the Chief Engineer. John Cameron MacDonald, aged fifty-two in 1874, was not only a magnificent technical organizer who had supervised the invention of the Walter press; he was also a man of wide experience, who had started life as a journalist. It was MacDonald who had been sent to Scutari to administer *The Times* Crimea Fund on behalf of Florence Nightingale. Nevertheless he was to exhibit grave weaknesses as a Manager. He was appointed 'to assist Mr Walter in the management'. The wording of the appointment was significant for it indicated that Walter intended to take a much greater share in the day-to-day running of the office. MacDonald, however, became powerful too. Because of his mechanical experience he was *de facto* Manager both of the newspaper and the printing works, which in Morris's day had been kept apart.

The most important post which Walter had to fill, and the hardest, was the editorship. Here he lacked the flair of his father. There was no obvious Editor designate. After some hesitation his choice fell upon Thomas Chenery who had written the diplomatic articles from Constantinople while Russell was special correspondent at the Front. Thus two 'Crimean veterans' were now in charge of the paper, as Manager and Editor respectively.

Chenery was a stop-gap Editor. He was fifty-one at the time of his appointment in 1878. This in itself was a departure from tradition, for Barnes and Delane had been young men when they came to the Chair. The new Editor was shy and erudite. 'Who will look after the social side of the business?' asked Disraeli. Small, rotund and meek-looking, Chenery was a phenomenally hard worker. For many years he had combined being Professor of Arabic at Oxford with writing for *The Times*. But he was slow of speech and his staff complained that he used to fall asleep over his desk.

Chenery was a foreign specialist and, to be fair to him, the foreign performance of *The Times* during his editorship was dazzling. He was in the Chair for only six years, but these were the years of Blowitz's Berlin scoop and Power's dispatches from Khartoum. In other respects he made the paper dull. With the best of intentions he tried to broaden its scope: his idea of effecting this was to cram it with articles on science and archaeology, written by experts for experts. Among the topics treated were Arabian antiquities, Semitic inscriptions, the Hittite empire, burial customs among primitive peoples, extinct birds of New Zealand

and the decomposition of chlorine. Readers complained that he was
turning the paper into a learned journal. '*The Times*,' wrote *Truth*, 'is
becoming a positive disgrace.' Chenery is 'making a mess of *The Times*'
wrote Lord Acton.

With the appointment of Chenery, Walter began to play a much more
active part in editing the paper. This did nothing to enliven it, and was
a factor in causing the disaster which was shortly to overtake *The
Times*. Nor was it any relief to the strain on Chenery who died in office
on 11 February 1884.

The account book is its own commentary on those six years:

	1877 (Delane)	1884 (Chenery)
Circulation	62,193	48,871
Gross advertising revenue	£234,518	£222,839
Total revenue	£406,663	£361,845
Total expenditure	£332,715	£321,658
Dividends	£79,600	£64,200

John Walter collected only £93,000 for printing. He put up the rent of
Printing House Square to £3,400 a year, presumably to offset the fall
in revenue. The year 1884 also saw the printing of the first twenty-four-
page paper.

The reserved ex-professor of Arabic cannot be numbered among the
successful Editors of *The Times* but he was certainly one of its distinguished eccentrics. Among modern languages he was fluent in French,
German, Greek and Turkish. His edition of the Assemblies of Al Hariri
published in 1867 was a distinguished work of Arabic scholarship while
his edition of the Machberoth Ithiel of Jehuda ben Shelomo Alkharizi,
published in 1872, testified to his equal accomplishment in Hebrew and
contained an introduction written in that language which was acclaimed
by Jewish scholars for its elegance and accuracy. His interests extended
to the publication of 'Suggestions for a Railway Route to India',
written between taking part in Oriental examinations at Oxford.

As Editor of *The Times* Chenery's erudition and zeal did not compensate for his heaviness of temperament and lack of professional
experience. He became overworked, tired and fussy. The paper would
be delayed until 3 am while he made minor alterations. His post-
prandial dozes became more frequent. MacDonald remarked that
he was 'very comatose at dinner and afterwards'. But he was awake to
events abroad as was shown by the coverage which *The Times* gave to
a story which broke during his final year in the Chair. It came from
Africa.

10 THE SIEGE OF KHARTOUM

(i) Frank Power is Recruited

The story of the rise of the Mahdi, the siege of Khartoum, and the murder of Gordon on the steps of the Governor's Palace has never ceased to fire the imagination of the British people and of writers, who have told and retold it in a spirit of adulation, of scepticism and even of impartiality. But little has been written of a young Irishman from Queen's County who shared with Gordon some of the last few months of his life and fell under the spell of his magnetism. This was Frank le Poer Power, *The Times* correspondent. Power was one of the two Britons cut off with Gordon in the beleaguered town, and he was killed trying to get a message out of Cairo. Like Russell's dispatches from the Crimea, Power's messages from Khartoum served to awaken the British public to the desperate state of the defenders. They were instrumental in compelling a reluctant Liberal Government at home to dispatch a relief force up the Nile, which tragically arrived two days too late. Power also wrote private letters home to his family. These have been preserved and describe with all the freshness of youth day-to-day life in Khartoum and the conduct and character of Gordon during the siege.

Frank Power was the son of a bank manager, but banking was not his talent. When he left school he took service with the Austrian army and later, as correspondent for the *Daily News*, won a name for himself at the siege of Plevna by the Russians in 1877. Here he gained much military knowledge which became useful to Gordon at Khartoum. Thereafter Power spent some years in Dublin and London as a journalist.

During his peregrinations of Fleet Street Power met Edmond O'Donovan, a well-established war correspondent on the *Daily News*. O'Donovan was about to go out to the Sudan for his paper and to write a book on Equatorial Africa. Power contrived to accompany him as his assistant. He also picked up a commission to make drawings for the *Pictorial World*. The two left London together on 17 May 1883; Frank Power was twenty-five years old when he embarked on this – his last – journey.

Power and O'Donovan reached Cairo on 3 June 1883. The city was then newly occupied by British troops who, under the command of General Sir Garnet Wolseley, had defeated the nationalist army led by

Arabi Pasha at the battle of Tel el-Kebir on 13 September the previous year. The reasons which had led a Liberal Government to sanction independent military action in the Sudan were complex, but now that the deed was done Gladstone's main concern was to withdraw as quickly as possible. In fact it was to be seventy years before the troops left, and from the outset the British found themselves obliged to think, not in terms of disengagement, but of further involvement. In particular the Government was faced with the need for an immediate decision about the Sudan.

In the early years of the nineteenth century Mehemet Ali, the independent Viceroy of Egypt, had sent an army into the Sudan, and Egyptian influence there was further extended by his grandson, the Khedive Ismail. But Ismail, having plunged himself and his country deeply into debt, was deposed in June 1879 as a result of pressure from his European creditors. The weakening of central authority was felt in the Sudan.

In June 1881 a holy man about forty years old called Muhammad Ahmad ibn Abdallah, who had for some time been teaching and meditating with his disciples on the island of Aba in the White Nile, publicly announced that he was the Mahdi, the leader chosen of God who would substitute a reign of justice for one of oppression and wrong. Avoiding attempts to suppress or capture him the Mahdi increased both the number of his followers and his reputation for sanctity. In January 1883 El Obeid, the capital of Kordofan, capitulated to the Mahdi's army. This brought him within striking distance of Khartoum from the south-west.

Was it possible for the remaining Egyptian troops in the Sudan to check the growing tide of Mahdism? And what assistance, if any, could Britain – now the *de facto* ruler of Egypt – give to prevent Egypt from losing this vast province to the forces of religious fanaticism?

Arrived in Cairo, Power and O'Donovan spent a social week such as any two young men out from England might have spent there at almost any period during the British presence in Egypt. They dined with Sir Edward Malet, the British Consul-General, soon to be replaced by the more famous Sir Evelyn Baring – 'Cromer of Egypt'. The 35th Foot, two of whose officers were Dublin men, invited them to mess. They lunched with the 19th Hussars, and rode out with the British Commander of the Egyptian cavalry to see the Pyramids. No doubt it was at one of these parties that they ran across Moberly Bell, *The Times* correspondent in Egypt. Bell was already a power in the land, the friend of the Khedive and the Prime Minister, and it was he who recruited Power to *The Times*'s service. We shall hear more of Bell later, when he became Manager of *The Times* at a tempestuous period in its history.

From Egypt, Power and O'Donovan travelled to Khartoum where they arrived on 1 August on the eve of a big Egyptian counter-offensive against the Mahdi. On their own initiative, and with no encouragement from the British, the Egyptians determined to strike back. For this purpose they received from the British Government permission to employ retired British officers. Their Commander-in-Chief in the Sudan was an ex-Indian Army colonel, Hicks Pasha, assisted by a medley of English, Irish, Austrian and South African mercenary officers. His army was largely formed from the Egyptian garrisons in the Sudan and the remnants of the Egyptian army which had been defeated by Wolseley at Tel el-Kebir. It also included locally raised battalions.

In Khartoum Power was given quarters with the foreign officers in Government House. His political opinions, ironically, were almost identical with those of Mr Gladstone, who saw in the Sudanese 'a people struggling to be free'.

I am not ashamed to say I feel the greatest sympathy for them [the rebels], and every race that fights against the rule of Pachas, backsheesm, bribery, robbery, and corruption [wrote Power]. It is the system, and not the Mahdi, that has brought about the rebellion. The rebels are in the right, and God and chance seem to be fighting for them . . . I hope they will hunt every Egyptian neck and crop out of the Sudan.

Power has left an account of Hicks Pasha's army, which shows that the offensive was more or less doomed from the start. His account is of historical importance since no other record of this tragic, ill-fated army exists:

We have here 9,000 infantry that fifty good men would rout in ten minutes; and 1,000 cavalry [Bashi-Bazouks] that have never learned even to ride, and these, with a few Nordenfeldt guns, are to beat the 69,000 men the Mahdi has got together . . That Egyptian officers and men are not worth the ammunition they threw away is well known, and the few black regiments we have will be left to garrison this place, as the Arabs and townspeople fear them . . .

Even our own officers and men (a cowardly, beggarly mob) believe that he [the Mahdi] is a prophet, and are less than half hearted in the business, so that the ruffianly though brave Bashi-Bazouks and the niggers are the only men to be relied on.

(ii) Hicks Pasha's Army
About 4 September Hicks's army crossed the Nile to the west bank, preparatory to its advance on El Obeid. The plan was to march south

parallel with the river as far as Dueim, and thence to strike westwards into the open desert for the 250-mile march to the objective. The army moved in an immense square, formed by some 11,000 fighting troops with, in the middle, 5,000 to 6,000 camels, two Krupp batteries, the Nordenfeldts, and twenty light guns. Power rode on 'a splendid dromedary', given him by the Egyptian Governor-General, Aladin Pasha, who accompanied the expedition. At night, they halted and built a zereba of thorns round the square.

The destruction of Hicks Pasha's army is one of the most macabre stories in military history. This immense force, marching in the formation of the traditional British square, disappeared into the wastes of Kordofan and was never seen again once it left the Nile. Indeed, not only was it not seen: it was not even heard of for nearly three months. Even today, little is known of its fate.

Hicks was optimistic when he set out. He impressed Power as an able man and perhaps this was a sort of boyish adulation. Power was less optimistic than the general. His earlier experience of fighting in the Russo-Turkish War at Plevna led him to doubt not only the quality and morale of the troops, but the feasibility of the plan. The first stage of the march, he pointed out, was to a well fifty miles away, where all the men, plus 6,000 camels and 3,000 horses, mules and donkeys had to be watered. This, and each successive well, was held by the Mahdi, could be poisoned, and had to be fought for.

The Mahdi had great numbers of troops, and did not worry about casualties. 'I believe their rush is wonderful,' wrote Power. 'They had only their spears and shields in the other battles, and in spite of the Nordenfeldts, Remingtons, &c. they swept over the square.' Since then the dervishes had captured 7,000 rifles, eighteen guns and a rocket battery, together with ammunition and gunnery instructors. They dominated the country through which Hicks had to march, their cavalry cutting off stragglers and preventing any messages getting back to the Nile.

Power's life was saved by dysentery. He could not walk or ride, and was strapped to a gun in 127 degrees of heat. Finally he was deposited at Dueim and sent back to Khartoum by river. O'Donovan of the *Daily News*, and Aladin Pasha, the Governor-General, went on to meet their death with Hicks's army.

When he got back to Khartoum Power, never idle, spent his convalescence learning Arabic and sketching for the *Pictorial World*. It was then that he offered his services to *The Times*. He and Colonel de Coëtlogan, the garrison commander, were the only British left behind in the town. They spent much of their time cruising up river to Dueim, trying to pick up news of Hicks Pasha. On 27 October Power wrote to his mother: 'It is now thirty-two days since Hicks Pasha and his immense army marched from Dueim, where I left, and since then not one word, good or bad, has been heard of him or his 11,000 men.'

Hicks was attacked by the Mahdi on 5 November at Kasghil, south of El Obeid. The news did not reach Cairo till 22 November. Power provided *The Times* with the only first-hand reports to be received by any newspaper. Of Hicks's army, almost all were massacred. First news of the disaster came from the Arabs. Then in December a black lay sister from the convent at El Obeid brought fuller accounts. On 14 December in a letter home Power wrote:

> The last that was seen of poor old Hicks was his taking his revolver in one hand and his sword in the other; calling on his soldiers to fix bayonets, and his staff to follow him, he spurred at the head of his troops into the dense mass of naked Arabs, and perished with all his men. They had fought for three days and nights without a drop of water, the whole day under a scorching sun on a sandy plain.

Later, on 24 January, a Greek merchant escaped with more details. According to these accounts the Austrian Baron Sheckendorff's batman, Klootz, who had deserted to the Mahdi some days before the battle, was the only European survivor. Father Joseph Ohrwalder, a priest who saw him in El Obeid, said he had 'socialistic tendencies'.

According to the Greek, the dervishes kept behind rocks and trees 'till the army was nearly annihilated with shot and shell. Then they charged and killed the staff. As each sheik was shown the dead body of Hicks, he was permitted to plunge his spear into it.'

(iii) The Arrival of Gordon

The destruction of Hicks Pasha's army caused consternation in England. The British Government were forced out of their policy of disclaiming all responsibility for the Sudan. That country had to be either abandoned or reinforced, unless someone could think of a third way out. In either of the first two cases, British troops were likely to be involved. Even evacuation of the remaining garrisons was not so simple. By this time the Mahdi had closed the route from the Red Sea to Khartoum by which Power had travelled in July. This would have to be opened up by force. There were even fears that the Mahdi would invade Egypt proper.

Power and de Coëtlogan suddenly became persons of international importance. They were the only men-on-the-spot who could advise Baring, or the Khedive – or Gladstone, for that matter – what the real situation in Khartoum was. Baring appointed Power British Consul, to look after such Hindu, Cypriot and Maltese interests as might remain. He wrote home that he was living in 'poor Hicks's' room in the Palace, and how 'the ignorance, the mind-darkness, and the wretchedness of the people sometimes makes one think that God has forgotten or turned His back on this land of misfortune . . . Wish some of the Irish agitators had a year of it.' Colonel de Coëtlogan and he were 'the last of the Mulligans'. All the consuls and other Europeans had fled.

What, however, was shaking the authorities were his reports, endorsed by de Coëtlogan, of the likely chances of holding Khartoum. He wired nearly every day to Baring and *The Times*. 'We have only 2,000 men to man four miles of earthworks and keep a rebel population of 60,000 Arabs quiet.' On Boxing Day the garrison of Fashoda, 600 miles up-river, came in by barge. This doubled the Khartoum garrison. The Egyptian Governor proposed poisoning 5,000 of the Mahdi's supporters in the town, but his suggestion was vetoed.

> 'You would be surprised how much influence being British Consul and *Times* correspondent gives me here. The people here have a very high opinion of the power of *The Times*. They say 'that it was not Europe but *The Times* deposed Ismail Pacha' (and in this they are au fond right), and say 'if this paper can change one Khedive, why not another?'

The reports from Khartoum were nowhere popular. This was not the kind of news governments wanted to hear. The Khedive wired that he could not get together a relief column, so de Coëtlogan and Power must depend on the neighbouring sheiks for assistance.

> This is really rich, as the Khedive knows very well that there is not a Sheik in the Sudan who would, or dare, help us; the Khedive telegraphs 'are the gates closed?', as if the place had walls. It is an open town, with garden fields, &c, and not a bit of defence round it till Colonel de Coëtlogan commenced the ditch, and yet they try to hamper our movements by trying to command us from Cairo.

Power's 'plain-spoken wire to Baring . . . has brought the Khedive to reason. Colonel de Coëtlogan has just had a private telegram from the Khedive telling him to do all the things suggested in the wire.' They planted the bottom of the ditch and side of the fortification with spear-heads and strewed the ground in front with caltrops, broken bottles and improvised anti-personnel mines.

Rather unfairly, de Coëtlogan was accused afterwards of being panicky. General Gordon had recently arrived in London, and to him everyone was beginning to turn as to a *deus ex machina* who, with his great authority and unrivalled knowledge of the Sudan, might be able to find some way out of the mess. He told a ministerial meeting at the War Office that the danger at Khartoum was exaggerated and that the two Englishmen there had too much whisky. 'He would be able to bring away garrisons without difficulty.' These were brave words and they were unfortunately what the British Government and public wanted to hear. De Coëtlogan was right, and Gordon was wrong. Gordon believed that his personal ascendancy could overcome all practical difficulties and paid for his mistake with his life.

The dispatch of Gordon emanated from his own over-confidence and the Government's wishful thinking. By sending this miracle-maker to the Sudan they hoped to find that third way out which would avoid those painful alternatives of reoccupying the Sudan by force or sending troops to cover an evacuation. The idea of sending Gordon to the Sudan had been mooted behind the scenes for some months. It appears first to have found public expression in a letter to *The Times* from Sir Samuel Baker published on 1 January 1884. An interview given by Gordon to W. T. Stead in the *Pall Mall Gazette* a week later, in which Gordon attacked the policy of evacuation, raised a public outcry in favour of his going.

Although the Government approved the Gordon mission many individual ministers were nervous about it. Gordon was temperamentally allergic to a policy of 'scuttle'. He was already throwing out hints through the *Pall Mall Gazette* that he intended to exercise a pretty free hand. Power commented from Khartoum on 24 January 1884 in a letter to his mother: 'Both *The Times* and the Government have given me leave to go if I wish. However, the order for a general retreat is given, and we shall march *together* to Berber. I hear that Chinese Gordon is coming up. They could not have a better man. He, though severe, was greatly loved during the five years he spent here.' Thus Power too seemed ready to fall under the spell of the miracle-maker. His own letters had clearly pointed out the physical difficulties of evacuating Khartoum without a major expedition to clear the Red Sea route. Gordon, no stickler for consistency, had made much the same point in the *Pall Mall Gazette* interview.

In Printing House Square the strong imperialist tendencies which were to appear a decade later had not yet developed. But the paper's contributor on imperial affairs, Demetrius Boulger, was a friend of Gordon, who kept in touch with him during January. The paper, warned by the Foreign Office of the impending appointment of Gordon, welcomed it in a leader dated 19 January but added: 'It would certainly be as well not to feel too great confidence at the outset as to the final issue of the enterprise. The Government will undoubtedly be felt to have largely increased its responsibilities by entrusting him [Gordon] with his present hazardous mission.' Thereafter, influenced by its Cairo correspondent, Moberly Bell, the paper began to advocate a more forward policy including the declaration of a formal protectorate over Egypt.

Gordon arrived in Cairo on 24 January and spent two days there. His main purpose was to see Baring, the Khedive and the Prime Minister, Nubar. He also met Moberly Bell at lunch with the Commander-in-Chief of the Egyptian Army, Sir Evelyn Wood. When their host introduced him as *The Times* correspondent Gordon 'made a mouth'. Later he sent him a message by Wood 'making', wrote Bell to *The Times*,

> the statement I wired you – that he would recommend holding on to the Sudan if the English Government would undertake expenses of conquest and subsequent government. I daresay, however, you know him well enough to be aware that it is rather dangerous to rely upon the opinions he may express at any given time.

Bell, who was an older and more mature man than Power, had met Gordon before. His attitude was friendly, but not uncritical. Nevertheless he gave steady support to Gordon in his dispatches.

Another sceptic was Colonel Stewart, 11th Hussars, who arrived with Gordon in Cairo as his military secretary; he was the War Office's choice, not Gordon's. Always perfectly loyal, he remained unaffected by Gordon's 'charisma'. He had shorter, but more recent experience, of the Sudan than his master. During the stay in Cairo, Baring authorized Stewart to report to him directly. Stewart was the third of the trio to be confined in Khartoum and killed.

In Cairo, Gordon settled with Baring and the Egyptians the measures he was to take on arrival in the Sudan. At his instigation, the Khedive appointed him Egyptian Governor-General there. This gave Gordon added authority, but a dual responsibility. Just after Gordon left Cairo, taking the route up the Nile, there was another appalling massacre of Egyptian troops by the dervishes. Valentine Baker had been trying to relieve Tokar from Suakin, on the Red Sea. As prophesied by Power, he had been 'Hicksed on the road'. 'The Egyptians,' wrote Bell from Cairo, 'did not make the resistance that a child would make against a man; they simply . . . lay down and howled until they were killed.' The dervishes allowed the European officers to walk away without drawing their swords. Thus the Red Sea route was closed. The news does not seem to have shaken Gordon, who by now had appreciated that disengagement from the Sudan was far more complex than he had declared it would be in London.

Meanwhile from Khartoum Power had been keeping up his stream of telegrams. 'I had a telegram from the Khedive asking me how it was he had to look for the news of his own province in an English paper [*The Times*] and why I could get news three days before his own Governor-General could telegraph it to him. I answered – I did not know, but that I went very much amongst the bazaars.' Baring was also appreciative of Power in his consular capacity. 'He tells me that the Council only know what is going on in the Sudan by my two wires a day to him.'

On 24 January Power received a telegram from Bell saying that Gordon would reach Khartoum in eighteen days. 'The shortest time on record is twenty-four days but Gordon (Sword and Bible) travels like a whirlwind,' he wrote to his mother. 'He and Colonel Stewart, 11th Hussars, will be tired when they arrive. We are going to give them a roast turkey, a leg of mutton, Bass's pale ale, and lager beer ... I don't believe the fellows in Lucknow looked more anxiously for Colin Campbell, than we look for Gordon.' Everyone had smallpox; 'smells are supreme'; the rebels had cut the telegraph wire.

By 14 February the wire was repaired and Power received a telegram from Gordon in Berber: 'Will be in Khartoum on Sunday.' Power thought it was civil of him to telegraph:

I hope Gordon will be a nice fellow. We will be living together, &c, and I hope I will get on with him. [His thoughts turned to Ireland.] Do you remember this night two years ago – At this hour your ball was in full swing, and you had put me on fatigue duty, and I had brought poor Mrs D. down to supper ... There are a great many of us dead since that night. I suppose we all have our appointed time when we are to go, and the only thing is to be prepared for it.

Gordon's arrival in the Sudan rather resembled that of Field-Marshal Montgomery's in the Western Desert. Without waiting to reach Khartoum, he sat down in Berber and the telegrams began to fly. Poor Colonel de Coëtlogan was simultaneously made a Pasha (a General), had his pay doubled, and was promoted Acting Governor-General of the Sudan. This meant of course that he was about to be sacked. On 16 February Power wrote in a letter to his mother: 'De C-Pacha is hard at work night and day: he today signed over three hundred orders, &c.'

Gordon knew by now that he could only evacuate the Sudan with honour, or even at all, if he came to an agreement with the Mahdi, or managed to set up a stable alternative administration, or if he secured military backing. The last was precluded by his terms of reference. Gordon's policy was to try everything, and to lose no time about it. He had to conciliate the local population. 'The town is posted up with placards saying that, by Gordon Pasha's orders, the taxes are reduced to half. Slavery is freely permitted, and the Mahdi is proclaimed King of Kordofan,' wrote Power. Bell, from Cairo, wrote cynically to his wife that the first order was 'dividing nothing in half', that the second was making a virtue of necessity, but 'will astonish Exeter Hall' – it did – and that the third 'is a case of thank you for giving me what I possess already'. All the same, he concludes, 'not a bad two days' work!'

A few days later, Gordon was in Khartoum, de Coëtlogan had left, and Gordon, Stewart and Power were living and messing together. Power need not have worried about how he and Gordon were to get on. Gordon promised him the Order of Osmanli, the Second Order of the Medjidji, and to take him with him to the Congo when the present business was finished. Baring telegraphed: 'HM Government highly approve of your action in the Sudan, and the aid you have given to General Gordon on his arrival. Lord Granville [Foreign Secretary] has intimated his wish that I send you this telegram.'

This showering of praises on *The Times* correspondent may not have been altogether altruistic. Gordon was a very press-conscious general. But to Power he was something more than that.

> Gordon [he wrote to his mother], is a most lovable character – quiet, mild, gentle, and strong; he is so humble, too. The way he pats you on the shoulder when he says, 'Look here, dear fellow, now what do you advise?' would make you love him. When he goes out of doors there are always crowds of Arab men and women at the gate to kiss his feet, and twice today the furious women, wishing to lift his feet to kiss them, threw him over. He appears to like me, and already calls me Frank. He likes my going so much amongst the natives, for not to do so is a mortal sin in his eyes. I often speak of you to General Gordon; he says he must make your acquaintance before we go to the Congo; he would like a day in Dublin. He is Dictator here; the Mahdi has gone down before him, and to-day sent him a 'salam', or message of welcome. It is wonderful that such a man could have such an influence on 200,000 people. Numbers of women flock here every day to ask him to touch their children to cure them; they call him the 'Father and the Saviour of the Sudan'. He has found me badly up in 'Thomas à Kempis', which he reads every day, and has given me an 'Imitation of Christ'. He is indeed, I believe, the greatest and best man of his century ... I stay on here to the end. I'll stop while he stays.

(iv) Siege and Death

Power's feelings for Gordon were probably reciprocated, although the General's comments on persons were apt to be terse – Power was 'a nice young fellow'. He telegraphed to Baring 'Power is a first-rate fellow.' And when he learned of his death: 'Power was a chivalrous, brave, honest gentleman. Can one say more?' He would hardly have offered to take him to the Congo if he had not thought highly of him.

Meanwhile there was work to be done, and he put Power to work. First, he made use of his military experience, which by now exceeded that of many regular soldiers. Gordon's striking force were his ten armed, and bullet-proof, wood-fired paddle boats – these were his cavalry. He used them for reconnaissance, for raiding cattle and grain, and, as Power put it, 'to let the rebels know there was kick in us yet'. Power was good at commanding these expeditions. Gradually, as the rebels brought more cannon down to the river, they reduced the flotilla's numbers. Or there were groundings. 'Last evening one of our steamers ran aground twelve miles from here, and as she was in danger Gordon sent me off with two steamers and strong hawsers to get her off.' They worked all night and had to take everything out of her, the fuel, the chains and the guns. Gordon was pleased when Power brought her back safely in the morning. If Gordon had preserved more of these steamers to the end he might have staved off the final assault until the relief column arrived.

More important, Gordon used Power to inform the British public of the true situation in Khartoum, and of his own views. This was a perfectly legitimate course, but it could back-fire. Power's dispatches to *The Times* tended to be more gloomy than Gordon's dispatches to his official superiors. Khartoum, Gordon said, was 'as safe as Kensington Park', but he did not disapprove of Power's more sombre messages. Not unnaturally the home government suspected them of collusion, and concluded that Gordon was trying to force their hand to send troops to annex the Sudan. Gordon, of course, had two audiences to address – the Sudanese and the British. As the Commander, he could scarcely let himself appear defeatist. On the other hand, it was important that somebody should be telling people at home just how serious his situation was. No doubt in his eyes Power served that purpose. The system could be counter-productive.

One of Power's best-known dispatches was sent on 3 March. Gordon was not progressing with his attempts to come to an agreement with the Mahdi. This was hardly surprising, since Baker's disastrous attack on the Mahdi's men at Tokar, delivered just at the moment when Gordon was setting out on his peace-making mission, can hardly have put the Mahdi in a placatory frame of mind. So he had to fall back on his alternative policy of finding a suitable leader to head a substitute administration in the Sudan. In Cairo he thought he had found such a one in Zebehr Pasha, who had been a most successful military commander in the Sudan before Gordon's first term as Governor-General there. Unfortunately Zebehr was a notorious slave-trader. Gordon was a realist. He had done his best to put down slave-trading and had actually been responsible for killing Zebehr's son, but he saw no other hope of an orderly evacuation.

In Cairo both Baring – after some hesitation – and Bell supported Gordon. So, in England, did Queen Victoria. Even Gladstone was privately in favour of following Gordon's advice. But the only hope of getting adopted a proposal which was certain to shock many liberal consciences, lay in keeping it secret for the time being. Unfortunately, Gordon laboured under the mistaken delusion that Baring was opposing him. He lost patience and began to make use of Power to forward his demands. On 5 March *The Times* published this obviously Gordon-inspired telegram sent by Power under a Khartoum dateline of 3 March:

> It is now admitted that Zebehr Pasha is the only man connected with the Sudan who is endowed with the ability and firmness necessary to head any government here. It is out of the question that General Gordon would leave Khartoum without first having formed a government which would in some measure stem the fearful anarchy that must eventually sweep over the Sudan. The arrival of Zebehr Pasha would draw over to his side the bands of rebels which are now scattered over the Sudan and his great knowledge of the tribes fits him more than any other man to take the place of the Egyptian Government. He would, of course, come here under certain stringent conditions. General Gordon has foreseen this ever since he left Cairo.

Publication of this message destroyed any hope of Gladstone's ever getting Zebehr's appointment through Parliament. The outcry was appalling. Even *The Times* leader writer thought that the proposed cure was worse than the disease. Gordon was almost certainly justified in his confidence in Zebehr, but he was utterly ignorant of politics at home. *The Times* at least was logical. On 31 March the paper was advocating sending troops. But the Gladstone Government, having willed the end, namely evacuation, was not prepared to will the means. It was a classic case of the difficulty of running a colonial policy under a democratic government.

Power had secured a nice scoop for *The Times*, and he followed it up by publishing a full-scale interview outlining Gordon's plans for the Sudan if Zebehr were sent. A more experienced journalist, knowing the English political climate, might have faced a conflict of duty in sending these dispatches. Power no doubt was confident that he was being helpful to Gordon. The interview, although asking for some military assistance, ended 'I am dead against any British expedition to reconquer the Sudan. It is unnecessary if HMG do what I recommend.'

On 23 March Power filed a message saying that the Mahdi had returned the robes of honour Gordon had sent him and spurned his offer of the sultanship of Kordofan. Thus both Gordon's attempts at a peaceful solution had failed. The alternatives were now only too clear, although Gordon did not himself yet know that his request for Zebehr had been turned down.

On 1 April Roland wound his horn almost for the last time. 'We are daily expecting British troops. We cannot bring ourselves to believe that we are about to be abandoned by the Government. Our existence depends on England.' The sound was heard in Printing House Square: 'If General Gordon be abandoned because he has not accomplished an impossible task, England will hold the Ministers of the Crown responsible for his life, and will exact the strict discharge of every fraction of that responsibility.'

By now the net was tightening round Khartoum. On 12 or 13 March the telegraph line was cut north of Khartoum and south of Berber, this time for good, but Power was still getting telegrams through for some time after this. Power's last message went out on 7 April and was published in *The Times* ten days later. Gordon, who had received no communication from outside since 10 March, had just received a message from Baring telling him that no troops were coming to his aid. From then on there was silence.

Power and Stewart left Khartoum on their last, and fatal, sortie on 10 September. Gordon had been out of touch with the rest of the world for five months, and he decided that at all costs contact must be re-established. During these months, the hottest of the year, the siege had dragged on in a ding-dong manner. Khartoum was closely invested, but not yet subjected, as it was to be, to artillery bombardment.

On 5 August Gladstone, though Gordon could not of course know it, had authorized the sending of a relief force. The main reason for delaying the decision so long was that Ministers were preoccupied with domestic affairs, particularly the new Reform Bill. But in the end Hartington, the War Minister, much influenced by Sir Garnet Wolseley, the Adjutant-General, threatened to resign if nothing were done. On 9 September Wolseley arrived in Cairo to take command.

The next day, Stewart and Power left on a forlorn hope to run the blockade down the Nile with messages from Gordon describing the true situation in Khartoum and asking urgently for troops to be sent. Both men had not wanted to leave. They felt they were deserting their chief, but Gordon persuaded them that it was their duty to go. They took with them the French Consul, Herbin, an Anglophobe editor of a scurrilous evening paper in Cairo, who had arrived in Khartoum in March. The party left in the steamer *Abbas*. According to a survivor, they were escorted past Berber by two other steamers, and towed four sailing boats with them. After passing Berber safely, Stewart sent back the escorts and cut loose the sailing boats. The *Abbas* steamed on.

Somewhere between this point and Merowe was Major Kitchener, forward intelligence officer of the relief force, destined one day to be the
conqueror of the whole of the Sudan. He was encamped with an escort
of bedouin. Kitchener had actually learnt of the *Abbas*'s approach and
tried, unsuccessfully, to get a message to Stewart advising him to cut
across the desert rather than continue by river because the riverside
sheikhs had gone over to the Mahdi. Even so, if Stewart and Power
had retained the sailing vessels, they might have proceeded downstream
safely by river, but by now they had only one small boat. They entered
into negotiation with a sheikh for camels. Possibly he knew, and told
them, of Kitchener's presence.

The rest of the story is told by one of the survivors, a stoker:

> Suleiman Wad Gam...being asked for camels...said that he
> would provide them, and invited Colonel Stewart and the two
> Consuls [Power and Herbin] to the house of a blind man,
> named Fakrietman, telling them to come unarmed, lest the
> people should be frightened. The camels were not given us. We
> all went unarmed, except Colonel Stewart, who had a small
> revolver in his belt.
>
> Presently I saw Suleiman come out and make a sign to the
> people standing about the village, armed with swords and spears.
> These immediately divided into two parties, one running to the
> house of the blind man, the other to where the rest of Colonel
> Stewart's party were assembled. I was with the latter. When the
> natives charged, we threw ourselves into the river. The natives
> fired and killed many of us, and others were drowned . . . I swam
> over to the left bank. The bodies were thrown into the river.

Power died, but Gordon fought on. On 26 January 1885 the dervishes
poured into Khartoum. The Nile had fallen, leaving a crumbled stretch
on the riverside extremity of the wall, which the townspeople were
too weak to strengthen. There were not enough steamers to cover the
river, and the garrison had little fight left in them. A few hours later,
Gordon's head was shown to Slatin Pasha, the Austrian former Governor of Darfur who had declared himself a Muslim and was now a
prisoner in Omdurman.

The Times was as deeply concerned at the loss of its own correspondent as it was with that of Gordon. The Government, in the paper's
view, were responsible for both. In Power they had lost a man of
character and exceptional potential. 'We feel bound to pay a tribute to
the memory of our brave and ill-fated Correspondent, Mr Power, who,
thrown on a sudden into the midst of great events and formidable
dangers, showed himself fully equal to the occasion.' Gordon's appoint-

ment was 'one of the most callous and unjustifiable speculations in human life that a responsible Government ever embarked upon'.

For *The Times* the Gordon episode was an important turning-point. From this time dates the beginning of its definitive identification with British imperialism. The formation of a colonial department in *The Times* was a result of the arrival in power of new men whose outlook was deeply coloured by the Gordon crisis. For the next half century the imperial theme, under Buckle and Dawson, was to be the dominating factor in the policy of the paper.

11 THE PARNELL CASE

(i) Houston and the Little Black Bag

In 1886, one year after Gordon's death, there occurred the first move in a series of events which ended in near-ruin for *The Times*. By this time a new Editor was in the Chair. John Walter III's experience with Chenery had persuaded him to revert to his father's and grandfather's recipe of appointing youthful editors. To find one, Walter had gone back to the older universities and the name which emerged with a warm recommendation after consultation in Oxford was that of a brilliant young scholar, George Earle Buckle. His father, Canon Buckle, a Fellow of Oriel, had been connected with Newman and the Tractarian movement, which would have constituted an added recommendation in the eyes of the Proprietor, who appointed him as an assistant editor in 1880 while still aged only twenty-five. Four years later Buckle became Editor.

The three leading Editors of *The Times* in the nineteenth century thus came from three different backgrounds. Barnes's was literary, Delane's sporting Irish, and Buckle's academic and ecclesiastical. A Wykehamist and scholar of New College, Buckle had won Firsts in both Greats and Modern History, added to which he won the Newdigate Prize with a poem on Livingstone. As a follow up, he had been elected a Fellow of All Souls, studied law, and been called to the bar at Lincoln's Inn. The only possible doubt that might have been raised over Buckle's appointment was whether his academic achievements were matched with the shrewdness and flair required for dealing with the labyrinths of politics.

It was in April 1886, shortly before the defeat of Gladstone's Home Rule Bill for Ireland, that Buckle, who had then been in the chair for just over two years, received a call from a twenty-three-year-old Dublin journalist with an unusual proposition. His caller, Edward Caulfield Houston, the son of a prison warder, had worked for the *Dublin Daily Express*, and had deputized for *The Times*, three years earlier, in reporting the trial of the murderers of the Chief Secretary for Ireland, Lord Frederick Cavendish and the Under Secretary, Mr Thomas Burke, in Phoenix Park. In the interval he had become Secretary of the Irish Loyal and Patriotic Union, a body formed to fight Home Rule in Ireland.

The story Houston told Buckle was as follows. While at the trial of
the Phoenix Park murderers he had become convinced that there was
complicity between Parnell, the leader of the Irish parliamentary group
in the Commons, and the terrorist gang, the 'Invincibles', which was
responsible for the killings. He was now on the track of some letters
which, he believed, would compromise Parnell, but had run out of
funds to complete his inquiries. Because of the danger of assassination
he insisted on withholding the name of the person from whom he
thought he could obtain these letters – a reticence which seemed reasonable to the Editor. The point of Houston's visit was to raise money to
enable him to secure the letters for *The Times*. He sought no reward for
himself.

Houston was not being frank with Buckle. He did not reveal that he
had already shown copies of the letters to W. T. Stead, Editor of the
Pall Mall Gazette. That veteran connoisseur of scandalous revelations
had refused to touch them. But Buckle was impressed by Houston. Any
evidence serving to identify the political wing of Irish nationalism with
the terrorists was welcome. He refused to pay out any money but he
temporized by telling the young journalist to come back whenever he
could produce the actual letters.

A man of more experience and shrewdness than Buckle would
probably have reflected that Parnell, although not morally disapproving of subversion, might be opposed to the activities of such
'angry brigades' as the Invincibles on grounds of policy and common sense. Furthermore, in listening to Houston's story, Buckle was
guilty of a curious omission. He neither called in, consulted, nor
informed J. Woulfe Flanagan, *The Times*'s expert and leader writer
on Irish affairs. Flanagan, a Catholic Unionist, was one of the most
knowledgeable men in the country on the tortuous intrigues and
personalities of Irish politics, pressure groups and newspapers. He
was a Balliol scholar and remained a leader writer till 1928. Failure
to consult him was a first false step which was to be followed by many
others.

Houston, not wholly dissatisfied after his first interview with the
Editor of *The Times*, went back to his principal. This was a notorious
scoundrel called Richard Pigott, who had guaranteed to obtain for
Houston the material which would incriminate Parnell. Pigott had been
a shady Dublin newspaper proprietor in the 1870s. Houston might be
expected to have known of his reputation, even though his most active
days were over by the time the prison warder's son had entered Dublin
journalism. The relationship between the two still remains something
of a mystery, but Pigott later declared that he took the young innocent
for a ride.

In appearance, Pigott was bald, bronzed and bouncy. Known as

'Old Neptune', he was a strong and keen swimmer and the life and soul of the Kingstown Model Yacht Club, though he seems to have spent more time in the bar than with the boats. He had started life as an office boy on a newspaper. By 1859 he had become business manager of the *Irishman*, a Dublin nationalist publication, but being both dishonest and incompetent, he landed the paper's proprietor in bankruptcy. The proprietor's revenge was to leave his property to the man who had been the cause of his troubles.

But now luck played into Pigott's hands. The British authorities in Dublin Castle chose this moment to ban the only other nationalist newspaper in the city, whereupon the circulation of the *Irishman* shot up from a mere 5,000 to 50,000, and Pigott found himself not only well off but a considerable figure in Irish politics. He had no loyalties. He took money indiscriminately from both the Fenians and the Castle, and was finally bought out in 1881 by Parnell and Patrick Egan, treasurer of the Land League. In the course of this negotiation Pigott possessed himself of, and preserved, letters written by both these men, of which he was now to make use.

Newspaper ownership was not Pigott's only métier. He was a blackmailer, a writer of anonymous letters, and a pornographer. He had, wrote an acquaintance, James O'Connor, 'a photographic apparatus' and his trade in pictures of every description – engravings, lithographs, woodcuts – 'was not of the purest character'. Forgery was the most secret of his activities. A compulsive letter-writer, with a remarkable facility for imitating other people's handwriting and signatures, he traded in forged bills. This ability of his was known to Egan and other nationalist leaders. Such was the man who was offering Houston, and through him *The Times*, highly damaging letters purporting to be written not only by Egan but by Parnell himself.

Edward Houston had first met Richard Pigott a year earlier, in 1885. At that time the Parnellites were still backing the Tories, and the Liberals therefore wanted to discredit the Parnellites in the November general elections. On behalf of the Liberal Chief Whip, Lord Richard Grosvenor, Houston purchased from Pigott for £60 a document, known as 'The Black Pamphlet', showing that £100,000 was missing in the Land League accounts. The inference was, of course, that it had been spent on objects such as the Phoenix Park murders. Grosvenor subsequently advanced to Houston a further £100 and told him to continue delving. After further conversations Pigott told Houston of the existence of the incriminating letters.

This was the position at the time of Houston's first visit to Printing House Square. After a second unsuccessful call, Houston persuaded Pigott to disgorge. This Pigott had previously been reluctant to do since he was travelling round the world on an expense account and a guinea a day, advanced to him by Lord Richard Grosvenor. For a man in Pigott's position of perennial insolvency this was something he was in no hurry to give up.

The letters were handed over in circumstances of suitable melodrama. Houston journeyed to a run-down hotel in Paris which went by the appropriate name of the *Deux Mondes*. It was a regular haunt of Pigott's. To lend moral support Houston brought with him Dr Maguire, Professor of Moral Philosophy at Trinity College, Dublin, and an active Loyalist who had been concerned in Houston's earlier deals with Pigott. In the uniformly frustrating sequence of events which is the hallmark of this story, the professor died before he could be called upon to give his version of the transaction to the judicial Commission of Inquiry which was subsequently ordered by the Government.

Pigott then submitted the letters for inspection to the representative of the Irish Loyal and Patriotic Union and the moral philosopher from Trinity College, Dublin. After scrutiny, the letters were pronounced satisfactory and Pigott explained that the two men, Maurice Murphy and Tom Brown, who had brought them in a 'little black bag' were downstairs. They were, of course, waiting for their money, but were, in the circumstances, too shy to meet the purchasers. Nothing more was ever heard or seen of Murphy and Brown.

However, the professor was sufficiently credulous or intimidated to dole out £500 to Pigott for Murphy and Brown and £100 for himself. Houston returned in triumph with the letters, but indulged in a little risky double dealing before delivering them at Printing House Square. He took them first to Lord Hartington, leader of the Liberal Unionist Party, the section of the Liberal Party which had broken from Gladstone over Home Rule. Hartington sent him to Sir Henry James, a former Attorney-General and the party's legal adviser. What Houston did not know was that Sir Henry James was also a part-time legal consultant to *The Times*. In showing the letters to him first Houston was therefore exposing himself to considerable risk.

Sir Henry James was more successful than the Editor of *The Times* in wringing information out of Houston. He found out that Pigott was the source of origin of the letters. He doubted their authenticity and declared that even if genuine they were inadequate in law to sustain a case against Parnell. Like Stead he would not touch them, and recommended Houston to communicate with Scotland Yard. In September Houston took the letters instead to the Editor of *The Times*. There were five purporting to be signed by Parnell and five by Patrick Egan, the man who had bought the *Irishman* from Pigott five years earlier and who later became treasurer of the Land League. Other letters were produced at a later date.

The most famous of the letters, No. 2, commonly called 'the Facsimile

Letter', related to the condemnation which Parnell, horror-struck, had issued on hearing of the Phoenix Park murders:

15/5/82

Dear Sir,

I am not surprised at your friend's anger but he and you should know that to denounce the murders was the only course open to us. To do that promptly was plainly ~~the only course~~ our best policy.

But you can tell him, and all others concerned that though I regret the accident of Lord F. Cavendish's death I cannot refuse to admit that Burke got no more than his deserts.

You are at liberty to show him this, and others whom you can trust also, but let not my address be known. He can write to House of Commons.

Yours very truly,

Chas. S. Parnell.

There were several points about this letter which might have caused a prudent man to be suspicious. Only the words 'Yours very truly' and the signature were in Parnell's hand. The rest was said to have been written 'by a secretary'. The crossing out of the words 'the only course' is curious. One might think that the writer of a letter of this importance who wished to make a correction of such substance would have rewritten the whole letter. The word 'this' is also inserted as an afterthought. The letter was a single folded sheet, making four pages. The text was written on the first page, the two inside pages were blank, and the words in Parnell's alleged handwriting were at the top of the back page. On the face of it, the inference is strong that whoever wrote the letter had obtained a single blank piece of notepaper with Parnell's signature upon it.

The second most important letter, No. 1, known as the 'Kilmainham letter', purported to have been written while Parnell was in Kilmainham gaol, before the Phoenix Park murders. It was a letter of incitement:

9/1/82

Dear E.

What are these fellows waiting for? This inaction is inexcusable our best men are in prison and nothing is being done.

Let there be an end of this hesitency. Prompt action is called for.

You undertook to make it hot for old Forster and Co.
Let us have some evidence of your power to do so.
My health is good thanks.

Yours very truly

Chas. S. Parnell

W. E. Forster, Chief Secretary for Ireland, was the British Cabinet Minister responsible for Irish affairs.

The letter looks more like the work of an illiterate rather than of an educated man like Parnell. Most of the other letters were undated, and few showed any address, or were sent to any named person. There were no envelopes. Other points made at various times were that the handwriting of the Egan letters and of the 'secretary' are similar, and that the dates appear penned by a different hand to the words.

Houston handed the letters over to Buckle for investigation. He asked for no personal remuneration, only for reimbursement. £1,780 was the sum eventually mentioned. As money was involved, the Editor sent Houston on to the Manager, John Cameron MacDonald – the 'Un-Canny Scot' as he came to be labelled after the affair. MacDonald showed the letters to the Chief Proprietor, John Walter III. Walter in turn consulted Joseph Soames, *The Times* solicitor, who played an active role in the transactions, handling large sums of the company's money. Still no one told Flanagan, the sole person on the staff who was conversant with all the *dramatis personae*. The omission still seems inexplicable.

Walter's working party, in the course of their inquiries, unearthed circumstantial evidence which led them to believe that the letters were genuine. They obtained a specimen of Parnell's handwriting by inserting in the agony column an advertisement, offering £10 for the autographs of twenty distinguished parliamentarians, Parnell being among the names listed. The device worked. Three specimens of his signature were obtained within a week. Gradually others followed. G. S. Inglis, the most celebrated handwriting expert of the day, was called in to compare them with the specimens on the letters, and on technical grounds pronounced them genuine. Altogether he studied forty examples.

Other arguments which actuated Walter and his assistants were, however, less rational. 'It was however upon the internal evidence of the facsimile letter', Walter wrote in a memorandum, 'that our conviction of its genuineness chiefly rested. Its whole tenor and composition appeared to us to negative the idea of forgery.' Nor did they appear to find anything unreasonable in Houston's refusal to divulge the name of the owner of the letters. In fact MacDonald may well have known Pigott's name from the beginning but not divulged it.

The Times was planning to publish the letters in order to ease the passage through Parliament of the Irish Crimes Bill and had fixed on 27 January 1887 as the date for publication in facsimile of Letter No. 2 when, not many hours before press time on the 26th, the management received their first positive warning of danger. MacDonald and Soames went to consult Sir Henry James on the legal aspects of publication. James already knew from Houston the source of the letters, and Soames now learned to his consternation of Houston's visit and the name of Pigott was mentioned for the first time. Sir Henry James's considered advice was against publication.

Buckle stopped the facsimile from going to press and sent for Houston. This plausible young man managed to convince the Editor once more that he had only been exercising normal discretion in concealing these important matters of fact from his knowledge. According to Houston, he actually offered to take the letters back, but Buckle refused. Sir Henry James's words to Soames did at least cause *The Times* to review their strategy. They were impressed by his argument that the letters, even if genuine, bore no legal weight. They decided therefore to back them up with an informed series of special articles entitled 'Parnellism and Crime'. Their publication would, it was argued, shift the basis of the indictment on to political, as opposed to legal, grounds. Ironically, the writer chosen to produce most of the articles was Flanagan. Others were contributed – anonymously, of course – by Sir Robert Anderson, who had been adviser to the Home Office on Irish affairs and was to become head of the CID at Scotland Yard. Anderson subsequently claimed that he had the permission of his superiors to write these articles, but this was denied by Asquith and others in the House of Commons debate that followed the disclosures.

The articles started on 7 March and contained no direct reference to the letters though making dark hints of a secret weapon yet to be revealed. Meanwhile, in March, Soames travelled to Kilmainham gaol to see the Governor. There he confirmed that the paper and ink used in Letter No. 1 – the 'Kilmainham letter' – were those normally used by Parnell when in prison. He discovered also that, on the date at the head of the letter, Parnell had received a visitor who would have been able to smuggle it out. This visitor was a medical student called Charles Russell who subsequently died in Brussels. The paper was manufactured in Dublin and was out of production.

His findings seemed to provide corroborative evidence of the genuineness of the letters.

Then, on 18 April, Buckle published the facsimile of Letter No. 2. To mark the solemnity of the occasion *The Times*, for the first time in its history, used double column headings.

(ii) 'Villainous Forgery'

If anyone in Printing House Square had doubts about the impact that *The Times* of 18 April 1887 would make on its readers, those doubts would have been banished next morning. Chamberlain, Parnell's bitterest enemy, found the facsimile hard to credit, but thought it almost impossible that *The Times* of all newspapers could have acted without being sure of its proofs. The nationalist MP, Captain O'Shea, whose wife was Parnell's mistress, said he thought the signature genuine.

The Prime Minister, Lord Salisbury, appeared to be convinced. He accused Mr Gladstone of mixing on terms of intimacy with 'allies tainted with the strong presumption of conniving at assassination'. 'There goes Home Rule, and the Liberal Party too,' remarked a Liberal friend of Parnell's over the breakfast table.

Almost the only person who remained outwardly unmoved was Parnell himself. Like many others, he saw the facsimile while reading *The Times* at breakfast. Throwing it to Mrs O'Shea, he remarked: 'Wouldn't you hide your head with shame if your King was as stupid as that, my Queen?' In the House of Commons that afternoon he affected not to have noticed it. Shown a copy of the paper he said: 'I did not make an S like that since 1878.' Compelled to make a statement in the House later in the evening, Parnell described the letter as 'a villainous and barefaced forgery'.

The Times challenged Parnell to sue them. But neither then, nor for a long time, did he make any move. This was taken by *The Times*, as well as by the public in general, as an admission of guilt. Various explanations have been put forward for his inactivity, the most common being that he could not trust an English jury. Perhaps he was waiting, in Kruger's phrase, for the tortoise to put its head out of the shell. Perhaps he was just disdainful – he was a very disdainful man.

The Government refused an inquiry, demanded by the Irish members, while *The Times* went steadily on with the publication of its articles on 'Parnellism and Crime'. So things continued until June when an obscure Irish ex-MP, Frank Hugh O'Donnell, wrote a letter to the paper to correct what he called 'mis-statements' in the articles. A leader commenting on this letter was taken by O'Donnell as being defamatory and he brought an action for libel. On the face of it his case was so poor that he was suspected of being a stalking horse for Parnell. When a year later, in July 1888, the case came to trial, the jury found for *The Times* without leaving the box. But the affair had gone on long enough to stir up all the old passions.

The Times was defended in this action by Sir Richard Webster, the Attorney-General, for at that time the Law Officers of the Crown

were allowed to practise also on their own. Webster took the opportunity of reading out another batch of the as yet unpublished letters,
including Letter No. 1, supposed to have been written in Kilmainham
gaol. This turned out to be an exceptionally injudicious move, for
Parnell immediately asked the Government for a Select Committee of
the House to inquire into the genuineness of the letters. The Government countered by offering a Special Commission, composed of three
judges, to investigate all the charges contained in the articles on
'Parnellism and Crime'.

After a bitter political fight as to the form the inquiry should take,
it was finally decided that there should be a judicial commission with
the widest terms of reference. *The Times* agreed to co-operate, although
from its point of view the procedure had grave disadvantages. In an
inquiry of this kind, there is neither plaintiff nor defendant, nor
prisoner in the dock. Win or lose, each witness must pay his own costs.
The Times would much have preferred that Parnell should have sued
it for libel. As it was, he did start a libel action simultaneously, but
in the Court of Sessions in Edinburgh, apparently choosing this course
because of his mistrust of English courts and the mistrust of English
public opinion for the verdict of an Irish one.

The Special Commission held a preliminary meeting on 17 September
1888, when it ruled that *The Times* must make good all the charges
contained in the articles. This meant that the entire burden of proof
rested on the paper, which found itself obliged to call 494 witnesses,
some of whom had to be brought from America, all at the paper's cost
– a shattering blow. The Commission then adjourned until 22 October.

But even before the inquiry opened *The Times* management had
their first real glimpse of the dangers ahead. The Attorney-General,
Sir Richard Webster, appearing once again to represent the paper's
interests, insisted on knowing the whole truth. Webster, like his second
counsel, Sir Henry James, appeared reluctantly on this occasion for
The Times, both men being held to their brief by Salisbury, who feared
that *The Times*'s case would collapse without them. Houston, reluctant
too, confessed the full details of how he obtained the letters from
Pigott. J. Woulfe Flanagan and E. D. J. Wilson, another leader writer,
who were at last told the story, knew Pigott by disrepute. There were
long faces in Printing House Square.

Webster, against the wishes of MacDonald, the Manager of *The
Times*, insisted on putting Pigott in the box. He could hardly have
done otherwise, though Pigott himself advised against this course, as
'I feel utterly unable', he wrote to Houston on 11 November 1888,
'from defect of memory and other causes, to refute satisfactorily the
many allegations founded on remote events of my career as a Nationalist journalist that are now certain to be brought up in judgment

against me.' Hauled into the limelight Pigott proved pathologically nervous. Even if innocent he would have seemed guilty. Desperate but ever resourceful, he had previously sought his luck with the other side. He had attended a meeting on 25 October arranged by the radical MP and journalist, Henry Labouchere, with Parnell and his solicitor, George Lewis. One may assume that Pigott tried to get money out of the opposition and failed. According to Pigott's evidence, Labouchere had suggested that he could avoid prosecution for perjury by admitting in the witness box that he had forged the letters. Pigott replied that 'nothing would induce me to come into the witness box and swear a lie'. Lewis had then advised him to write to *The Times* acknowledging that the letters were forged. *The Times* would then naturally withdraw them, and he might not have to go into the witness box at all.

The inquiry was conducted by three judges, presided over by Sir James Hannen, President of the Probate, Divorce and Admiralty Court. Parnell was represented by Sir Charles Russell (afterwards Lord Russell of Killowen), the foremost advocate of his time who became the first Catholic Attorney-General since the Reformation. He was supported by, among others, H. H. Asquith, the future Liberal Prime Minister.

Among witnesses for *The Times* were Captain O'Shea who, when it came to the point, was not very positive about recognizing Parnell's signature, and a remarkable secret agent from America, Henri Le Caron, whose real name was Thomas Willis Beach and who came forward of his own accord. Le Caron spent twenty-five years infiltrating the Irish secret societies and testified that a year before the Phoenix Park murders he had been sent over to Parnell as an emissary. Parnell had remarked to him that he had long since ceased to believe that anything but force of arms would ever bring about the redemption of Ireland. He had, by implication, encouraged Le Caron to raise money in America for purposes of insurrection in Ireland. Le Caron was by far the most damaging witness that Parnell had to face, and recent research has tended to uphold his veracity.

(iii) The Case Collapses

On Thursday, 14 February 1889, five months after the opening of the inquiry, the Commission approached the one subject in which Parnell, and the public, were most interested – the letters. *The Times* called MacDonald, Soames, Inglis (the handwriting expert), Houston and Pigott. The decision to call the Manager rather than the Proprietor rested on *Times* protocol, but he was not the best man to put in the box. MacDonald was ageing and losing his grip.

The mainstay of *The Times*'s case was intended to be that the letters could be proved genuine on internal evidence alone. For this they would rely on Inglis. As for the source of the letters, they would argue that this was bound to be tainted if letters of this kind were ever to be obtained at all. At best this was a lame argument. In the event the Commission was not to allow *The Times* to deploy the case on the lines it had planned. Inglis never even had a chance to give evidence.

Soames went into the box first. He gave formal details about the acquisition of the letters, and revealed that Pigott had asked for £5,000 to testify that the letters were genuine. Later it came out that he had demanded the same sum from the other side to testify that they were forged. By the time Soames stepped down, Russell had done something to undermine confidence in the authenticity of the letters. For the first time the public began to wonder whether *The Times* was on such sure ground as they had assumed. Worse was to follow.

The next witness was the Manager, J. C. MacDonald. He was cross-examined by H. H. Asquith, who severely shook the court's faith in the reliability of *The Times* management. The climax of Asquith's inquisition was reached when he pressed the witness to state what steps he had taken to establish the provenance of the letters:

'Did Houston say that he had paid £1,780 for these eleven letters?' – 'Yes.'
'He did not tell you to whom?' – 'No.'
'Or how?' – 'No.'
'Or when?' – 'No.'
'Or where?' – 'No.'
'Showed you no voucher or receipt?' – 'None whatever.'
'No particulars, whether in items or a lump sum?' – 'No.'
'Did he represent to you that he was ready to let *The Times* have the letters for publication on being recouped?' – 'Yes.'
'Nothing more?' – 'No.'
'And you have not, as I understand, up to this moment investigated the details of Mr Houston's alleged expenditure?' – 'I have not.'
'You have taken his word for it throughout?' – 'I have.'

When Asquith sat down, he left the impression on the court that *The Times* was managed by a nincompoop. He had also contrived to suggest that Houston was a confidence trickster.

MacDonald's discomfiture in the witness box may have been in part due to the fact that he found himself unable to give his evidence as he had intended. A document in *The Times* archives, which appears to be his preliminary draft of his account of events, states that: 'At the very outset of our negotiations, in October 1886, Mr Houston informed me that he had obtained the letters through the agency of Mr Pigott, formerly editor of the *Irishman*; but Mr Pigott is still personally quite unknown to me, and I have had no direct relations with him.'

In the witness-box, however, MacDonald denied that Houston, when he first brought the letters to him in October 1886, told him whom he got them from. He said that he only learnt the name of Pigott 'a very considerable time afterwards'. Under cross-examination he admitted that his pledge of secrecy as to the source of the letters referred to Houston alone. When pressed to give the date when he first learned that Houston had obtained the letters from Pigott he said that he could not 'fix the exact date', but agreed that it was 'somewhere about' March 1887, which was when the 'Parnellism and Crime' articles began.

MacDonald also got into difficulties when he was pressed under cross-examination to give the names of those besides Flanagan who had contributed to these articles. Webster and James clearly felt that Sir Robert Anderson's name must not be revealed, but Anderson himself had no objection as long as he had the opportunity to go into the box to give evidence. On 14 February, the day before MacDonald's first appearance as a witness, he wrote to him:

'One thing you said to me weighs much with me – I mean your nobly generous resolve to suffer rather than divulge my name. I earnestly beg of you not to do that. You appealed to me to put myself in the hands of Webster and James, and I did so. I now appeal to you in return to leave yourself in the hands of the Court in this matter, and if Sir J. Hannen says you are to answer any q. about me, do so ... You may take it from me that Sir James's fears are wholly based on misapprehension of the facts.

A letter also exists from Buckle to MacDonald, dated 17 February, which, referring to Anderson's desire to give evidence, throws some light on MacDonald's hesitations in the box: "That Webster and James as politicians are inclined to keep him out of the box on political grounds, I quite understand. But surely it is common prudence on our part to avail ourselves of his offer, if he is willing. We used not care [*sic*] for the susceptibilities of Whigs or Tories.'

The inquiry now took a turn which proved fatal in the eyes of Printing House Square. The Attorney-General, on behalf of the paper, rose to call the handwriting expert, but Russell objected. He maintained that the Commission should first pursue the matter of the origin of the letters and the Commission agreed. Webster, however, insisted on calling Inglis as a witness. But after he was sworn in, the absence of photographic copies of various documents prevented him from giving his evidence and Houston took his place in the box.

Houston, as would be expected, was a confident witness. His story was none the less damaging. He admitted that he had taken the letters from Pigott in much the same way that MacDonald had taken them from him – on trust. He had made no cross-checks. He admitted – what he later denied – that he knew Pigott by name as a former Irish newspaper proprietor.

The moment now came which the court, their interest in the mysterious Pigott now thoroughly aroused, were impatiently awaiting. On 20 February he took the stand, appearing, as one onlooker remarked, like a coarse and cheapened Father Christmas. 'The rat caught in the trap at last,' grunted Parnell.

Pigott's evidence took one more wrapping off the parcel, but still did not reveal what was inside. He had obtained the letters from Maurice Murphy, the man who was supposed to have waited downstairs while Houston paid over the money in the Hotel des Deux Mondes. Murphy had been a compositor on the *Irishman*, Pigott's paper, and was an agent of the Clan-na-gael, the American-Irish terrorist society. The rest of Pigott's evidence was concerned with his conversations with Labouchere, Parnell and Lewis, endeavouring to establish whether Pigott had tried to extort money from them, or whether, on the contrary, they had tried to bribe him.

On the evening of the second day Sir Charles Russell rose to cross-examine. He began in a disarmingly inconsequential way. He told Pigott to sit down and write – 'livelihood,' 'likelihood,' his own name, 'Proselytism', 'Patrick Egan,' 'P. Egan,' and 'hesitancy – with a small "h"'. Picking up the paper on which Pigott had written, Russell turned to other matters.

Pigott was a compulsive letter-writer, and one of the involuntary recipients of his correspondence for many years had been Dr Walsh, Roman Catholic Archbishop of Dublin. On 4 March 1887 the Archbishop had received a letter from Pigott. The date was just three days before publication of the first of the 'Parnellism and Crime' series. Russell, having induced Pigott into swearing that he did not know about the intended publication of the articles and the facsimile, proceeded to read out his letter to Dr Walsh. In it Pigott warned the Archbishop of an impending attack on the Irish nationalists, and claimed that the writer knew of a means by which it could be foiled. The inference was that the attack he referred to was the imminent publication of the articles on 'Parnellism and Crime', supported by the incriminating letters. The further inference was that Pigott could nullify the effects of the attack by revealing that the letters were forgeries. On this, Russell pressed him hard:

'Then if . . . you had not the letters in your mind, what had you?' – 'I have no idea.'
'Can you give their Lordships any clue of the most indirect kind as to what it was?' – 'I cannot.'

'Or from whom you heard it?' – 'No.'

'Have you ever mentioned this fearful matter, whatever it is, to anybody?' – 'No'.

'It is still locked up – hermetically sealed in your own bosom?' – 'No, because it has gone away out of my bosom.'

Then, for the first time, a ripple of laughter was heard in court which sound became more common as the examination of Pigott turned into some of the best entertainment to be had in London.

The following morning Russell produced copies of letters written by Parnell and Egan to Pigott, presumably in relation to their purchase from him of the *Irishman*. He was able to point out that many of the phrases used in these letters were identical with phrases in the letters sold to *The Times*. He put it to Pigott that he had copied these phrases by placing tissue paper over them. To use the same phrases on the same day of the same month in recurrent years – did the writer have a kind of anniversary of phrases? How else could he account for their recurrence? Mercilessly, Russell harried his quarry as a traitor, a liar, a forger, and a bungler.

In the course of the day the proceedings developed almost into a riot. One of the judges had hysterics. Pigott was wringing his hands. 'The breath of the hounds was on him, and he could bear the chase no longer,' wrote Morley. 'It was all very funny', wrote a more merciful observer, 'but I could not help recalling Becky Sharp's "it is easy to be virtuous on 5,000 pounds a year".' In the afternoon, Russell moved in for the kill.

'Yesterday you were good enough to write down certain words on a piece of paper, and among them was the word "hesitancy" . . . did you notice that you spelt it as it is not ordinarily spelt?' – 'Yes, I fancy I made a mistake in the spelling.'

'What was it?' – 'I think it was "a" instead of an "e" or *vice versa.*'

'You cannot say what was the mistake, but you have a general consciousness that there was something wrong?' – 'Yes.'

'I will tell you what was wrong . . . you spelt it with an "e" instead of an "a" . . . Have you noticed the fact that the writer of the body of the letter of the 9th of January, 1882 – the alleged forged letter – spells it in the same way?' – 'I heard that remark made long since, and my explanation of my misspelling is that having it in my mind I got into the habit of spelling it wrong.'

'Did your Lordships catch that answer?'

The President: 'Oh, yes.'

Having established Pigott's contention that he picked up the habit of spelling 'hesitancy' with an 'e' from Letter No. 1 itself, Russell picked up another letter and gave it to Pigott to read.

'You have already told me that that letter is yours?' – 'Yes that is right, that is my letter.'

'But you did not become possessed of this valuable letter (Letter No. 1) until the summer of 1886; and this letter is prior to that. The wrong spelling had not got into your head then?' – 'No. I say that spelling is not my strong point.'

'Did you notice that in this letter you spell "hesitancy" in the same way?' – 'No, I did not.'

As Pigott left the box that evening, Parnell observed to George Lewis: 'That man will not come into the box again.' Nor did he. The case against Parnell had collapsed. It remained only to pick up the pieces.

(iv) Cost and Consequences

There was an interval of three days before the Commission reassembled. When it did, Pigott failed to answer to his name. He had fled to Madrid, having eluded a police watch on his hotel. Characteristically, Pigott made two contradictory confessions before leaving. To Labouchere, in the presence of George Augustus Sala, he made a simple confession of forgery; to Shannon, an Irish solicitor, he made a qualified one. Some of the letters, he said, he had obtained from a man named Patrick Casey – yet another name dragged in – and these he believed to be genuine. The others he and Casey had forged together. Pigott's main concern with Shannon was to raise money for his children, of whom there were four.

The Times withdrew the letter unconditionally. But it did not withdraw the general allegations against Parnellism made in the articles. No one questioned the paper's *bona fides*. 'I have to say, and have said, many hard things of *The Times*. I am not going to say that they believed that these [letters] were forged when they put them forward,' remarked Sir Charles Russell, Parnell's leading advocate. He could afford to be magnanimous. Michael Davitt rubbed in the lesson from the nationalist point of view. Speaking of *The Times* he declared:

> These men, with the salaries of the rich in their pockets and the smiles of London Society as their rewards, have been carrying on a deliberately planned system of infamous allegation against political opponents who have been striving to redeem the sad misfortunes of their country, in efforts to bring to an end a strife of centuries' duration between neighbouring nations.

It was a grotesque description of the solemn men who managed Printing House Square, but their obtuseness had laid them open to any and every form of obloquy.

The inquiry dragged on till November. But the rest was anticlimax. The Land League were unable to produce their accounts. The Loyalists then refused to produce theirs. Sir Charles Russell threw up his papers and walked out. In February 1890, a year after Pigott's cross-examination, the Commission published its report. The Commissioners exonerated Parnell from complicity in the Phoenix Park murders and declared all the letters to be forgeries. Overnight, Parnell became a hero.

What of the other actors in the drama? As we have already seen, Pigott reached Madrid, where, in one of the equivocal coincidences which stud this story, he ran across O'Shea, already meditating the next move against his wife's lover. When the police caught up with Pigott he blew out his brains. In Printing House Square there lingered on an oral tradition that Pigott had been spotted years later in a Fleet Street public house and bolted. The coffin in Madrid, it was said, was filled with stones.

As a consequence of the exposures in a letter of 10 March 1889 Buckle offered to resign. Walter naturally turned down the offer. MacDonald, worn out with overwork and worry, died at his desk before the report was published. Soames later became the first solicitor to Captain O'Shea in the divorce proceedings in which he cited Parnell as co-respondent, but was advised to turn the case over to another lawyer. The divorce ruined Parnell as the Commission had failed to do, and he died in the following year, 1891. So passed the only Irish leader who might have achieved a peaceful settlement for Ireland without partition of the island or separation from Britain.

The Commission cost the paper over £200,000. In addition, there was Parnell's libel action in Scotland, but this was settled by compromise for £5,000. The paper had no financial reserves. Had the shareholders not insisted on grabbing Walter's nest egg of exactly that sum several years before the situation would not have been so gloomy.

The Times accounts show payments out of current account to Soames of over £50,000 in 1888. For the first time since the beginning of the century the paper went into deficit, with a loss of £13,335. Soames – 'on a/c Special Commission' – received £60,000 in the following year. *The Times* managed to show a small profit – £5,000. The year 1890 shows payments of £45,000 for Soames and the Special Commission, £600 for editorial expenses on the Commission and £250 for Houston. In 1891 the payment to the Special Commission had tapered off to £12,000. Walter met some of the costs out of his own pocket. From this time, however, dated the financial troubles from which *The Times* has never wholly shaken itself free.

To what extent was there collusion between the Government and *The Times* during the Parnell episode? When the nature of the intended tribunal was under discussion, John Walter wrote to Balfour on 12 July 1888 about 'the proposal you mentioned to me last night'. If the Government, argued Walter, for reasons of state policy, made such a proposal to Parliament, *The Times* would expect Parnell to be plaintiff and to go into the witness box. They would expect also that the whole case included in the title of 'Parnellism and Crime' would be as thoroughly investigated as before an ordinary tribunal. There is a letter from Balfour, apparently in reply, making three points. Parnell would go into the box; the inquiry would cover the whole ground of the Attorney-General's speech; the Attorney-General was distinctly of the opinion that the Tribunal was as good as or better than any existing one.

Further light is cast upon Walter's negotiations with the Government by a conversation held between John Walter and his son Arthur at Printing House Square on 4 March, 1889, three days after Pigott's suicide. The record of this conversation is endorsed by Arthur's 'manuscript of notes, made same afternoon on return home' and is worth quoting in full for the light it throws on his father's relationship with W. H. Smith, head of the great publishing firm whose fortunes had been so closely linked with those of *The Times*. Smith was, at the time we are now discussing, Leader of the House of Commons, a position of considerable power when the Prime Minister was a member of the House of Lords.

Conversation at P.H.S.   March 4, '89

J.W., A.J.B., and W.H.S.

1. A.J.B. called one evening at dinner time and announced proposal of Commission. Asked J.W. to think over it and let him know his opinion. J.W. said he would do so: not being prepared to express himself offhand on the question. After considering the matter with Soames J.W. wrote A.J.B. that he did not object provided he was not put in a worse position than before ordinary legal tribunal.

No mention of answer to this letter.

2. First interview with W.H.S. had reference to appointment of new Bp. of Oxford. Probably took place on day that retirement of Mackarness was announced.

J.W. doubts if Commission mentioned at all.

J.W. and W.H.S.

The object of second visit to W.H.S. was to enquire about character of proposed Comm. To insist that as Parnell had declined to avail himself of ordinary proceedings open to him, the govt. ought to be able to make out a strong case in justification of such special commission: and that certainly we ought not to be placed in a worse position than we should be in an action for libel.

I understand this to mean that we ought to be placed on the defensive rather than the offensive: the point being that P. shd. have no chance of avoiding the witness box.

3. The third visit was made simply with the object of eliciting information as to whether it had been decided to appoint a Commission: and if so as to its character and probable mode of proceeding.

4. The object of J.W.'s fourth visit to enquire if anything was known by the Govt. as to supposed disappearance of H. Campbell, and where he had gone to.

Manuscript of notes, made same afternoon on return home.

A.F.W. March 4,
'89.

(Mr Campbell was Parnell's secretary, who was assumed to have written the text of the facsimile letter.)

A suggestion has been made that the Government undertook in advance to reimburse *The Times* for any expenditure incurred by the paper in the conduct of the case. The main evidence for this seems to rest on the statement made many years later by a disgruntled police officer, W. H. Joyce, who was appointed by Dublin Castle to assist *The Times* in the preparation of its case before the Commission. Joyce is quoted by Mr Leon O'Broin in his book *The Prime Informer* as stating that Soames and MacDonald impressed upon him that the Government had given a secret pledge to Mr John Walter that 'the expenses would be defrayed by a Parliamentary subsidy'. Soames denied this in a written paper.

On this subject Arthur Walter's notes are of interest, but not conclusive. 'I spoke to my father', he wrote on 18 March, 're the commission and our financial prospects. I said we should be cleaned out by the end of the inquiry. He thought we should get back a large part of our expenditure.' Some days earlier Arthur had also discussed this aspect with George Lewis, who had given him cold comfort. Parnell's solicitor 'did not think the Government would pay the cost of witnesses, or in any way contribute to defraying the expenses of the case. The Commission differed from others in this respect: that our witnesses were brought by ourselves, of our own motives, and not under order from the Court.'

A year later, in February 1890, when the Commission had reported, the Editor himself wrote to Salisbury inviting assistance. He quoted £60,000 as the sum expended on witnesses. The Cabinet were scarcely sympathetic to the proposal. By that time even W. H. Smith had harsh words to say about *The Times* in Parliament. It was evident that the House would not countenance such a vote of credit, nor was it ever introduced. There seems enough evidence to suggest that someone had put it into Walter's head that he would recoup some of the outlay, but not enough to prove any actual commitment so to do.

The nationalists, of course, were able to meet some of their expenditure by contributions from sympathizers. A fund was started to raise money for *The Times*, but Walter proudly refused it. Another aspect which did not escape criticism was that, as a result of the procedure of the Commission, most of these vast sums of money went into the pockets of the lawyers and none into those of the aggrieved persons.

In one respect the Government did help *The Times* extensively. They allowed Soames access to the criminal files at Dublin Castle, both before the O'Donnell case and for the Special Commission, and indeed opened up the prisons to his inquiries. W. H. Joyce has left a long memorandum on this subject, now in the National Library in Dublin. According to this memorandum, written in 1910, Joyce was detailed as a liaison officer to aid *The Times* in preparing its case. His evidence is difficult to corroborate, owing to destruction of records. No letters from Soames to Joyce survive in Printing House Square, though there is a short note dated 3 November 1885, also in the National Library. On 13 June 1892, a Mr Davies removed the bulk of the files from Dublin Castle, and only the indexes remain to show what he took away. An interesting point is that the date on which the files were removed coincides with that on which the Government announced the dissolution of Parliament, and Davies was, moreover, the name of the private secretary to the Under-Secretary, Sir Joseph West Ridgeway. It is tempting to conclude that Balfour ordered the removal to prevent the opposition examining the files when they came into office. However, there is no question that the Government did everything within its power to aid *The Times*. It was unfortunate from the point of view of the paper that its servants made such bad use of the facilities afforded.

Soames was indefatigable in acquiring a mass of irrelevant information while overlooking the main point. Ridgeway recorded with disgust that he was actually handed the papers on Pigott but 'seemed to pay little or no attention to them'. Perhaps he was hardly to be blamed. MacDonald, characteristically, had never told the solicitor of Pigott's involvement in the sale of the letters.

In estimating the degree of collusion between the Government and *The Times* it is essential to bear three points in mind. The first is that Walter and his associates were strong Unionists and needed no encouragement from government or anyone else in exploiting what to them seemed a heaven-sent opportunity of discrediting Parnell. The second is that to Buckle, as a new Editor, the opportunity of bringing off a noteworthy journalistic coup must have presented itself as irresistible. To plan publication to coincide with the division on the Crimes Bill is evidence not of political collusion but of good journalistic timing. A third, and more general point, is that *The Times* in 1886 was probably less in touch with government than was usual in its history. Buckle had not yet been in the Chair long enough to establish links, nor was he ever an Editor of sufficient calibre to carry great influence in the corridors of power. Walter, it is true, had his friendship with W. H. Smith. But the relationship was of a somewhat formal kind even by Victorian standards. Although Smith knew of the existence of the letters before publication, his correspondence was with MacDonald not Walter, no doubt because of Walter's illness. It was all very different from the days when Delane would get out his horse and hack round to see 'Pam', or even, later, to Dawson's telephonic *coups de foudre* to Halifax. The Government no doubt saw an apparently golden opportunity of putting the paper to its own uses, and sadly miscalculated.

Some of the Ministers would have liked to help Walter out of his difficulties, but only if this could be done without inconvenience to themselves. Indeed on 21 May 1888 W. H. Smith wrote to Lord Salisbury recommending him for a peerage: 'The public would not now connect it [the peerage] in any marked manner with Parnellism and Crime, but if you wait until the [O'Donnell] trial comes off, it will take the appearance of being either a reward or a consolation.' Nothing more was heard of this project, which may have been mooted also in 1865 and in 1878. Nor can it be assumed that Walter would have wanted a peerage, especially in view of his coldness to his eldest surviving son.

Within Printing House Square the attempt to fix responsibility for the debacle has led to some controversy. The official *History*, written under the influence of Buckle and Houston, states that 'the chief conduct of the negotiations with Houston had been taken into Walter's hands'. This is contradicted by an undated memorandum by Walter himself, written some time after the event, in response to attacks made on the 'conductors of *The Times*' by Sir William Harcourt, the Liberal leader. In his statement, Walter relates that he was first shown the letters by MacDonald in November 1886:

> In the course of this business, I had no communication, direct or indirect, with reference to the letters with anyone but Mr MacDonald and Mr Soames. I was unable, even had I been so disposed, to take any active part in the matter, beyond doing my best to verify the signature, and to satisfy my mind as to the internal evidence, in consequence of ill health, by which I was

partly confined to my room, and partly compelled to go abroad
for four months out of the five which elapsed between my first
sight of the facsimile letter and its publication.

There can be no doubt that the Manager, MacDonald, was the man
who preserved all the strands in his own hands. He is a shadowy figure.
A letter written to Walter, who was apparently at the time in Egypt,
and dated 10 April 1888, reveals something of his views and activities.
He was, it is clear, in regular correspondence with Walter, and in the
habit of passing on to Buckle instructions as to the line the paper
should take on such subjects as the Local Government Bill and
diplomatic relations with the Pope. 'I dislike the Romish Church as
much as mortal man can,' he interpolates. He discusses the purchase
of a further letter from Pigott, which, if genuine, 'will be a cheap £1000
worth or even more'. And he reports that Soames has had on the whole
a satisfactory visit to Dublin and 'returns assured of all the support
that Mr Warrill, the Head of the Constabulary there, can give him'.

From this letter it is apparent that Buckle was a subordinate figure
in the Chair. Nevertheless, Buckle's own memoranda to MacDonald
make it clear that the Editor was an enthusiastic supporter of publication of the letters. This view is borne out by Houston – albeit an
admittedly unreliable witness – in an undated memorandum written
probably in the late 1920s. According to Houston it was Buckle who
made the decision to carry on with publication of the letters after he
had received the vital warning from Sir Henry James.

After the unmasking of Pigott it was the miserable Soames who was
in danger of becoming the scapegoat. Described by an eminent
colleague as 'a dull but very respectable solicitor,' Arthur Walter tells
us that it was the general opinion of the legal profession that he ought
to have been struck off the Rolls. But Soames, like Flanagan, might
have saved his superiors if they had trusted him more. It was the lack
of communication within the office that ruined them.

In the background lurks the figure of Houston, a congenital liar, a
romanticist, and always very keen on money. In contrast to the
scriveners' copperplate of the other protagonists, Houston's hand
embellished the expensive Cork Street notepaper on which he wrote,
with the frills, flourishes and furbelows of the exhibitionist. Self-
important and conspiratorial, he obviously revelled in his clandestine
relationship with the great in Printing House Square. Pigott went to his
death declaring that he had deceived Houston. But Ed. Caulfield
Houston, as he was wont to sign himself, required no deceiving by
others; he was eminently capable of deceiving himself. It does not
appear that he made much money out of *The Times*. The records show
that they were niggardly in dealing him out cash. (The rumour that

he was paid £30,000 is due to a misprint for £3,000.) But he remained as an incubus, and even in the 1930s was influencing Buckle when he was working on the history of *The Times*.

John Walter and Buckle continued to believe that at least the facsimile letter was genuine. The fact that Inglis, the handwriting expert, did not give evidence and the refusal of the Attorney-General to allow Sir Robert Anderson into the witness box, prevented them making the best of their case. But it does not appear that either would have produced any fresh evidence on the authenticity of the letters. Inglis's report is a masterpiece of technical gobbledygook, concerned with the shape and slant of the letters, but failing to take account of the possibility that the letters might have been traced through a window glass by a clever forger. Anderson's evidence would no doubt have strengthened the case against the Irish Nationalists: but it would scarcely have strengthened the case for *The Times*. On the authorship of the letters he had hypotheses but no proof.

Although *The Times* suffered heavily in the financial sense, it suffered less, perhaps, in authority than has sometimes been made out. The sudden shattering of confidence in its accuracy and reliability was only temporary. In the political sense, the Commission was important in the history of *The Times*. It marked its final progression from radical beginnings into the camp of the Conservatives; the heart of the paper no longer beat left of centre. This was the doing of John Walter III, and the tradition was to be carried further by George Buckle.

The history of *The Times* is like a tapestry continually unfolding. The characters displayed upon it are woven in contrasting colours, some strong and flamboyant, like Barnes, William Howard Russell and Blowitz; others muted and faded, like MacDonald and the John Walters. But they all form part of the same evolving pattern.

In the 1890s appeared a new figure, that of Flora Shaw, the first professional woman staff correspondent, and the first Colonial Editor of *The Times*. She emerges sharply outlined, standing stiffly in the black silk dress which she habitually wore, and which became as much her uniform as were Russell's commissariat cap and butcher boots in the Crimea. Her silhouette was to loom large in the background of events during the decade when South Africa replaced Ireland as the centre of controversy.

Flora was one of those journalists who go a long way beyond their professional brief of reporting and commenting. She was by instinct a crusader and an intriguer, who liked now and then to leave her desk in order to put a spoke in the wheel of history. By her powerful mind and compelling personality she directly influenced policies and statesmen, and did much to restore the somewhat battered image of *The Times* bequeathed by the episode of the Pigott forgeries. Even she eventually got *The Times* hauled before a commission, but, when she did, she managed things much better than poor MacDonald.

Her first excursion into journalism occurred in 1886. She was in Gibraltar. Scrambling up the cliff one day, she came upon a little dwelling set in the rocks, where Zebehr Pasha was detained in exile. This chance encounter was to have important consequences for her. Zebehr, it will be recalled, was the Arab soldier and slave-trader whom Gordon had wanted to succeed him as Governor-General of the Sudan. Flora, seeing the journalistic possibilities, asked for, and obtained, an interview which was published by Stead in the *Pall Mall Gazette*. Zebehr was released and returned to Egypt, firmly convinced that he owed his freedom to Flora Shaw's article.

In Flora the incident aroused a passionate desire to learn more about Africa. Two years later she went to Cairo, this time with the status of an accredited press representative, with a commission from C. P. Scott to write articles for the *Manchester Guardian*, which had a particular interest in the Egyptian cotton market. On arrival, the first person to greet her was Zebehr, now restored to the grandeur of a Cairene pasha. He invited her to his palace, and took her through the harem where the women struck her as 'plain'. She found Zebehr melancholy, and the visit depressing: 'He keeps the appearance of a soldier, the long and spare black hands with which he wraps his coat about him seem made for the rein and the sword.'

More important for her, however, was her meeting with the egregious Moberly Bell, *The Times* correspondent who had 'discovered' Frank Power. An imperialist of the new kind, his thinking was in harmony with that of men like Joseph Chamberlain. In Flora Shaw he recognized a kindred spirit. She visited him at his home in Alexandria to collect material for her articles on the cotton market, and they would sit up far into the night discussing and arguing about history and politics. Flora's was the superior intellect, but Bell had experience and fire. These meetings were to have their *lendemain*.

By 1890 things were happening in Printing House Square which were profoundly to alter the lives of both Moberly Bell and Flora Shaw. After the death of MacDonald, John Walter III, who was now seventy-one and wished to retire from active participation in executive work, appointed his eldest surviving son, Arthur Fraser Walter, as Manager. Arthur Walter, himself now forty-nine years old, was a reserved, unimaginative man with a good scholastic record at Eton and Oxford, interested mainly in country pursuits. His father had never brought himself to regard Arthur as filling the void left by the death of his eldest son, John. Arthur therefore lacked a thorough training in the business although he had held the nominal post of Joint Manager.

The Walters had formed a high opinion of Moberly Bell, whom they had met whilst visiting Egypt in the same year as Flora Shaw. When Arthur, who had mistrusted MacDonald, became Manager, he summoned Bell home to be Assistant Manager, and in effect to manage the paper on his behalf. The printing works were to be managed by his half-brother, Godfrey Walter. Bell now became responsible, under *The Times* constitution, for running the foreign department. Having been a foreign correspondent for twenty-five years he had long ago come to the conclusion that the days when a Manager could exercise direct control over foreign correspondents were past. He therefore set up a new foreign department, under a director of its own, answerable to him as Manager for administration but to the Editor for the foreign policy of the paper. Arthur Walter agreed to this scheme. Buckle was persuaded.

The man chosen to head the new department was Donald Mackenzie Wallace, who had been Blowitz's assistant at the Berlin Congress and had made the famous journey to Brussels with the Berlin Treaty stitched into the lining of his coat. Since those days he had served *The Times* in St Petersburg and Constantinople. He was a diplomat and scholar as much as a journalist and currently was acting as political adviser to the Viceroy of India. He was a good administrator, had an exceptional grasp of foreign affairs, and brought distinction to the new department.

Bell, who foresaw that colonial affairs would dominate the minds of the British public during the coming decade, determined to follow the institution of a foreign department by setting up, in addition, a colonial department, and there is no doubt whom he had in mind for the job. But he had to go carefully. He began by securing Wallace's agreement in principle to the appointment of a 'colonial expert'. For the next step there was the awkward matter of Flora Shaw's gender to be overcome. Mrs Norton, it is true, had reviewed for *The Times* under Delane. But the thought of appointing a woman to the permanent staff was likely to alarm the ultra-conservative Arthur Walter, and probably many others.

Moberly Bell and Flora Shaw now co-operated – not for the last time – in a comedy of deceptions. Bell wrote to the Colonial Office asking them to recommend a young man to write articles for *The Times* on colonial topics. The Colonial Office wrote back that they had no such man in mind, but recommended a woman – 'you could not possibly do better than engage her'. Moberly Bell burst in on Flora waving this letter in the air, and declaring 'If you were a man you would be Colonial Editor of *The Times* tomorrow.'

They began by a policy of infiltration. Flora wrote a trial article on Egyptian finance, which Arthur Walter read with approval. He remarked to Bell that 'whoever wrote it is the sort of fellow we ought to get on *The Times*'. It was some time before anyone dared reveal the sex of *The Times* colonial expert to Arthur. Step by step Bell built up Flora Shaw's position on *The Times* until she became *de facto* Colonial Editor, not only writing articles and leaders, but organizing a system of 'stringers' and occasional correspondents throughout the Empire. Meanwhile Flora gave up her work for other papers, unregretted by Stead who considered her too cold a writer for the *Pall Mall Gazette*: 'Flora did not want to bring a lump to your throat,' he said. But Bell approved the austerity of her style – 'You don't seem even to have mentioned anything about the dominion on which the sun never sets.'

Flora Shaw soon established the routine of a weekly visit to the Colonial Office – a habit which was to get her and others into trouble before long. She developed her friendship with Cecil Rhodes, whom she had already met when he came to London in 1889. Rhodes outlined to her his schemes for forming the Chartered Company and went into the financial details with her. Why, she asked him, did he spend so

much time on a project which would bring such small and slow returns?
Rhodes, who had long since passed the phase when merely increasing
money afforded him any satisfaction, replied: 'Some men collect butterflies. I do this. It interests me.' Among the butterflies which he was
contemplating adding to his collection at that time were Rhodesia,
Bechuanaland, and the Transvaal.

In 1892 Bell decided that it was time to give Flora first-hand
acquaintance with some of the lands about which she was writing –
Africa, Australia and Canada. She was to start with South Africa, the
country which was the most likely to occupy public interest, leaving
England in April 1892, and travelling via the Cape to Johannesburg.
There she stayed with Lionel Phillips, local representative of the gold-
mining firm of Wernher-Beit and President of the Chamber of Mines.
Two years later Phillips, the driving force behind most activities on
the Rand, was the first of the mining tycoons – the 'Randlords' as they
were called – to give money to the Transvaal National Union, a body
formed to secure representation for the Uitlanders, the gold-miners who
had poured into the Transvaal and who had been denied political
representation by the Boer Government.

Flora, writing to Bell just before the establishment of the National
Union, found that Johannesburg 'at present has no politics. It is
hideous and detestable, luxury without order, sensual enjoyment without art, riches without refinement, display without dignity. Everything,
in fact, which is most foreign to the principles alike of morality and
taste by which decent life has been guarded in every stage of civilization.' She much preferred the sleepy old capital of Pretoria where she
met President Kruger. She was received first by his wife on the stoep of
a 'pretty little house surrounded by flowers'. The President, who shortly
afterwards returned from the Volksraad (Parliament), sat down as he
was and stared at her. 'Rough to ruggedness, with keen eyes and
shrewd, pleasant features,' he kept his tall steeple hat on, and 'smoked
all the time, knocking out his pipe ashes and spitting about the floor
as seemed most convenient to himself; but he showed himself shrewd,
keen and enlightened in conversation as well as doggedly determined –
his yes and no were always emphatic'.

After she had returned to Cape Town Flora Shaw annoyed the local
press by scooping them over the provisions of the Franchise Bill. Their
attack fell rather flat 'as,' she remarks loftily, 'the Government had
not given me the information and I had got it for myself where any
Cape journalist who chose to try could have obtained it too'. Perhaps
she did not quite make allowances for the tendency of colonial politicians to favour a handsome woman correspondent representing
England's 'leading journal'.

Moberly Bell's protecting arm was never far from her. While at the

Cape she received a letter in which he asked her to appoint 'some ordinarily trustworthy but not brilliant man' who could send her news when she returned to London, and to do the same in all the centres she visited. 'When you come back with all the glory and experience of the Colonies in your mind, you will practically become a sort of Colonial D.M.W. [Donald Mackenzie Wallace].'

Before leaving South Africa she visited Natal, most British of British colonies. Here, in one of her dispatches to *The Times*, she gives an account of the predicaments of a woman correspondent in South Africa at that time:

> I was fast asleep . . . when a whistle and the sudden slackening of the train informed me that we must be near Durban. I jumped out, pulled on my shoes and began hastily to comb my hair when, just at the critical moment when the hair was neither up nor down, but was all gathered in my left hand, while my right worked away with the comb, the door was suddenly opened by a gentleman whom I afterwards found to be the General Manager of Railways, and I was informed 'The Mayor has come to meet you and put his carriage at your disposal.' There stood the Mayor, there stood the General Manager with a circle of railway officials gathered respectfully around – and there, alas, stood I. The shock had brought my hair unconditionally down, but I still held the comb with a convulsive grasp and had not the presence of mind to drop it. The Mayor blushed, the General Manager laughed a hearty laugh and banged the door shut again, with a promise to meet me at the next station which was three minutes along the line.

By this time she was dressed in her 'ordinary black silk garb and was ready to accept with becoming dignity the offer of his very comfortable victoria'.

When she returned to London, Flora Shaw set up her colonial department on the monastic site once dedicated to the Black Friars. 'In the hurry of editorial work,' wrote Bell, 'considerations of sex must disappear.' But in the privacy of the Bells' own home a disapproving leader writer snubbed her in the presence of Mrs Bell. 'Ladies should not talk politics, or,' he added, 'meddle with them.'

The knowledge that a reform movement such as the Transvaal National Union existed in Johannesburg compelled both the Imperial Government in London and Cecil Rhodes in Cape Town to consider what action they should take if the reformers were to revolt and, possibly, find themselves in danger of being suppressed by the Transvaal Government. Since the Uitlanders were predominantly of British origin the

British Government could not decently wash their hands of the matter. Nor did they acknowledge the Transvaal as a wholly sovereign state. Moreover, if they did not intervene there was the fear that Germany would. As a matter of fact, the interest displayed by Germany in the Transvaal from 1894 on was a political bluff – but neither the British Government nor Kruger knew this at the time. They took it at its face value.

Cecil Rhodes had economic, as well as ideological, reasons for supporting the Uitlanders. His dream was to establish a federal union in South Africa dominated by the British, and only Kruger stood in his way. The difference was that, while the Liberal Government at home dreaded having their hands forced, Rhodes would have welcomed it. Flora in London kept in touch with Rhodes and continued to explain the Uitlanders' grievances to *The Times* readers.

In 1894, two years after her visit, the pot began to boil. That summer Kruger conscripted British subjects for a native war. Seven men, persuaded with great difficulty by the Transvaal Union, refused to serve. The British High Commissioner in Cape Town, Sir Henry Lock, travelled up to see the President. There were rowdy scenes in Pretoria. Kruger climbed down, but the High Commissioner was advised not to invite more trouble by visiting Johannesburg, and he took the advice.

The sequel was ominous. The Rand magnates, led by Lionel Phillips, began secretly to finance the Union. The High Commissioner, also secretly, asked Britain for troops, in case of trouble. Later that year, in October, Rhodes saw Kruger in Pretoria. Shortly afterwards he dined at the Rand Club in Johannesburg where all the mining 'Establishment' were present. He took aside another key member of the Union, Frederic Hamilton, Editor of the *Johannesburg Star*, and confided to him that he had come to the conclusion that no deal with Kruger was possible.

This visit of Cecil Rhodes to Pretoria and Johannesburg was the turning-point. From then on, by hook or by crook, Rhodes intended to secure control of the Transvaal, and laid his plans accordingly. He began to busy himself with what came to be known as the Jameson Plan. The essence of this plan was – first, that a rising, either spontaneous or engineered, should take place in Johannesburg; second, that a force based on Rhodes's private army in Rhodesia, the Matabeleland Mounted Police, should enter the Transvaal from Bechuanaland to assist the revolutionaries; and third, that Rhodes should obtain from the British Government, under pretext of building a railway into Rhodesia, the whole or part of Bechuanaland as a jumping-off point for this force. The raiding force was to be commanded by Dr Starr Jameson, Rhodes's closest friend, a Kimberley doctor then serving as administrator of the Chartered Company in Rhodesia. Dr Jameson was known as a man of strong character, dash and popularity, and also as a gambler.

In furtherance of these aims, Rhodes at the end of 1894 went to London to negotiate with the British Government (still a Liberal one) the cession of Bechuanaland. He took with him Dr Rutherfoord Harris, Secretary of the Chartered Company, who was, like Jameson, a politically minded doctor from Kimberley. An indefatigable go-between and busybody, Flora Shaw later described him to J. L. Garvin as 'the mischief maker of the whole affair'.

While Rhodes was in London the Moberly Bells gave a dinner party for him, to which they invited Mackenzie Wallace and Flora Shaw, but not the Editor. The omission is significant. Buckle was to be kept in the dark over most of their subsequent transactions.

That Rhodes continued to impress Flora Shaw may be adduced from a letter she wrote at the time to a Captain Lugard, whose work in Africa she much admired. (Five years later, by which time both had become better known to the British public, they were to marry.)

> I cannot help thinking [she wrote to the future Governor of Nigeria], that if you were brought into personal touch with Mr Rhodes and could realize, as I do, the absolutely unsordid and unselfish nature of the devotion which he gives to the imperial cause, you would acknowledge the ennobling influence of a great conception, and much of your prejudice would disappear.

Early in 1895, Rhodes went back to Cape Town, having extracted satisfactory promises from the Colonial Office over Bechuanaland. In June British politics took a turn which delighted the imperialists. The Liberals were out, the Conservatives were in, and Joseph Chamberlain, at his own request, became Colonial Secretary. Not only was this the first time that a front-rank political leader had graced this office; the new Minister was known to be a dedicated imperialist. 'The change at the Colonial Office was marvellous,' Flora Shaw told Garvin. 'It was a total transformation; the sleeping city awakened by a touch.' For Rhodes the change was a mixed blessing. Chamberlain was likely to sympathize with expansionary designs, but it meant also that there were now two prophets in Israel, and the new prophet was likely to have ideas of his own.

In Johannesburg, too, there were interesting events that June. The year had been marked by an unprecedented gold boom which had distracted minds from politics. But now the leaders of the 'Reform Movement' met in conclave. Lionel Phillips invited Frederic Hamilton to a dinner *à trois* with Jameson, at which the doctor outlined his plans. Johannesburg was to arm, and rise in December. Wernher-Beit, Phillips's firm, was to finance the Johannesburg end. Rhodes and the Chartered

Company would pay for Jameson's force. Asked his opinion of the plan, Hamilton found much to criticize. The people had lost interest in politics because of the boom; they had no leader. Phillips replied that by winter the boom would be over, and the miners would have plenty of time to brood. The leadership question was being looked after also. Frank Rhodes, Cecil's brother who was a regular soldier, was coming up, ostensibly as local manager of Consolidated Goldfields, to organize the military side. To clinch the matter Hamilton was assured that the Colonial Office would further the scheme by all possible means. Hamilton went away impressed, but still uneasy about the lack of organization. The assurance of Colonial Office support naturally weighed heavily with him. As for Frank Rhodes, he was at least a professional soldier and a man of great charm. But he was not, like his brother, a man of dedicated endeavour.

Jameson's visits to Johannesburg were, of necessity, rare and hurried. Their principal object, one might have thought, would have been to meet the military leader of the Johannesburg rebels. But on his second visit, in November, the only communication which he received from the colonel was a pencilled note left on the hall table: 'Dear Jimjams, sorry I can't see you this afternoon, I have an appointment to teach Mrs. . . . . . the bike. Yours ever, Frank.' Back in Printing House Square, nobody grasped just how half-baked this conspiracy was. Had they done so, Moberly Bell and Flora Shaw might have been less enthusiastic in their support.

13 THE JAMESON FIASCO

(i) Lines from Africa

One of the most warmly disputed questions in African history is the degree of complicity of Joseph Chamberlain in the plans of Cecil Rhodes, the Johannesburg reformers, and the Jameson raiders. Inseparable from that inquiry is the examination of the charge that Flora Shaw was the intermediary between the Colonial Secretary and the conspirators, for it is this second allegation which immediately concerns *The Times*.

The ubiquitous Dr Rutherfoord Harris, described by J. L. Garvin as the Figaro in the case, arrived again in London in the summer of 1895; this time alone. His purposes were threefold. The first was to persuade Chamberlain to honour the promises given to Rhodes by the previous government to hand over Bechuanaland Protectorate, in part or in whole, to the Chartered Company's administration. Chamberlain ceded the required strip of territory on the Transvaal border to the company on 6 November. Harris's second purpose, which he concealed from Chamberlain and Flora Shaw, was to purchase arms for the reformers. This mission, as we know from other sources, he bungled. The third was to supply Flora Shaw with a copy of the company's code, together with a telegraphic address – 'TELEMONES'. Her use of these facilities quite naturally rendered *The Times* suspect of collusion.

During the negotiations over Bechuanaland Harris, in pressing Rhodes's case, claimed to have made a 'guarded' allusion to the 'Jameson plan' – that is, to support for the rebels with armed help from outside the Transvaal. Later Chamberlain was adamant that when Harris announced 'I could tell you something' he had halted him immediately, saying: 'I am here in an official capacity. I can only hear information of which I can make official use.' Whether Harris succeeded in saying what he intended and, if so, whether or not Chamberlain heard, has since been a subject of much controversy. But the inference is clear. Whether words were conveyed or not the Colonial Secretary anticipated the gist of what Harris was trying to tell him.

Meanwhile the situation was muddied by a side issue. In August Kruger, who was waging a commercial war over railway freight charges with the Cape, closed the 'Drifts' – river crossings – which carried road traffic between the Transvaal and the territories to the south. The action was a breach of the convention regulating the status of the Transvaal, and the British Government was prepared to go to war if Kruger refused to reopen the crossings. Troops were diverted to the Cape. Chamberlain made it clear that Rhodes, as Prime Minister of Cape Colony, would be expected to provide money and 'a fair contingent of the fighting force'. Kruger climbed down in August, but in reading conversations and communications made at the time it becomes difficult for the historian to discern whether possible action over the Drifts or over the Jameson plan is referred to. Certainly the conspirators made the best of any ambiguity in retrospect.

Rhodes had at least three lines to Chamberlain and the Colonial Office. One was through the Chartered Company's own London office, where the principal executive was Dr Rochfort Maguire. After Harris's return to Cape Town on 30 November 1895, Maguire continued to see Fairfield, the head of the African division in the Colonial Office, and to communicate the substance of their exchanges by cable. Secondly, as Prime Minister of the Cape, Rhodes communicated through the British High Commission in Cape Town. A third, and more clandestine, channel was Flora Shaw. She continued to make her weekly calls at the Colonial Office, talking either to Chamberlain or to Fairfield, and after Harris's departure she made good use of the Chartered Company's code book, aided by Moberly Bell.

Flora and Bell were acting of course in the interests of the paper; they wanted to be sure of getting the news. But they were also ideologically committed to the expansion of the British Empire. From time to time they crossed the line between the strict duties of a journalist and the temptation to take a direct hand in events. Just how much did they know about Rhodes's plans? Did Flora Shaw act as a secret go-between for Rhodes and Chamberlain?

Flora Shaw certainly knew of a plan to support a revolt in Johannesburg either with imperial troops or with Rhodes's company police, which were now stationed at Pitsani on the Bechuanaland border. In Printing House Square Arthur Walter and Moberly Bell were enthusiastic about it; Buckle and Mackenzie Wallace less so. Dr Rutherfoord Harris had spoken to Flora on the subject in the autumn. He told her that 'we must be ready to go in to the help of the Uitlanders if need be. It's all right – Chamberlain knows all about it.' She told him she would speak to Chamberlain, but Harris said in alarm 'Oh, you mustn't do that: it's absolutely confidential.' This does not mean that Flora knew in November that Rhodes was deliberately fomenting trouble in Johannesburg or that Harris was buying arms. She later stated that she knew arms were being bought by the Uitlanders, but not that Harris was the agent.

On 4 November Harris cabled Rhodes: 'I have already sent Flora to convince Chamberlain support *Times* newspaper and if you can telegraph course you wish *Times* to adopt now with regard to Transvaal Flora will act.' The next day he cabled: '... We reported your letter to A. Beit during the month of August to these and Flora we have these solid.' On 26 November he cabled: '... Flora suggests December 16th celebrate Pretoria district 1880.' And on 29 November, on leaving for South Africa: 'We have given code to Flora . . . Keep her well informed.'

In interpreting these cables, it is legitimate to suppose firstly that Dr Harris was trying to represent himself to his boss as being more influential than he really was and, secondly, to accept that the Chartered Company's code contained code-names for phrases as well as for words and was therefore capable of ambiguities. Later Harris, under examination, claimed that the first two cables referred respectively to the Drifts crisis and the transfer of Bechuanaland, not to the Jameson plan. He was probably lying. The Drifts crisis ended on 7 November, three days after the first cable was sent.

The third cable contained an historical allusion – 16 December was Dingaan's Day, the Boers' national day when they celebrated their victory over a native chief of that name. In 1880 they had chosen that day to declare their independence from Britain, thus starting the First Boer War. Flora Shaw subsequently admitted that she suggested that Dingaan's Day would be a good day for the Uitlanders to revolt against the Boers, her explanation being that it was a joke. If so, it was rather a sick joke.

(ii) The Centre of Secrets

Meanwhile in Johannesburg the market had slumped. Rumours of impending revolution were rife, and Jameson paid a flying visit from Pitsani on 20 November. On this occasion Charles Leonard, a lawyer who was President of the Transvaal National Union, gave Jameson a letter which was later to cause Flora Shaw, and not only her, the deepest embarrassment. Known as the 'women and children' letter, it was an appeal from the Union to Jameson for help. The date was left blank, for Jameson to fill in when the time came.

Thousands of unarmed men, women and children of our race [it ran], will be at the mercy of well-armed Boers, while property of enormous value will be in the greatest peril. We cannot contemplate the future without the gravest apprehensions. All feel that we are justified in taking any steps to prevent the shedding of blood, and to insure the protection of our rights. It is under these circumstances that we feel constrained to call upon you to come to our aid.

Without such an invitation, Jameson had complained, he would be no better than a pirate if he crossed the Transvaal frontier with his column.

Frederic Hamilton, lunching with Frank Rhodes and Jameson, expressed the view that the doctor would meet with much stronger resistance than he expected. Jameson replied hubristically that he would get through 'as easily as a knife into butter,' that they did not know what the Maxim meant. He would draw a zone of lead a mile each side of his column, and no Boer would be able to live in it. Told about the undated letter, Hamilton replied, 'Charlie, you must be mad.' Leonard and the other signatories, however, honestly believed that Jameson would not use the letter without a genuine invitation from them. The twenty-ninth of December was fixed provisionally as the date of the rising.

In November Moberly Bell decided it was time to station a special correspondent in Johannesburg. The man he chose was Captain (later Sir) Francis Younghusband. Younghusband had just made a name for himself as *The Times* correspondent with the Chitral expedition. On despatching him to Africa on 21 November Bell supplied him with a code. His professional instincts remained uppermost – having heard that the revolt was likely to start on a Saturday, Bell instructed Young-husband to impress on Rhodes that the 'New Company' should not 'commence business' on a Saturday 'because of Sunday papers.'

When he arrived in Johannesburg Younghusband put up at Frank Rhodes's house, where he was certainly following Mr Tonans's precept of 'sticking to the centre of the secrets'. He immediately, and rightly, reported home to *The Times* that Johannesburg was singularly lacking in revolutionary ardour. The situation did not, in his opinion, warrant the expense of cable costs. His amiable host, no doubt, was still teaching ladies to ride bicycles. Both he and his house guest were regular army cavalry officers and, as such, they would be likely to talk freely to each other.

Younghusband's report must have disappointed Flora Shaw. She continued to write articles enumerating the Uitlanders' grievances and giving warning that the days of Boer despotism were numbered. But she must have felt some misgivings about the seriousness of the con-spirators' intentions. She began sending Rhodes what came to be known as the 'hurry up' telegrams. 'Can you advise,' she cabled on 10 December, 'when will you commence the plans, we wish to send at earliest opportunity sealed instructions representatives of the London *Times* European capitals.' Bell felt depressed when Flora received the reply 'We do think about new year.'

Two days later Flora Shaw sent a hastener: 'Delay dangerous sympathy now complete but will depend very much upon action before

European powers given time enter a protest which as European situation considered serious might paralyse government.' Then, on 17 December: 'Chamberlain sound in case of interference European powers but have special reason to believe wishes you must do it immediately.'

This cable was prompted by a worsening in the international situation which had nothing to do with South Africa. On December 17 the President of the United States threatened Britain with war over the British Guiana–Venezuela frontier dispute, and Britain's rivals in Europe were poised to make the most of it. The wording of the cable was later adduced as damning evidence of collusion between Flora and Chamberlain. In reply she maintained that it was based on deductions from a talk with Mr Fairfield at the Colonial Office. On hearing of the American threats Chamberlain, who was in Birmingham at the time, had reached the conclusion that unless the Uitlanders were to revolt by the end of the year, it would be preferable that they should postpone any action indefinitely. The deduction of his attitude by Flora on the information available to her was certainly remarkable, but probably not beyond the powers of any capable journalist keeping herself well abreast of a developing political crisis. What she could not know was that Maguire too had seen Fairfield and sent a similar cable three days later – the text of which is only known by hearsay. So quick off the mark was Flora Shaw in this case that intuitive deduction seems the only logical explanation. What is undeniable is that *The Times* correspondent was egging Rhodes on. Almost plaintively he replied 'Thanks. Are doing our best but these things take time. Do not alarm Pretoria from London.'

Plaintive he well might be. He knew that Johannesburg was going sour on him. On 13 December he had cabled his brother Frank: 'Dr Jameson wishes most strongly to urge no postponement of shareholders' meeting, and let J. M. Hammond [another member of the Johannesburg Reform Committee] inform weak partners any delay most injurious. The London *Times* also cables confidentially to that effect. Postponement of meeting would be a most unwise course.' On 23 December, having read Maguire's cable, he telegraphed to Jameson: 'Company will be floated next Saturday [December 28].' Yet by that date Rhodes had received clear warning from *The Times* Johannesburg correspondent, Younghusband, that the reformers were in no mood to rise. Younghusband had by now been admitted to the inner council of the reformers, about whose effectiveness he remained a complete sceptic. The degree of fighting spirit in Johannesburg may be deduced from the fact that miners and their families were beginning to stream out of Johannesburg in order to avoid trouble. Any secrecy moreover about the coup had long since been dissipated.

(iii) *Muddling towards Disaster*

But more than mere apathy was involved. Characteristic of the bung-
ling in this conspiracy was the failure of the conspirators to define their
aim before they took action. In Johannesburg the reformers were quite
clear that the object of the revolt was not to place themselves under
Britain but to reform the Transvaal Government from inside with
British help. They would continue to live under the flag of the South
African Republic, the *Vierkleur*. They were in fact the forerunners of
the UDI movement. Not for one moment did they contemplate exchanging Kruger for Whitehall as a master. Of the sixty-four members of
the Reform Committee, nearly half were foreign or South African-
born. They had to live with the Boers, in the same way that their
compatriots did in the Cape, and many of the Boers shared their
feelings. Kruger, who was an extremist, survived in power by the
narrowest of majorities, the opposition leader, Joubert, favouring co-
operation with the Uitlanders.

But back in London Chamberlain and *The Times* assumed that the
revolt would take place under 'the Flag'. Early in November, while
still in England, Harris had been questioned about this by supporters
of Rhodes and had cabled 'We have stated positively that results Dr
Jameson's plan include British flag. Is this correct?' Reassuringly
Rhodes had replied: 'I of course would not risk everything as I am
doing excepting for British Flag.'

On 22 December Younghusband arrived in Cape Town as the
emissary of the Reformers to clear up this matter. He seems a strange
choice, though after all Frank Power had brought out Gordon's last
messages from Khartoum. Younghusband's message to Rhodes was
quite simple – the reformers would not revolt under the British Flag.
He gave a gloomy picture of revolutionary preparedness. 'Is there no
one in Johannesburg who will risk being shot and will lead the mal-
contents?' Rhodes asked. Younghusband replied that there was not.
Rhodes then invited him to do it himself. 'Do you mind being shot?'
Younghusband replied that he had no interest in the proposed revolution and would not dream of leading it. By this time Rhodes was driven
almost to distraction. 'All right, if they won't go into it they won't,
and I shall wire Jameson to keep out.'

But he did nothing of the kind. He sent Harris posting after Younghusband to tell him that 'when any rising takes place it must be under
the British Flag'. Next day, 23 December, as we have seen, he telegraphed Jameson: 'Company will be floated next Saturday.' There
were now five days to go. All parties were muddling towards disaster.

On Christmas Day the reformers heard Younghusband's report.
Finally, relates Frederic Hamilton, who was present at the meeting, a

letter was produced from Flora Shaw, 'purporting to relate an interview with the Colonial Secretary, at which he had said that he would not stir a finger to substitute one Dutch Board [government] for another'.

The reformers now sent two more emissaries, Frederic Hamilton and Charles Leonard, to tell Rhodes quite plainly that without the assurance about the *Vierkleur* the reformers would not move. These two arrived in Cape Town early on the morning of the fatal Saturday, 28 December. Rhodes was conciliatory; he promised to wire at once to Jameson forbidding him to cross the frontier. Half-heartedly, Rutherfoord Harris, during the course of the day, dispatched a number of messages on Rhodes's instructions – 'It is all right if you will only wait' – then closed his office and went home. Desperately the reformers sent messengers by horse and train to stop Jameson, with whom they had no direct communication.

On the same Saturday Jameson sent his famous telegram to Cape Town where it lay in the Post Office until 11 am on Sunday: 'Unless I hear definitely to the contrary shall leave tomorrow evening.' Harris's clerk called at the Post Office to pick it up, together with a later one, dispatched that very morning, announcing: 'Shall leave tonight for the Transvaal.' The first telegram had been lying in the office since 6 o'clock the previous night, and Harris has understandably been suspected of deliberately omitting to make any special arrangements to keep the cable office open after hours. As the representative of the Prime Minister he could quite easily have done so, and he knew very well that Sunday was 'D Day' for the raid. The line to Pitsani, where Jameson was camped, was still open until midday on Sunday, had anyone wished to send Jameson a peremptory order to halt. Flora Shaw was right when she described Harris as 'the real mischief maker'.

On Monday morning two sets of people awoke with headaches. Jameson's troopers had been given thirty-six cases of champagne by the ebullient doctor as a 'jumping powder' before setting out on the raid. A drunken trooper cut a wire fence in mistake for the telegraph line with the result that news of their departure was quickly known in Pretoria. In Cape Town those in the know awoke to a far worse headache. They learnt that the column had marched but the reformers had failed to rise.

Stunned though they may have been they did not lose their presence of mind. Rhodes immediately summoned Hamilton, the *Johannesburg Star*'s Editor, one of the two delegates from the Reform Committee, who was still in Cape Town. He received him in the billiard room at Groote Schuur, looking ill and haggard. 'This is the end of me and my work,' he declared. Then, becoming brisker: 'We have twenty-four hours' start of public opinion, and you must write every leading article that appears in Cape Town this afternoon and tomorrow morning.'

Hamilton's description is as clear evidence as can be, were any needed, that Rhodes never intended to launch Jameson into the Transvaal in the circumstances in which he actually marched.

Rutherfoord Harris, meanwhile, had not forgotten Flora Shaw. Some weeks earlier he had asked the Doctor for a copy of the 'women and children' letter given him by Charles Leonard in Johannesburg. Jameson, mindlessly dating it 20 December, had duly sent it. Harris altered the date to the 28th and cabled it to Flora Shaw at her private address, together with a brief communiqué announcing that, in consequence of this appeal, Jameson had crossed the frontier with 700 men (in fact, because of desertions and other reasons, the number was only about 400).

Flora Shaw heard the news of the raid in Wernher-Beit's London office on Monday too. She immediately went round to alert the Colonial Office. It was the first they had heard of it. Chamberlain, preparing to attend a servants' ball at Highbury, outside Birmingham, took the midnight train to London.

Next morning, Tuesday, 31 December, at 5.30 am, Flora received Harris's cable. This was followed by a brief release cable, dated the same day – 'You can publish letter'. On New Year's day *The Times* carried the news and the letter as from 'Our Correspondent in Cape Town'. The result of Flora Shaw's efforts had been to give the paper one of the most sensational scoops of history, if of a somewhat dubious kind. Later she complained that Harris had duped her.

Over this critical week Flora Shaw had been receiving, besides the messages for publication, a spate of private advice from Cape Town. On 27 December Harris signalled that everything was postponed until 6 January: 'We are ready but divisions at Johannesburg.' On Monday 30 December, the day after Jameson started, three more telegrams were dispatched. The first informed her that Jameson had moved and that the 'letter' was on the way; it asked her to withhold publication for the time being: 'We are confident of success. Johannesburg united and strong on our side.' This was a palpable lie, as *The Times* well knew from Younghusband's reports.

The next telegram was a queer one. Signed 'F. R. Harris for C. J. Rhodes, Premier,' it ran: 'Inform Chamberlain that I shall get through alright if he supports me, but he must not send cable like he sent to High Commissioner in South Africa. Today the crux is, I will win and South Africa will belong to England.'

The cable which this message complains of was sent from the Colonial Office on Chamberlain's instruction at 5.30 p m on Sunday, 29 December, and was occasioned by an encounter between Fairfield, Head of the African division, and Hawksley, London solicitor to the

Chartered Company, on Friday evening. Hawksley alarmed Fairfield by observing that he and his friends were being much chaffed about the fizzle of the Johannesburg revolution. 'He seemed to think,' reported Fairfield to Chamberlain, 'that Rhodes (whom he does not like much) might be driven into an attitude of frenzy and unreason, and order Dr Jameson to go in from Gaberones [a town near Pitsani] with the Company's police and manipulate a revolution.' On the strength of this report Chamberlain instructed the High Commissioner in Cape Town, if necessary, to warn Rhodes that in such an eventuality Chamberlain would revoke the Company's Charter. This warning arrived too late to have any effect except to exasperate Rhodes. From Chamberlain's point of view it was a two-edged weapon. That he should have sent such a message exonerated him from any complicity in the Jameson Raid as it occurred, but strongly suggested that he was privy to the conspiracy which prepared the way for it.

Flora, under cross-examination later, claimed that she took no action on this impertinent telegram. She had divined from its wording, she maintained, that it was sent by Harris on his own initiative. Alfred Beit had subsequently told her that Rhodes could not have sent it because he was out all day on 30 December. Flora Shaw's general line was that the wording of the telegram was a piece of impudence. She replied roughly to the effect that Chamberlain was 'awfully angry'. Flora's divination here was at fault. We now know from Frederic Hamilton that Rhodes was in all morning and gave lunch at his home to the English cricketing team – 'God knows what I can say to them with this on my mind,' he exclaimed. The tone of this telegram accords very much with the tone of his conversation with Hamilton, and no doubt the gist of it was dictated by him to Harris.

On the following day, Tuesday, Rhodes cabled under his own name:

> Unless you can make Chamberlain instruct the High Commissioner to proceed at once to Johannesburg the whole position is lost. High Commissioner would receive splendid reception and still turn position to England advantage but must be instructed by cable immediately. The instructions must be specific as he is weak and will take no responsibility.

Rhodes, in effect, was merely blustering. That same afternoon he told Hamilton, in the presence of Rutherfoord Harris, that his special train had steam up and he proposed to go to Pretoria himself to see Kruger. Hamilton replied that they would hang him. 'Hang me!' exclaimed Rhodes. 'They can't hang me! I'm a Privy Councillor! There are only two hundred of us in the British Empire.' Hamilton thought, silently, 'there will soon be only 199.' 'Well, anyhow,' said Rhodes, 'I have got Chamberlain by the short hairs.' (Only, writes

Hamilton, the expression was even more colloquial.) 'Then he really is in it, Mr Rhodes?' 'In it? Up to the neck!' he replied.

Meanwhile events in the world outside were moving quickly. Arriving in the Colonial Office on Tuesday, 31 December, the same day that this conversation took place, Chamberlain, without consulting his colleagues, ordered the High Commissioner in Cape Town publicly to repudiate Jameson. He virtually declared him an outlaw. This decision saved Chamberlain's political career but the immediate public repercussions were hostile. The next day, 1 January, on the publication of the 'women and children' letter in *The Times*, there was an immense upsurge of British opinion in favour of Jameson. Nobody in England yet realized that the raid was nothing but a humiliating and bloody fiasco. For on 2 January Jameson was rounded up by the Boer commandoes and surrendered: casualties – 17 killed, 35 missing, 55 wounded. The Boers had been merciful. They did not shoot the raiders down like dogs as they had the redcoats in 1881. No one in Johannesburg had stirred a finger to help Jameson. The wretched Hamilton, returning there by train from Cape Town, found that his friends had included his name *in absentia* on the list of the Reform Committee. He and Charlie Leonard joined the raiders in Pretoria gaol.

The following day, 3 January, the Kaiser took a hand:

> I express to you [he telegraphed Kruger], my sincere congratulations that without calling on the aid of friendly Powers you and your people, by your own energy against the armed bands which have broken into your country as disturbers of the peace, have succeeded in re-establishing peace and defending the independence of the country against attacks from without.
>
> Wilhelm I.R.

In England, there was another violent revulsion in favour of Jameson, even stronger than that caused by the 'women and children' letter. It was intelligent anticipation of some such foreign reaction which had caused Bell and Flora Shaw to send 'sealed orders' briefing *The Times* correspondents in Europe on the Jameson plan.

The 'Kruger telegram' has led subsequent historians to see in the Raid a cause not only, immediately, of the Boer War, but also, remotely, of the war with Germany. The Kaiser had wanted to declare a protectorate over the Transvaal and to send marines to Pretoria. He was restrained by his Ministers, who only wanted to use colonial affairs as a lever to influence Britain's European policy.

(iv) Post Mortem

After the Raid, the *post mortem*. Official inquiries were held in Pretoria and Cape Town. The raiders were handed over to the British authorities and tried in London. Jameson went to prison for fifteen months.

But the full-dress inquiry was that ordered by the British Government, and this was the one in which *The Times* was interested. The telegrams were bound to be produced. The public were also inquisitive about how *The Times* came into possession of the 'women and children' letter. Flora Shaw, it seemed certain, would be called.

The inquiry took the form of a Select Committee of the House of Commons and did not meet till over a year later – February 1897. The Select Committee's brief was:

> To inquire into the origin and circumstances of the Incursion into the South African Republic by an Armed Force, and into the Administration of the British South Africa Company [the 'Chartered'] . . . and Report what Alterations are desirable in the Government of the Territories under the Control of the Company.

The composition of the committee was curious. Chamberlain who, if anybody, should have been in the dock, was a member, though he had on occasion to step down to be examined. Other members included Sir William Harcourt, leader of the Liberal opposition, and Labouchere, the Radical MP and journalist who will be remembered from the Pigott case. *The Times*, in a leading article, argued against his inclusion as being unlikely to give an impartial verdict; but this was ignored.

Flora had seen Rhodes since the Raid, and found that he would be 'conciliatory to Chamberlain'. This meant that he would do his best to suppress any telegrams in the possession of the company which might suggest complicity. In return, Chamberlain forbore to put into effect his threat to revoke the company's charter. Time, and the Kruger telegram, had led to a closing of the ranks. But before the inquiry opened Chamberlain instructed his private secretary to ask Flora Shaw a question: 'I should myself like to know beforehand what her answer would be if I asked her, whether she had ever, in the course of any conversation with me, mentioned what is now known as Jameson's plan . . . I do *not* believe that she ever said a word on the subject.'

The Times Colonial Correspondent went to see the Colonial Secretary. Here is the record of her memory of their conversation as given to Chamberlain's biographer:

> I said to him, 'It is absolutely necessary for me to know the truth. I put you on your honour to answer me. Did you know about the Raid beforehand or not?'
> Chamberlain said . . . 'I can hardly say what I knew and what I did not. I did not want to know too much. Of course I knew

of the precautions, the preparation, if you like, in view of the
expected trouble in Johannesburg, but I never could have
imagined that Jameson would take the bit between his teeth.'
'Then you did not know about the Raid?'
'I did not.'

Flora Shaw and Rhodes were not the only principals in the drama
whom Chamberlain saw after the Raid. He also went secretly to see
Jameson in prison. To his Sovereign alone did this man of arcane and
even furtive stratagem reveal the visit.

Tensions began to develop between Flora Shaw and Buckle. A
French paper published a story about the 'hurry-up' telegrams. The
Editor had not been informed of these, and was disconcerted when he
learnt the truth. Flora in a letter circulated among the staff explained to
the Editor that she had sent them 'in a personal and friendly capacity
to a correspondent in Cape Town . . . it is important to place on record
the fact that the telegrams were sent without your knowledge or that
of the Managing Proprietor [Arthur Walter] and that they were private
communications paid for by my private funds'. She did not, it will be
noticed, include the name of the Manager among those kept in ignorance.

Bell gave her some friendly advice before she appeared at the
inquiry. 'It was your business to get information, and you got it. . . If
it appears that at a later date you urged that it should be done quickly
I think there was sufficient of what you knew of the state of Europe
to explain it.' Buckle wrote her the following lengthy, damaging and
somewhat pompous letter, not best phrased to lend confidence to a
witness about to undergo a daunting test. Nor was Flora the sort of
person who needed advice on how to conduct herself before a public
inquiry:

Private   The Athenaeum,
                                          24th May, 1897.

Dear Miss Shaw,

I have been thinking a great deal over our conversation yesterday, and over the turn which your examination may take.
Naturally, what I am most concerned for is the reputation of
The Times, and in its interests I am convinced that it is of the
utmost importance to keep, if possible, Mr Bell's name out of
the matter of the telegrams. I quite recognize that this may not
be possible; but I think you should bear it steadily in mind as a
thing to aim at.

It occurred to me after our meeting whether it might not be
desirable for you to prepare and put in a written statement; but

on reflection I have come to the conclusion that to do so would be to seem to claim for yourself the position of a protagonist in the 'plan', which you were not.

A point which we did not discuss, but which is important, is that you should make it clear that you were not originally in the secrets of the conspirators; on the contrary that, from your knowledge of the situation in South Africa and of the general views of Mr Rhodes and others, you were able to make a shrewd guess at the kind of game that was being arranged, and so to worm the truth out of Dr Harris.

I should certainly decline positively, if I were you, to re-construct your cables from your memory. If they exist, the Committee can get them. If not, *tant mieux*.

With regard to the Paper and your cables; the way I think the matter should be put is: that you sent them on your own respon-sibility and at your own expense, that you had no instructions to do anything of the kind, the action of *The Times* being limited to sending correspondents to report events; that they were sent without the knowledge or concurrence of the Editor (if Mr Walter authorizes you, you can add the Managing Proprietor); that the Editor only discovered what you had done in April, when the Steevens telegram about *The Times* appeared, and that he expressed his strong disapproval of what you had done (if Mr Walter authorizes you, you might add the Managing Proprietor here).

It is important that you should let the Committee know you were severely blamed, especially as you are going – rightly, if that is your true feeling, though I confess I cannot understand it – to maintain that everything you did was entirely right and justifiable. That, as you know, is very far from being my opinion or the opinion of the Paper; and the Committee and the public should not be left to think it was.

You are quite right, I am sure, in your view that you should be quite frank about your personal actions, but that you should refuse to disclose confidential communications between yourself and Ministers, and yourself and your chiefs in *The Times* office. And with regard to the latter, I should put in early a suggestion that the inquiry was travelling rather beyond the province of the Committee. The negative statement that you never discussed or mentioned 'Jameson's Plan' in your talks with Mr Chamber-lain seems to me also important.

Let me warn you again against proffering too much unsolicited information, and making speeches to the Committee. You are a journalist dealing with Colonial subjects and therefore bound to be informed on important Colonial matters, but not one engaged in getting up this plan, though you subsequently approved and, I fear, we must say, aided it. Therefore your air should rather be that of one who is called to speak on one or two points, than that of one who is full of important information to give to the Committee. Accordingly it would be well mainly to confine yourself to answering direct questions.

Flora never replied to, or forgave, this letter.

There were two occasions when she was called before the Committee, at which, after Rhodes, she was the star turn – she even once made Mr Chamberlain laugh, which was more than anyone else could do. By now she was a person much talked of and surrounded by an aura of mystery. George Wyndham, a Conservative MP and member of the inquiry, told his cousin Wilfrid Blunt that he had been seeing a lot of the 'gang that have been running the Transvaal business . . . with Buckle, *The Times* editor, and Miss Flora Shaw, who is really the prime mover in the whole thing, and who takes the lead in all their private meetings, a very clever middle-aged woman'.

She appeared, accompanied by her sister Lulu, who wore 'a seasonable hat'. Flora, by now more matronly than when she interviewed Zebehr Pasha, still wore the black dress with white lace and chiffonerie round the collar. There was nothing severe, or 'tweedy' about her, and reporters were mildly surprised that she was not a 'frump'.

Flora Shaw's first examination before the Select Committee caused her few anxieties. The object of the inquiry was to assess Rhodes's responsibility for the Raid, and one or two members of the Committee, particularly Labouchere, wished to prove that Chamberlain was implicated. Harcourt, the leader of the opposition, was not one of these. Flora was only being examined because she appeared to be a link between Chamberlain and Rhodes. While, therefore, she had to protect Printing House Square and her superiors against incidental revelations she did not need to fear direct attacks.

Flora omitted to mention the telegrams sent to her by Rhodes just after the Raid, which referred to Chamberlain by name. In reply to Harcourt she said that she had communicated information to the Colonial Office on one occasion, the Monday after the Raid, when she called to tell them what had happened. They had got their own information soon afterwards. She admitted she knew that a bloodless revolution was expected shortly in Johannesburg and that Jameson was holding his force on the border in case the situation got out of hand. On one subject she was emphatic. She did not know that the rising in Johannesburg was being actively promoted by Rhodes from Cape Town. This seems impossible to credit, both because of the tone of the telegrams, her intimacy with Rhodes, and the fact that Young-husband was actually living in Frank Rhodes's house and being used as an emissary between the Reform Committee and his brother Cecil. Younghusband's name was never mentioned in the inquiry, nor was he called.

At one point Harcourt asked Flora whether she had inspired a leading article, to which she administered a slight – ever so slight – snub: 'I do not feel as if I could give any answer about what takes place in *The Times* office.' Another member came to her rescue: 'I understand you would rather not answer questions as to your relations with or your communications to *The Times* newspaper?' Flora agreed, and so did the Committee.

Pressed on the degree of her responsibility, Flora declared that the telegrams were not written in consultation nor dictated to her by any-body. When she got home, she must have reflected that some of these telegrams were actually in the office written out in Bell's hand.

The Colonial Correspondent of *The Times* stepped down. She had passed through her ordeal without giving anything away and had stuck as closely to the truth as was possible without getting everybody into hot water – which nobody but Labouchere would have wanted. She had even established a degree of domination over the Committee, which by the time of her appearance was becoming rather worn down by strain. Congratulations poured in. But she was not out of the wood yet.

Rochfort Maguire, the Chartered's London representative, made the surprising statement that after Harris returned to Cape Town at the end of November, Flora Shaw was his chief, if not only, source of information on the progress of the plot. The Committee thereupon ordered the telegraph company to produce copies of the December telegrams between Rhodes and Harris in Cape Town and Flora in London. Miss Shaw was recalled. She was faced with the difficulty of explaining not only the references to Chamberlain in the telegrams, but how she had forgotten to mention such important ones as those instructing her to intervene with Chamberlain after the Raid. It was a question of maintaining her credibility.

She faced her interlocutors with aplomb. The extreme rapidity of her speech was noted. She made a pretty little speech: 'There has been so much of what I may call mystery-mongering about all this business that the evil of keeping anything back is infinitely greater than the evil of producing everything and allowing the public to form its own opinion upon it.' She explained that she had been under such pressure at the time that she had ignored and later forgotten the telegrams. This is not so unlikely as it might seem today. One has to remember that Flora Shaw was operating largely from home, without secretaries, typewriters, carbon copies and modern filing systems. Nevertheless she was pushing the Committee's credulity in feminine vagueness to the extreme. In order to drive home the genuineness of her desire to tell all, she produced a receipt for a telegram sent on 1 January, but could not for the life of her remember what it said.

Harcourt and Labouchere pressed her very hard over the mention of Chamberlain. How did she know that Chamberlain wanted the rising to happen quickly? Obstinately she stuck to her story that she had inferred it from a remark of Fairfield's. How did she know that Chamberlain was 'sound in case of interference by European powers'? She had put this in lest anyone in South Africa should think that Mr Chamberlain was still a Little Englander; it was here that Chamberlain laughed. As for Rutherfoord Harris's abjurations to 'inform Chamberlain', she did not take orders from Dr Harris. The doctor himself was out of the country and could not be recalled. Onlookers remarked on her asperity whenever she referred to him. He had lied to her barefacedly over the 'women and children' letter.

Flora's loyalty throughout to Printing House Square was unfaltering. The responsibility was hers; she had not informed the Editor of her telegrams. She had shown one to the Manager after sending it – this was an understatement, since the draft is in Moberly Bell's own hand. Labouchere she snubbed: 'It is not etiquette to speak in public of what is done in the internal organization of any large paper.' No doubt the Committee could have made it harder for her to defend *The Times*, but *The Times* was not the object of the hunt.

The Report, when it came, condemned the Raid, blamed Rhodes for everything except Jameson's crossing the frontier without orders, exonerated Chamberlain, and omitted mention of *The Times*. Labouchere put in a minority report in which he found Flora Shaw's memory 'somewhat defective'. She went home exhausted physically and mentally, but the heroine of the hour. Congratulations on her conduct poured in. The combination of masculine gifts with feminine personality and charm created an overwhelming impression on Victorian society.

The Jameson Plan had turned out, as Chamberlain had at times feared, a 'fiasco'. Frederic Hamilton, writing forty years after, summed up thus:

> Looking back on it, I am amazed afresh at the sheer craziness
> of the adventure. It seems preposterous that grown men should
> have associated themselves with it, and incredible that they
> should have risked ruin and a sporting chance of the hangman's
> rope in order to further it . . . I doubt whether the scheme was
> ever presented in its entirety to any one person in Johannesburg.
> In my experience there was always a margin of mystery where
> innuendo took the place of exact information, and as to which

it was understood that details could not prudently or decently
be demanded. It was openly stated that the plan had the blessing
of Mr Chamberlain, but there were hints, altogether unauthorized
and baseless but none the less impressive, that behind Chamberlain and the Colonial Office even greater personages and forces
were involved.

Geoffrey Robinson, later Dawson, future Editor successively of the
Johannesburg Star and *The Times*, was assistant private secretary to
Chamberlain at the Colonial Office from May until September, 1901.
Writing to Stanley Morison, *The Times* historian, in 1941, he had this
to say about Chamberlain's involvement:

> The impression I formed, when I first came into this business,
> was that Chamberlain *himself* was *not* au courant with all
> Rhodes's plans, though some of his subordinates undoubtedly
> were. He knew that something was in the wind, but in my
> opinion was very careful not to know too much. There was a
> great deal of discussion at the time about the 'damping down'
> of the Commission of Inquiry . . . I always understood that this
> had to do with . . . highly placed personages.

There have, it is true, been modern instances of senior civil servants
keeping Ministers in the dark over matters that vitally affected their
political survival. But even so, a careful study of documents now available cannot but lead to the conclusion that Chamberlain knew quite
precisely (a) that Rhodes was the driving force behind the conspiracy,
and (b) that the company's police under Jameson were stationed there
to assist the rebels after – though not of course before – they had risen.
He simply hoped that Rhodes would pull the chestnut out of the fire
without compromising him. As for the damping down of the inquiry,
the Liberals, if the matter had been probed too deeply, would have had
great difficulty in convincing any impartial body that they had not at
least listened to plans much resembling the 'Jameson Plan' while they
were still in office.

And what of the part played by *The Times* Colonial Correspondent?
Flora Shaw was certainly more than a reporter and commentator; in
matters affecting the Empire she was a crusader. To say that she 'aided
and abetted' the conspirators would be a wrong description of her role;
rather did she goad them on. 'The time is past,' proclaimed *The Times*
in a leader on 16 December, 'even in South Africa, when a helot system
of administration, organized for the exclusive advantage of a privileged
minority, can long resist the force of enlightened public opinion.' Such
exhortations were legitimately part of her job; but she went outside her
terms of reference as a journalist when she preceded such articles by

sending cables to Rhodes proclaiming 'delay dangerous'. At times, as we have seen, she even flew ahead of Chamberlain.

To suppose that she was the sole secret channel between the Colonial Secretary and Rhodes would be to go too far. Communicate what she understood to be Chamberlain's feelings she certainly did; and by her regular visits to the Colonial Office she was able to keep herself tolerably well informed of what these were. How much of the incoming traffic she transmitted to Chamberlain is less certain. She herself, as will be recalled, stated on oath that she only communicated information to the Colonial Office once.

How much was Flora told about the conspiracy? She herself steadfastly maintained that she was ignorant of Rhodes's real function as leader. There was a streak of naivety in Flora Shaw. On one occasion – over the 'women and children' letter – she allowed herself to be deceived, and indeed made to look foolish, by Rutherfoord Harris. Nevertheless, with her thorough knowledge of the personal and political conditions in South Africa, not to mention her feminine intuition, she can scarcely have failed to appreciate that nobody but Rhodes was capable of organizing a movement on this scale. Her attempts to explain away her knowledge, which was implicit in the wording of all her cables to Rhodes, ring singularly hollow. With Flora Shaw one is constantly faced with the choice of thinking her either a liar or stupid, but there is nothing in the rest of her career to suggest that she was anything but preternaturally intelligent. She was also a very loyal woman – both to her employers and to her country. So far as she could, she protected them from damaging revelations.

14 DECLINE FROM GLORY

(i) Falling Circulation

The Times had been in decline since the death of Delane, but from 1890 on the dissipation of its reserves by John Walter III and the costs of the Parnell Commission placed it in mortal danger. The paper had met and overcome such a challenge once before in its history, at the time of the repeal of the taxes on knowledge, but the threat which now developed was far more grave and was to end with the sale of *The Times* in 1908 to an entirely new proprietor.

In the year of Delane's retirement the circulation stood at 62,000. During the 1880s, under his successors Chenery and the young Buckle, this was reduced by one-third to 41,000. In the 1890s the decline continued at an even, but much slower, rate. In 1904 the circulation reached its lowest point – 32,000. By superhuman efforts Moberly Bell managed to restore it to 44,000 in 1906. The dividends paid to proprietors sank in proportion. From the highest peak of £93,000 in 1876, they fell to £36,000 in 1890, to £17,800 in 1900, and to £6,400 in 1906 when no dividend was paid for the second half of the year. In some years the paper showed a loss, though this never exceeded the costs, £32,000 a year, charged by the Walters for printing it.

Various explanations have been offered to explain the decline of *The Times* in this period. Great changes were certainly taking place in the British press. Three enterprising newspaper proprietors – George Newnes, Alfred Harmsworth and Arthur Pearson – developed a style of popular journalism aimed at the lower middle classes and the better-educated working classes, who now had more money to spare and greater leisure to read. This popular journalism was livelier, more entertaining yet more trivial than that of the existing national daily newspapers. Modern techniques, moreover, enabled the proprietors to mass-produce the new-style papers and sell them at a halfpenny. Their publication coincided with rising consumer demand which served to aid their finances by providing plentiful consumer advertising.

The rise of popular journalism can have had but slight direct effect on *The Times*. In the first place it was aimed at a totally different readership, and in the second place it developed long after the most serious period of decline was over. This, as has been seen, was in the 1880s, whereas Harmsworth brought out the first halfpenny national daily, the *Daily Mail*, in 1896. The spectacular success of this publication, which soon reached a circulation of nearly a million, was comparable to the performance of *The Times* in a previous generation, but it is unlikely that it won over many *Times* readers. Certainly it took readers from the other serious papers, such as the *Daily Telegraph*, and no doubt they in turn gathered some from *The Times*. But the earlier losses of *Times* circulation in the 1880s must have been mainly to these serious national dailies. This is to some extent borne out by the figures. The *Daily Telegraph* and the *Standard* gained 50,000 readers each between 1880 and 1889, and it is fair to assume that many came from the 20,000 which *The Times* lost.

The Times, in fact, was suffering from the delayed effects of the abolition of the taxes on knowledge. These effects had been staved off by the brilliant talents of Delane and his circle. But their successors, under an ageing Chief Proprietor, a dying Manager, and an inexperienced Editor, were unable any longer to hold out against their competitors. Personalities aside, technological innovations favoured the more cheaply produced newspapers. The development of news agencies relying on the electric telegraph meant that news, and foreign news in particular, was available to them at a more economical rate. *The Times* was spending vast sums on maintaining what was admittedly the finest foreign news service in the world, but the average newspaper reader was content with something less.

In printing technology, where for nearly a century *The Times* had ruled supreme, other papers were already introducing more up-to-date machinery, some of it from America. In the case rooms Linotype and Monotype machines, which cast type in solid lines and in single letters respectively, were making their appearance. These enabled newspapers to print more quickly and in the long run more cheaply. *The Times* laboured on with the Kastenbein mechanical typesetter of the 1870s, which meant that its case room was out of date – and with circulation falling the Walters could see no point in purchasing expensive new machinery, especially as their contract ensured them a steady profit so long as *The Times* continued to be printed at all. Other papers were using cheaper newsprint, manufactured mechanically from wood pulp, but *The Times* continued to use high-grade paper.

Thus on almost every count the future of *The Times* as a high-quality newspaper and as a national institution was threatened. 'People bought cheap papers not because the price was low, but because their contents were low,' complained Moberly Bell to J. L. Garvin. The gibe was only partially true. The price of *The Times* at 3d was prohibitive, yet the paper, according to Arthur Walter, cost 6d to produce.

(ii) The Grey Nineties

The men of *The Times* were now involved in a struggle to save their newspaper from extinction. The story of the rearguard action which they fought, and of how they ultimately sold to a commercial proprietor a paper which had grown to be regarded as a national institution, remains one of the most dramatic episodes in the history of British journalism. The senior executives of *The Times* at this period were not men lacking in intellectual ability or force of character. What they all lacked, however, was practical experience of journalism outside Printing House Square. Their backgrounds respectively were All Souls College, the Alexandrian cotton market and the English country house. Their professional knowledge was 'in-bred'.

George Earle Buckle, the Editor, was a tall, thick-set man with an auburn beard – a 'genial Viking', one of his editorial staff called him. He was shy, modest, and, in comparison to Delane, unsocial, though he was a regular diner-out in London during the season. Still wearing his white tie and waistcoat he would return to the office and refresh himself during the small hours with copious draughts of soda water. He had a resonant voice, and an even more resonant laugh. Harcourt Kitchin relates that when going through the letters to the Editor he showed Buckle one discussing that well-worn subject – 'which side of the pavement should one walk on?' The letter was sent in by Lord Grimthorpe, and was signed 'An Old Street Walker'. Buckle laughed so loudly that he could be heard down in the machine room.

Buckle had outstanding academic ability, quick discrimination in judging articles and writers, and familiarity with the ins and outs of Westminster and Whitehall politics. He had a few, but well-chosen, friends in politics, such as Lord Rosebery, John Morley and Arthur Balfour. None upon his staff could 'gut a Blue Book' as quickly as he, and his handling of a domestic political crisis grew to be masterly. He was sound and impartial, but not brilliant or original. Under him, *The Times* became reliable, encyclopaedic, and conservative. He once told a colleague he had been responsible for moving the paper 'from left of centre to right of centre'. In newsgathering the emphasis was on accuracy rather than speed. '*The Times* thinks that news, like wine, improves by keeping,' remarked Northcliffe.

The greatest scoop that Buckle ever obtained was the news of the resignation in 1886 of Lord Randolph Churchill, communicated to him by Churchill in person. Colleagues said it positively embarrassed him. No doubt Buckle's early experience in the Pigott case discouraged him from taking risks. He was conscious that he lacked the intuitiveness which so often saved Delane from error. He succeeded in restoring the authority of the paper and the faith of the public in its reliability, but at the cost of liveliness. He lacked wit, flair, and imagination, and in consequence *The Times* in the 'gay nineties' was anything but gay.

In the evolution of *The Times* Barnes gave the paper its national standing, and Delane its standing in Europe. Buckle increased the range by giving it standing as the paper of Empire, though much of the credit for this must go to the Manager, Moberly Bell. W. T. Stead once wrote to Flora Shaw that Buckle was the 'editing editor' and Bell the 'managing editor' of *The Times*. There was truth in this, though Stead overstated the case.

Ever since the death of Delane, it had been realized that the growth of editorial administration was putting too heavy a strain on the Editor. The early death of Chenery confirmed this view. A scheme was therefore put up, and wisely vetoed by John Walter III, for dividing the editorship between an 'executive assistant' and a 'literary director', both to be subordinate to the Manager. Bell drily remarked of this proposal that 'the doctrine of the Trinity however suitable for Heaven is unfitted for Printing House Square'. The scheme was shelved, but the problem remained. Other papers have adopted the doctrine of the Trinity, but for a paper with the principles and role of *The Times* the indivisibility of the editorship is of necessity sacrosanct.

Now, with the appointments of Buckle and Bell, the difficulty was met by the Manager undertaking most of the editorial administration, including 'hiring and firing' of journalists. In theory Bell upheld the supremacy of the Editor, but Bell was a maverick, and in practice the temptation to conduct an editorial policy on his own was apt to carry him away, as it did with the Jameson Raid. Not unnaturally the Editor resented these intrusions, nor did he trouble to hide his resentment. On the other hand, he was glad enough to have the administration taken off his hands.

Moberly Bell was the strongest personality among the upper hierarchy of Printing House Square. He was a man of great courage, power and authority, who ruled his subordinates by harshness tempered with charm. As Manager he had his weaknesses. In his daily routine he was unbusinesslike to a degree. He wrote everything out himself in longhand, did his figures on an old envelope, and was over-accessible to the staff for the efficient conduct of his work. He had no training in newspaper production, advertising or promotion; but life had given him an aptitude and natural zest for negotiation which was to serve *The Times* well in its hour of danger.

Too much of Bell's boundless and frequently misdirected energies was spent indulging the passion of an ex-foreign correspondent for cutting a figure in foreign affairs. But he had also a thorough understanding of how a foreign service should be organized. The correspondents he recruited constituted a roll of honour in journalism. The trouble was that *The Times* was not earning enough, either in sales or advertising, to afford such a galaxy.

A further reason for the failure of *The Times* to survive under its original ownership lay in the organization of higher management and in the character of the new generation of Walters. With the death of John Walter III in 1894, there had been changes in the condition of the Walter family. Under the will of the first Walter, it will be recalled, three properties and two proprietorships had been left. The properties were the buildings, the printing works, and the newspaper. Of these the first two were under the sole proprietorship of John Walter, while *The Times* itself was owned by a number of shareholders, known as the 'small proprietors', who were mostly relations of the Walters, with John Walter as Chief Proprietor and Manager.

The system worked satisfactorily until the death of John Walter III. His eldest son having died young, his second son, Arthur, succeeded to the joint ownership in 1885. In later life John Walter married a second wife and the eldest son by this marriage also died young. A third son, Godfrey, was intended for the army. John Walter III in his will sub-divided the proprietorship once more. Arthur was left two-thirds and his half-brother Godfrey one-third of the buildings and printing works. These two men, whom circumstances had placed in charge of the most influential newspaper in the world, were without training or experience in newspaper production. For this inexperience many were to suffer. In practice Arthur was Chief Proprietor and Manager of the whole complex, while Godfrey managed the printing works. Moberly Bell, as Manager of the newspaper, had no control over Godfrey Walter's activities, and could only approach him through Arthur – the weakest link in the chain.

The mechanical supremacy of *The Times* had been built up by the first three Walters, all of whom were printers, and by MacDonald, the Chief Engineer, who had become Manager and died in 1889. Since the Walter press had come into operation in the late 1860s there had been no innovation apart from the introduction of the Kastenbein typesetting machines. Neither Arthur nor Godfrey were printers or engineers. In 1895 Godfrey imported the new Hoe printing presses from America, but the faster typesetting machines being introduced by other papers gave them an advantage over *The Times*. The printing costs, charged by the Walters' printing press, were higher than the printing costs of the new papers started by proprietors like the Harmsworths.

(*iii*) '*Made Up with a Shovel*'

It was not only the managerial and mechanical side of the paper which exhibited weaknesses. Harcourt Kitchin, Moberly Bell's assistant, has left a revealing account of what it was like to be a sub-editor on *The*

Times in the 1890s. He shows both the strength and the weakness of the paper at the time.*

A modern newspaper possesses, under the Editor, a general staff which ensures that newsgathering, make-up, and appearance are coordinated into a single streamlined operation. Within this general staff are the news editors, and the night editor and his planning staff. In Printing House Square in the 1890s none of these posts existed. Little had changed since the days of Delane, with the exception of the headings and cross-headings which had been developed, albeit with restraint, to break up the massive columns which mid-Victorian readers had been content to plough through with Spartan determination. To them the reading of *The Times*, like family prayers, had been a daily ritual. 'Room Seven', where the sub-editors worked, was 'a cavernous back room with a smell of sour meat', ill-ventilated and cheerless. Junior sub-editors earned five pounds a week and, given the low rate of income tax, the remuneration was not ungenerous. From 'Room Seven' the copy was delivered direct to the printer.

Because of the lack of planning, the paper was always grossly overset. One sub-editor, therefore, was brought in early to bring up to date the over-matter – that is, material which had been set up in type but failed so far to find its way into the paper. As the presses were unable to print the paper in one operation *The Times* was divided into an inner and outer sheet. Into the outer sheet, printed early, went the up-dated over-matter. It was Kitchin's first job to go through and revise this over-matter, much of which had lost all topical interest by the time it got into the paper. But as a measure of economy, nothing was ever thrown away. Indeed, Kitchin relates that when later he became assistant manager 'I was going through proofs of long standing matter which was congesting the case room. I chanced upon an article of my own which had been lying in type for more than six years. After that lapse of time even I had not the courage "to bring it up to date".' To Bell such practices may have seemed an economy, but they were steadily driving away younger readers.

While 'Room Seven' was sending out the general home news to the printer in uncontrollable quantities, other departments were doing the same. From the Editor's room – in which sat the assistant editors – leaders, special articles and reports poured out. The law, parliamentary and City offices added their quota. Only the foreign department had any planned or guaranteed area of space in the paper. All this went into the inner sheet, printed later in the night. Once the copy was received in the composing room, the printer put it into the paper according to his own convenience. *The Times*, in fact, 'was made up with a shovel'.

* Harcourt Kitchin: *Moberly Bell and his Times*, Philip Allan, 1925.

Both the Editor and the Manager were aware that the system was unsatisfactory. Complaints flowed in from readers, many of whom abandoned *The Times*. 'It is sufficiently obvious', wrote Moberly Bell in 1894, 'that we have to deal with a steady and continuous decline. There is no reason to suppose that we have reached rock bottom.' In this forecast the Manager was correct.

Both Bell and Buckle were handicapped by their lack of control over the printing department. When remonstrated with, the Printer maintained that to adopt a system of editorial, as opposed to mechanical, make-up was technically impossible. Neither All Souls, nor the Alexandria cotton market, nor Bear Wood dared override him. Nor could the Printer be entirely blamed; he was trying to catch trains with antiquated machinery. And so the old system went on. The paper continued to lose readers and the profits continued to dwindle.

Most inefficiently run organizations contain a grossly overworked backroom executive who somehow holds the fabric together. In *The Times* editorial department this was the assistant editor, J. B. Capper. He was, writes Kitchin, 'the high priest of the religion of accuracy in detail'.

Capper had no control over planning because, as has been seen, there was none. But he read for accuracy every proof and every word that went into the paper.

> For a quarter of a century and more [writes Kitchin], he never got to his bed on a working day till four o'clock in the morning after. Yet he was always alert, and I never remember him to have been ill . . . I am sure that Capper enjoyed what would would have been to most men a job of unspeakable dreariness . . . Anyone can turn up a file of *The Times* in the 'nineties and reckon up for himself the prodigious nightly task which it was Capper's dreadful job to get through.

He read not only for accuracy, but for lapses of taste, discretion and judgment, and in so doing had developed a nose for blunders which was unerring.

The health and the sickness of *The Times* invariably reflect the robustness or pallor of editorship or management. But behind both in the nineteenth century stood the all-powerful shadow of the Walters. Unfortunately in the 1890s, as has been seen, the remedy lay within the sole power of two inexperienced men. Nothing could be effected unless the newspaper and the printing works were combined under unified management and accounting, and this would have put an end to the system of robbing Peter to pay Paul by which the Walters ran their business. Restructuring of management would have cleared the way for renovating the case room, whose out-of-date machinery was

at the root of much of the trouble. All these measures were subsequently put into effect by Northcliffe, but had the Walters themselves
initiated them they might have retained control of the paper.

Moberly Bell, the Manager, could have cut costs by pruning the
foreign department, where expenditure was needlessly, and sometimes
heedlessly, extravagant, but he was determined to maintain the superiority of *The Times*'s service in face of the universal resort to agencies,
such as Reuters, upon whom *The Times*'s rivals were now able to rely.
His efforts in one sense were successful. Never has the foreign service
of any newspaper been so brilliant as was that of *The Times* under
Mackenzie Wallace and Valentine Chirol, who succeeded him in 1899.
But Bell went beyond all reason, considering that the revenues were
falling at a rate of £9,000 a year and that foreign news of high quality
was an attraction to a very small minority of potential readers.

In 1906 *The Times* had to sell out its last meagre securities in order
to meet the bill for newsprint. Bell had increased the revenues of the
company in the previous five years through special publications, but
these were now falling off and no alternative revenues were as yet
provided for. Unless they were, *The Times* would have to be sold or
cease production. What the paper needed was a Manager who managed.
Moberly Bell moreover would have saved money by hiring a managing
editor with experience of modern journalism to help Buckle and
Capper sort out the chaos of the editorial operation, though even this
would have served no purpose so long as Godfrey Walter and the
Printer were allowed to pursue their own way independent of editorial
requirements.

(iv) Desperate Remedies

Nevertheless Bell could see clearly enough that desperate remedies were
called for. Unable to control Godfrey's printing works, and unwilling
to curb his own expenditure on Wallace's foreign department, the
Manager sought a way out through adventitious aids.

Few newspapers, he argued, paid their way, or ever had. In the
eighteenth century John Walter I had accepted subventions from
government. In the 1890s subsidies to other newspapers came chiefly
from political parties. Bell determined to provide his own form of
internal subsidy. He turned his attention to developing the special
publications department, which had been making modest profits out of
The Times Law Reports and *The Times Atlas*.

In 1897 Bell first received a visit from two American booksellers,
Horace Hooper and W. M. Jackson. They were the leading exponents
of modern methods of mass book selling and specialized in cheap
reprints, direct selling by mail order, payment by instalments and high-
pressure advertising. These two proposed to Moberly Bell that under

cover of *The Times*'s name they should extend their operations to Britain. Bell listened, was impressed, and agreed.

Their first joint enterprise was sponsorship by *The Times* of a reprint of the ninth edition of the *Encyclopaedia Britannica* in 1898. The results exceeded Bell's wildest hopes. By 1905 *The Times* had made £108,000 out of the deal and from 1902 to 1904 was able to pay a slightly increased dividend.

But there were dangers. Hooper's trans-Atlantic advertising techniques offended the readers of *The Times* and also its small proprietors, whose dividends in 1905 resumed their downward trend. There were criticisms also of the ethics of Hooper's business methods. The *Encyclopaedia* had been commissioned twenty years – and printed ten years – earlier. In order to silence the reproach that *The Times* was promoting shoddy goods Bell set up a special department to produce supplementary volumes for the *Encyclopaedia*, with two men of fine intellectual calibre to run it – Mackenzie Wallace and Valentine Chirol.

Encouraged by the good results of Hooper's methods Bell, in 1904, applied them to *The Times*; he offered the newspaper by subscription at a discount. This was a mistake. The regular readers, who must have been better businessmen than was the Manager of *The Times*, simply abandoned direct purchase and went on the subscription list. Bell lost more money by these transfers than he gained by new readers. Kennedy Jones, Northcliffe's newspaper adviser, remarked waspishly that Moberly Bell could not count up to more than five, but Bell's principal motive was probably to attract advertising by 'buying circulation'.

On the advertising side Hooper's advice was helpful. *The Times* had suffered some losses in its advertising during the years of its decline. The *Daily Telegraph* had appropriated its near-monopoly in small advertisements, though the personal column still held its own as a national institution, serving many authors like Conan Doyle in the *Adventure of the Red Circle*, as the starting-point for their stories:

> Sherlock Holmes . . . took down the great book in which, day by day, he filed the agony columns . . . 'Dear me!' said he, turning over the pages, 'What a chorus of groans, cries, and bleatings: what a rag-bag of singular happenings! But surely the most valuable hunting-ground that ever was given to a student of the unusual.'

Under Bell display advertising had increased to take the place vacated by the 'smalls'. Horace Hooper developed this type of advertising further, though not without complaints from readers who thought it vulgar. All the same, Walter appointed him Advertising Manager.

The most encouraging aspect of an otherwise threatening situation was the circulation. Thanks to Bell's enterprise, and his dogged refusal to accept defeat, sales in 1906 exceeded 40,000 for the first time in fifteen years. But by now it was too late.

Unfortunately Bell and Hooper had over-reached themselves. The year before, in 1905, they started a lending library called *The Times* Book Club, with the object of increasing annual subscriptions to the paper. As an inducement subscribers were offered membership of the club, which not only lent new books to them, but also sold them, when still relatively new, at second-hand prices. It soon became evident that any profits would come out of the selling, not the lending, side of the business. But neither Bell nor Hooper really understood the intricacies of the British book trade, and they soon had the publishers up in arms.

The British Book Publishers Association maintained that for a publishing company to buy up new books in bulk and retail them at second-hand prices was an unfair trade practice. They retaliated by drawing up an agreement, binding on its members, by which a book might not be sold as second hand until after six months, and they refused to supply *The Times* Book Club except at the full price.

The controversy was waged with extreme bitterness; some writers, such as Bernard Shaw, supported *The Times*. Reviews in *The Times Literary Supplement* of books published by hostile firms asked subscribers 'to abstain from ordering the book so far as possible'. The publishers retaliated by withdrawing advertising to the tune of £10,000. In 1908 the publishing firm of John Murray brought a libel action against *The Times* which had printed letters accusing him of extortion. The prosecution were able to show that *The Times* had underestimated the costs of book publishing, won their case, and were awarded £7,500 in damages. This was virtually the end of the Book War, which had proved a disaster for *The Times* and indirectly sealed its fate. For while Bell was battling against the outside world, internecine strife had broken out within the walls of Printing House Square.

15 *THE TIMES* IS SOLD

(i) *Appointment of a Receiver*

The small proprietors of *The Times* – those multiplying beneficiaries of the first John Walter's will – had been growing restive. So long as profits were high they remained amenable to sole management by a member of the Walter family, but when their dividends began to shrink they became more demanding. In their defence it must be pointed out that, while they shared in the profits of *The Times*, they also had an un-limited liability for its losses. As dividends were reduced to a third of what they had been in the 1870s, alarm began to spread that they might be converted into actual losses. Moreover, since the Walters never disclosed their accounts the small proprietors suspected them of feathering their nest by charging exorbitant rents and printing costs.

Foremost among the small proprietors was a Mrs Sibley, who for over twenty years had conducted a guerrilla war against her cousin Arthur Walter. In 1885 she had objected when his father appointed him as joint manager. In the 1890s she had conceived the tactic of testing whether it was legal to sell a *Times* share outside the family during the lifetime of the shareholder. She chose as her guinea-pig Alfred Harmsworth, to whom in 1898 she offered a moiety of her own holding. Harmsworth went to see Walter. He accepted the advice given by Joseph Soames, still the company lawyer, that the transaction was illegal, but from then on Harmsworth maintained a watchful eye on the fortunes of *The Times*, which it became his ambition to buy.

In 1900, after much agitation, Mrs Sibley obtained permission to inspect the books of the company, which the Walters had hitherto kept to themselves. But Moberly Bell's rudimentary methods of book-keeping revealed little of what she wanted to know, and in the following year she and her son brought against Arthur their first action in the courts. This was to test the legal position over the sale of shares to outsiders. Although they compromised by selling a part of a share to Godfrey Walter, they made an important point by establishing the price of her one-fortieth share at £2,200, which was later used as a basis for calculating the total value of the paper. Then there was a pause in the Walter skirmishing until another, and more formidable, female Walter cousin raised the standard of revolt. She was a Miss Brodie-Hall, and her faction claimed the backing of the *Wiener Verein-Bank*.

It was at this point, in 1905, that Mrs Sibley issued her second, and more serious writ, and now she was supported by others of the small proprietors who repeated the demand for inspection of the accounts, asked that Hooper's schemes should be halted, and applied for a transfer of *The Times* property to a limited liability company.

To save *The Times* from the indignity of being dragged through the courts, and possibly ending up at public auction, Arthur Walter at last summoned the small proprietors to a meeting at Printing House Square. To one of his retiring disposition this decision must have been painful indeed. Surprisingly, the meeting went off well. No doubt for the first time the silent majority had an opportunity of making its views heard and no doubt it counselled moderation. Walter and the small proprietors agreed to settle out of court, and in a friendly manner, the details for the formation of a limited liability company. This was to be called *The Times* Limited. The pending legal action was withdrawn.

Unfortunately Arthur Walter could not easily bring himself to tell people unpleasant truths, a failing which was to get him into trouble on several subsequent occasions. On this one he forbore to tell the meeting that only one month previously he had signed a renewed agreement with the hated Hooper by which, among other things, Hooper was appointed Advertising Manager. When the small proprietors discovered this concealment they finally lost confidence in Walter and the legal action went forward.

On 7 July 1907, Mr Justice Warrington sanctioned the plan of dissolving the partnership and ordered the paper to be sold. Arthur Walter was appointed Receiver.

(ii) The Anonymous Bidder

Once the 'For Sale' board went up at Printing House Square a number of groups began manoeuvring for position, though few of them were serious contenders. It was easy enough to find people ready to put up money for *The Times*, but for practical purposes the buyer had to be someone with experience of running a newspaper. The object of Arthur Walter, as Chief Proprietor, and his colleagues was to sell the paper privately, and with satisfactory guarantees that its traditional character would not suffer by the change of ownership. As the Receiver it was Walter's business to arrange for a sale of *The Times* which the judge would approve.

The first scheme to be considered was put up by Moberly Bell and Horace Hooper. This was to form an amalgamated company consisting of *The Times*, the *Encyclopaedia*, the Book Club, and all Hooper's interests. Arthur Walter promptly turned it down, but, foolishly, he omitted to tell Bell of this rejection. Bell first heard of it from Hooper, and it is easy to imagine his feelings. He began visiting his friends in the City, including Lord Cromer and the Rothschilds.

Miss Brodie-Hall persevered with her German friends. The rumours of a German syndicate trying to buy *The Times* grew with the telling, until finally it was believed that the Kaiser in person had tried to obtain control. A group with German banking names did in fact consider the project, but it was knocked on the head by Sir Ernest Cassel.

Meanwhile Godfrey Walter was following a line of his own. Godfrey was a more determined man than his half-brother, and particularly disliked Bell whose ambitions for the paper conflicted with his printing interests. Indeed, the way things were organized in Printing House Square seemed deliberately devised to promote friction between the manager of *The Times* and the manager of the printing works. Godfrey came to an agreement with Arthur Pearson, the youngest of the 'Big Three' of popular journalism, to purchase *The Times*, leaving the Walters with a stake in their family business. During these negotiations Arthur Walter was away ill at Bear Wood.

C. Arthur Pearson was the least successful of the three popular newspaper owners. He had now started the *Daily Express*, but neither this, nor his other paper, the *Standard*, was prospering. Northcliffe's own ambition to buy *The Times* went as far back as 1898, when he had offered to purchase a controlling interest, but Walter had turned him down. Now a lucky chance put him on the scent. Impatiently, he had cancelled a dinner invitation because of fog, but hearing that Paderewski was to play after dinner, he changed his mind and went. Next to him at table sat Sir Alexander Henderson, the City magnate who had actually brought Pearson and Godfrey Walter together. Their host let out a hint which was enough to tell Northcliffe that Pearson was in negotiations for, or might even have bought, *The Times*.

When he had received confirmation of this rumour through the assistance of his solicitor, Sir George Lewis, he played a forcing card. Northcliffe realized that if it was known publicly that Pearson was bidding for *The Times* there would be an outcry on the grounds that a paper of dignity and seriousness was passing into the hands of a leader of 'the yellow press'. So he caused J. L. Garvin, the Editor of his Sunday paper, the *Observer*, to insert the following paragraph in the issue of 5 January 1908:

It is understood that important negotiations are taking place which will place the direction of *The Times* newspaper in the hands of a very capable proprietor of several popular magazines and newspapers.*

* Reginald Pound and Geoffrey Harmsworth: *Northcliffe*, Cassell, 1959.

The trick worked. On Monday all London was alive with rumours, most people believing that the prospective buyer was Northcliffe. Godfrey Walter panicked. He feared that the small proprietors of *The Times* and the whole of the City would take fright if they thought that Northcliffe, the biggest of all the 'yellow press' newspaper owners, was about to purchase the paper. Accordingly Godfrey instructed Buckle, much against his inclinations, to insert a counter-statement:

> Negotiations are in progress whereby it is contemplated that *The Times* newspaper shall be formed into a limited company under the proposed chairmanship of Mr Walter.
>
> The newspaper, as heretofore, will be published at Printing House Square.
>
> The business management will be reorganized by Mr C. Arthur Pearson, the proposed managing director.
>
> The editorial character of the paper will remain unchanged, and will be conducted, as in the past, on lines independent of party politics.
>
> The contemplated arrangements will in all probability require the sanction of the court before they become definitive.

By inserting this paragraph without warning, Godfrey Walter antagonized almost everybody whose co-operation he most urgently required. Buckle, who had many and powerful contacts in London, began to work against him. The small proprietors saw in the announcement just one more example of the high-handedness of the Walter brothers. Even more important, the judge of the Chancery Court, in whose hands lay the decision as to who should purchase *The Times*, considered that he had been treated with contempt.

Moberly Bell was out of London that weekend. He first read the announcement, which amounted to one of his own dismissal, in proof on Monday night. He had a stormy interview with Godfrey, who sensibly advised Arthur to get Bell out of the office as soon as possible, but Arthur characteristically took no action. The result was that now in Printing House Square the Walters had a bitter enemy whose hands were on most of the levers. On this issue Bell and Buckle were as one; so were the rest of the staff.

Meanwhile Northcliffe, though lying low, was not inactive. As was his habit when preparing a coup he had left for France. But his capable lieutenant, Kennedy Jones, went to see Hooper at the Savoy on the very day when Pearson was holding a premature victory dinner in the hotel, at which the table decoration was *The Times* clock in ice. But the ice was melting as rapidly as Pearson's hopes.

(iii) Northcliffe's Bargain

When Moberly Bell returned home on the night of Monday, 6 January 1908, having read the proof announcing his own replacement, he appeared to his family 'simply stunned'. 'What is the use of being bitter?' he asked. He then sat down to write a letter of reproach to Arthur Walter. He resolved to 'smash' the Pearson deal. This was not merely because of personal mortification, but because of all the newspaper owners in London Pearson seemed to him the worst choice. He was in a receptive mood, therefore, when Hooper called on him after leaving Kennedy Jones. At first he jibbed at the prospect of encouraging Northcliffe; it seemed to him a case of King Log and King Stork. But reflection convinced him that the best practical solution now left would be a purchase of *The Times* by Northcliffe, subject to guarantees of continuity in journalistic standards and editorial staff. This would mean Bell and Buckle remaining in office. He decided to see Kennedy Jones himself.

In the meantime opposition to the Pearson deal was building up outside Printing House Square. Northcliffe, who as yet did not know whether or not the agreement was 'signed, sealed and delivered', filled the *Daily Mail* with congratulatory articles praising Pearson as a 'hustler'. This course had the double advantage of showing good will should Pearson succeed, and rousing just those fears in the minds of the Establishment which might cause the judge to refuse the sale. At the same time Buckle was working away successfully in the Athenaeum. By the end of the week the Carlton also was dead against Pearson. Arthur Walter began to wobble.

In the following week Bell and Kennedy Jones drew up a draft agreement. The latter was having difficulty in communicating with Northcliffe, storms having brought down the lines between London and Paris. Secrecy was all important, and all telegrams to Northcliffe were addressed to his valet Brunnbauer.

The following Sunday, 12 January, Northcliffe once more made use of the *Observer* to damn Pearson with loud praise. He drafted an article which his chief of staff, George Sutton, took in to J. L. Garvin. 'Where did this come from?' asked the Editor. 'It just blew in the window,' replied Sutton.

The case of *Walter* v. *Sibley* was due to be heard on 30 January, but matters were now so uncertain that the judge granted a postponement. In the meantime Bell secured Arthur Walter's support for his own scheme, without revealing the name of the effective purchaser; Walter however guessed that he was Northcliffe. In this transaction Bell was not candid. He sold his scheme to Walter under assurances about the editorial independence of *The Times* which he had no warrant to give.

'X', as the unknown purchaser was described, was meanwhile paying flying visits to London *incognito*. On 3 February he made his first firm offer. From the offices of his accountant in Sackville Street, he wrote in his own hand to Hooper: 'I am desirous of purchasing *The Times* on behalf of myself and others, and I authorize you up to 30 June 1908, to negotiate for the purchase of the copyright thereof for any sum up to £350,000.' On the following day, Moberly Bell, assuming his character-istic role of cloak and dagger, called upon 'X' secretly. Northcliffe did not fail to sustain the dramatic tension of the meeting.

'Mr Bell,' he said in greeting, 'I am going to buy *The Times*. With your help, if you will give it me. In spite of you, if you don't.'

'I will help you,' answered Bell.

Northcliffe was conciliatory over guarantees on the character of the paper and the security of the staff. Bell would be Managing Director. In subsequent conversations Northcliffe confessed that he had been moved by the way in which Bell had asked everything for the paper and the staff and nothing for himself. But there were still ditches to be cleared, and quagmires into which the riders nearly fell. One technical difficulty was that any proposal submitted to the judge had to originate from one of the Proprietors. Bell as Manager had no legal standing in the case, nor could Walter, as the Receiver, sponsor the scheme. General Sterling, a moderate reformer and grandson of the man believed to have coined the phrase 'The Thunderer', came to the rescue. Having formally abandoned Pearson, he agreed to introduce Moberly Bell's proposal without asking questions. Walter thereupon braced him-self to tell Pearson that in view of mounting opposition among the small proprietors he could no longer support his bid. On 14 February Pearson officially withdrew.

Preservation of secrecy was another cause of anxiety. If the real identity of 'X' once became known then all the animus which had been aroused against Pearson would be transferred to Northcliffe. Unfor-tunately the latter learnt through Bell that Arthur Walter had assured Sir Alexander Henderson – the originator of the Pearson scheme – that the new purchaser was not Northcliffe. Being quixotic, as well as tough and shrewd, Northcliffe insisted that Bell reveal to Walter the truth. When told, Walter agreed to keep the real name of 'X' secret; but he passed it on, first to Godfrey and his own son John, and then to Buckle, who told W. F. Monypenny, the Assistant Editor. Bell was beside him-self with anger and worry; he longed for the day of decision. This was to be 16 March.

But the worst hitch of all, which might well have ruined the whole project, came through a disagreement between Bell himself and Northcliffe. The Manager's first interest was all along to preserve the standards of *The Times*. In pursuit of this objective he had persuaded the purchaser to insert into the agreement a preamble guaranteeing in very general terms the 'efficiency, reputation and character' of the paper. Moberly Bell now over-reached himself. He attempted to define, in a draft letter sent to Northcliffe for signature, what these phrases meant. The definition went into such details as maintaining the price of the paper at 3d.

The response from Northcliffe was swift and unfriendly. On Sunday morning, 9 February, Sutton appeared on the doorstep of Bell's home carrying a brief case. Bell was in a coloured dressing gown, looking, said Sutton, 'like a brigand'. In the case were two letters; one was Bell's own document, returned unsigned, the other a draft for Bell to write. This read:

> It is understood that in the event of your acquiring *The Times* newspaper, I shall act as Managing Director for 5 years and carry out your absolute instructions.
>
> But you express your desire that the present policy of the paper in Home and Foreign Affairs should be continued under the Editorship of Mr Buckle and Mr Valentine Chirol.
>
> In my former letter I desired to make no *conditions*. I merely wished to express what I believed to be your ideas.

Sutton explained that he also had in the case all the papers relating to the transaction. His instructions were, if Bell did not agree, to hand them back.

Moberly Bell had now gone too far to retrace his steps; he wrote the letter. In doing so, he was betraying his promises to Walter, Buckle and numerous others. But he meant also to mislead Northcliffe, for he had no intention of keeping the undertaking given under *force majeure*.

In other respects the negotiations had a happy ending. Northcliffe, as an expression of appreciation, trust and friendship, paid over into Bell's personal account £320,000 for the purchase of *The Times*. Bell paid in to Court £32,000 as deposit, and on 16 March the Bell-Northcliffe agreement was approved. Arthur Walter became Chairman of the new company, *The Times* Publishing Company; members of the Board being Moberly Bell, George Earle Buckle, Valentine Chirol and W. F. Monypenny. None of the other contenders put in an offer. The judge refused Miss Brodie-Hall's request for an adjournment.

There remained one piece of unfinished business after the sale - the fate of the printing works and buildings at Printing House Square. The whole object of forming the new company was to unite all these under one proprietorship, yet in the struggle over the sale of the newspaper the details of this transaction had been overlooked, and the Walters had managed to retain the lucrative part of the business for themselves.

The small proprietors had put in a claim against the Walters for

£100,000 in respect of excess profits derived from printing *The Times*, but Bell had persuaded the judge to strike this claim out of the agreement. Now the Walters were making high demands; they proposed to retain the printing works and buildings and charge *The Times* Publishing Company £40,000 a year for them. Bell wrote a stiff letter to Arthur Walter. Kennedy Jones described the Walters' machinery as 'old scrap'. Arthur Walter retorted that Bell was accusing him of being 'a Shylock', which indeed he was. Now that the sale of *The Times* was completed Bell was in a mood to bear hard on the family which had tried to dismiss him from the management.

This time he dealt them a body blow. He persuaded the Court to rule that the claim against Walter for £100,000, although it was void so far as the small proprietors were concerned, was transferred by the agreement to *The Times* Publishing Company. In other words, if Walter proved difficult over the printing works he risked being sued by 'X' for £100,000. He capitulated, and handed over the works for an allotment of shares in the new company. Of the three properties into which the business had been split by the will of John Walter I only the buildings now remained in the hands of the family. 'X' could congratulate himself that in purchasing the paper and the machinery he had made a good bargain. In this Bell had been his principal ally.

The year 1908 saw the end of the old *Times* as founded by the Walter family. The paper had started as a commercial enterprise and grown into a national institution. Northcliffe's purchase underlined, in the eyes of both its staff and its readers, a fact which they did not like to face – namely, that the inescapable condition of its survival as an independent journal of comment was commercial success.

16 THE CHIEF TAKES OVER

(i) A careful start

'The easy part is finished, now we've got to keep him in order.' So said
Moberly Bell on learning that the sale of *The Times* to 'X' had gone
through. This patronizing remark shows how little he had taken the
measure of the new Proprietor. To Northcliffe, harassing an opponent
into an early grave came as second nature. In this case he did so
reluctantly, for he had come to relish the heroic eccentricity of Bell's
personality.

Unfortunately for himself Bell's weakness was love of power. He
would rather work himself to death than relinquish the reins to someone else; nor could he believe that either Northcliffe or the Walters or
Buckle knew what was good for *The Times*. Only he did. The effort of
living up to his beliefs killed him.

What sort of man was this new Proprietor whom Bell had fought to
get in, and now fought to keep out? In conversation with the staff
Northcliffe often compared himself to John Walter II and Barnes. The
comparison was perceptive, and it proved, in spite of success on a scale
which might have destroyed most men's balance, that Northcliffe
preserved his sense of historical proportion.

Like the founders of *The Times* he had come upon the scene just at
a time when journalism was ripe for another forward leap, and like
John Walter II and Barnes he had the qualifications for grasping the
opportunity. But in taking on *The Times* Northcliffe was setting himself the hardest test he had ever encountered.

Adaptation is always more difficult than initiation. Satisfying the
needs of a new mass readership was one thing; refashioning an élite
newspaper to meet twentieth-century trends was another. In dealing
with his recently acquired property Northcliffe for the first time was
navigating in waters where he could not instinctively identify the landmarks. 'I am sorry, Alfred, you have lost your horizon,' his mother
told him. He understood, none better, the techniques for improving a
newspaper, but the background of his life was far removed from that
of the people who produced *The Times*, and of those for whom they
produced it. In the end Northcliffe did succeed, and succeeded bril-
liantly, but cynics would observe that the effort cost him his sanity and
possibly his life.

To *The Times* staff their new Chief appeared an intimidating character. His means of ruling were devious, and he could be brutal to the point of sadism. One of the myths he encouraged was that he perused *The Times* every morning for two hours, starting at 6 am. Northcliffe undoubtedly could gut a newspaper quickly, and often did. But at 6 a m he could be otherwise employed. At 38 Sackville Street, in a back room, there sat an experienced journalist, S. J. Pryor, whose duty it was to make a detailed analysis of *The Times* each morning, comparing it with other papers. On Pryor's reports were based the sometimes tactful but at other times pungent memoranda which the Chief sent to Bell, Buckle and other members of *The Times* staff. 'Such an analysis, even trained as I am, occupies at least two hours,' he wrote shamelessly to Bell.

The Chief made an equally close scrutiny of the cost sheets. There was, in Garvin's words, 'a long purring before he showed his teeth'. Dismissals followed, which it was left to Harcourt Kitchin, the Assistant Manager, to carry out. 'This man,' wrote Kitchin, 'though he was capable of great generosities, could torture those who served him without giving a thought to the pain which they suffered. He was to me like a boy pulling the legs off flies.' This was the unpleasant side of Northcliffe's nature.

The new Proprietor had no love for the generation of Walters from whom he had purchased *The Times*. 'They behaved,' he wrote to Buckle on 14 August 1908,

> like petty hucksters . . . At a most delicate period of the negotia-
> tions, when I felt in honour bound that my name should be
> disclosed to Mr Walter . . . [he] gave his solemn word of honour
> that he would not mention my name and broke his word within
> 24 hours . . . they have extracted from the paper the maximum
> old-fashioned and outrageous printing charges . . . I have en-
> deavoured to explain to the other proprietors that these are only
> the unbusiness-like habits of a country squire unused to business
> . . . During the whole of this time we have never heard one
> word from Mr Walter in regard to *The Times* itself as an institu-
> tion, or the staff of *The Times*. The matter has been dealt with
> as though it were the buying and selling of a public house . . .
> had it not been for the splendid spirit shown by you and your
> staff the sordid story of the last two or three months would have
> wearied me of my enthusiasm for the maintenance of this
> national institution.

According to Harcourt Kitchin *The Times* staff as a whole shared these sentiments. Fortunately for the paper Northcliffe was to conceive very different feelings for Arthur Walter's son, John. When he became

Chairman a new and fruitful relationship began between the new and the old tradition.

Northcliffe's protestation to Lord Esher that he regarded *The Times* as a hobby was probably a smoke screen, intended to be relayed to the King. The conclusions of Arthur Bates, the Chief's trusted secretary, are nearer the truth. Years later he put down on paper for the benefit of *The Times* historian what he conceived to be Northcliffe's real intentions:

> My impression then was, and is still, that he intended ultimately, though not immediately, to have some influence on the news and views of the paper, assuming that this would be possible, without friction, through the editorial staff. At the same time he was prepared, if necessary, to go further and to control. For the time being, however, and until the prejudice against the name of Harmsworth subsided, he decided to concentrate attention on the great improvements needed in the mechanical departments and the business organization. But beyond any question his main aim was to see *The Times* again the great national organ.

For five years Northcliffe took no drastic steps to reform *The Times*. For at least a year he never even visited Printing House Square. Because of the machinations of Bell, who deliberately kept them apart, he never spoke to the Chairman of the company, Arthur Walter, who died in 1910. The Walters' misfortune was that Arthur, the least effective of the clan, should have been at the head of affairs when strong leadership was most required. Perhaps if his father had been less cold to him in his youth he would have had a better grasp of the business when he entered upon his heritage in middle age. As it was he was aloof, autocratic, ignorant of the newspaper industry, and unimaginative. Opposed to all change, he resolutely refused to grasp the many nettles that needed uprooting.

After the sale the Old Guard in the editorial department – the 'Black Friars' or 'Brethren' as Northcliffe called them – continued doggedly to resist innovations. In them they saw nothing but the thin ends of countless unwelcome wedges. With Buckle – that great bear of a man must have been hard to quarrel with – Northcliffe's relationship was friendly. But trivial incidents irritated the Chief. The sight of the Editor opening his letters with his thumb, and putting papers together with pins instead of clips, used to drive this paragon of modern business efficiency to distraction.

For a long time the name of the new Proprietor was supposed to be a secret. But 'the Chief', as he liked to be called, employed every artifice to assert his influence. He tried to use one member of the staff against another and, when that failed, as it usually did, he would sack

him and put in a nominee. Harcourt Kitchin left early to become
Editor of the *Glasgow Herald*. Reginald Nicholson, one of Northcliffe's
oldest followers, a man of ability and charm, took his place. He became
the Chief's spokesman in Printing House Square and did much to
minimize friction; but it was an unhappy office. The 'harrying reign of
the invisible autocrat', as Garvin described it, was carried on through
a barrage of always pertinent, but sometimes contradictory, criticism.
'Northcliffe,' wrote the new Chairman, John Walter IV, 'knew his own
mind at any given moment, though his mind might change with startling
rapidity.' In the first three months, everybody was encouraged to spend.
Then, they were chidden for extravagance. In spite of brave words,
'Old Bell' turned out a quisling rather than a resistance leader so far as
'the Brethren' were concerned. Northcliffe had in his pocket the letter
of absolute submission extracted by Sutton, which Bell had never dared
show to any of his colleagues, since he had won their support for the
sale by giving assurances that the paper would continue essentially
unchanged. Whenever there came a crunch Bell advocated caution,
moderation and compromise. He could scarcely do otherwise.

Greatest progress was made in the printing works. Kennedy Jones
ripped out the Kastenbeins and Hoes, replacing them with Monotype
typesetters and Goss presses. In the editorial department S. J. Pryor,
Northcliffe's secret weapon from Sackville Street, was brought into
advise on home news and make-up.

At this point an important new influence was introduced. George
Murray Brumwell, a *Times* sub-editor and former secretary to Buckle,
was promoted to organize the day planning of the paper. Like Capper
he was to serve as the unseen anchor-man of *The Times* for a generation – planning the make-up, co-ordinating the departments, and
reading every word that went into type. A Northcliffe selection, he lived
to be the greatest traditionalist of them all.

There were other newcomers too, and in a way John Walter IV, the
new Chairman, was one of them. Untainted by the guilt of the past, he
had the usual Walter background of Eton and Oxford. But he had other
things too – sensitivity, common sense, and humour. Another of his
qualities, which served him well in his present circumstances, was a
realistic knowledge of his own limitations. Having acted successfully
as temporary correspondent in Paris, he was urged to apply for the post
of staff correspondent when the existing incumbent died. Wisely he held
back on the grounds that he was entirely unequal to the assignment.
Later his wisdom was confirmed when Bell indicated that had he
applied he would have been rebuffed. Instead, he was posted to Madrid.

His relations with the Chief were distant but, he reckoned, friendly.
'I got on best with him,' said Walter, 'on paper.' 'You look on me,'
Northcliffe once burst out, 'as a cuckoo in your nest.' The Chief,

Walter felt, treated him as a busy father treats his son, indulgently as a rule, but with wrathful impatience if opposed. There exists in the files of *The Times* a letter from Northcliffe to Bell, dated 13 March 1909, which shows that Walter's interpretation of Northcliffe's friendly feelings towards him were not wide of the mark:

> I had about an hour's chat with John Walter today. I like him extremely. He does not seem to have had a chance, and seemed quite pleased to get an appointment on *The Times*. I believe that if he had two years' education in the mechanical and editorial part of the business he would be able, *with good advisers*, to take charge of *The Times* . . .
>
> If he shows any capacity in Madrid, and any desire to regain *The Times* for his family, I should certainly feel disposed to leave my interest to him on very easy terms, and would indeed prefer that to my present scheme of forming the control into a national trust.
>
> I am impulsive and sometimes too quick in my judgments, but I do not think I have made a mistake in John Walter.

The letter shows the finer side of Northcliffe's nature – the generosity, the fair-mindedness, and the genuine dedication to the future welfare of *The Times*. Is there also a tinge of regret that there was no son of his own to carry on the tradition?

Walter was an essentially modest man and realized that as Chairman he was bound to be little more than a rubber stamp for Northcliffe. But he was determined, if he could, to preserve the family connexion with the paper. With this in mind he bought in his uncle Godfrey's shares and went to his intimidating self-appointed foster-father with a novel proposal. This was that he should support him through thick and thin so long as Northcliffe remained the Proprietor, in return for which the reversion of the paper would be guaranteed to the Walters. The Chief took some time – years, in fact – to ponder this suggestion, although, as can be seen from the letter just quoted, it was already in his mind. In the interval he himself bought out Kennedy Jones, who he felt was becoming too independent. Finally, in January 1913, he agreed in essence to Walter's proposals. In return for his proffered support, he would give or leave Walter the option to repurchase *The Times* on his death 'at the market price'.

From his agreement Northcliffe received one immediate benefit. By a readjustment of holdings Walter waived his right to arrears of dividends for his preference shares, which the company had been unable to pay since it was still virtually insolvent five years after the sale. John Walter's deal with the Chief did much to clear the air. A happier and more prosperous period began for *The Times*.

Meanwhile Buckle, now fifty-eight (the danger age in Printing House Square) had been putting out hints about early retirement. When taken at his word he was disconcerted, but at least he, Moberly Bell and the Chief were in agreement on the choice of a successor. This was the Editor of a South African paper, a man in his late thirties, then called Geoffrey Robinson. The choice was Northcliffe's, but Robinson had qualifications, as a fellow of All Souls and a latter-day imperialist, which commended him to both Buckle and Bell. Like Barnes, Delane, and Buckle himself, he was to hold the Chair for a good quarter of a century. Today he is better known by the name of his adoption, Geoffrey Dawson.

(ii) The New Editor

The new Editor has been described by Northcliffe's biographers as 'a Yorkshire squire with a donnish mind'. This, no doubt, is how he appeared to Northcliffe's circle, but it is a good example of the dangers of applying labels to individuals. It would have been equally true, and just as superficial, to describe him as the self-made son of a country bank manager. His forebears were in fact Yorkshire gentlefolk who had been deeply involved in banking and commerce for over a century, one having been Mayor of Liverpool. Geoffrey was a squire only in that he was fond of walking, riding and shooting, and inherited a landed estate from his aunt, Margaret Dawson, in 1917 when he was forty-three and already Editor of *The Times*, changing his name by deed-poll.

Geoffrey Dawson was primarily a man of affairs. On going down from Oxford he worked for two years in the Colonial Office, but was carried off in 1901 to South Africa by Lord Milner, the High Commissioner, who employed him as a private secretary. Thus from his earliest days he was accustomed to work at the centre of power and amid the turmoil of events.

The selection by Milner was a turning-point in his life, for he became one of that élite group of young men known as the Milner Kindergarten, nearly all of whom were to achieve high position afterwards. Several of them – Leo Amery, Edward Grigg (later Lord Altrincham), and Lord Brand – were, like Dawson, to join *The Times*.

After some years with the High Commission, he was, on Milner's recommendation, appointed Editor of the *Johannesburg Star*, and it was here, in charge of a colonial paper, that he was able to acquire that all-round experience of journalism which was to equip him for editorship of a national daily. Here, also, he began his connexion with *The Times*, for in 1906, at the invitation of Leo Amery, he became its 'stringer' in South Africa.

Dawson's South African experience is essential for the understanding of his life. He served there during the period of reconstruction after the Boer War, and imperial interests and constitutional solutions remained basic to his outlook on politics. Equally important were personalities. The special relationship with Lord Milner remained fundamental to all his major judgments and decisions. After they left South Africa Geoffrey exchanged letters by almost every mail with Milner and Amery, who had succeeded Flora Shaw as Colonial Editor of *The Times*. Northcliffe had marked Amery out as the next Editor, but the latter, preferring to pursue his career in politics, introduced Dawson to the Chief as a potential alternative choice.

At the end of 1910 Dawson returned to England – after resigning the editorship of the *Star* – without firm plans. 'Lord Milner at Brooks's,' he notes in his diary for 30 December, 'where we talked till midnight . . . He anxious I shd. go to 'the *Times*', as a job wh. wants doing and is not being done well and consistently.' During the first week of the New Year he saw Moberly Bell and John Walter, and then, on 5 January, 'went down to Sutton [Lord Northcliffe's country house] . . . & was plunged into a children's party'. Northcliffe did not come down till dinner. There followed days of long talks about *The Times* and its difficulties. On 7 January 'More and more talks w. Ld. N. who frankly offered me a place in the Times. . .Rather nervous about it, but much too attractive to refuse.'

Dawson joined *The Times* in the spring. On 28 July of the following year he was appointed Editor, at the age of thirty-seven. Although in the end they were to part, Northcliffe never regretted the appointment. 'One of the ablest men in England,' he once called him, and the Chief was a good judge of able men.

Later Geoffrey Dawson's critics were to point out that he had no experience in European affairs, which were to dominate British politics during most of the time that he was in the Chair. These criticisms would not have troubled Northcliffe when he appointed him in 1912. *The Times*, with a foreign staff of unparalleled brilliance headed by Valentine Chirol, had no need for reinforcement in this department. Moreover, waiting in the wings in Vienna was a young correspondent of glittering attainments, Wickham Steed, whose knowledge of Europe was already profound, and the Chief had his eye upon him, too, for accelerated promotion.

Throughout these early years Northcliffe's 'interferences', as they appeared to *The Times* staff, had stopped short of dictating editorial policy in the leaders. Harassing as they were they could be defended as being well within the Chief Proprietor's province. It was really Bell's false assurances which caused the staff to regard them as unconstitutional. But in 1911 the Chief took a more active line; he attempted to interfere with editorial policy over a matter of international politics, the

A CENTENARIAN AND A HALF.

Interviewer. "TO WHAT, SIR, DO YOU ATTRIBUTE YOUR REMARKABLE HEALTH AND LONGEVITY?"

The Old Squire. "TO REGULAR AND METHODICAL HABITS, A GLASS OF PURE NEWS EVERY MORNING, AVOIDANCE OF OVER-EXCITEMENT, AND — THINKING BEFORE I SPEAK."

Sir Bernard Partridge celebrates 150 years.

Max Beerbohm's impression of evenings in Printing House Square with Northcliffe at the centre.

Vicky 1950

"... BUT WE'LL ROW FOR EVER
STEADY FROM STROKE TO BOW
AND NOTHING IN LIFE SHALL SEVER
THE CHAIN THAT IS ROUND US NOW "
— ETON BOATING SONG

take THE T*MES*

Vicky (1959)

" WHAT WOULD YOU SAY WERE I TO TELL YOU
THAT THOSE BRILLIANT TURNOVERS WERE IN
FACT WRITTEN BY CLEVER LITTLE ME?"

4. iv. 64.

Osbert Lancaster (1964)

Air raid damage to the Queen Victoria Street building.

Printing House Square in 1964 after rebuilding.

The Walter Press of 1868.

William Howard Russell

Flora Shaw

Henry Crabb Robinson who after serving the paper abroad in the early years of the nineteenth century was for a short time appointed editor.

SOME VERY SPECIAL CORRESPONDENTS

Henri Stefan Opper Blowitz

During the Napoleonic War *The Times* engaged a light cutter to run between France and England and was thus often able to publish important news before official intelligence reached the government.

GETTING THE NEWS TO LONDON

During the Russo-Japanese War *The Times* chartered a fast steamer and used wireless telegraphy. The first wireless press message from ship to shore was despatched on 14th March, 1904.

occasion being the ratification of the Declaration of London, which limited the Royal Navy's rights to search neutral shipping in time of war. Northcliffe, who regarded its provision as damaging to national interests, instructed the *Daily Mail* and his other papers to oppose it. *The Times* had already taken up a position in favour of ratification. Northcliffe indicated that he would accept resignations rather than allow the paper to pursue a course which he regarded as unpatriotic. The Editor and Chirol naturally saw this as a flagrant incursion on the editorial prerogative.

In this incident Moberly Bell urged compliance on Buckle, and the matter was settled by compromise, with the paper adopting an indeterminate line. Northcliffe never attempted such interference again until Buckle and Bell were out of the way and his relationship with Printing House Square had become much closer. In retrospect it seems plain that he was motivated entirely by his strong sense of national duty, and not by any machiavellian desire to make a test case of his powers. The Declaration of London was thrown out by Parliament, and Northcliffe had fair reason for feeling that he had saved the paper from committing a serious error.

Nevertheless, the conflict had its significance in the history of *The Times*. For the first time a dispute between the Proprietor and the Editor had been dragged into the open. A novel and rightly disquieting aspect of the affair was that the Proprietor of *The Times* was now the Proprietor of many other papers. *The Times*, some feared, was not only being coerced into changing its policy but was also being forced into line with a block of centrally controlled journals.

Whether Northcliffe's action was really so much out of line with practice in the past may be doubted. John Walter IV believed that the Walters had always maintained their unspoken right to dictate leader policy and to 'have the last word'. His view is borne out by history. Editorial independence was a matter of custom, not statute. John Walter II withdrew from direct editorial responsibility for convenience's sake, not principle. This history has shown numerous examples of the Walters taking the lead in editorial policies, particularly when young editors were in the Chair. What is lacking is evidence of violent disagreements, arbitrary overrulings, or threats of resignation. The régime, steeped in paternal constitutionalism on the one side, and dignified service on the other, precluded such public manifestations of differences. But once it was established that *The Times* was a property which could be bought and sold, the need for codifying the relationship inevitably arose.

The clash over the Declaration of London was therefore a turningpoint. It emphasized this need, which was eventually realized in 1922 by the written charter of editorial rights insisted upon by Dawson when he embarked on his second term of editorship.

(iii) *A Penny for The Times*

In 1911 Moberly Bell slumped forward and died at his desk. He was never cut out to be a newspaper manager in a modern sense, but he had carried the flag high in adversity and in his conduct of the negotiations for the sale he had shown skill and determination. If he had equivocated, it was because he was operating from a position of weakness. He was sixty-four when he died. Reginald Nicholson slid easily into his chair. Chirol retired and Steed was brought home as acting Foreign Editor. So, by 1913, Northcliffe, by hook and by crook, had ensured that an entirely new team was in control of *The Times*, led by an Editor of his own choice and presided over by an amenable Chairman.

The Chief was now determined to move forward. Since his acquisition of the paper he had, he felt, achieved nothing. Its appearance was much the same, its content little altered, the circulation almost static around 40,000, while advertising had actually fallen away; the annual accounts showed only £20,000 profit, and no dividends were being paid on ordinary shares. This was failure, bleak and plain. Alfred Harmsworth was not used to failure, and would not tolerate it now.

His outward resolution was to make the paper pay, and his inward determination to assert personal control of the policy. There was no problem in diagnosing what was wrong. The price of the paper crippled the circulation and the low circulation drove the advertising away to the *Daily Telegraph* and the *Morning Post*, both serious papers sold to the middle and upper classes at a third of the price of *The Times*. But Northcliffe had to walk warily. This was not just a matter of irritating old fogies by lowering the standards of their favourite journal. He was the Proprietor not only of *The Times* but of a mass-circulation popular, the *Daily Mail*, and if he turned *The Times* into a successful popular daily he might well ruin the paper which he himself had created.

In 1913 he conducted an experiment. *The Times* was already sold to subscribers at 2d, 1d less than the 3d which was the cover price on the stalls. He lowered the price to a flat rate of 2d and backed the reduction with an intensive promotional campaign. The result, as he suspected, was a rise in circulation of only 5,000 – not enough to attract more advertising – and a loss in revenue caused by lowered sales' receipts and added production costs.

The dénouement was fast approaching. Northcliffe reckoned he could attract the 'small ads', particularly the 'job ads', away from the *Morning Post* and to a lesser extent the *Telegraph* provided that he could raise the circulation from 47,000 to 100,000 or more. On the editorial side, he argued that if the *Morning Post* could attract 150,000 Tory and upper-middle-class readers with a product sold at 1d, so could

The Times. There was no need to lower standards, only to lighten the style.

As usual, Northcliffe retired to Paris when about to strike. From there the first shot fired was a telegram dispatched on 25 January 1914: 'Humbly beg for light leading article daily till I return Chief.' Thus the man who was accused of destroying *Times* traditions started a new one – the Light Leader – which was to endure until 1967. Hundreds of thousands of *Times* readers were to derive delight from the anonymous wit poured out from the pens of such writers as Bernard Darwin, Harold Child, Douglas Woodruff and Peter Fleming. Quotations from Dickens, it used to be said, were Darwin's preserve – any other light-leader writer whose steps strayed into Dingley Dell used to be firmly warned off.

One incidental consequence of the plan to lower the price to 1d was the breaking of the age-old custom by which Printing House Square had been a 'non-union' house. The passing of '*The Times* Companionship', as the house union was known, was lamented by all; but it was realized that the print order might be so large that it could not be handled in Printing House Square alone. The *Daily Mail* presses would have to be called upon and the unions would co-operate under no other terms. It was to John Walter IV that Northcliffe entrusted the conduct of this delicate negotiation, and Walter put it through with minimum disturbance to individuals. The Companionship continued as a welfare organization; it may already have outlived its usefulness as a union. Plainly by the 1890s the composing room at Printing House Square had become just as restrictive as those of the unionized houses. But from now on the printers and compositors of *The Times* were to have divided loyalties, to *The Times* and to their unions.

On the night of Sunday, 15 March 1914, the new Goss presses began turning to print the first 1d issue of *The Times.* The paper was a twenty-four-pager which included a light leader, a Book Page (reviewing Henry James's *Notes of a Son and Brother*) and a handsome Court Page under the Royal Arms. The 'Bill Page', opposite the leaders, contained the most important news, both home and foreign. Northcliffe's personal influence might be detected in the article, unsigned, of course, by Bernard Darwin on 'Golf for Women', which combined under one head two of the Chief Proprietor's main private interests in life. Another article on Paris fashions announced that 'the commoner class of French women do make up, but not the better. This class now spends a fortune on massage.' To reassure traditional readers, the correspondence columns carried two letters from bishops attacking the compulsory public recital of the Athanasian Creed.

The first penny edition of 'The Thunderer' was universally acclaimed as a handsome and worthy production. Congratulations poured in. Sales reached 150,000, far above expectations, and were maintained at an average of 145,000. On 4 August the paper once again received the fortuitous bonus of another war. Sales jumped to 278,000.

Northcliffe supported the price-cut with full promotional backing from the *Daily Mail*, including an article written by himself. In it, with one of those characteristic gestures of his, which cost nothing but made people love him, he gave the whole credit for the coup to John Walter IV. Perhaps in his complicated mind he was sending a salute back to John Walter II who, on that morning almost exactly a hundred years earlier, had walked into the press room to announce 'Gentlemen, *The Times* is already printed – by steam!'

17 THE FIRST WORLD WAR

(i) A Strong Régime

Both Northcliffe and *The Times* entered the First World War in good shape. Both, in their different styles, had been warning readers for over a decade that a war with Germany was coming, and they were proved right. Northcliffe had been accused of warmongering, because of his emphatic mode of conveying the warnings; but he was not just responding to jingoist sentiment – he knew the country well. Two of his aunts were married to Germans, and he had visited Germany on several occasions. He was right also about the duration of the war. From the first day he insisted that it would last three years at least. The Editor, in common with most people, was expecting a short war.

In one respect only did the Chief show lack of judgment. He opposed the dispatch of an Expeditionary Force to France on 4 August, though fortunately on this point he allowed himself to be overruled. This was a concession from one who was coming more and more to lay down lines of policy. For by August 1914 the Chief Proprietor had become not only 'the Chief' but also *de facto* Editor-in-Chief. The vital editorial conferences held during the days before war was declared were chaired by Northcliffe, not the Editor. Sometimes Marlowe, the Editor of the *Daily Mail*, joined them, and it was he who persuaded Northcliffe to support the dispatch of the Expeditionary Force.

From now on the Editor – and the Manager – were bombarded as never before with instructions from 'the Chief'. Taken as a whole, and until his mental faculties began to decline, these instructions were practical, constructive, concise and amiable. They show professional grasp and wide range. Occasionally they could be pungent, as this one, dated 27 January 1917:

> Today's *Times* came as a very great surprise to the Principal Proprietor. It contained a leading article which is practically a censure of the Women and National Service matter on the same page. It is halting and weak. It is exactly like one of those leading articles which brought *The Times* down to 27,500 a day, and necessitated the introduction of the Encyclopaedia and the Book Club.
>
> In future, when the Editor is away, I propose having a liaison

between my other newspapers and *The Times* to prevent them contradicting each other as they do. This morning *The Times* not only contradicts its own news, but criticized my own newspapers of the two previous days. It is the sort of thing which cannot and will not happen again.

Otherwise the paper was excellent, with some interesting articles.

The combination of Northcliffe and Dawson at this period provided one of the strongest régimes *The Times* ever enjoyed. However, Northcliffe's paramount position did not prevent Dawson from maintaining his authority as the permanent incumbent at Printing House Square: 'Steed in particular pouring out volumes of incoherent "Europeanism". I got Grigg enlisted for an article on the Empire.' Evelyn Wrench, his biographer, considers that relations between the two men were at their happiest in 1916.

Censorship was one of the office's chief concerns, especially during the early days of the war. Kitchener (with the support of *The Times* and its formidable military correspondent, Colonel Repington) was Minister of War and was therefore in charge of war correspondents at the front. His ruling was, in effect, that there should be none. Stale news was to be served up from GHQ by an official 'Eye-Witness'. This was Colonel Swinton, the distinguished soldier-author who wrote under the nom-de-plume of 'Ole Luk-Oie'. H. W. Nevinson described one of his contributions as 'hogswash':

> Within sight of the spot where these words are being penned, the chauffeur of a General Staff motor-car is completing his morning toilet in the open. After washing his hands in a saucepan minus a handle he carefully brushes his hair with an old nail-brush, using the window of the car in which he has slept as a looking-glass.*

At first *The Times* could get no news from the Front. Then towards the end of August it had some luck. Two British correspondents – *The Times*'s own man, Arthur Moore, and Hamilton Fyfe of the *Daily Mail* – working in cars, ran across the 4th Division of the BEF in the retreat from Mons. They drafted dispatches which they entrusted to the purser of a cross-Channel steamer at Dieppe. Arrived in Printing House Square Moore's message was sub-edited and cut in accordance with what the sub-editor judged to be the requirements of censorship. The finished product was then submitted, late on a Saturday night, to the Press Censor, F. E. Smith (later Lord Birkenhead). To the surprise

---

* Hamilton Fyfe: *Sixty Years of Fleet Street*, W. H. Allan, 1949.

of Printing House Square 'F.E.' not only passed the message but restored some of the deleted paragraphs, adding a sentence or two of his own, with a written request to publish.

It is important that the nation should know and realize certain things [ran the published report]. First let it be said that our honour is bright. Amongst all the straggling units that I have seen, flotsam and jetsam of the fiercest fight in history, I saw fear in no man's face. It was a retreating and a broken army, but it was not an army of hunted men. Nor in all the plain tales of officers, non-commissioned officers and men did a single story of the white feather reach me . . .

Since Monday morning last the German advance has been one of almost incredible rapidity . . . The British Force fought a terrible fight – which may be called the action of Mons though it covered a big front – on Sunday. The German attack was withstood to the utmost limit . . . The French supports expected on the immediate right do not seem to have been in touch . . .

The Germans, fulfilling one of the best of all precepts in war, never gave the retreating army one single moment's rest. The pursuit was immediate, relentless, unresting. Aeroplanes, Zeppelins, armoured motors, and cavalry were loosed like an arrow from the bow . . .

Our losses are very great . . . The men are battered with marching . . . but they are steady and cheerful . . . The regiments were broken to bits, and good discipline and fine spirit kept the fragments together, though they no longer knew what had become of the other parts with which they had once formed a splendid whole.

The German commanders advance their men as if they had an inexhaustible supply. Of the bravery of their men it is not necessary to speak . . . Our artillery mows long lanes down the centres of the sections . . . but no sooner is this done than more men double up, rushing over the heaps of dead, and remake the section.

This piece of military narrative, conveying as it does the authentic feel of an army in retreat, awakes echoes of Crabb Robinson's description of the retreat from Corunna and Russell's tribute to the sufferings and stoical stolidity of Raglan's men before Sebastopol.

At the end of the message, F. E. Smith pencilled in: ' [The BEF] has suffered terrible losses and requires immediate and immense reinforcement. The British Expeditionary Force has won indeed imperishable glory, but it needs men, men and yet more men . . . We want reinforcements and we want them now.'

Hitherto the disasters befalling the Allies during the opening stages of the war had been hidden from the public. This dispatch, published in a special Sunday edition of *The Times* on 30 August, shook the nation.

F. E. Smith may have passed the message because he wished to jolt the Government out of what he considered its apathy. The man who took the message to him commented that it was 'After dinner – you know what that means with him.' Sad to record, when attacked in the House of Commons next day, 'F.E.' disavowed *The Times*. A night's sleep had brought second thoughts and he inferred that he had not had time to consider the message properly. Kitchener summoned the Editor and, as Dawson wrote in his diary, 'discoursed on the damage done to wh. however the answer was complete'.

One consequence of the war was that Dawson began to look outside the office for expert advice. No doubt an Editor's best 'brains trust' should be his own staff of leader writers and specialists, though not all Editors of *The Times* have recognized this (it will be recalled that Buckle's failure to consult his staff was a main factor in landing *The Times* in the Pigott case). But Dawson was conscious of gaps in his knowledge. He had come to *The Times* with a deep understanding of the problems of Africa and of Empire, and quickly acquired an instinctive grasp of domestic affairs, but Europe was beyond his horizons and he did not have much military knowledge.

So grew up a body of outside advisers, which called itself the 'ginger group'. Its central figure was Lord Milner; and the whole group, which met each Monday evening from January 1916 onwards, had a strong Milner Kindergarten flavour. The permanent members included L. S. Amery, F. S. Oliver (described by Evelyn Wrench as 'a refreshing and unorthodox man of affairs who combined the direction of one of the most successful firms of drapers in London with the hobby of writing history'*) and Edward Carson, best known as the organizer in 1914 of Protestant resistance in Ulster. Later Waldorf Astor, Conservative MP for Plymouth and heir to the first Viscount Astor, joined the group. Besides their regular private meetings, usually held at Milner's house in Great College Street, the 'ginger group' occasionally invited to join them 'advisers' such as Field-Marshal Sir Henry Wilson, another prominent Irish Unionist, who in 1918, with Milner's support, became Chief of the Imperial General Staff.

A larger and more permanent 'brains trust', of which the Editor was an active member, was the 'Moot'. This, too, had as its nucleus ex-members of the Kindergarten. The Moot met at large country houses such as Astor's seat, Cliveden, and Lord Lothian's, Blickling, and published a

---

* John Evelyn Wrench: *Geoffrey Dawson and our Times*, Hutchinson, 1955.

quarterly magazine, the *Round Table*, which still survives as a valuable learned periodical dealing mainly with Commonwealth topics.

No account of the editorial structure of *The Times* during the First World War would be complete without further reference to Colonel Charles à Court Repington, the military correspondent. He was in many ways the most influential, and certainly the most controversial, of the writers on the paper's staff and he had the added distinction of being a force in his own right in British politics – 'the twenty-third member of the Cabinet' as the Irish leader Dillon called him in the House of Commons. Repington was the first of the paper's professional military – as opposed to war – correspondents. He was less interested in military reporting than in shaping defence policy at the highest level, and thus introduced a new genre into British journalism which was perpetuated later by writers such as Basil Liddell Hart.

Moberly Bell recruited Repington to *The Times* in 1904 and his commentaries on the Russo-Japanese War first brought him to public notice. Like his fellow Rifleman Sir Henry Wilson he was a pioneer in promoting closer co-ordination with the French and in urging the preparation of an expeditionary force capable of operating in Europe. His policies brought him into conflict with Buckle, Valentine Chirol, and Thursfield, the naval correspondent, all of whom belonged to what was then known as the 'blue water' school, which regarded continental military entanglements as anathema. Repington advocated these not merely on paper but acted as a secret negotiator between the British and French General Staffs. In 1911 the War Office tacitly reinstated him in the Service, from which he had been forced to resign after running away with a British official's wife in Cairo, by making him the editor of an official quarterly review and giving him a room in the War Office. The outcry in Parliament when it was discovered that *The Times* military correspondent was actually collecting inside knowledge from that point of vantage compelled the dropping of the arrangement.

Forced to choose between Whitehall and Printing House Square, Repington chose the latter, although he was never a man who gave his full loyalties to *The Times*. He was a publicity hunter and an intriguer, who regarded the paper primarily as a useful *point d'appui* for pushing his own policies. His presence in the War Office harks back to the days of Reeve, with his place in the Privy Council office, though unlike Reeve, Repington was not trusted by his colleagues. But though they may not have trusted him the soldiers continued to use him and to supply him with secret information. When war became imminent he was the first to suggest in public the appointment of Kitchener as War Minister. He was a persistent advocate of conscription, and it was his dispatch from France on 14 May 1915, on the shortage of high explosives which started the 'great shell scandal', the source of which was generally supposed to have been Sir John French, the Commander-in-Chief.

To Geoffrey Dawson the military correspondent was a constant source of harassment. He combined all the qualities the Editor disliked most – he was 'viewy', vain, and unamenable to office discipline. To begin with he impressed Northcliffe, but in January 1918 Repington, after repeated disagreements over the sub-editing of his articles by the Editor and others, resigned and joined the *Morning Post*. Northcliffe, at a later date, refused to reinstate him.

(ii) The 'Knock-out' Policy

Northcliffe's power during the First World War was immeasurably greater than that of any other newspaper proprietor in the country. In all his campaigns the *Daily Mail*, with its circulation of nearly a million, was used to influence the masses, putting the case with Northcliffe's characteristically unbridled vehemence. Dawson in *The Times* provided the follow-up with moderate, reasoned argument aimed at the governing classes. On all major issues, such as conscription and the need for a stronger government organization to fight the war, the two papers functioned in concert. On minor issues, particularly in the case of attacks on individuals, *The Times* might pursue its own line. The combination of the two papers exerted a formidable influence which neither the Government nor individual politicians like Lloyd George could ignore.

The two papers sometimes aroused violent hostility, but Northcliffe was prepared to sacrifice both popularity and circulation if he thought this necessary in the public interest. Because of an attack on Kitchener the *Daily Mail* was burned in public, while *The Times* found itself banned from service clubs.

The main objective for which the Northcliffe press campaigned was all-out prosecution of the war ending with the total defeat of Germany – the 'knock-out' policy as Lloyd George called it. This was by no means the tone of Asquith's Governments (Coalition after 26 May 1915). In the First World War, as in the Second, there was an element of 'business as usual' during the opening stages. This, Northcliffe did his best to fight.

The Northcliffe press set itself four cardinal war aims, which it adopted early on in the war and consistently pursued:

1. The improvement of the munitions industry in order to ensure an adequate supply of shells, especially high explosive, to the forces.

2. The introduction of conscription.

3. Support for the advancement of Lloyd George into positions of greater power and responsibility – the Ministry of Munitions, the War Office, and finally the Prime Ministership.

4. Opposition to attempts at a compromise peace.

At no stage of the war was the influence of *The Times* more apparent than in the days of crisis which led to the resignation of Asquith and the formation of Lloyd George's Coalition Government. In this drama Dawson's leader of 4 December 1916, one of the most famous ever published in *The Times*, played a key part. But the circumstances in which it was written continue to puzzle historians. Was it deliberately prompted by Lloyd George, as Asquith believed, or was it an example of Dawson's capacity for following the game very closely for some days and then suddenly relying on intuition to choose the moment to strike?

The year 1916 was a bad year for the Allies, particularly for Britain. Heavy casualties on the Somme, the disappointment of Jutland, disasters in the Dardanelles and Mesopotamia, the death at sea of Lord Kitchener – all combined to weaken the reputation of the Asquith Government. As this was a coalition of parties, the stresses showed secretly inside the Cabinet rather than publicly in parliamentary debate. Thus the press, and particularly its largest component, the Northcliffe press, became the principal vehicle for public criticism of government. Furthermore, it was clear to all the politicians that in any proposed government reconstruction the support of the Northcliffe press would be essential.

Matters came to a head in mid-November. This is not the place to give a blow-by-blow account of the fall of the Asquith Government; suffice it to say that almost everybody concerned agreed that a small inner war council or committee, consisting of three, four, or at most five members, should be constituted to prosecute the day-to-day conduct of the war. Some thought that this committee could function without the removal of Asquith as Prime Minister; others that there should be a clean sweep. Should this happen the most obvious successors to Asquith were Bonar Law, the leader of the Unionist (Conservative) Ministers in the Coalition, or Lloyd George, who had proved his worth as an energetic and capable Minister for War. But Bonar Law shrank from a confrontation, while the intentions of Lloyd George were opaque. Both had familiars urging them forward to drastic action. In the case of Law this was his fellow Canadian, Max Aitken, at that time a rich, influential but freelancing backbench Tory MP, who was secretly acquiring the controlling shares in the *Daily Express*. At Lloyd George's elbow was Sir Edward Carson, the rebel Unionist who had resigned from the Government in October through discontent over its handling both of the Irish question and of the war. Further to stiffen the resistance to Asquith, Aitken had access to Lloyd George. In his capacity as Canadian military representative overseas he had acquired a room in the War Office, which gave him that geographical propinquity to the

Minister so useful to an intriguer. Carson, it wil be recalled, was a member of the Milner-Robinson 'ginger group'.

On Monday, 27 November 1916, the beginning of the week in which the crisis was to break in earnest, Dawson recorded in the diary: 'An immense series of interviews at the Office . . . & an important dinner at F.S. O[liver]s, Ld. M[ilner], Carson, W.A[stor], and Henry [Wilson] at wh. we definitely counselled the much harassed Carson to pull L.G. out rather than go on w. the present indecision about everything.'

One of the Editor's concerns was the relationship between Lloyd George and Northcliffe. Although the Chief was whole-heartedly in support of a thoroughgoing reconstruction of government he was not on good terms with the Minister for War. He supported the generals against the politicians, and Lloyd George's Liberal colleagues took good care to ensure that he knew this by repeating malicious gossip. 'I would as soon go for a sunny evening stroll round Walton Heath with a grasshopper,' Lloyd George told Aitken, 'as try and work with Northcliffe.'

So on Thursday, 30 November, the Editor records:

> I got hold of Northcliffe later in the day – his weekly visit to London – and impressed him with the importance of having no minor squabble w. L.G. at a moment when it was really necessary to reconstruct the Govt. and only L.G. cd. do it. He undertook to see him tomorrow.

Northcliffe was as good as his word. Frances Stevenson, Lloyd George's secretary and mistress, observed vindictively in her diary for 1 December: 'Northcliffe has turned up again, grovelling, and trying to be friends with D. [Lloyd George] again.' At this meeting Northcliffe pledged his backing to Lloyd George as the only man who could save the country.

During the week Dawson continued to urge 'my old point about the proper form of Govt. for war'. He kept in touch with Lloyd George through Arthur Lee, the Minister's secretary. His Saturday morning leader was particularly harsh, indeed insulting, to the Asquith Government. On Saturday morning he had a talk with Milner who had seen Lloyd George two days before. But since then much had happened. Lloyd George had submitted to Asquith a written proposal for a War Committee of three members, one of whom was to be chairman. The Prime Minister was to be excluded from the committee, 'which was to have full powers, subject to the supreme control of the Prime Minister, to direct all questions connected with the war'.* Asquith replied the same day accepting most of the proposals but insisting that the Prime Minister must be chairman. The situation was thus deadlocked.

* Roy Jenkins: *Asquith*. Collins, 1964.

To continue the Editor's diary, for Saturday, 2 December:

> A talk w. Ld. Milner, to whom Asquith was now almost affectionate in his appeals for help, a visit to the Aunts, & a brief lunch w. N. & Leo [Amery]. N. had seen L.G. whose ultimatum was apparently unsatisfactory to the P.M. Thence to Eton... to see an excellent field game... Taxi'd out to Cliveden to dine & sleep.

Next morning he records 'Up late after writing late.' He was writing the draft of the leader for Monday, or at any rate a portion of it.

Sunday was the crucial day. That afternoon Asquith and Lloyd George reached agreement on a formula for the War Committee by which the former could remain Prime Minister and Lloyd George stay within the Government as chairman of the committee. The Prime Minister would have supreme control of war policy, with the right of veto and the right to attend, but would not be a member of the committee. This was in fact a concession to Lloyd George, induced no doubt by a visit from Bonar Law earlier in the day which convinced Asquith – rightly or wrongly – that the Unionist Ministers had now definitely come down on the side of Lloyd George.

Next morning, Asquith read Dawson's leader in *The Times*. This stated that the country was now in sight of the small War Council which the paper had always pressed for. The gist of Lloyd George's proposal, the Editor went on to say, was that Asquith himself would not be a member – 'the assumption being that the Prime Minister has sufficient cares of a more general character without devoting himself wholly . . . to the daily task of organizing victory'. His closest supporters, the leader went on, must have convinced the Prime Minister that his own qualities 'are fitted better, as they are fond of saying, to "preserve the unity of the nation" (though we have never doubted its unity) than to force the pace of a War Council'.

With this ineffable flip of contempt the Editor completed the destruction of the Asquith Government. When the Prime Minister read it in the morning he jumped to the conclusion that he had been double-crossed by Lloyd George, who, he deduced, had betrayed the secret of Sunday's agreement to Northcliffe. He therefore revoked that agreement, and on Tuesday resigned, in the hope of being able to form a new government with himself as Prime Minister. In this hope he was disappointed. By this time Asquith's credit had sunk too low and it was Lloyd George who formed the new government.

Did Lloyd George leak to *The Times*? Dawson always maintained that the only person with whom he had communication before writing the leader was Carson. Yet it must be admitted that the circumstantial evidence of the diaries is incriminatory. Lloyd George saw Asquith between 4 and 6.30 p m when he returned to the War Office and met Northcliffe. Here is the relevant entry from Dawson's diary for the day:

> ...back to the office [from Cliveden] at 4 for a strenuous night. I was again writing intermittently till nearly 1.30. A visit to Carson and dined w. N. who had again seen L.G. But the situation changed fr. hour to hour & Asquith announced 'reconstruction' at midnight ...

If the Editor did know about the agreement, he could hardly have heard of it from Carson who evidently saw him before Asquith and Lloyd George had met. On the other hand he could, on the timing, have heard it from Northcliffe, if Lloyd George had indeed told the latter when he saw him at 6.30 pm.

Lloyd George, Dawson, and Northcliffe have all left evidence on the subject. Lloyd George, in his *War Memoirs*, maintained that he 'had not communicated any information as to the negotiations which were going on with Mr. Asquith or the agreement arrived at with him to the proprietor or editor of that paper [*The Times*] either directly or indirectly'. Dawson, in a memorandum dated 16 December, stated categorically: '[The leader] was absolutely "uninspired"...I had not seen, or held any communication with, Lloyd George himself for several weeks. Carson, on the other hand, I had seen constantly.' Northcliffe apparently told Tom Clarke of the *Daily Mail* on the Monday that he 'came to town, saw L.G., and then wrote a two column article on the political crisis'. In 1931, according to A. J. P. Taylor, in his life of Beaverbrook, Wickham Steed wrote to Lady Asquith assuring her that Lloyd George was guiltless.

The credibility of these witnesses is, of course, variable. The Editor's memoranda, even when written after the event, are reliable, though it is conceivable that in this instance his wish to play down Northcliffe's exaggerated claims led him to over-emphasize his own independence. Tom Clarke's story is too garbled to be considered as serious evidence. Steed's letter was written many years after the happenings it refers to, and it is by no means certain that Dawson, who was a secretive man, would have confided in his Foreign Editor.

Internal evidence tends to exonerate Lloyd George and to confirm the Editor's testimony. To a suspicious man like Asquith the leader certainly bore the inference that the writer had inside information, though this is nowhere explicit. The influence of Carson is apparent in the leader:

> We may be allowed to add that he [Lloyd George] has also a great opportunity of re-establishing a personal position which has, perhaps necessarily, been obliterated by recent political

events. It must be counted as fortunate that a period of quasi-opposition has never broken Mr Bonar Law's old relations with Sir Edward Carson. The latter – most unwillingly, we are sure so far as his personal inclinations go – forms an essential part of Mr Lloyd George's scheme of reform.

It is also curious, to say the least, that Dawson, if he had positive knowledge of the true situation, did not bring the Parliamentary Correspondent's story up-to-date. This, running alongside the leader, stated: 'At night matters stood thus. The Prime Minister had not accepted Mr Lloyd George's proposal . . .' The Editor was never backward in revising the Parliamentary Correspondent's story. In those days he occasionally wrote it himself.

Historians in general have acquitted Lloyd George of intentionally leaking to *The Times*. But one would still like to know what he said to Northcliffe, what Northcliffe guessed as a result of the meeting, and what he passed on to the Editor over dinner before the latter returned to Printing House Square to polish up his leader.

On Monday evening (4 December), the 'ginger group' had their weekly dinner. 'Asquith was still negotiating. The point now was to keep L.G. firm and this Carson was doing.' On Tuesday, when both Asquith and Lloyd George resigned, the Editor 'saw L.G. in *articulo resignationis*', and there were further talks with him throughout the week. In Lloyd George's reconstructed government Carson got the Admiralty, but not a seat on the War Council. However, in the Editor's eyes, this was more than balanced by the appointment of Lord Milner to the Council as Minister without Portfolio. 'The breadth and sincerity of his judgment, his wide outlook, and his firmness of purpose fit him exactly for the duty to which he is called,' proclaimed *The Times*.

With two out of its half-dozen members appointed Ministers the 'ginger group' had not come badly out of the fray. However there was one more annoyance the Editor had to bear before the dust settled. On 12 December one of Northcliffe's other papers, the *Globe*, came out with an article headed 'The Greatest Dictator – Lord Northcliffe's supreme journalistic feat'. The article declared:

> Lord Northcliffe has just brought down the Asquith Cabinet . . . the fact remains that it was after reading the now famous leader in Monday's *Times* that Mr Asquith sent in his resignation. By that alone Lord Northcliffe . . . has achieved probably the greatest feat in history. He has out-lioned all the famous lions of *The Times* itself . . .

The Editor had the fortune – or misfortune – to overhear the Chief congratulating the author on this effusion.

(iii) Dawson Resigns

The years following the government crisis of 1916 saw a change in the relationship between Northcliffe and the Editor. 'The Chief' became more concerned with his role as a public figure than with that as a newspaper proprietor. In 1917 he left England for the United States as leader of the British War Mission there. Colonel House, President Wilson's confidential adviser, considered that Northcliffe did more than any other Englishman to bring America into the war. On his return, Lloyd George offered him the post of Secretary of State for Air, but he declined, publishing his refusal in a letter to *The Times* attacking members of the Government. However, in February 1918 Northcliffe accepted the post of Director of Propaganda in Enemy Countries. This was then a novel form of warfare which he had long urged upon the authorities without success. 'Our business,' a member of the General Staff had commented earlier when rejecting the proposal, 'is to kill Germans'.

Meanwhile *The Times* was again ailing. In spite of five price changes in five years, circulation was falling and the paper's finances were unsteady. Northcliffe's health, too, was deteriorating and he was becoming increasingly erratic, though it would be difficult to pinpoint the stage at which eccentricity gave way to mental unbalance. Dawson was just as strong a character as Northcliffe, and having inherited the property in Yorkshire was financially independent. Northcliffe's long absences had accustomed him to running the office in his own way. As soon as the war ended the Chief began once more to deluge him with comments, criticisms, and instructions. Northcliffe was becoming more frustrated and the Editor less patient and less easily moved. They were heading for a clash.

The causes of friction were both personal and political. The latter have been more publicized, but the personal resentments may well have been deeper, because less openly expressed. In any case, persons and policies were identified with each other in Northcliffe's mind. Once more he turned against Lloyd George, whereas Dawson remained faithful to Milner, Astor and the 'ginger group', which continued to support the Prime Minister.

Dawson spent much of his leisure time at Cliveden with the Astors, a friendship which Northcliffe had always resented. Now it was reported to him that Dawson had joined in 'disloyal' criticisms of his Proprietor at the Astors' table. It appears that someone who was a regular guest at Cliveden was in the habit of repeating Dawson's conversation to Lord Rothermere, who disliked what he termed 'strong editors' and passed on the gist to his brother, Northcliffe, who sent Campbell Stuart, Managing Director of *The Times*, to remonstrate, accusing Dawson of discussing his private life at dinner parties – a subject on which he was of course vulnerable. Dawson did not take the accusation well. North-cliffe, on his side, was conscious that with all his power, his money, and his brilliance he had failed to win that acceptance within the British Establishment which Dawson's less spectacular but more solid qualities secured for him.

There were a number of reasons for Northcliffe's now fanatical hostility to Lloyd George. To begin with he had thought that Lloyd George intended to preserve his department after the Armistice to act as a public relations organization for the Paris Peace Conference. This plan never materialized. During a private talk between the two men Lloyd George gained the impression that Northcliffe wanted something more – namely a permanent place on the British Peace Delegation itself. It seems extremely improbable that this is what Northcliffe intended to convey, but the two men had a capacity for misunderstanding each other and the incident widened the rift.

Another cause of discord was Northcliffe's nagging the Prime Minister to supply him in advance with a list of proposed Ministers as a condition of support from the Northcliffe press in the general election at the end of 1918. Yet another cause of offence was Milner, always suspect because of his German blood and German schooling and still a Minister in Lloyd George's Government. He gave a press interview just before the Armistice in which he drew the distinction, often to be echoed in the days of Hitler, between 'good' Germans and 'bad' Germans. To Northcliffe this doctrine was, of course, anathema. Milner, he declared, was 'semi-German'.

For such reasons both Lloyd George and Milner drew upon themselves the wrath of the Northcliffe press. Since Dawson did not join in the vituperation Northcliffe accused him of sacrificing the 'independence' of *The Times*. It is arguable that the Editor's loyalties to Milner influenced him too closely, and that the independence which he was asserting in 1918 was against his stable-mates in the Northcliffe group of newspapers rather than against the Government.

Lloyd George's overwhelming victory in the General Election of December was probably the last straw. 'I beg you to do either one of two things – endeavour to see eye to eye with me, or to relinquish your position,' wrote Northcliffe soon afterwards. In February 1919 Dawson resigned. 'Parting with dear Robin,' wrote the Chief to the new Editor, Wickham Steed, 'is a personal grief to me.' He was perfectly sincere when he used these words. His relationship with J. L. Garvin, another editor with whom he had parted company, had proved many years back that his friendships could survive professional ruptures. Dawson had been his own choice for the editorship, and the best choice since Delane. They had weathered many disagreements and achieved many successes in the eight years of their partnership.

From Dawson's standpoint he chose the right time to leave. Wickham Steed would have to cope with the chaos created by the final disintegration of the Chief Proprietor's personality. By disassociating himself from Northcliffe at this time Dawson saved himself a great deal of mental wear and tear and ensured his own return to the Chair when the Chief died three years later.

18 THE DEATH OF NORTHCLIFFE

(i) Wickham Steed as Editor

Wickham Steed, like Chenery, was promoted into the Chair after a quarter of a century's service on the staff, whereas Delane, Buckle and Dawson had all been specially selected and groomed for the part. Also, like Chenery, Steed was a savant; but there the likeness ended. The new Editor, aged forty-eight at the time of his appointment, was an arresting personality, with wit, panache, and style. Tall, handsome, with a small, neatly trimmed beard, he seemed to his fellow countrymen the pattern of a cosmopolitan Englishman. He was a great conversationalist, lighting up any company in which he appeared, and could keep a discussion going in three or four languages at once.

His education had been entirely different from that of other editors of *The Times*. The son of a solicitor's clerk in East Anglia, he had attended Sudbury Grammar School but had received the main part of his education in German universities and at the Sorbonne. He had, in a long and distinguished career, served the paper in Berlin, Vienna, and Rome, before becoming Foreign Editor. His expertise lay in his understanding of Central European affairs. Just as Dawson understood the Empire, but not Europe, so Steed understood Europe, but not the countries outside it. With America he was unfamiliar, and he failed to foresee the magnitude and permanence of the Russian Revolution.

Steed was a committed man. He believed passionately in self-determination and the rights of small nations. In his approach to the problems of Central Europe he was a Slavophile, and some of his communications reveal anti-Semitic prejudices.

> Five years' experience [he wrote from Vienna before the war],
> has taught me one thing . . . every Jew in this part of the world
> is a strong pro-German . . . I have studied them high and low,
> rich and poor, learned and ignorant – in their heart of hearts
> they are pro-German to a man.

To Wickham Steed there could be no peace in Europe without the dismemberment of the Austro-Hungarian Empire; this was cardinal to his creed. While working in Northcliffe's Department of Propaganda during the war he persuaded his superiors that the propaganda put out should include the promise of independence to the subject peoples of

227

that empire. Though this was done primarily with a view to encouraging desertion from the imperial armies, it also became a long-range policy decision, and so inevitably pre-empted the British stance at the Versailles Peace Conference. Steed did not seem to see – as Lloyd George did – that the fragmentation of Central Europe, by encouraging future German expansionism, was as liable to be a cause of future war as the existence of the Austro-Hungarian Empire had been of the last. Unlike almost all his predecessors in the Chair, Steed's approach to public affairs was logical, almost ideological, rather than pragmatical. It was a symptom of a continental, as opposed to an Oxford, training.

Wickham Steed was a consummate journalist. With unrivalled access to information he combined an intuition that penetrated beyond the known facts. He could be discreet when it paid; but, as will be seen, there was also a streak of Blowitz about him. He was a prolific writer, and in the last phase of his editorship wrote an average of four leaders a week for twenty-three weeks. While this may not seem abnormal for an ordinary leader writer it is a great deal for a man who is also editing a paper.

Steed was not married. An important influence in his life – perhaps not fully realized at the time of his appointment – was his Egeria, Madame Clemence Rose. Madame Rose, who came from the Balkans, acted as hostess for him and was described as his 'political secretary'. That she helped to mould *Times* policy is certain. On coming to London she took a dislike to Lloyd George who she thought had snubbed her. This helped to widen the breach, already serious, between *The Times* and the Prime Minister.

Steed's social, cosmopolitan and slightly Bohemian background was more congenial to Northcliffe than the atmosphere that surrounded Dawson, so redolent of 'Church and King' – always providing it was the King approved by the Editor. The Chief also shared some of Steed's racial feelings; he disliked the Germans and felt at home in France. While Steed was an intellectual anti-Semite, Northcliffe had a crudely contemptuous attitude towards Jews.

Northcliffe had not ousted Dawson in order to install another editor who would thwart him. The Chief Proprietor took good care to extract from the new Editor in advance, as he had from Moberly Bell, complete and unequivocal acknowledgement of his subordination. The Managing Director, Campbell Stuart, after offering the editorship to Steed on Northcliffe's instructions, wrote to the Chief: 'He would regard himself as your trustee as far as the policy of *The Times* was concerned, and would do everything in his power to safeguard and develop your property and especially to guard and increase your reputation.' The words, he adds, are an exact quotation of Steed's message.

This was the most explicit surrender of editorial independence ever made in Printing House Square. But for Steed there was compensation. He was to be responsible for the policy not of *The Times* only, but of Northcliffe's other papers – the *Daily Mail*, the *Evening News*, and the *Weekly Dispatch*. This solved the problem, which had always worried Dawson, of *The Times* being an 'appendage' of the *Mail*. Wickham Steed was, in fact, to be what would later be called 'editorial director' of the Northcliffe press.

In his haste Northcliffe had omitted one step; this was to consult John Walter about the new appointment. Walter, who had been for three years in Spain in charge of British war propaganda, was summoned belatedly to Menton, where Northcliffe had gone to rest. Walter approved of Northcliffe's choice (though probably not of Dawson's resignation), but pointed out that the procedure adopted violated the articles of association of the company by ignoring the Chairman.

During Wickham Steed's editorship *The Times* rendered one of its greatest services to history. The paper may rightly claim to share with King George V a great part of the credit for bringing about the Irish Treaty of 1921, setting up the Irish Free State with the constitutional status of a Dominion. 'It was,' wrote J. A. Spender, 'one of the most powerful efforts in the journalism of my time.'

The Irish question returned to the fore again just before the First World War. Dawson was then Editor and Ireland occupied his mind, as it did those of most of his fellow countrymen, even to the exclusion of the Sarajevo crisis. With his acute knowledge of imperial constitutional issues Dawson could no doubt have made a useful contribution to an Irish settlement, although by then there were fewer options open than in Buckle's day. But the outbreak of war caused legislation to be shelved.

Wickham Steed, with his belief that small nations had a right to be emancipated, brought to bear on Irish problems a mind favourably attuned to the concept of Home Rule. What was right in Central Europe was, in his view, right in the United Kingdom. Nor, in this case, was the Chief Proprietor an obstacle to the Editor. Northcliffe, half Irish himself, had an instinctive grasp of Irish needs. Much more important, however, in Northcliffe's mind was the need for Anglo-American co-operation over the War Debt, over Europe, and above all over a settlement on naval problems and the relationship between England, America and Japan. To obtain these objectives, settlement of the Irish question on terms acceptable to American public opinion was essential. But on this, as on other issues, Northcliffe was not always consistent – the 'grasshopper' in him made its appearance, in Irish affairs, as in everything else. His mother ('the Old Lady of Totteridge') exerted her influence, and she was an ardent Unionist. 'Alfred,' she cabled when he was in Java in the course of a world tour, 'I will not have Ulster coerced.' She was the only living person who could shake him. Cables and letters poured forth from Java, but in his absence Mrs Harmsworth sent for executives of *The Times* and 'gave them a piece of her mind'. However, barring such matriarchal incursions, Steed could generally count on the Chief's support for his Irish policy.

The Editor was also fortunate in having at his right hand as Irish expert a brilliant Irishman who had been introduced into the office by Campbell Stuart. This was Captain R. J. Herbert Shaw, a barrister with a distinguished war record in the Connaught Rangers. In 1916, at the time of the Easter Rising, he had been invalided home and found himself in Dublin. The authorities chose him to be defending officer at the court martial of James Connolly, the Irish socialist leader. Shaw was a high-minded sceptic, a man of vision, with a deep love and human understanding of Ireland and the Irish. Happily, too, he wrote excellent prose. During the whole of the negotiating period in 1920 and 1921 he was able to maintain his underground contacts with the Irish nationalists because of his efforts on behalf of Connolly, and was thus of service not only to *The Times* but to the Government – a good example of the anonymous heroes of Printing House Square.

In their approach to an Irish settlement Wickham Steed and Shaw had to reckon on one serious drawback; Lloyd George was by now pathologically hostile to Northcliffe and *The Times*. Any suggestion emanating from Printing House Square was liable to be *ipso facto* rejected on that account. Steed and Shaw worked out a constitutional blueprint for Ireland which the Editor sent to Lloyd George through an intermediary with the promise:

> You may tell your colleagues in the Cabinet . . . that if the Government will take this scheme as it is, or improve it, they will be able to count upon the support of *The Times* . . . We shall never claim credit for having helped to promote a settlement, if a settlement is reached on such a basis.

So far from responding to Steed, Lloyd George attacked *The Times* for criticizing without offering any constructive alternative.

In a leader four columns long, written jointly by Steed and Shaw, *The Times* now publicly declared its proposals:

> The basis of our suggestions is that there should be created in Ireland two Provincial or State Legislatures. They should be set up by an act in substitution for the Home Rule Act – one Legislature for the three southern provinces, the other for the province of Ulster . . .
>
> Upon the two State Legislatures we suggest there would be bestowed full powers of legislation in all matters affecting the

internal affairs of their respective States . . . There would be provisions for the eventual establishment of an Irish Parliament . . . The reservation to the Parliament of the United Kingdom of the powers not transferred to the Irish State Legislature or to the Irish Parliament . . . necessitates the retention of an Irish representation at Westminster.

This scheme was the basis of the Government of Ireland Bill passed in December 1920, setting up a separate Parliament in Ulster and opening the way to the foundation of the Irish Free State.

Shaw was in contact with the Irish leaders through a Dublin business-man, Patrick Moylett, the envoy in London of Arthur Griffith, later to become first President of the Free State. Meanwhile the Editor kept in touch with Lord Stamfordham, the King's Private Secretary. The burden of his message to the King was that, if George V would take an initiative over an Irish settlement, *The Times* 'would go bail for him'. This precisely is what the King in his tactful way did. In an effort to find an intermediary acceptable to both parties recourse was had to the Dominions, and Field-Marshal Smuts was asked to intervene.

The Anglo-Irish Treaty of 1921 was a much less perfect document than *The Times* blueprint, but the latter had at least served as a con-structive basis for discussion and set the ball rolling. By 1921 any hope of Home Rule for a united Ireland was dead, and had probably died, as Churchill believed, with the final wrecking of Gladstone's Home Rule Bill in the 1890s. Imperfect as the 1921 Treaty was, it gave Ireland peace for nearly fifty years and, until 1969, relieved England of the need for armed intervention. The settlement also contributed, as Lord Northcliffe had hoped, to the flowering of Anglo-American relations between the wars. *The Times* could congratulate itself on the not un-important role it had played in the settlement, and also reflect that it had finally made its *amende honorable* to the shade of Parnell.

(ii) Introduction of Pictures

During Wickham Steed's short editorship much history was made. In the years 1919–22 Europe was in process of being refashioned after the First World War, and the Editor and *The Times* played their part in covering the Paris Peace Conference and the other conferences which emanated from it.

But this period also saw an important technical innovation which caused a stir in the printing department at *The Times*. In fact it was Northcliffe, not Steed, who was responsible for the formation of the picture department. In later years the paper was famed for its pictures as being some of the best photo-reproductions of any daily paper in the world, but at the time the introduction of pictures encountered much opposition both within the office and from readers. Northcliffe was not deterred by this obscurantist attitude, and it is another tribute to this remarkable man that he successfully forced through the complicated but successful embellishment of the paper in spite of political preoccupations, illness, and approaching insanity and death. The human instrument of this office revolution was U. V. Bogaerde, and the story of his achievement is as dramatic in its own setting of the newspaper world as are some of the parts that have been played by his son Dirk Bogarde on the screen.

Northcliffe – who had been the pioneer of the picture paper when he published the *Daily Mirror* in 1903 – had always intended to introduce pictures to *The Times*. When he bought the paper in 1908 there had been dark rumours among older readers, who already objected to black and white line drawings in advertisements, that he would make a 'three-penny Mirror' of *The Times*. The objections seem strange considering that fine drawings of ships, funerary catafalques and housing schemes had been printed in *The Times* in the early nineteenth century.

For the time being, Northcliffe held his hand. But in 1912, when he had already made up his mind that radical changes were needed, he took the first steps towards introducing a picture department. J. O. P. Bland, whom he had brought in to reorganize the mechanical side, was authorized to hire Bogaerde, who had been working as a designer of stained-glass windows, to improve the line drawings, and a year later T. W. Lascelles, who was producing photogravures on *The Illustrated London News*, was recruited to print pictures for *The Times Weekly Edition*. The two were installed in an iron birdcage in the basement to experiment with mechanical screens and photogravure cameras. So secret was their work that only the two inmates had keys to their cage.

The war called a halt to these experiments – but Northcliffe did not give up. He was much impressed by the use the Germans made of press photography as propaganda, and until he was mobilized in 1917 Bogaerde was employed as Art Editor and press photographer for *The Times History of the War*. For this publication, which was Northcliffe's brainchild, he took photographs of the damage after the German bombardment of Scarborough and the Hartlepools. In the army Bogaerde continued to exercise his calling. He was employed by the Royal Artillery to make reconnaissance drawings from aircraft over the German trench system at Passchendaele.

In March 1919, when Bogaerde returned to *The Times*, Northcliffe pressed on with his plans for producing pictures in *The Times Weekly Edition*. The cover page on 25 July consisted of a photograph of the Peace Procession passing down Whitehall. From the first number he was insistent that women's fashions should be presented.

From the *Weekly*, pictures spread to *The Times* itself. Northcliffe's first idea was to produce illustrated insets, but this idea was abandoned because it took three days' work to produce one inset. Instead, scattered individual photographs were introduced for special occasions; these included the Royal visit to Belfast in 1920 and the crew of the Vickers-Vimy biplane which attempted, on behalf of *The Times*, to fly from Cairo to Cape Town. Photographs were also introduced into the estate pages to attract advertisers.

On 1 March 1922 the Chief, recently returned from his world tour, decided to consummate his plans. This he did in his usual theatrical fashion. At eight o'clock in the morning Bogaerde received a telephone call ordering him to prepare a full page of topical news pictures for publication in the next day's *Times*. The page proof, complete with captions, was to be submitted to Lord Northcliffe for approval by midday at his house in Carlton House Gardens.

By telephone and taxi Bogaerde rounded up staff, engravers and picture agencies so that he was able to bring the proof, still wet, to the Chief, only five minutes late. Northcliffe examined the pictures, rejecting one but passing the rest. Bogaerde noticed that the Chief had prudently invited George Isaacs, the printing trades union leader, to be present at the little ceremony, which concluded with Northcliffe's instruction that the page should be printed that night and that from now on there should be a full page of pictures in *The Times* on every day of the week.

These instructions were faithfully implemented, though not without opposition from inside Printing House Square. Lints Smith, the Manager, and Murray Brumwell, the Deputy Editor, sent for Bogaerde and told him that he had been gravely disloyal to the Editor and management in going behind their back to Northcliffe. The night staff tried to overturn the forme of the new picture page on its way to the foundry. Northcliffe was compelled to intervene personally to secure the necessary staff, equipment and accommodation for Bogaerde, now appointed 'Art Editor'. So long as he was still in the country the Chief continued to visit or telephone the new department daily; it was his last great contribution to the paper.

Readers wrote in to object to the innovation. But the picture page continued to appear six days a week and, like the light leader, in due course took its place as an institution in the national life of Britain.

The Chief did not live to see that day. In July Bogaerde, by chance, caught a glimpse of him on the last occasion in which he was seen in public. The Art Editor was saying goodbye to some friends at Victoria Station when he noticed a group near the continental arrivals platform. He was shocked to see Northcliffe stumbling through the barrier, supported on either side by two of his travelling companions. The Chief was returning to his London house to die.

(iii) Steed Falls from Favour

Despite the successes of *The Times* during his editorship, Wickham Steed did not enjoy an easy three years. Northcliffe was breaking up physically, and the effects on his mind were evident. His throat, his heart, and his eyes all gave him trouble. Steed believed that he had syphilis, and possibly Northcliffe believed it himself. The numerous doctors who attended him, however, have insisted, both officially and in private, that there were no traces of the disease and no reliable evidence has been produced since to prove them mistaken or untruthful. For Northcliffe's generation syphilis held a morbid fascination. It was a 'judgment'. Northcliffe's friend J. L. Garvin used sombrely to hint at the 'fearful price' which he paid for his fondness for women, but the fact is that a Wasserman test proved negative.

Steed began to fall out of favour. 'Pinhead' was Northcliffe's favourite epithet for him now. The Chief complained unceasingly of the financial burden of *The Times* and at the end of 1920 threatened to sell it. Steed believed that the prospective purchaser was Rothermere, but Northcliffe may have been bluffing. If he really had any such intention the family believed that his mother put a stop to it. Steed had a different version. He reported the story to Sir Robert Hudson, the friend of Lady Northcliffe, in the belief that he would pass it on and that she would then intervene with her husband. This, he concluded, is what happened.

Then, capriciously, the Chief veered round. He was all smiles, and in July 1921 dragged the Editor off, at a few hours' notice, on the first leg of a world tour. In the United States the two were responsible for a well-publicized fiasco. On their arrival the New York journalists naturally wanted to interview the world's most famous newspaper proprietor. Northcliffe could not resist the publicity but he also wanted to play golf and so deputed Steed to do the talking. The Editor, unfamiliar with American journalism, fell into an elementary trap. After giving an anodyne interview to the *New York Times* he added some indiscreet remarks 'off the record' which the interviewer published in a separate message. They included an account of an alleged exchange between King George V and Lloyd George, which ran as follows:

'Are you going to shoot all the people in Ireland?'

'No, your Majesty,' the Premier replied.

'Well, then,' said the King 'you must come to some agreement with them ... I cannot have my people killed in this manner.'

Further to confuse matters, Northcliffe, without having read the text, instructed the New York office of *The Times* to cable the interview to London as given not by Steed but by himself personally. Campbell Stuart killed this message in London as soon as he saw it, but he was not quite quick enough; it slipped into the early edition of the *Daily Mail*, which naturally went to Ireland, the place where such an indiscretion was most likely to do harm.

Steed's anecdote was in essence true, but its publication left Palace and Premier little choice but to deny it completely. Northcliffe was made to look a fool in public. Rothermere blamed Wickham Steed and advised his brother to sack him. Any two junior reporters who had contrived to get themselves into the position that Steed and Northcliffe had landed themselves in would indeed have been fired.

In the spring of 1922 Northcliffe once more drove the Editor out of London, this time to the Genoa Conference. Here again Steed gaffed. He reported that in a confidential talk with Barthou, leader of the French delegation, Lloyd George had denounced the Entente. Steed probably divined the spirit of the talk correctly, but unfortunately he confused the details, and this put him in a weak position when he was officially repudiated by both men. Lloyd George took especial satisfaction in catching out *The Times*. In his memoirs Steed claimed that he had documents to prove that he was right but he was unable to vindicate himself publicly at the time. Northcliffe now found another epithet for Steed – besides 'pinhead', he was a 'dupe'. 'Arrange for Steed's resignation,' he wired to Campbell Stuart. No doubt Steed after all this time in the office had rather lost his touch as a foreign correspondent.

The Editor was not the only one who was finding life difficult with Northcliffe. By May 1922 John Walter was finding it so unbearable that he was driven into an act of surprising folly. He decided to sell out his shares to the Chief Proprietor and thereby sever all further connexion with *The Times*. Northcliffe purchased the shares on 7 June, and it was agreed and confirmed in writing on 15 June that Walter's option to purchase Northcliffe's own shares on his death should be forfeited. Northcliffe asked him to continue as Chairman, but this Walter declined to do.

The timing could hardly have been worse, for by now most of those concerned realized that Northcliffe was displaying symptoms of mental derangement. Ironically Walter, the Chairman of the company, was the last to learn the truth; and when he did, he tried desperately to prevent the completion of the sale on the grounds that Northcliffe was not of sound mind when the deal was agreed. The lawyers ruled against him. He tried also to recover the option in return for the withdrawal of his refusal to continue as Chairman, but received no answer from Northcliffe.

By this time it was too late. In a matter of weeks Northcliffe was dead, but Walter meanwhile had thrown away his right to repurchase on favourable terms the enterprise with which his family had been associated since 1785. Only great good fortune was to save him from the consequences of this decision.

(iv) Northcliffe's Madness

On Thursday, 25 May 1922, Northcliffe went abroad. The object of his journey was to write a series of articles on Germany. Since his normal behaviour was so eccentric, people still found difficulty in recognizing that he was on the brink of a total breakdown. But before he left England three people closely associated with him had been forced to this conclusion – they were his solicitor, his head gardener, and the gardener's wife who was the housekeeper. The solicitor, Sir Charles Russell, warned that Northcliffe was 'so abnormal that he considered him incapable of business and unlikely to live long'. At Elmswood, the country house in Thanet which he had bought in 1890 with the profits from his successful popular weekly *Answers*, Northcliffe sent for the gardener and announced that arsonists were coming down from London to set fire to the house. The couple were so alarmed by his behaviour that they gave notice.

Northcliffe set out for Germany in his Blue Butterfly Rolls-Royce, accompanied by Pine, the chauffeur who had been with him most of his life, by Sandy Thomson, his golf professional, and by a temporary valet, William Brown. As they sped along the pavé from Boulogne to Brussels the Chief pulled out a pistol and made target practice on the trees. A Walter Mitty spirit had entered into him: 'I shoot from the hip,' he said.

In Brussels he ate some ice-cream, which upset his stomach. This was a mishap which was to loom larger in his mind as the days wore on. Northcliffe's delusions harked back to his past life. His obsessions, conscious or unconscious, expressed or suppressed, were struggling out into the open. Suspicion of Germany was one, and he became convinced that Germans had poisoned his ice-cream.

From Brussels he pursued a zig-zag course to Cologne and Boulogne, where Douglas Reed, then a junior member of the staff in charge of the telephone system, was sent by *The Times* to act as secretary. He found the Chief living in a back room under the alias of Leonard Brown. After a few days of some very odd dictation Northcliffe gave him £150 and told him to go back to London to buy himself a silver-fitted crocodile suitcase. By the time he left Boulogne Northcliffe's condition had taken a marked turn for the worse. He conceived the idea that Douglas Reed had attacked him with a bottle of Perrier water. This hallucination again was symbolic of his anxieties. All his life he had been plagued with demands for money from his crippled brother St John, who had bought the firm of Perrier and never succeeded in making a real business success of it.

The departure from Boulogne on Saturday was spectacular. According to the valet, William Brown, Northcliffe had collected a crowd at the station, insulted the railway officials, and loudly declared that Reed had accused him and William Brown of homosexuality and also that he had attempted to assassinate him.

Steed, summoned from London, went round to Northcliffe's hotel in Paris on Sunday evening. There he was met by Gouldie, the *Daily Mail* representative, who had just been appointed to succeed Lints Smith as Manager of *The Times*. Gouldie warned him to be prepared for a shock. 'The Chief is not himself,' he said. The Editor found Northcliffe in bed, in a darkened room. He seized Steed by the hand, and related the story of the attempted assassination with a Perrier bottle. Reed, he was convinced, was a partisan of Lloyd George. Previously, he told Steed, he had been poisoned by the Germans. He then showed his tongue, which was black. His lower lip bore a black scab 'as though it had been burned'. 'His eyes,' noted the Editor in a long memorandum dictated on 17 June, 'were wild, and I noticed, when for a moment the light was turned on, that his left eye had a strange squint in an upward diagonal direction.'

After discussing a niece of Lady Northcliffe's who had caused him much anxiety in Germany by becoming engaged to a middle-aged army officer, the Chief then went on to assure Steed that he loved him dearly, though he had given him great trouble. If he wanted to leave, he could have £100,000 or £200,000 down. The attempts to remove him from the editorship had been the work of 'rascals like Mr John Walter and villains like Lints Smith,' who had tried 'to jew him' out of a £50,000 contract for £5,000. He then accused Steed of speaking in the most disgusting way about Lady Northcliffe. She and all her friends, as well as all his friends and the whole of *The Times* staff, were in revolt against Steed. Nevertheless he, Northcliffe, intended to support him.

At 8.30 next morning Northcliffe and his entourage left to join Lady Northcliffe at Evian, travelling in a special railway coach provided by the Manager of the P.L.M. The journey gave no respite to Steed or his companions. In the special carriage, wrote Steed, Northcliffe hid until the train started. Then:

> He summoned Mr Sisley Huddleston, Paris correspondent of *The Times*, to his compartment, and told him that he was no gentleman because he had a red silk pocket handkerchief, his teeth were bad, and his mouth stank. Mr Sisley Huddleston was much upset by this reception, and left the train at Dijon. Lord Northcliffe consented to his departure, but declared that Mr Huddleston's railway fare must not be paid.

For nine hours of the journey, Steed sat with Northcliffe in his private compartment, while the latter dictated telegrams and talked incessantly. Part of his conversation, Steed recalled, was filthy beyond repetition, but 'in it there were intervals of uncanny lucidity'. At luncheon Northcliffe told dirty stories to the telephonist, Miss Rudge. 'Did I go a little too far with that girl? Don't you think I am mad? Am I mad?'

On arrival at Evian he had his first meeting with his wife:

> Lady Northcliffe, who saw him immediately, told me afterwards that he had been rude to her. She was much upset. He also refused to see Sir Frederick Treves, calling him an old imbecile. Sir Frederick Treves summoned the local French doctor . . . A strong injection of morphia quietened Lord Northcliffe for a time . . . but he continued to talk until 1 a m. He had in fact been talking almost without a break since 5 a m on the Monday morning.

Even so, the unhappy Editor was summoned by the Chief at seven o'clock the next morning and reviled for appearing unshaven.

Still the spate of telegrams carrying instructions to London continued. Steed's problem was to warn *The Times* and the *Daily Mail* what the real situation was. He dispatched a telegram to *The Times*:

> From Wickham Steed . . . Disregard entirely unpublish anything received directly or indirectly from here unless signed at beginning and at end by George Sutton or by me. Warn Daily Mail.

But, with the cunning of the lunatic, Northcliffe read his mind: 'Somebody in London is playing me tricks.' He dictated a telegram purporting to come from Steed himself. It ran as follows:

> Lints Smith Times London
> From Wickham Steed . . . You are a rascal and a thief. I will have the law on you. If you don't leave the office immediately I will come with the police to turn you out. Acknowledge receipt to me here. Wickham Steed, Hotel Royal, Evian-les-Bains.

Steed took this to the Post Office and substituted a harmless message of identical length. Immediately he returned, Northcliffe asked for the receipt, which he took from Steed. 'Quite right – forty-nine words!'

There now occurred an incident which remained, and still does, a subject for historical dispute. While in Paris Steed had wired for help from Northcliffe's oldest friend and factotum, Sir George Sutton. Although this angered the Chief, he sent Steed to the station at Bellegarde to meet him. According to Steed's account, during his absence a nerve specialist was summoned from Lausanne and examined Northcliffe in company with the local French doctor. When Steed got back to the hotel, the specialist had already left. But the French doctor told him that he had signed a certificate to the effect that Lord Northcliffe was out of his mind. This is the only record of his ever having been medically certified insane. Afterwards the Harmsworth family cast doubt on the authenticity of the story. As, a little later, the patient was so rude to the French doctor that he too left, the certificate was never seen, nor does anybody appear to have remembered the names of either doctor. Those who discredit the story point out that Wickham Steed could have had motives for proving the Chief insane. Some of the insults hurled at him were, like so much of Northcliffe's ravings, not wholly divorced from fact. Steed's reputation as a journalist had been injured by the New York and Genoa interviews. In the previous month he had been virtually sacked.

But in general the Editor's narrative stands up to scrutiny. Most of what he relates took place in front of witnesses; much is corroborated by documents which have survived. Whether Northcliffe was certified or not, Steed evidently believed that he was insane, since while passing through Paris on his journey home, he requested the authorities not to put difficulties in the way of the patient's return through France, as they well might have done if the certification had been notified to them.

After Wickham Steed's departure from Evian on 15 June Northcliffe still had two months to live. He was brought back to his London home, 1 Carlton House Gardens, where he was immured in a bedroom in the care of male nurses. But even so, the drama was not ended. The house was full of telephones. Most of these were cut off. Despite this he managed from time to time to elude his guardians and communicate with the outside world.

Lints Smith – still occupying the Manager's chair in defiance of repeated dismissals – received one morning the transcript of a telephone message from the Chief. The recipient was George Beer, the news editor.

> Do you know that Steed's private telephone is still connected [it ran]. Will you have it cut off at once. Do it yourself.
>
> Have you seen Gordon Robbins in Fleet St. wearing a tall hat, strutting up and down. He has been trying to become editor of the *Daily Mail* with a salary of £5000 a year. But he won't. He has been rude – that young man has – to my relatives. Find out why he wears a tall hat. Tall hats are only to be worn on special occasions. I know more than you think. My men tell me.

Lord Northcliffe then went on to instruct Beer to have Wickham Steed, Douglas Reed, and Price (his secretary) turned out by the police. 'This fellow Reed. Do you *know him*? . . . Tried to knock my eye out. If I had had my gun I would have taken his leg off.

'Have you got these instructions? You have a very very great opportunity my dear boy. Have you courage? Are you a shrimp or a brewer?'

'This,' George Beer interpolated, 'refers to the fact which he undoubtedly remembered that the inns of Broadstairs (near his home Elmswood) were plastered with Shrimp Brown Beer made by the Gravesend Brewery and that I was born at Gravesend.'

More serious, however, than these lunatic exchanges was his successful attempt to smuggle out a new will. Northcliffe, a rich man with a large family, many friends and no heir, was continually making amendments to his will. The will operative at this time had been drawn up in March 1919. Its principal features were that the estate was divided up into hundredths and the income was allotted to legatees in units of these hundredths. Three points in it are of significance to this story. First the will of 1919 preserved the option on *The Times* for John Walter. This would not have mattered, of course, had not John Walter forgone his option in *The Times* agreement by selling his shares. It was for him a second, and unexpected, line of defence in claiming the option. Secondly, the will penalized Lady Northcliffe should she remarry. As she had almost certainly formed the intention of marrying Sir Robert Hudson after her husband's death she had a strong motive for persuading him to make a new will before he died. Thirdly, Sir Campbell Stuart, the Managing Director of *The Times*, was given a small legacy. As Managing Director he had no *locus standi* over disputing Northcliffe's will; as a beneficiary he did. It was to be useful to him in the next fight for ownership of the paper.

While at Evian, Northcliffe had stated that he would probably have to make an entirely new kind of will. He had sent for a copy of his existing one. But Wickham Steed had not transmitted the request. Early in July, according to the affidavit of a male nurse, Leslie Richardson, Northcliffe made a new will which he scribbled in pencil. He asked Richardson to witness it. The nurse stated that he complied in order to humour him. One of the doctors, Seymour Price, found it lying on a table.

The new will was a short one. In the preamble, the patient referred to himself as 'being in good mental state, though suffering from one dangerous disease, Indian Jungle Fever, and another unknown to any doctors in Great Britain, poisoning by ice-cream supplied on the Belgian Frontier, where I was unfortunately known first'. In this will, he bequeathed everything he possessed to his wife 'to use exactly as she chooses under Sir Robert Hudson's guidance'. 'I particularly desire that the darling wife should remarry if she wishes. She and I,' he continued, 'both know who we desire she should marry.'

In the will he abused other members of his family. When he started the *Daily Mirror*, Rothermere, he wrote, 'ran for his life'. There were certain other bequests, including £10,000 a year to his mother. There was a mention, too, for the niece about whose marriage he had made such a fuss in Germany. Later, a typed and legally re-phrased version made specific mention of *The Times* as being part of the bequest to Lady Northcliffe. Northcliffe signed this revised version 'Harmsworth', which was later held to invalidate it. The witnesses were a doctor and a male nurse. Lord Horder, who had been brought in as a consultant, when asked, refused to add his signature. 'I never saw Lord Northcliffe,' he declared, 'in a state of mind capable of understanding the nature of a legal document from the day of his arrival in England up to his death.'

Northcliffe died on 14 August, at the age of fifty-seven. He had lived just two years longer than Barnes, that other great servant of *The Times* whom he admired so much. And one year longer than Mowbray Morris, the Manager of *The Times* in its most prosperous days, who also died mad. The cause of death was given as ulcerative endocarditis, a disease which eventually causes damage to the brain. Lord Horder, who seems to have been outspoken about the case, subsequently confirmed this diagnosis to Campbell Stuart in private conversation.

Northcliffe's last thoughts were for the two things that mattered most, his mother and *The Times*: 'I wish to be laid as near Mother as possible at North Finchley . . . In *The Times* I should like a page reviewing my life work by someone who really knows and a leading article by the best man available on the night.' The Editor himself undertook the leader.

In assessing the debt which *The Times* owes to Lord Northcliffe it is necessary to look first at his permanent legacy to the paper, and secondly at his handling of its commercial problems. *The Times*, when he took it over in 1908, was still a paper of the highest integrity and intellectual quality. Within the limits of what the paper set out to do, it did it well. But editorial methods were archaic, and the mechanical equipment overdue for replacement. The circulation stood at 38,000, the lowest figure since its early days, and although the paper was scarcely being run at a loss (taking into account the money the Walters received for the printing contract), it was on the verge of bankruptcy. The price was 3d, which potential readers found prohibitive.

Northcliffe introduced to the editorial department of the office up-to-date methods of news-gathering and news-processing, which it lacked. The appearance of the paper was made more attractive by improving the make-up and starting a picture page. The scope of the leaders and features articles was widened, making the paper lighter in tone and more interesting, particularly to women. In Geoffrey Dawson he provided an Editor supremely competent to supervise modernization and deal with the policy requirements of the day. Northcliffe re-equipped both the composing room and the press room with up-to-date machinery, and saw to the modernizing of the office in many other ways, such as telephones and communications.

On the commercial side, Northcliffe saved the paper from bankruptcy. His production of *The Times* at 1d in 1914, leading immediately to a vast increase in circulation, must rank as one of the most successful management decisions in the history of journalism. But Northcliffe, like other successful newspaper proprietors, was better at exploiting favourable conditions than at devising counter-measures against bad ones. It may be surmised that the success of the penny *Times* would not have been so great but for the First World War.

After the armistice *The Times* was struggling against rising costs and wages on the one hand, and increasing financial stringency throughout the country on the other. Unpopular policies, such as support for Home Rule in Ireland, helped to lose traditional readers, and by 1920 *The Times* had no cash and an overdraft at the bank.

Towards the end of his life, Northcliffe seemed to recognize that for all his success he had been unable to solve the problem of how to keep *The Times* a quality daily and make it pay.

Not the four thousand square miles in Newfoundland [he wrote to Campbell Stuart at the end of 1920], with my ships and railways, social problems of the increasing population; nor the Paper Mills at Gravesend; nor the Amalgamated Press with seventy publications; nor the *Daily Mail* whose sale has increased even in December, cause me even one feather-weight of annoyance. Some day there will come a limit to my capacity to stand *Times* annoyance.

There remains one final aspect of Northcliffe's ownership to be examined – its influence on the relationship between Proprietor and Editor. Here Northcliffe acted as a catalyst. The relationship in the days of the Walters had never been defined. How it was exercised remains to a large extent among the arcana of Printing House Square. The veil lifted on the transactions between Editor and Prime Minister more often than it did on those between Editor and Chief Proprietor. Northcliffe, by dragging his disputes with the Chair into the open, destroyed the century-old co-operation which had been governed by unspoken law and custom. After his death the next Editor was to ask for, and obtain, a written constitution laying down rights and obligations on both sides. He could scarcely do less for his own protection.

19 THE ASTOR PURCHASE

(i) The Struggle for Ownership

The death of Northcliffe plunged *The Times* once more into a struggle for ownership comparable to that in 1908. The contenders included some famous names – Lloyd George, Sir Basil Zaharoff, Lord Rothermere, and Major J. J. Astor. As matters turned out, only the last two were enabled to bid.

The situation was complex and obscure. To John Walter IV, the question of the option was all important, for if *The Times* were put up for sale in the open market the bidding would probably go outside his reach. On the other hand, if he still had the option to purchase at 'the best price obtainable', this was interpreted as meaning that all he had to do was to match any other offer that might be made. Walter had abjured the option on 15 June 1922, having previously sold his shares to Northcliffe. But he was unaware of the contents of either of the two conflicting wills. In March 1919 Northcliffe had made a will which included a clause asserting the option; and then, on his death-bed, he had made another which did not mention the option and left *The Times* to his widow.

If the first will was proved to be valid, then there were two possible rulings. Either the judge might hold that Walter retained his option or he might rule that, by specifically abjuring it on 15 June, he had *ipso facto* invalidated his right to benefit from it under the will also. Of all this Walter himself was in complete ignorance until it was revealed to him by the lawyers after Northcliffe's death.

Lord Rothermere, too, had his problems. If the option were approved, he might buy *The Times* more cheaply. If the option were destroyed, he would be more certain of getting it, because he had the longer purse. There was also a time factor. One of the trustees, Sir George Sutton, was also appointed administrator of the estate until the matter could be sorted out. But the Inland Revenue were pressing him for early payment of estate duties. Walter's option gave him three months in which to make up his mind. During that period, Sutton would have to borrow money to help to pay the tax.

Lady Northcliffe had a strong card. The death-bed will bequeathed virtually everything, including *The Times*, to her, and although the will might not appear the work of a man in his right mind, she realized that for that very reason the Harmsworth family would not like to see

243

it made public. They had taken great pains to avoid risking their brother being certified as insane, and these efforts would be wasted if the whole story of the death-bed will were dragged through the law courts, especially in view of Horder's attitude. Without actually trying to prove this will, therefore, she might obtain a favourable compromise out of court.

The Walters, and others at Printing House Square, were taking counsel even before Northcliffe's death on how they could arrive at a stable solution over ownership of *The Times* while maintaining the Walter interest. John Walter's uncles, Hubert and Ralph, sought advice from Geoffrey Dawson's old friend Sir Edward Grigg. Grigg, who had once been Colonial Editor of *The Times*, was now private secretary to Lloyd George, still Prime Minister. But the Coalition Government was threatening to dissolve, and its leader might very well soon be out of office. It would be a remarkable coup if the man who had so consistently been attacked in *The Times* were to gain control of the paper. Various schemes were set on foot to raise money which would retain John Walter as Chairman with Lloyd George possibly as Editor. In spite of strong backing from Lloyd George's political circles the money was not forthcoming, and these efforts proved abortive.

The germ of the final solution seems to have originated with Bruce Richmond, Editor of *The Times Literary Supplement*. He and his editorial colleagues were aware of the possibility of Rothermere buying the paper. After consulting Wickham Steed and George Freeman, the Deputy Editor, Richmond went to see two friends of his, General Neill Malcolm, and Owen Hugh Smith, a director of Hay's Wharf. These passed him on to the bankers Sir Guy Granet and Robert Grant, of the New York and Boston firm of Lee Higginsons, who told him that they had a man who, as Richmond wrote in a letter to Stanley Morison, 'was very anxious to save *The Times*, knew quite well that he could never hope to make a penny out of it, and would stand by waiting for us to let them know when the chance came'. Richmond and his friends believed the man to be Waldorf Astor. They had no idea at that stage that it was his younger brother. For the time being they took no action.

Such was the state of play when Campbell Stuart, the Managing Director, arrived back from a visit to Canada, just before Northcliffe's death. Campbell Stuart, who was still only thirty-three and who was to prove an important figure in the subsequent negotiations, was one of the three men who held Northcliffe's power of attorney during his absence abroad. The other two were Sir George Sutton and his solicitor, William Graham. Campbell Stuart was also Managing Editor of the *Daily Mail*, though he immediately resigned this position on returning to England.

Stuart has already figured in this story on a number of occasions. His appointment of Managing Director, which made him Northcliffe's mouthpiece in the office, was unprecedented in Printing House Square. Another unusual element in Stuart's appointment was that he was a Canadian. The time would come when a Canadian would own *The Times*, but in 1919 it still appeared strange that what was then described as a 'colonial' should hold sway in Printing House Square.

'Campbell Stuart,' Northcliffe once told Steed, 'is the only person I have yet found who understands the harmonizing of my newspapers, that is to say, chiefly stopping the pin-pricking.' The same quality that commended him to Northcliffe naturally drew resentment from the Editor, who used to call him 'The Senior Wangler'. Stuart, like Moberly Bell, regarded it as his job to hire and fire editorial staff, thereby interfering with what Steed regarded as the editorial prerogative.

But Stuart served the paper well. One of his great qualities was that he could stand up to Northcliffe. He probably did him as great a service by knowing when to countermand orders as by seeing that they were carried out. On one occasion (as was related by J. S. Maywood, who worked for *The Times* for sixty-seven years and was largely responsible for the creation of the library, or 'Intelligence Department' as it is called) Northcliffe, highly suspicious of *The Times Literary Supplement*, ordered it to cease publication. Stuart got wind of this just in time. He went straight down into the case room and stopped the printers inserting an announcement to this effect. But for his prompt action there might well be no *T.L.S.* today.

Shortly after Campbell Stuart returned to England, Richmond went up to his room and suggested ringing up Guy Granet, which he did, with, as Richmond observes 'fateful results'. They then learnt that the banker's unknown client was J. J. Astor, who, like Richmond, the Walters, and many others in this story, had been educated at New College, Oxford. This formed a link. Campbell Stuart determined to back the scheme by which John Walter would bid for the shares, while Astor, rather like Northcliffe in 1908, acted as the 'X' in the case – the unseen backer who put up the money for the purchase.

(ii) Rival Bids

Fortunately for Stuart, the wishes of the Harmsworth family played into his hands. They were unwilling to bring into court any dispute which would expose to the public the state of Northcliffe's mental derangement when he wrote his last will. Stuart, as a beneficiary of the 1919 will who was not mentioned in the later one, was in a position to provoke action in court. The trustees therefore negotiated a compromise by which the 1919 will was accepted as the operative one, while

Lady Northcliffe was given a much larger capital sum than that will allowed her. All the beneficiaries agreed to this compromise, except for one litigious ex-secretary of Northcliffe's, Miss Louise Owen, who brought an action against the trustees. Thus Walter's option survived.

Stuart's next move was to discover the price which Rothermere was prepared to offer for the paper, for, whatever it was, it was essential that Walter should be able to match it. Theoretically, according to the terms of the option, he would have three months to raise the money. But Stuart was taking no chances which, as matters developed, was just as well. As a preliminary, he bought in on behalf of Astor at a low price a large minority holding owned by Sir John Ellerman.

Rothermere, who was still ignorant of the identity of Walter's backer, was equally curious to know how much the opposition would put up. Earlier he had mentioned £800,000 to Stuart as being a reasonable price. His brother, it will be recalled, had given about £300,000 in 1908 for the newspaper without the printing works. In an effort to discover more, Rothermere persuaded Sir Robert Hudson to invite Stuart to dinner. Hudson, who had been Lady Northcliffe's constant companion, was shortly to marry her. As it turned out, the tête-à-tête dinner which ensued early in October was a most fortunate event for Stuart, Walter and Astor.

The dinner lasted long and the wine flowed freely. Hudson asked Stuart whether he and his friends could go beyond a million, a large sum in view of the estimated commercial value of the property. Private advice to Astor was that *The Times* was not worth more than £800,000, the same sum mentioned by Rothermere. The latter, however, believed (optimistically) that properly managed the paper could earn an average profit of £250,000 a year – an average, let it be said, which no previous or subsequent management of *The Times* has been able to sustain. But in the eyes of John Astor the prestige of *The Times* justified his paying a substantial, though not unlimited, price in excess of its commercial value.

Stuart indicated that he would be able to go as high as £1,250,000. At that point the telephone in the hall rang. It was one o'clock in the morning, and Hudson left to answer it, without closing the door. The caller was Sir Charles Russell, Rothermere's solicitor, asking for a progress report. Through the open door Stuart heard Hudson tell him that the Walters were prepared to go to £1,250,000 and that Rothermere would have to top that figure. Next morning he immediately reported the conversation to Astor's adviser, Robert Grant, who took steps to ensure that the necessary sum would be available if needed.

Matters now moved swiftly to a climax. On 12 October Rothermere wrote to Sutton, the administrator of the estate, making a formal bid for *The Times*. No price was mentioned. All Rothermere said was that the bid would have to be rejected or accepted in a short space of time. say a week.

On 19 October the rival parties appeared in court before the judge. Only Sutton and Rothermere's representatives were heard. Walter sat there listening, secure in the knowledge that he had very much greater backing than anyone there could have guessed. On the matter of the option, Sir George Sutton's counsel, F. H. Maugham, KC, the future Lord Chancellor, rose to propose a compromise. He suggested that it would be fair, as the will had not yet been proved, to recognize Walter's 'right of pre-emption', but to limit it to a very much shorter period than three months. This, he must have felt, would effectively baulk Walter, who would not be able to find the money in the time.

Then, amid a hushed court, he declared Rothermere's price – £1,350,000. All save John Walter, who had been forewarned by Campbell Stuart, were staggered when they heard it. Peat, the accountant for the Northcliffe estate, described it as a 'fancy' price but recommended his clients to accept. The judge ruled that this was a final figure, and that no third party, other than Walter, might intervene. 'I cannot,' he replied, in response to requests from the representatives of Lord Rothermere and Lady Northcliffe, 'conduct either a negotiation or an auction.'

The day was a Thursday, and at Walter's request the court adjourned till Monday. Over the weekend Robert Grant rang up John Astor, who was in Scotland, for instructions. Astor told him to go ahead and buy. Thanks to Campbell Stuart's early warning, Grant was able to lay his hands on the necessary cash in the time required. When the court reassembled on Monday, Walter's representative cut short the wrangling by announcing that 'Mr Walter will exercise his option here and now . . . That is an absolute contract made now today.' To a still more astounded court, the judge then pronounced the contract approved.

For the second time in a century, *The Times* had been sold and bought. Astor's total bill, including costs, was £1,580,000. But the thread of tradition, inherent in the Walter connexion, had been preserved throughout both sales.

The handling of the case by Stuart had been masterly. Critics of it have maintained that Rothermere never intended to buy the paper, but was only trying to raise the price in the interests of the estate. Such a theory seems scarcely tenable. If it were true, Rothermere was taking a risk which even he might have shrunk from. Moreover, there is evidence that he was concurrently in negotiation with Bonar Law, who was in process of forming a Conservative government, over the support to be given him by *The Times*.

(iii) *The Return of Dawson*

The sale of the paper was only the first step. There remained to be settled the questions of who should edit it and on what terms. Astor, Walter and Stuart were all agreed that Steed should leave. There were a number of reasons for this decision, probably not shared identically by all three. The intention was to make an entirely new start – or rather to return to the pre-Northcliffe pattern which left the Editor a free hand in the editorial domain. In the eyes of the world Wickham Steed was too closely associated with Northcliffe for this to be possible if he remained in the Chair. In the eyes of the new proprietors he was also too flamboyant and opinionated. If they were to hand over so much editorial authority they preferred that it should be to someone more reliable, as they saw it, and less unpredictable.

Astor took counsel with his friend Robert Brand, the banker. He seemed on all counts eminently qualified to advise, and it is hardly surprising that he advocated the recall of Geoffrey Dawson, an old friend and colleague in South Africa. The former Editor had been filling in his time as estates bursar of All Souls and secretary of the Rhodes Trust, a position to which he had been appointed on the instigation of Lord Milner.

Various other names were discussed, including those of J. L. Garvin, who might have become Editor in 1919 had Wickham Steed refused, and J. A. Spender, the well-known Liberal journalist who might have done so in 1908 if Pearson and not Northcliffe had bought *The Times*. John Walter IV, however, agreed with Astor that Dawson was the more suitable. Stuart was less certain.

Sounded out at Oxford by Robert Brand, Dawson, for his part, was not so certain either. He had recently married and started a family, and was enjoying the life of a country gentleman in Yorkshire. Was he to abjure his new-found life of freedom and happiness for a return to the treadmill of a newspaper office? As always, when in doubt, he consulted Milner, and it was on Milner's advice that he accepted the offer, subject to conditions. These were that there should be a written definition of the Editor's sphere of power and responsibility *vis-à-vis* the Proprietors, the Board, and the Manager. Accordingly he submitted a long memorandum, based on a draft by Freeman, the Deputy Editor, summarizing his views. Astor and Walter accepted these terms unconditionally, and at the end of November 1922 Geoffrey Dawson once more became Editor of *The Times*.

There were consequential results of Dawson's appointment. Steed did not take his dismissal lightly. He had in his possession a personal letter written to him by Northcliffe in 1919 just before the Chief underwent an operation. It gave him a five-year contract and highly favourable pension terms. The Board refused to regard it as binding. A compromise was reached by which they paid what they considered fair, while the Northcliffe estate made up the balance.

There was the position of Stuart to be considered. He, of all people, personified the overshadowing of the Editor by management. In the background lay the incident of Dawson's indiscreet remarks about Northcliffe at Cliveden. Both men realized that it was impossible for the one to remain as Managing Director if the other were to be appointed Editor. Yet Stuart had deserved exceptionally well of *The Times*, of Astor and of Walter. But for him Rothermere would almost certainly have been in control. Stuart himself resolved this difficulty by voluntarily standing down.

> Lunch w. Freeman [noted Dawson in his diary], bearing olive-branches fr. Campbell Stuart, but also a v. dift. view of organn. fr. mine...He [Campbell Stuart] of course realized that it upset the position of M.D. if my scheme were accepted. We argued v. friendly...By this time [22 Nov.] C.S. had abdicated.

Stuart was to remain a director on the Board, and an active one, for forty years.

(iv) *New Constitution*

The Times was now to be furnished, for the first time in its history, with a detailed written constitution, governing the relationship between Proprietors, Board, Editor and Manager, and regulating any future transfer of controlling shares. At the apex of the pyramid were the two co-Chief Proprietors, John Astor and John Walter. They were the owners of the controlling shares, and they alone of the directors and board members were responsible for editorial policy. This meant in effect that they were responsible for the hiring and firing of the Editor. Astor, as the majority shareholder, was also Chairman of *The Times* Publishing Company.

The exact sense in which the co-Chief Proprietors were responsible for editorial policy was laid down in Dawson's memorandum, on which of course he had consulted Milner. The memorandum, dated 18 November 1922, is an attempt to reduce into words what it was believed was the relationship of the Walters to the Editors in the best days of *The Times*.

> I am anxious [wrote Dawson], that there should be no sort of misunderstanding about my conception of the duties and responsibilities of the Editor and of his relations both with the Proprietors and with the Manager of *The Times*. None of them, as I recognize, can be defined precisely. The conduct of a newspaper differs from every other business in the world inasmuch as

it has two quite distinct objects which are ultimately both dependent on one another, yet are in constant opposition. They can
only be achieved by the closest co-operation and by daily com-
promises . . . These two objects are (1) to reflect and guide public
opinion by producing a good newspaper and (2) to make money
by producing a profitable newspaper.

Dawson then proceeded to instance activities where Editor and
Manager might clash. They included the allocation of space between
news and advertisements, the character of the advertisements, and the
breadth of columns. He regarded these as primarily questions for the
management, 'but the Editor should certainly have a voice in their
discussion'. He should certainly have authority to strike out any
advertisement which he thinks mischievous – 'such as the political
manifesto masquerading as an advertisement'.

The general question of the amount of expenditure required to make
a good paper was treated as one 'in which the Editor's views should
carry equal weight with the Manager's in its decision by the Proprietors'.
They were to be the 'ultimate arbiters and Court of Appeals'.

Dawson then came to the question which had been the cause of so
much friction in the past, particularly in the days of Bell and Northcliffe, namely the appointment of staff. The Editor, he stated, must be
ultimately responsible 'for the selection of his assistants at home and
abroad, and for the allocation of their duties'. But it was the business
of the Manager, subject to the Proprietors or their Board, to say what
the paper could afford to pay and to make the formal appointments.
The Proprietors, he added, should act only through the Editor or
Manager when dealing with subordinate staff.

Dawson then gave his views on the composition of the Board. The
Editor and Manager, he considered, should attend board meetings as
of right. But he went further. He thought it arguable that 'no salaried
administrative officer at all, whether on the managerial or on the
editorial side', should be included in the Board. No doubt at the back
of his mind was a desire to ensure that directors should not have the
expertise to interfere with him. But in staging this principle, the prospective Editor was going beyond his brief, and laying up trouble for
the future. The absence from the Board of members familiar with the
practical working of newspapers was to constitute a serious weakness
in later years.

To Dawson's surprise, his definition of the Editor's functions was
accepted without question or modification by the Chief Proprietors. It
now remained to top the edifice with trustees who should be responsible
for overseeing any future transfer of controlling shares in the newspaper.
The two Chief Proprietors, who owned the controlling shares, were

constituted as a holding company which in effect controlled *The Times* Publishing Company. A committee of trustees was formed which should have an absolute veto on the transfer of shares in the holding company to any outside individual or interest. The object of this provision, it was announced in *The Times* of 7 August 1924, was 'to ensure so far as is humanly possible, that the ownership of *The Times* shall never be regarded as a mere matter of commerce to be transferred without regard to any other circumstance to the highest bidder, or fall, so far as can be foreseen, into unworthy hands.'

With this object in view, the trustees were to be ex-officio, 'precluded by their position from active party politics, and should represent various elements . . . in the national life'. They were to be: the Lord Chief Justice, the Warden of All Souls, the President of the Royal Society, the President of the Institute of Chartered Accountants, the Governor of the Bank of England.

The trustees of *The Times* came to be regarded in public mythology as something other than they were. Misconceptions arose as to their importance in deciding questions of policy and appointing Editors, in neither of which functions had they any part. Even the role allotted to them was, as their terms of reference wisely forewarned, only effective 'so far as is humanly possible'.

In spite of some weaknesses the constitution of *The Times*, as settled in the years after the Astor purchase, was a workmanlike attempt to learn from the successes and failures of the past, and to systematize the lessons for the future. The architects wrought well. The constitution lasted for nearly half a century, and many of its features are still present in the organization of Times Newspapers Limited. It also served as a model on which other newspapers both at home and overseas based their own constitutions.

20 DAWSON'S FRESH START

(i) *Return to Stability*

When Dawson resumed the Editor's chair in Printing House Square at the end of 1922 a period of consolidation set in. By the terms of his agreement the Editor had more power more firmly guaranteed than any of his predecessors. Nor was he the man to let his power be eroded. The Manager no longer had any control in editorial matters, though his responsibility for agreeing salaries of editorial staff gave him some indirect influence.

The reinstated Editor made no startling staff changes. He realized that what the paper needed after the alarms of the Northcliffe–Steed era was order and stability. The three senior members of the editorial staff, George Murray Brumwell (Night Editor), George Freeman (Assistant Editor) and Harold Williams (Foreign Editor) were left secure in their offices. Brumwell became Dawson's trusted chief staff officer, and Dawson came greatly to depend on him.

Stabilization in turn produced financial buoyancy. One of Northcliffe's last acts had been to bring the price of the paper down to 1½d from 3d. The circulation responded. From a level of 110,000 in 1921 it rose to 163,000 in 1923, reaching the 180,000s in the following year and staying at about that figure until the financial crisis of 1931. Profits, too, rose steadily from £17,000 in 1923 until they reached £331,000 in 1929, the highest so far ever attained. At that point they began to dwindle under the influence of economic depression.

With the change in fortunes went a change in style. In Steed's writing there had been a touch of Barnes's thunder. Dawson, like Delane, tended to adopt a more restrained approach. For limpidity of style and economy of words he was unequalled. His weapons of attack were irony, devastating understatement and the sudden throw-away phrase, like 'the corridor for camels', by which he dismissed the token access to the sea permitted to Ethiopia under the Hoare–Laval pact.

In national politics, as at *The Times*, a new era was beginning. Dawson supported the dissolution of the Conservative–Liberal coalition, which had outlasted the war, and advocated return to a party system. He approved the choice of Baldwin (a man 'singularly free from self-advertisement') as leader of the Conservative Party. When the general election of December 1923 failed to give the Conservatives an overall majority over both opposition parties, he was in favour of giving the first Labour Government a trial run. 'Nothing,' he wrote to Lord Robert Cecil, 'is more dangerous than the existence of a large party in the State who have never had the responsibility of office and consequently do not know what can and cannot be done by the Government.'

In foreign affairs revision of the Treaty of Versailles and collective security through the League of Nations were the twin pillars of *Times* policy. With the return of Milner's pupil, the rabid anti-Germanism of the Northcliffe–Steed days was swept away – a change which had far-reaching implications for the future of the paper. But it was to the Dominions, as ever, that Dawson turned for the solution of Britain's problems. In Imperial Preference he saw a means of assisting the country's economic difficulties, and in the co-operation of the Dominions in imperial defence a means of reducing its armaments.

From Washington correspondence was maintained by the powerful personality of Willmott Lewis. Recruited to *The Times* in 1920 by Northcliffe, Lewis had previously served as correspondent for a number of American papers. The questions at issue between Britain and America in those years seem strange and artificial in the light of history. The United States were intent on establishing a naval ratio of $5:5:3$ as between themselves, Britain and Japan. To Britain, already reducing her own Navy, this policy of further drastic cuts seemed an affront to national pride, and *The Times* supported the Government in resisting it. The Americans continued to press for a reduction in the number of British warships, a policy Willmott Lewis dubbed as 'Faith, Hope and Parity'.

In a memorandum dated December 1925 Dawson summed up the editorial goals of his second editorship:

What *The Times* wanted first and foremost was a period of obvious steadiness, even stodginess, before it could become an active force again . . . The process of startling the public had been carried rather too far . . . In the last three years *The Times* has endeavoured to return to the tradition of fair play for the Government of the day without by any means following them at every point.

(ii) Tutankhamun

In fact the first question to which Dawson had to address himself on resuming the editorship was the contract for exclusive rights in reporting the excavation of Tutankhamun's tomb. Its discovery in November 1922 had been the subject of Wickham Steed's last leader written as Editor. From Lord Carnarvon and Howard Carter Dawson purchased exclusive world rights for the first season's excavations, at a cost of £5,000. *The Times* were at liberty to recoup what they could by selling the syndication rights. What it amounted to, from Carter's point of view, was that he had appointed *The Times* as his press agents, and, as he hoped, relief from the distractions caused by other newspapers and visitors to the Valley of the Kings.

At first all went well, but by the time the second season started, jealousy had grown among other journalists at what they regarded as a *Times* monopoly.

> After a week . . . our rivals began to get restless at getting very little news. Having been nice to us all, [they] now changed their tactics. Morton [*Daily Express*] arranged a meeting in his room at the hotel, attended by Weigall [Sir Arthur Weigall, formerly on the staff of the Egyptian Department of Antiquities], Valentine Williams [Reuters], Badstreat and an Egyptian press-man, the outcome of which was 'to do everything possible to break *The Times* agreement' – Weigall apparently wiring Egyptian authorities at Cairo, protesting . . . and many champagne dinners were given, presided over by Mr Valentine Williams who apparently was now becoming a sort of News Editor for the rival Press.

Situations of this kind are not unusual when a newspaper secures exclusive rights to an important expedition. They are difficult to deal with since so many people know what is going on and the prevention of leakage is in practice hard to assert. On these occasions everything depends on the attitude of the leader of the expedition. *The Times* was fortunate in that Howard Carter was determined to honour his contract both in the letter and the spirit.

> Friday [17 February 1923] was the great day at the Tomb as it was apparent to everyone that some opening would be made before the Queen and Allenby [British High Commissioner] went up on the Sunday. All the correspondents were sitting on the parapet at 8.45 a m . . . and the breaking down of the inner chamber could of course be heard. One of the native workmen collared by the combine during the afternoon said 8 mummies had been found, and other workmen said 3 mummies had been found. This spurious information specially sent out by Mr Carter as a blind confused our rivals very much.

Frustration among the 'combine' became so great that recourse was had to desperate expedients:

> Mrs Valentine Williams being the chief gleaner, learning apparently that a Press man, M. Fath, representing the Egyptian

Press, might have got *The Times* story, she cornered him and even, to use Fath's own words, squeezed his hand . . . Sunday, on the visit by the Queen, Mrs Valentine Williams was caught looking over Mr Merton's shoulder at his writing pad. Merton, noticing this, wrote on his pad 'it is unladylike and rude to look over my shoulder' – exit Mrs Valentine Williams.

These events, trivial though they may appear, prompted the other British correspondents to stir up opposition to Carnarvon and Carter from the Egyptian Government, already jealous that the Tutankhamun treasures were being excavated by foreigners. The row assumed international importance.

To add to the troubles of *The Times*, Lord Carnarvon died on 5 April 1923, from an infected mosquito bite followed by pneumonia, which meant that a new contract had to be negotiated with his executors and a further £2,500 paid to continue *The Times*'s agency over the next season's diggings.

Opposition from its rivals became so strong that the paper had to defend its position before the Newspaper Proprietors' Association:

I am not here to apologize for anything we have done nor to labour the fact that unless *The Times* had obtained the contract it might have gone abroad [declared *The Times* spokesman]. I understand that exception was taken to our having obtained the rights to deal with all news and pictures relating to the excavations and it was even suggested that a boycott should be instituted against us. I am not concerned with the illegality of the proposal nor seriously with the proposal at all. I am, however, rather surprised that it should have been suggested at this Council that private newspaper enterprise should be restricted – especially coming from the quarter that it did. If I am rightly informed, the objection was made on the ground that the excavations are of national interest and there should be free access financially and otherwise. I go further and say that they are of international interest but is that a reason for condemning our contract? . . . I want to say at once that the Earl of Carnarvon has no desire whatever to make money out of the contract – any money which is obtained for the rights will not go into his own pocket but towards the liquidation of part of the expenses he has incurred.

This unjustifiable attempt by members of the NPA to use collective machinery in order to strangle the enterprise of an individual member failed.

The team sent to Luxor from Printing House Square consisted of two correspondents and one photographer. A balance sheet made up to the time of Carnarvon's death shows that the £5,000 paid to him, together with the salaries, expenses and cable costs of the correspondents, had amounted to £8,560, while sale of news services and photographs had brought in returns of £5,903, leaving a loss of £2,657 to be paid by *The Times* – an outlay well justified by the magnificent material obtained.

In February 1924, opposition from the Egyptian Government became so intransigent that Carter was compelled temporarily to close down the tomb. *The Times* was left with news liabilities to some of its syndication clients which it could not satisfy. Not until 1928 was the work on the tomb finally completed. By this time, however, *The Times* had had the best part of the news, and faithfully distributed it to the press of the world. That it should have recouped a proportion of its expenses in doing so seems reasonable.

(iii) The General Strike

The summer of 1926 saw a threat to the production of *The Times* such as had not been known since 1810. This was a threat of stoppage by trade-union action as a consequence of the General Strike. Although both the Editor and the Manager were abroad when the strike broke out the paper surmounted the danger triumphantly. In many ways it was a personal victory for the new Chairman, Major Astor, who, if he had remained a shadowy figure to some of the staff hitherto, was now to make his personal powers of leadership forcefully felt. The conduct of both management and strikers at Printing House Square provides a fascinating commentary on the social attitudes of the period.

For over a year an industrial dispute had dragged on in the coal industry, when the TUC decided, in default of a settlement, to declare a General Strike in support of the miners. The executive of the General Council hoped, by these unconstitutional means, to coerce the Government into a settlement. That the attempt would prove a failure, and in the long term an unmitigated disaster for the trade-union movement, was foreseen by many of the Labour leaders, notably J. H. Thomas, but they were unable to halt the militants. 'Zero Time', as the TUC called it, was fixed for midnight Monday, 3 May.

An essential part of the plan was to silence the independent, or 'capitalist' press, while the TUC's own organ (*British Worker*) continued to be published. The printing unions were in the forefront of the movement. Consequently it is hardly surprising that it was an incident in a newspaper office, that of the *Daily Mail*, which triggered the strike off a day earlier than planned. Operatives there, led by a spokesman from Natsopa (the National Society of Operative Printers and Assistants) objected to the wording of Sunday night's leader called 'For King and Country'. They demanded alterations which the Editor refused to authorize. An unofficial strike started and the *Daily Mail* ceased publication.

Dissatisfaction spread to Printing House Square. One of the overseers, Frank Easto, reported to the Night Editor that a deputation of Fathers of Chapels (shop stewards) from the packers and machine-men had intimated that they objected to printing an official appeal for volunteers to maintain essential services in the event of a strike. The Night Editor, who in the evening is the hardest-pressed man in the office, was too busy to see them and deputed Easto to reply that 'no alteration in the paper would be made under threats, and that they must either get the edition out as it stood or leave it alone'. Easto returned to argue with the objectors. According to a contemporary account, 'this he did at great length, meantime entertaining them with beer and cigarettes in order to make it impossible for them . . . seriously to affect the output from the Egyptian Government, already jealous that the Tutankhamun

The TUC officially disowned these acts of indiscipline but the Government, unwisely in the view of *The Times*, made the stoppage at the *Daily Mail* a *casus belli*. They refused last-minute negotiations with the strike leaders.

In the absence of Dawson and Lints Smith, Major Astor took command. A tall man, of modest yet commanding demeanour, John Astor had started life as a regular soldier and served throughout the war with the 1st Life Guards and as a gunner. He had been many times wounded and had lost a leg, though this disability did not deter him from shooting, swimming and playing tennis. He was now Conservative MP for Dover. In a crisis such as the present one he was in his element, as he was to show again in 1940 when Printing House Square was physically threatened in the Blitz.

Astor's diary for Monday records:

1 p m NPA [Newspaper Proprietors' Association] summoned to meeting at the Treasury. Chancellor of the Exchequer [Churchill] in the chair. He explains that in view of the fact that the Printing Trade is among the first to be called out, it is essential that at any rate one newspaper should be maintained and asks for suggestions. He says the most desirable way is, of course, for papers if possible to do it themselves, either singly or jointly. Esmond Harmsworth announces that the *Daily Mail* is prepared to go on, regardless of expense, if they are assured of protection. Winston promises full protection, and everything else the State can provide. The question arises as to who, under any composite arrangement to which the government gave help, would be responsible for policy. Burnham [Lord Burnham, *Daily Telegraph*] says that we, the newspaper proprietors, cannot be

expected to take any responsibility. [Lord] Riddell [Chairman of *The News of the World*] sees no chance of getting skilled men – that it takes at least 6 months to a year to train a machine minder. I came away with the clear impression that any paper that could start up on its own could get from Winston what it needed – except, of course, skilled men.

Major Astor continues with the narrative:

Staff from 18 CHT [Carlton House Terrace, the Chairman's town house] to move to PHS at once. Farm lorry and driver, and 8 men [gardeners] to come up from Hever [Hever Castle, his country seat in Kent]. 18 CHT to be a general dormitory.

At PHS meet the FOCs [Fathers of Chapels], 'Situation beyond us. Part as friends and hope to meet as such before long. *The Times*, being above party or class, does not recognize the right of anyone to dictate policy or course of action and will carry on – so far and as long as possible – goodbye and good luck.' (Loud applause.) (Tongue in cheek?)

Meanwhile Akerman [Assistant Manager] is busy installing 6 multigraphs and operators. Everyone except compositors is to go out at midnight, but men who came on before that hour can finish their shift. . . Our reserve motors are parked up a side street.

All play up – a 16-page paper is printed and published in the ordinary way.

As Shaw [Captain R. J. H. Shaw, the Chairman's political secretary] and I were driving off, about 2 am, Easto came up and said about 100 of them were stranded, and 'if my car was doing nothing' could it help to take some home. Send it straight back and ring up Akerman, who sends remainder home in reserve motors, which had not been required to carry papers.

Monday was the last night on which *The Times* was published by normal means until the strike was ended. On Tuesday night issue No. 44,263, familiarly known as the 'Little Sister', was printed by multigraph. This was not a satisfactory process. Only 48,000 were run off, practically all of which were sold in the London area. Nevertheless the 'Little Sister' allowed the management breathing space in which to assemble and train pensioners and volunteers to get a rotary press into action on the following night.

On Wednesday there was an attempt at sabotage, when strikers set fire to paper in the basement, an incident which drove home the lesson that *The Times* must look after its own security. A static 'garrison' was formed. This was backed by a mobile reserve under the command of Harry Pirie Gordon, son-in-law of the former editor, G. E. Buckle.

Pirie Gordon was a tall, burly man, wearing gold-rimmed spectacles, who combined serving as a foreign sub-editor on *The Times* with editing *Burke's Peerage*.

His subordinates in the Printing House Square 'shock brigade' were drawn from the Sporting Room. Among them was Bob Lyle, the Racing Correspondent, whose tips for the Chester Meeting were much canvassed by the pickets. (Unhappily for all, this meeting was cancelled because of the strike.)

By Wednesday night, thanks to the recall of pensioners, the retention of apprentices, the retraining of editorial staff, and the help of outsiders, one rotary machine was running. W. F. Casey, a future Editor of *The Times*, had learnt to produce eminently satisfactory moulds out of the damp 'flongs' in the imposing machines. Major Astor and Ralph Walter, emulating his ancestor who had once set a late issue of *The Times* with his own hands, were working away with chisels in the foundry. The machine room, under the direction of W. H. Tanner, a retired head of the department, was manned by a mixed company of chauffeurs, undergraduates, a sea captain, and the sixteen-year-old son of R. McNair Wilson, the Medical Correspondent. 'No wonder,' continues one report, 'that Mr Tanner felt faint and had to have recourse time and again to restoratives.'

Leading members of the Establishment rushed forward to help at PHS in the roughest and dullest of tasks. Among those shown on the roster are Brigadier-General M. Clifton Brown, Mr A. Duff Cooper, Captain H. F. C. Crookshank, Mr R. S. Hudson, Captain W. E. Elliott and Captain H. D. R. Margesson, all from the House of Commons; Lord David Cecil from Wadham; Lord Cranborne from the Travellers' Club; and Mr A. P. Herbert from the Savile.

The ladies' list was headed by two Duchesses:

The Duchess of Sutherland	Transport
Violet, Duchess of Westminster	Transport
Lady Diana Duff-Cooper	Subscription Room
Lady Maureen Stanley	Transport
Viscountess Massereene and Ferrard	Transport
Viscountess Maidstone	Subscription Room

Occasionally, with so much pent-up amateur energy released, mistakes occurred. A sea captain, for example, one night put a can of purple ink, intended for posters, into the front-page duct, and as it could not be taken out in time 'a good many copies of the paper went down to the provinces with the front page printed in a rich sombre purple'.

Relations with the pickets, in spite of the odd scuffle, remained friendly. They continued to be sustained with sandwiches and beer from the staff canteen and the Chairman noted that 'they always touched their caps' to him as he passed their lines. In mid-week those with money owing were paid out, Astor and Captain Shaw acting as paying cashiers.

A far more serious threat to *The Times* than that offered by the pickets came from the production by Winston Churchill of the *British Gazette*, the government 'throwaway' sheet printed on *Morning Post* machines. While praising the 'most brilliant and courageous effort' of *The Times* in being the sole national newspaper to remain in action, Churchill very nearly brought it to a standstill by requisitioning a quarter of its stocks of paper.

Dawson, who had arrived back in London on 7 May immediately saw the Prime Minister, Stanley Baldwin, and at his instigation wrote him the following letter to show to the Cabinet:

> Official propaganda is always suspect. If the result of pushing the circulation of the *British Gazette* with all the resources at the disposal of the Government should be to drive every independent newspaper out of existence, I do not think that the policy would easily be defended or commonly approved.
>
> I feel bound to add that if the real purpose of this commandeering of newsprint is to limit by general action the amount available for the TUC and their organ, then the policy seems to me to be equally disastrous. Rightly or wrongly the impression is current that the immediate *casus belli* precipitating the strike was an attempt by a trade union to suppress the free expression of opinion by a newspaper . . . The incident has emphasized the fact that the Government is standing for liberty as well as order . . . There is ample power to deal with seditious and revolutionary propaganda when published; but to attempt to prevent any public expression of opinion in advance seems to me to knock down gratuitously one of the main pillars of the Government case.

On 15 May, when the strike was over, the *New Statesman* pronounced what may well be accepted as a final judgment on the stand taken by *The Times* at this testing period of its history:

> One of the worst outrages, which the country had to endure – and pay for – in the course of the strike, was the publication of the *British Gazette*. This organ, throughout the seven days of its existence, was a disgrace alike to the British Government and to British journalism – in so far as journalism can be said to have had anything to do with it. It made no pretence of impartiality; it exaggerated, distorted or suppressed news, speeches and opinions for propagandist purposes. It was suppposed to be supporting the authority of Parliament, but it gave us nothing worth

calling a report of the proceedings either of the House of
Commons or the House of Lords. For that we had to go to *The
Times* . . . It [the *British Gazette*] boasted in its final issue of its
gigantic circulation, but this was largely achieved by the pushing
of unsolicited copies into our letter boxes. Moreover, the offence
of its appearance was aggravated by its wholesale commandeer-
ing of newsprint – it was scandalous that *The Times* should have
been deprived of its paper supplies in order to enable Mr
Churchill to poison public opinion. We can only offer our gratitude and our congratulations to *The Times* for the struggle which
it made in face of this robbery, and for the way in which it
selected the comparatively small amount of news it was able to
print, and maintained the best tradition of truthfulness and
impartiality.

The public showed its appreciation of *The Times* by purchasing as
many copies as it could lay hands on, although the size of the paper
was reduced to only four pages. Normal circulation, before the strike,
was running at 186,000. The figures for the strike period were:

Date	Sales	Centres of Motor Distribution
May 5	48,000	2
6	78,000	27
7	96,000	31
8	166,000	36
10	269,000	67
11	317,000	88
12	342,000	94
13	381,000	102
14	398,000	121
15	405,000	142

In spite of the ever-increasing radius of distribution by volunteer car
drivers, London naturally consumed the larger proportion of copies. A
few were sent to the north by air. On the day that the strike ended, *The
Times* produced one of the few special afternoon editions in its history.
This was an issue of 83,000 copies, sold almost entirely in London.

(iv) The National Government

The conduct of *The Times* during the General Strike illustrated the
immense strength of its position in the country in the mid-twenties. Not
only was it universally commended for the fairness and independence
of its views, but as an institution it showed itself stronger than either
the Government or the TUC. In 1926 the Editor was able to find an
ally in the Prime Minister against his own Chancellor in the matter of

press freedom, while the management, although scrupulous in observing the rules in its dealings with the unions, was able completely to frustrate their intention of closing down the paper. The vast majority of its employees in those days put loyalty to the paper before loyalty to their union, though the management was careful not to exploit this. Everybody concerned emerged from the ordeal with dignity and credit, and pride in the accomplishment lasted into the thirties and beyond.

By the end of the decade both Dawson and *The Times* were at the height of their power. When the financial and political crisis of 1931 arrived, *The Times* (editorially) and Dawson (personally) exercised an influence over events equalled only by the King, the leaders of the three parties, and the Bank of England. At the same time Dawson was not an instigator of the National Government. He believed, with Baldwin, that the Labour Government 'should get themselves out of their own mess'. The general theme of the leaders in the last days of Labour was 'the case for revising the whole policy of extravagance' in the light of 'the critical financial state of the country'.

On 23 August, the day of crisis, Dawson recorded in his diary that Clive Wigram, the King's Private Secretary, 'was on the telephone at dawn, just arrived fr. Balmoral w. H.M. I had a preliminary talk w. him and saw him in the late aftn. when Ramsay [MacDonald], Samuel [the acting leader of the Liberals], & Baldwin, had been to the Palace. Meanwhile S.B. arrived at my house about 11 & stayed talking till lunchtime, when we drove to the Travellers.'

J. C. C. Davidson describes events from the Conservative point of view:

> The discussions at my house that evening [August 22] were inconclusive . . . S.B. was deeply reluctant to envisage a new Coalition . . . Neville Chamberlain became very impatient with S.B.'s attitude. He made it quite clear that he could see no other way out of the situation . . . On the next morning he [Baldwin] decided to talk the situation over with Geoffrey Dawson. Shortly after he left my house, Clive Wigram rang to ask S.B. to come and see the King. The King had returned to London determined to see the leaders of all the Parties that morning.*

It is now a matter of history that Baldwin could not be found in the morning because he and Dawson had left for the Travellers' Club, with the result that the Liberal leader saw the King first, and it was at this meeting that the formation of a National Government was first broached by Sir Herbert Samuel. Later Stanley Baldwin told the King, who had now become convinced of the necessity for a National Government,

---

* J. C. C. Davidson: *Memoirs of a Conservative*, Edited by Robert Rhodes James, Weidenfeld & Nicolson, 1969.

that he would be ready to do anything to assist the country in the present crisis.

Next day Dawson saw Ramsay MacDonald who, having been 'on the point of throwing in his hand last night, had perked up again this morning. A "National Govt." was in process of formation.' Whether this would have happened if Stanley Baldwin had seen the King before Sir Herbert Samuel remains one of the speculations of history.

The National Government had been formed as an emergency measure to deal with the financial crisis. Probably none of the participants intended it to last. But the financial crisis did not abate. On 12 September the Fleet mutinied at Invergordon in protest at the pay cuts, and on 21 September Britain went off the gold standard. The necessity for a general election, which would give the Government in power a popular mandate, became pressing. The question was whether the National Government should go to the country and seek re-election as a coalition, or whether the three parties should contest against each other separately. The Conservatives had much to gain by such a course, since they were likely to win. Moreover Baldwin disliked coalitions on principle. He had destroyed one and did not wish to form another, he had told Davidson on 22 August.

Dawson set out to convince the Conservatives of the wisdom of the opposite course. On 10 September he had a long talk with Stanley Baldwin on 'the importance of going to the country as a National Govt. & not in 3 parties. He was very receptive, said it had carried his own ideas much further, & warmly approved my putting it to the P.M.'

Three days later he lunched with MacDonald at Chequers and had 'a couple of hours heart-to-heart'. He, too, was 'v. candid and receptive'. Having discussed the economic side with Lord Brand (who constituted for the Editor his link with the banking world), and tried out his ideas on cronies at the Travellers' Club (whom he was sometimes inclined to mistake for a cross-section of the British public) Dawson launched on 16 September the first of his leaders calling for a general election on a non-party basis, and returned to the subject on 21, 26, 28 and 30 September. The only basis, he argued, on which a general election was tolerable was 'an appeal by Mr MacDonald, as head of a National Government, for a popular mandate to go ahead with the work of reconstruction, and to use any and every means, including a tariff, which may be found to be necessary'.

The tariff was the sticking point for the Liberals. Nothing would persuade them to abandon their ideological adherence to Free Trade, and in order to include them in the appeal it was necessary for the National Government to go to the country with what was known as 'the doctor's mandate', which meant a very broad and vague undertaking to set matters to rights, with no mention of tariff reform.

The Times continued to hammer the theme throughout the election campaign. Polling day was on 27 October, and as Dawson learnt the election returns he found that they 'grew more and more wonderful as the day went on', as well he might.

The results were an overwhelming victory for the National Government. The Conservatives gained 208 seats. Only one of the former Labour cabinet ministers who had refused to join the National Government was returned to Parliament. This was George Lansbury. It was fourteen years before the Labour opposition would regain power. The Liberal Party was riven into three groups.

Dawson, for good or ill, had been a prime mover in fashioning the political structure with which Britain was to tackle the problems of the 1930s, including the threat posed by German rearmament and the rise of Hitler. The structure was to consist of a continuing and predominant middle-of-the-road consensus government, National in name but largely Conservative in substance. Although vigorous and vocal opposition parties and groups remained in being, the Labour Party took time to recover, and meanwhile the ding-dong of conventional party rivalry was virtually smothered. Both Baldwin and Dawson were to prove past-masters at protracting this structure.

21 RE-DRESSING *THE TIMES*

(i) Staffing Problems
The 1920s had been, as Dawson intended, a period of consolidation. *The Times* regained its reputation for reliability, which had been eroded in the later years of the Northcliffe régime, while maintaining – and if anything enhancing – its political influence. The management, under Lints Smith, was sound, if tight-fisted, and profits rose in a spectacular fashion up to the onset of the financial crisis. The profit of £331,000 achieved in 1929 was not to be reached again until the 1950s (by which time the real value of the pound had been halved).

Behind this impressive façade there were, however, incipient weaknesses which were to require attention in the 1930s. There was little advance in the content or appearance of the paper. Around tables where journalists gathered the remark was often heard that *The Times* was 'living on Northcliffe'. People forgot the tantrums and inconsistencies of 'the Chief' and remembered only the great professional journalist.

The perennial conflict between profitability and cost of staff continued. Dawson, when he returned in 1922, remarked that *The Times* had only three first-class foreign correspondents left. He made assiduous efforts to recruit brilliant young men, drawing on his connexions with All Souls and the north of England press. On the whole his efforts were successful, but the rate of turnover was too high. At the turn of the decade it was common for young men to spend a few years in the sub-editors' room before leaving to become writers, MPs and ambassadors. Graham Greene, Douglas Jay, Ivor Thomas and Goronwy Rees were examples. Although individuals tended to deny it, economics no doubt played a part in decisions to leave. In the mid-1930s £200 a year was a fair starting salary, £470 was the National Union of Journalists minimum after three years, and trainees were paid nothing. At that period it was possible for a bachelor, sharing a flat in London and with a family home to return to at weekends, to subsist in reasonable comfort in these terms, but it must have been difficult for a married man on his own and starting a family. Of course not many of the younger members of the staff were married in those days. A few, no doubt, had private means, but the Manager frowned on any attempt to earn money outside.

During the 1920s Dawson brought in Colin Coote as political leader writer. Coote, who had a distinguished war record and had been a Conservative Member of Parliament, remained in this key position throughout the 1930s but left after Dawson's retirement to become, ultimately, Editor of the *Daily Telegraph*. Douglas Woodruff, who developed the light leader on lines which made it some of the wittiest reading in London, joined in 1926, but later transferred his exceptional journalistic talents to the editorship of the Roman Catholic weekly, *The Tablet*.

Of the senior staff and writers, most had served as infantry officers in the trenches, many with exceptional gallantry, and this experience, not unnaturally, dominated their attitudes. Some of the younger members of the staff took it for granted that they were living in a pause between two phases of the same war. But to those who had served during 1914–18, the prevention of a second world war was an objective which outweighed all others, and unless this is realized it is impossible to understand the conduct of *The Times* in the 1930s.

Financial stringency played a part in the Editor's failure to fill two key vacancies, those of Foreign Editor and Defence Correspondent. When Harold Williams, the Foreign Editor, died in 1928, Dawson tried to rationalize the failure to appoint a successor on the grounds that the Imperial and Foreign Department could be adequately administered by a Foreign News Editor, leaving the conduct of foreign policy to the Editor. But the arguments which he adduced were valid neither in theory nor in practice; as well run a government without a Foreign Secretary as *The Times* without a Foreign Editor. The failure to find a suitable person within the staff to fill the appointment was a reflection on the extent to which the foreign staff had been run down in the past, and the failure to find one from outside was a case of false economy. Ralph Deakin, the Foreign News Editor, continued to control the Foreign News Service with thoroughness and imagination, but it is hardly surprising if he developed a sense of suppressed grievance which was sometimes noticeable to his colleagues.

Lack of a Foreign Editor created a gap at the top which was to a great extent disguised by the arrival in October 1927 of a man whose influence was to be powerful in Printing House Square for the next twenty years. This was R. M. Barrington-Ward, the new Assistant Editor.

Brought in originally with the intention of writing leaders, Barrington-Ward arrived at a time which coincided with or immediately preceded the loss by resignation or death of several senior men. In addition to Williams these included Gordon Robbins, the Day Editor, and J. W. Flanagan, the principal leader writer, who had been working in Printing House Square since the days of the Parnell Commission. Barrington-Ward, a man of preternatural energy and industry, absorbed most of their functions, as he was to absorb in addition those of Brumwell, the Deputy Editor, when he retired in 1934.

The new Assistant Editor came from a different background from Dawson. The son of an Inspector of Education who took Holy Orders later in life, he was one of a brilliant family of brothers who attained distinction in medicine, the railways, scholarship and the law. But Robin Barrington-Ward obtained the greatest distinction of them all, that of becoming Editor of *The Times*. Schooled at Westminster he went up to Balliol as a scholar but had an uneven career at the university. On the one hand, he succeeded in being elected President of the Union; on the other he failed to win more than a third-class degree in his final schools. This shattering dénouement was due, not to any lack of talent, but to a propensity, present until the end of his days, to overstrain his physical and nervous resources.

It was Sir Edward Grigg who first realized the inherent potentiality of Barrington-Ward as a journalist, and introduced him to Printing House Square in 1913 when he was reading for the Bar. In February 1914 Dawson appointed him to the post of editorial secretary, a position normally reserved for young men marked out for future high promotion. As a nominee of Grigg, and a protégé of the Editor, his was a most auspicious start in journalism. During the war, which almost immediately removed him from Printing House Square, Barrington-Ward made a second career for himself which few civilians can have emulated. He won both the DSO and the MC and was ultimately selected to write large sections of the official infantry training manuals.

When he was demobilized Barrington-Ward did not, strangely enough, return to *The Times*. Instead he accepted a tempting offer from J. L. Garvin to be his Assistant Editor on the *Observer*, with a brief to write leaders, exercise executive control, and deputize in his absence for 'the Chief', as Garvin was known in the office in deference to the Northcliffe tradition. Possibly Dawson did not encourage him to return then because he foresaw, in 1919, his own imminent resignation.

His new appointment did not, however, remove Barrington-Ward from the orbit of *The Times*. The *Observer* was owned by Waldorf (Viscount) Astor, Dawson's friend, and Barrington-Ward thus became a close friend of the Cliveden Astors. When the time came to return to Printing House Square he was able to do so with the good will both of Dawson, who was eager to re-enlist his services, and of Garvin, who was delighted to see the young assistant, for whom he felt a deep and lasting affection, marked out to be one day the successor of Barnes and Delane. Although the loss was to him a serious inconvenience at the time Garvin never held it against Barrington-Ward.

Barrington-Ward made an immediate impact on *The Times*. He was a thoroughly professional journalist and an innovator by temperament.

268 THE STORY OF THE TIMES

Among the tasks to which he addressed himself, apart from daily writing and administration, were the typographical re-dressing of the paper, supervision of the supplements, organization of the official history, and introduction of the crossword and of the women's page. Such measures were needed to modernize *The Times* in terms of the 1930s.

(ii) *Times New Roman*

At the end of the 1920s, a decision was taken which marks another technical landmark in the history of *The Times*, of newspaper production, and of typography. This was the complete re-designing of *The Times* type and typographical lay-out by Stanley Morison, who had recently been appointed typographical adviser to *The Times*. A committee was formed, under the chairmanship of the new Assistant Editor, Barrington-Ward, with the object of completely 're-dressing' the paper and all its subsidiaries. In a memorandum to the committee Morison defined his object as:

> by articulating the problem of a new type with relevant detail of past and present practice, to assist the committee towards the adoption of a Fount which shall be English in its basic tradition, new, though free from conscious archaism or conscious art, losing no scintilla of that 'legibility', which rests upon fundamental ocular laws, or of that 'readability' which rests upon age-long customs of the eyes.

After various experiments, the committee, advised by Morison, preferred to go ahead with the designing of an alphabet which would be a modernized version of one of the 'old faces', namely that used by the early Dutch publisher, Plantin. A modernized version of Plantin had already been designed for book-printing by the Monotype Corporation.

Morison was fortunate in finding in the publicity department of *The Times* a skilful collaborator, Victor Lardent, who made the actual drawings of the letters, for Morison was not himself a technically trained draughtsman. Some doubt exists as to the identity of the model which Lardent used for making his drawings. Nicolas Barker, Morison's biographer, concludes that it was the 'Gros Cicero' type of the French punch-cutter Robert Granjon, dating from about 1568. This type was never used by Plantin in its entirety but was acquired by his successors. The modernized version has the long letters shortened, and the use of oblique stress makes it economical in horizontal space. The drawings prepared by Lardent, and revised by Morison, were sent to the Monotype Corporation for cutting. A lavish number of trial 'punches' were cut, and it is probable that members of the Monotype Corporation played their part in modifying and improving the design. The letters had to be strong enough to stand up to the strain of being printed at speed on a curved stereotype, a requirement which is not of course present in book printing. Great trouble was taken over ensuring that the type conformed to what Morison called the 'fundamental ocular laws'. For this purpose he made use of the Medical Research Council's 'Report on the Legibility of Print' issued in 1926 and he submitted proofs to Sir William Lister, the leading eye-specialist of the day, for comment.

Stanley Morison's principal *bête noire* was the Gothic title-piece at the top of the front page. Here he was on dangerous ground, for the traditionalists regarded it, together with the Royal Arms (to which incidentally the paper was not entitled), as immemorial hall-marks of *The Times*. Triumphantly Morison was able to show that the earliest issues of *The Times* had Roman, not Gothic, title-pieces, and so the hated 'gothick' – fit, in his view, only for the outmoded taste of Strawberry Hill – was banished from the front page and replaced by Roman titling in keeping with the rest of the paper. But he was unsuccessful in his desire to modernize the Royal Arms – which, he objected, still quartered France and Hanover. The archaism survived for some years. *The Times* had adopted them because they appeared on the pediment of the old King's Printing House bought by John Walter I in 1784.

On 3 October 1932 *The Times* first appeared 'dressed over-all' in Times New Roman, as the new type was called. Apart from the immense labour of re-designing the title-piece, captions, capitals, lower-case lettering, and all the various series of type required in a newspaper, the consequential technical and mechanical adjustments required to carry out the changes constituted in themselves a feat of organizational management of which all rightly felt proud. Times New Roman was an instant success; versions of it for use in book-production and other printing activities were later designed and cut, so that Morison's type became one of the most widely used of modern times. Whether, as he claimed, it was completely 'new' may be disputed, for like all types that descend from Gutenberg it is derivative in a sense. But this is something that can be left to the 'typographical pundits' whom Morison affected to despise.

Stanley Morison has not lacked his critics. He was a great showman and his sales promotion was good. Without it Times New Roman might not have won the recognition in the world that it did. He was accused of extravagance, but the total cost of the change-over appears to have been £29,000, of which £11,000 was spent on type, salaries and wages, and £15,000 on publicity. This does not seem excessive in view of the accomplishment.

Although admirably suited to the use for which it was designed, namely the standard type for the world's premier newspaper in the

1930s, Times New Roman had its limitations. Barrington-Ward once described it as 'aristocratic', and he was right. The lettering is designed for printing on high-grade paper in a dignified newspaper to be read by people with some leisure. Allen Hutt pointed out in the *Journal of Typographical Research* that its use on cheaper paper printed at high speeds produces a 'grey' effect.

In 1953, in response to the pressures of paper-rationing, Morison himself produced a modified and slightly more condensed version, together with a smaller-sized set of type known as Claritas, suitable for use in small advertisements and tabular matter, such as Stock Exchange Dealings.

In acquiring Morison as a typographical adviser, *The Times* had also acquired, did its proprietors but know it, one of the archetypal figures of Printing House Square in the mid-century. He was to fulfil in turn the roles of *Times* historian. editor of *The Times Literary Supplement*, honoured friend of the Chief Proprietor, and *éminence grise* to one Manager (Francis Mathew) and two Editors (Barrington-Ward and Casey). With his pebble spectacles, round black hat, and his tall, stooping figure draped in semi-ecclesiastical suiting, he was, in many senses the *geist* of *The Times*.

> Met Stanley Morison at Yarmouth [wrote Barrington-Ward when Editor, many years later]. An astonishingly versatile, gifted, simple human and stimulating creature. Even apart from that, invaluable to me. He is the one man with whom I can discuss anything to do with *The Times*, its policy and its staff and be sure of a detached and instructed comment.

22 THE ABDICATION

(i) *The King's Design*

In the autumn of 1936 the attention of those in power was diverted from Spain, Hitler and Mussolini, to a domestic crisis as brief, strange and painful as any in British history. This was the abdication of Edward VIII.

In the legend which grew up in the aftermath Dawson was cast as one of the leading and more sinister figures. He was alleged to have headed a conspiracy of silence among the British press to keep the news out of the papers until the crisis was settled to Stanley Baldwin's satisfaction. Stanley Baldwin, the Prime Minister, Cosmo Gordon Lang, the Archbishop of Canterbury, and Geoffrey Dawson, the Editor of *The Times*, were subsequently accused, moreover, of forming a conspiracy to oust the King. But there is no need to invent a conspiracy in this case. The King was determined to marry Mrs Simpson, and in the political and social context of the 1930s such a marriage was outside the bounds of practical possibilities.

Unfortunately, there was a double misreading of the situation in the early stages. The King failed to appreciate how deeply rooted was the objection to his marriage among the English people. The Government – and indeed many of the King's friends – failed to realize that the King's feelings for Mrs Simpson were those of an enduring love and not a passing fancy.

The Crown in England touches atavistic, often subconscious, springs of human emotion. The leaders of opinion, when they saw the Crown threatened, spontaneously coalesced to contain the explosion and ensure that it did as little damage as possible. But the case is full of paradoxes, one being that the King himself co-operated in this process of containment. From the point of view of those who supported the King (including Lord Beaverbrook) the King was 'a cock that would not fight'. He had too much respect for the constitutional responsibilities of his position.*

Baldwin's difficulty was that the underlying reasons for opposing the

---

* A common assumption has been that Beaverbrook was only drawn in because of his feud with Baldwin, but his biographer, A. J. P. Taylor, maintains that this was not so, and that he responded, very reluctantly, to the King's plea for help merely out of good nature. A. J. P. Taylor: *Beaverbrook*, Hamish Hamilton, 1972.

marriage were so intangible that they were difficult to express in words. They were even more than religious or constitutional, and they were particularly powerful among the women. The British in the 1930s were an extremely conventional and traditional people. To them Mrs Simpson did not have the background to make her welcome as the Queen of England. She was regarded as an intruder. For many reasons the Prime Minister could not say this.

This explains the extraordinary solidarity of nearly all sections of British opinion against the marriage. It was not only the opposition of the Government, the Archbishop and *The Times* that blocked the King's design. Equally decisive was the opposition of Mr Attlee, the leader of the Labour Party, and of Sir Walter Citrine and the TUC. Their hostility to the marriage meant that the King could not challenge Baldwin to a showdown, even had he so wanted. He would simply have been compelled to fight the whole battle over again, this time with the Opposition. He was thus up against a stone wall. Indeed, the Labour Party were if anything more implacable than the Conservatives. They were more puritan, less emotionally attached to the institution of monarchy, and did not take the King's concern for social distress at its face value.

Nor was British opinion the only factor to be considered. The King was also king of five separate Dominions. Their governments had equal rights with the British Government in advising the Sovereign, and were all hostile to the marriage.

The 'King's friends', as those who supported him came to be known, tacitly recognized this position. Both Lord Beaverbrook and Esmond Harmsworth, the son of Lord Rothermere, knew it was hopeless to attempt to make Mrs Simpson Queen. They were either playing for delay in the hope that the King's passion would cool or that Mrs Simpson would withdraw, or for a compromise such as a morganatic marriage.

The organization of a 'King's Party' against this plethora of opposition never had any chance of success. The two considerable public figures who attempted it, Winston Churchill and Lord Beaverbrook, were both lone wolves, outside the main stream of contemporary political trends and regarded as confirmed supporters of lost causes. According to A. J. P. Taylor, Churchill told Beaverbrook years later that perhaps they had both been wrong.

Baldwin, as Prime Minister, although he knew the state of public feeling, still had to find practical and definable reasons for stopping the marriage. He could not find them in constitutional law. The King, by an anomaly, was the only member of the Royal Family free to marry whom he chose (provided she was not a Roman Catholic). But the Archbishop did have definable reasons. He was bound to oppose the

marriage of the head of the Established Church to a divorced person,
and in taking this stand he had a great body of public opinion behind
him, although not as much as he would have liked. Divorce therefore
became the ostensible reason on which official opposition to the marriage was based.

It is against this background that the actions of Dawson and *The
Times* – but particularly of Dawson, who within the office conducted
this battle almost alone – must be judged.

Soon after the abdication Dawson himself put down on paper a
record of events, just as Steed had done after the death of Northcliffe.

> The whole of the record [he remarks], cannot be told, except
> perhaps by the King himself and Mr Baldwin, and without access
> to secret Cabinet papers. But the British Press has received so
> much applause and also so much abuse for its conduct in the
> matter that it seems worthwhile to set down a private diary
> covering the period while it is still fresh in the memory.

Since then, in 1947, the Duke of Windsor has published his own
account in *A King's Story*. The *History of The Times*, the last volume
of which appeared in 1952, consigns the subject to an appendix. Much
other information has come to light since that history was written. But
Dawson's private memorandum, which *The Times* historian had read,
gives an unrivalled personal narrative by one who stuck 'close to the
centre of the secrets', though not quite as close as popular imagination
has claimed.

In May the King took the first overt step. On the afternoon of 27
May the Court sub-editor at Printing House Square was handed the
Court Circular at the usual time in the afternoon. Scanning quickly
through the list of guests at the Royal dinner party for that night, he
saw, with some surprise, the names of Mr and Mrs Ernest Simpson.
He immediately marked it straight for the Editor to read before sending
in to the printer. George Anderson, the chief sub-editor, could not
understand why.

The Prime Minister and Mrs Baldwin were also guests that night,
and indeed it was before this party that the King had given his first
intimation of marriage to Mrs Simpson by remarking 'It's got to be
done – sooner or later my Prime Minister must meet my future wife.' It
may seem strange that he should have asked the Baldwins to an official
dinner party where Mr Simpson was present when he had already
formed the intention of marrying the latter's wife.

The next stages in the move towards marriage were a royal dinner
party at which Mrs Simpson was present, this time without her husband;
the King's August holiday cruise in the Mediterranean in the yacht
Nahlin, and his subsequent stay at Balmoral. On all these occasions

Mrs Simpson accompanied the King without her husband. The second dinner party was interesting in that the Duke and Duchess of York were present to meet the King's future wife. The other guests were nearly all people whom he hoped to enlist in forwarding his project. They included Lady Diana Cooper, Lady Oxford, Winston Churchill, Sir Samuel Hoare, and Lady Colefax, who had given a number of dinner parties for the King and Mrs Simpson.

But it was the Mediterranean cruise which most of all unleashed publicity in the American and foreign press, since both the King and Mrs Simpson were constantly exposed to press photographers. In the 1930s the sight of the King in shorts only and Mrs Simpson in a bathing dress, was matter for scandalized comment. Throughout all this period the British press maintained a discreet silence.

It was the next step, the notification that Mrs Simpson was about to divorce her husband, which compelled the taking of decisions. The case was due to be heard at Ipswich on 27 October. Official notifications were circulated on 12 October. To those familiar with the divorce laws of the country the timing was suggestive. Under the law then existing it took six months for a decree *nisi* to be made absolute, thus releasing the divorced parties to marry again. The Coronation was to take place on 10 May 1937. With the decree made absolute on 27 April, there would just be time for the King to marry Mrs Simpson before he was crowned.

The Editor came back from holiday in mid-September to find an accumulated pile of letters and newspaper cuttings from America awaiting his perusal:

> The stream of cuttings gradually swelled to a flood, and the letters began to include a number which were abusive and contemptuous of the British press for its silence and others which were frankly distressed. These last came mainly from English men and women living in the States and across the border in Canada, where the papers were just as reticent as our own in spite of the full impact of American scandal. One effect of all this was a certain amount of pressure in England itself, where many people were receiving a similar mail, for some comment in *The Times* that would put an end to the mischief or bring it to a head. There was an obvious risk of some unfortunate explosion elsewhere, and I remember Barrie, who was my neighbour at a Literary Society dinner on 5 October, telling me of his fear even at that stage that one of his own compatriots might think it is his duty to become another John Knox and denounce the sins of the court from the pulpit.

It is sometimes forgotten by his critics that Dawson suffered during all these weeks the unpleasant apprehension, common to all good journalists in possession of a state secret, that some other paper would steal a march on him. 'For the moment,' he concluded, 'it seemed to me better to go on taking the risk, though it soon became impossible to think of anything else.' He took to writing soothing letters to correspondents in America. This was a mistake. One of them got blown up in the American press into a denial that 'Edward would wed Wally' and he had some difficulty in explaining away his alleged statement.

Commenting in retrospect on this press silence the Editor declared that:

> there was in fact neither censorship nor collusion from first to last. The nearest approach to interference from high quarters was probably the customary request from Buckingham Palace (as old as Queen Victoria) that the Sovereign's privacy should be respected by the Press during his annual holiday abroad . . . The Prime Minister probably saw a great deal more of me at this time than he did of any other journalist; but that was due rather to an old friendship and habit of discussion than to the slightest desire to influence me. He never in fact told me any secrets, nor did I ask for them.
>
> The only collusion with other papers, so far as *The Times* was concerned, consisted of three or four conversations, of a purely personal character, with journalist friends.

One of these was a talk with H. A. Gwynne, Editor of the *Morning Post*; another was a telephone consultation with Lord Camrose, proprietor of the *Daily Telegraph*.

This passage is revealing in that it shows both the strengths and weaknesses of Dawson's position. He was, indeed, the only Editor with constant access to the Prime Minister and the Archbishop of Canterbury. But in other respects he was out of touch. He appears to have been in ignorance of the activities at the time of the King and Lord Beaverbrook, directed at muzzling the popular press. As early as 12 October Theodore Goddard, Mrs Simpson's solicitor, had requested Beaverbrook, in response to an inquiry, to keep the notification of the Simpson divorce case out of the papers.* He had assured Beaverbrook, no doubt in all good faith, that the King had no intention of marrying her. Beaverbrook did not accede to Goddard's plea, whereupon the King rang him up and personally persuaded him to help 'in suppressing all advance news of the Simpson divorce, and in limiting publicity after the event'.

In company with Mr Monckton (Attorney-General to the Duchy

* Lord Beaverbrook: *The Abdication of Edward VIII*, Edited by A. J. P. Taylor, Hamish Hamilton, 1966.

of Cornwall) [writes Beaverbrook] I visited Esmond Harmsworth. He was Chairman of the Newspaper Proprietors' Association. There and then, under his leadership, we decided on the
plan of campaign. Most of the British papers consented without
much difficulty to the policy of discretion. Sir Walter Layton, of
the *News Chronicle*, hesitated, but I went to see him . . . The
King sent a letter of thanks for his co-operation.

Beaverbrook then got on to the provincial, the Irish and the French
press by telephone. It appears that *The Times*, the *Morning Post*, and
the *Daily Telegraph*, were purposely left out of these discussions on
the grounds that their discretion could be assumed. The assumption
was correct.

This was the pattern of British press reaction to the King's story.
There was certainly no censorship, but whether what took place is best
described as spontaneous co-operation or collusion depends on one's
approval or disapproval of the methods adopted.

The Times was not left entirely unapproached by the King's servants.
But again, this was for consultation rather than direction. The approach
came not to Dawson, but to the Deputy Editor, Barrington-Ward.
'B.W.' was an old friend of Walter Monckton, who rang him up on 19
October. Monckton would have known by then that the 20th was to be
a crucial day, for Baldwin had asked to see the King and there could
be no doubt what he intended to speak about. In his diary Barrington-
Ward wrote:

Before dinner a call from Walter. More about the case – and the
press. My advice: don't ask for suppression but for no prominence, and no connexion with HM. Indeed, in an ordinary case,
such treatment would be grossly unfair and would go near libel
on the third party.
V. difficult. Third party very fond and obstinate. Might sacrifice
everything to the infatuation. This, with all the world looking for
salvation to British constitutional democracy, would be a vast
catastrophe.

This incident, if it does nothing else, effectively disposes of the theory
that press silence was induced by Baldwin and Dawson in order to
thwart the King.

(ii) The Crisis Breaks

Not until Monday, 26 October, the day before the hearing of the
Simpson divorce case, did the Editor make direct contact with the
Palace. The occasion for doing so was the receipt of a letter for publica-
tion from a British subject living in New Jersey, which he thought

summed up American press comment and its damage to British prestige so aptly that it was worth showing to the King.

> I am one of those [ran the letter] who had a deep admiration for the present monarch when he was Prince of Wales; and looked forward to the day when he would bring a new vision and a new inspiration to the task of kingship. In common, I fear, with a great many others I have been bitterly disappointed . . . Of course, the really serious, even tragic, aspect of the affair is not so much what is said of the King as an individual, but what repercussions these stories have upon the international scene . . .
>
> It may be presumptuous, and even impertinent, for a person far removed from the centre of events to propose a remedy; but I cannot refrain from saying that nothing would please me more than to hear that Edward VIII had abdicated his rights in favour of the Heir Presumptive. In my view it would be well to have such a change take place while it is still a matter of individuals, and before the disquiet has progressed to the point of calling in question the institution of monarchy itself.
>
> Yours faithfully,
>
> *Britannicus in Partibus Infidelium*

Dawson went down to Buckingham Palace, and gave this letter to Alec Hardinge, the King's Private Secretary. Hardinge, a very worried man, was no doubt grateful for being provided with such useful ammunition.

Since the spontaneity of this letter, which was published anonymously, has been impugned, and the suggestion made that Dawson concocted it in the office, it may be well to state that there is no truth in this allegation. The original letter is preserved in the Archives, as is also the acknowledgement:

Private and Confidential   October 28th, 1936

Dear Sir,

I am very grateful to you for your long letter of October 15. It is one of several on the same subject that have reached me lately, but the only one that summarizes clearly the growth of the campaign in the American press and forms a reasoned estimate of its effect. I had myself seen most of the paragraphs and articles which you describe, but they are of little value without the penetrating deduction which you have drawn from them in regard to the impression created in the public mind. So important, in fact, did I think your letter that I had it copied at once (omitting only your signature, which is known to me alone) and took steps to have it read in what are known as 'the highest quarters'. I can only hope that it will produce its effect.

Meanwhile I should not like you to think that this is a 'forbidden theme' in the English press in the sense that any pressure has been exerted upon the newspapers to suppress it or that English opinion regards it as trivial. So far as *The Times* is concerned, you will realize that its make-up and traditions debar it from anything in the nature of hints or personal gossip and that no intervention is possible save something in the nature of a serious and solemn warning. It may, unhappily, come to that, and I can assure you that the prospect is constantly before me. But there has been no definite occasion for it yet; and on the other hand there are obvious reasons why there should, if possible, be a definite interval before any such warning could follow on yesterday's proceedings, with which it could in no case be associated.

I am writing to you in confidence because it is clearly better that every method of private representation should be exhausted in the first instance. But I should not like you to think that I am not grateful to you for so exhaustive a statement of the case, or that I am not making the fullest possible use of it.

> Yours very truly,
> Geoffrey Dawson

Hardinge, having read the letter from America, told Dawson that 'he had thought it best hitherto to say nothing to the King on his own account, but to maintain relations with him as Private Secretary and thus be able to facilitate the access of Ministers and other more weighty advisers'.

Dawson, having signified his agreement with this course of action, went on to deliver a second copy of the letter to the Prime Minister. Here Dawson heard for the first time that the Prime Minister had, on his own initiative, already visited the King at Fort Belvedere, his home near Windsor, on 20 October. 'He told me,' writes Dawson, 'more fully than he ever spoke of later events, about his first private conversation.'

He cannot, in fact, have had very much to tell. The main object of the visit was to ask the King to persuade Mrs Simpson to call off the divorce proceedings, which the King had refused to do. But one of the remarkable points about this meeting was that neither the King nor the Prime Minister mentioned the possibility of marriage. Neither was prepared to introduce the topic which was at the back of their minds while they talked.

Dawson's memorandum continues:

On the following day I lunched with Neville Chamberlain [Chancellor of Exchequer], saw S.B. again for a few minutes, and went on to a party at the Vincent Masseys' for the express purpose of having a word with Mackenzie King, who had had an audience of H.M. in the morning. It had been hoped, as I knew, that the P.M. of Canada might have said something on this occasion about the growing anxiety in his own country. He was in a strong position to give such a warning, but it was quite clear from his conversation with me that he had done nothing of the kind – had indeed, if anything, made matters rather worse by discoursing on the King's popularity in the Dominions.'

The Times reported the granting of the decree *nisi* to Mrs Simpson under headlines of studied sobriety:

Undefended Divorce Suit
Case at Ipswich Assizes

'The Judge didn't like the evidence,' grumbled Brodribb, one of the Assistant Editors, as he read the proof before passing it for publication. Dawson continues:

Oct. 28 – I lunched with Edward Halifax [Lord Privy Seal] at Brooks's and talked of nothing but the prevailing topic without being able to see much daylight.

Oct. 30 – Nov. 1 – Then came a hurried week-end visit to Langcliffe for the consecration of our churchyard extension by the Bishop of Bradford [Dr Blunt], who was eventually to play so conspicuous, if unintentional, a part in precipitating the crisis on to the public stage.

Nov. 2 – Lunched with Lord Dawson [the King's physician], who was interesting on the subject of His Majesty's obsession from the medical point of view. The Literary Society, with whom I dined that evening, was also absorbed in the same subject (to the complete exclusion of literature).

Nov. 5 – There was a 'Round Table' dinner at which we wondered when the trouble would come to a head and how it would fit the dates of that difficult quarterly.

The Editor, meanwhile, was at work on the draft of a leader for use in emergency. The existence of this leader became something of a legend in Fleet Street, and even got to the ears of the King. 'I was constantly writing and rewriting odds and ends of comment,' says Dawson.

His description of Archbishop Lang scarcely suggests a conspirator:

Nov. 11 – a talk also with the Archbishop at Lambeth, where he was sitting quite remote from the principal actors in the crisis, having made up his mind (wisely, as I thought) that any intervention on his part would do more harm than good. Apart from his ecclesiastical position, his friendship with the late King had put him out of court . . . He had not met King Edward since July, but had seen Queen Mary once or twice.

It was at Lambeth, on this occasion, that the Archbishop alluded to King George V's having 'had many distressing talks with him about his successor's infatuation, which he thought had definitely shortened his life'.

In the evening the Editor looked in again on the Prime Minister.

This [writes Dawson], and another visit on the following evening, were devoted largely to discussing the possible value of publicity. There were likely to be further popular demonstrations during the impending visit to South Wales and to the Fleet. If newspaper criticism were to begin before these engagements it might be taken as an attempt to undermine HM's popularity in advance; if immediately after them, as an attempt to minimize his influence. It was a very difficult problem, on which S.B. professed himself quite unable to give advice. The press is an unknown world to him, and he wondered vaguely, supposing it should ever become necessary for him to explain the position to the newspapers as a whole, what machinery was available for his use.

The Times did, in fact, take the opportunity of commenting upon some words uttered by the King to the miners in South Wales to remind him of his constitutional obligations. The leader might have been interpreted as a warning shot. But it went no further. In giving the visit this treatment Dawson was, of course, fully aware that, whether he liked it or not, he was setting out guidelines which other papers would follow.

The weekend from Friday 13 November to Monday 16 November was a turning-point. During these days the crisis came rapidly to a head:

Next day [Friday], I paid another visit to Alec Hardinge at Buckingham Palace and he showed me, since I happened to be there, the draft of a letter to his Royal Master which he had felt impelled to write after a sleepless night. It was his first and only intervention – an admirable letter, respectful, courageous, and definite – a warning that the Press could not long be kept silent and that Ministers were about to take counsel together, a plain statement of the constitutional position, and an appeal to the King to get Mrs Simpson out of the country quickly. He sent it off

to Fort Belvedere that same Friday afternoon – and never had
the slightest response or reference to it either in writing or by
word of mouth.

Dawson did not, as is sometimes suggested, make any amendments
to the letter.

There was little sleep for the King that night, either, after he received
it. He was shocked and angry with Hardinge at the impersonal method
of approach. From now on he asked Walter Monckton to be his personal adviser and liaison officer. He also summoned Beaverbrook back
from New York, where he had arrived only that morning.

Dawson spent the weekend at Chevening in Kent with Lord Stanhope.

> Walter Runciman [President of the Board of Trade] was in the
> party – my impression was that he was in favour of some public
> discussion at once, and he entirely approved of the sort of line
> that I had drafted from time to time as an opening gambit. There
> had been a meeting of the Prime Minister and some half-dozen
> of his colleagues (not a Cabinet meeting) on the Friday morning;
> so that Alec Hardinge's warning was by no means premature.

On Monday morning the Editor saw Gwynne of the *Morning Post*,
who was seeking guidance. Here we discern the anxiety of the professional journalist breaking through. Gwynne was in favour of simul-
taneous publication by all the newspapers at government discretion.
Dawson disagreed, but 'the main point to me was that the *Morning
Post* was not going to do anything without a lead'.

That evening Baldwin saw the King and for the first time broached
the question of the marriage, while, also for the first time, the King
told him of his determination to marry Mrs Simpson and of his 'readiness to go' if necessary.

The Prime Minister summoned the Editor the same night.

> It was a difficult moment in the production of the paper but of
> course I went down at once to the House of Commons and found
> him unusually depressed and worried. He told me nothing definite
> of his talk with the King, but broke out impatiently once or twice
> about his 'obsession'. Meanwhile he made it clear for the first
> time that any press comment at this moment might weaken his
> influence, such as it was.

On Tuesday evening, 17 November, Walter Monckton had half an
hour's talk with Barrington-Ward and told him what Baldwin had
omitted to tell Dawson, namely that the King was determined to marry,
and had told the Prime Minister so. 'W. thinks, rightly, that any

publicity just now will make the present decision, and all the consequences, certain.' Monckton went on to describe the infatuation, obstinacy and loneliness of the King: 'Says he cannot do the job without her.' If *The Times* had really been seeking the King's abdication, as opposed to prevention of the marriage, Monckton's information would have provided an incentive for publicity rather than continued silence.

On Friday 20 November Baldwin again saw Dawson, as an adviser rather than as a newspaperman: 'He wanted to clear his mind on a number of cardinal points – to what proposal, and at what stage, the Cabinet (if it became a Cabinet question) could properly make formal objection; what would be the reaction to such a course in the country etc.'

Tuesday 24 November gave Dawson the opportunity to write another leader aimed obliquely at the King. Patrick Duncan, another former member of the Milner Kindergarten, had just been appointed Governor-General of South Africa: 'I took the occasion to introduce one or two passages on the importance of keeping the Crown and its representatives remote from "glaring public scandal" and above "public reproach or ridicule". '

Two days later the Editor again saw Stanley Baldwin, who told him that the King had now broached the idea of a morganatic marriage, that is, a marriage in which Mrs Simpson would be his wife but not Queen. The Prime Minister attributed this suggestion to Esmond Harmsworth: 'My only other talk that day was with Margot [Lady Oxford] who was full of Mrs S's good sense and good influence on HM.'

Over the weekend, Dawson, who had cancelled a visit to Yorkshire, patiently tried to influence one of the Dominion governments, though he was only preaching to the converted. The question of the morganatic marriage had, at the King's request, been referred by Baldwin to the Dominions' Prime Ministers. Dawson called on S. M. Bruce, the Australian High Commissioner in London, who was ill in bed. He found the High Commissioner completely cut off from news by doctors' orders, but told him briefly what the position was.

> On several occasions afterwards he expressed his gratitude for my visit, and told me that it had enabled him to give his government his own views on what they should say. To judge from his conversation they were refreshingly robust, though he said on one occasion that Lyons's [the Australian Prime Minister's] strong Roman Catholicism had made his draft even stiffer. So my enforced stay in London may not have been altogether useless after all.

About this time Dawson sent to all the *Times* correspondents in the Dominions a somewhat loaded inquiry: 'Cable briefly regularly reactions

King news. Best opinion here solid against proposed marriage in any guise. Dominions support valuable help peaceful outcome.'

On Sunday Dawson dropped in on the Archbishop, finding him anxious, but 'still taking no hand in public affairs'. Later Arthur Mann, Editor of the *Yorkshire Post*, arrived at Printing House Square. This was timely, as it was in his area that the storm next day was about to break. Dawson found him 'perfectly clear and sound'. Colin Coote, the political leader writer, was instructed to include in his survey of the parliamentary week an exhortation to the House of Commons to prove itself 'a Council of State, which is able to demonstrate its solid strength in any crisis that may arise, whether foreign or domestic'.

(iii) *The Nine Days' Wonder*

Tuesday 1 December was the beginning of what is sometimes called 'the nine days' wonder', which opened with Dr Blunt's tactless speech at a diocesan conference in Yorkshire and ended on 10 December with the King's formal assent to his own abdication.

That night Dawson found on his desk the report of a speech by the Bishop of Bradford, Dr Blunt, 'in which he expressed his hope that the King was aware of his need for God's grace at his Coronation and his wish that he gave more positive signs of his awareness'. With the report was an agency message carrying a long quotation from the leader due to appear in next morning's issue of the *Yorkshire Post*, which went much farther than the Bishop and revealed the whole course of the scandal in the American press. Arthur Mann had circulated this through the agencies in advance of publication so that the London papers would have an opportunity of reporting it if they wished.

For a keen professional journalist such as Dawson, who was also pre-eminently conscious of his public duties according to his own lights, the situation was a nightmare. It was enough to drive him for once to ask advice from other editors rather than to give it:

> I had always felt very strongly that we must be the first to speak. The rest of the press had quite openly been looking to us for a lead. And now the floodgates had unquestionably been opened . . . so I took the (to me unprecedented) course of ringing up Camrose of the *Telegraph* and Gwynne of the *Morning Post* and asking them plainly what they meant to do about it . . . Gwynne had left the office before dinner, giving instructions that nothing was to be said . . . Camrose was reluctant even to report the Bishop's address . . . After thinking things over . . . I told him (1) that it was quite impossible in my opinion to withhold publication of a pronouncement which would certainly become historic, and (2) that I had made up my mind to refrain from

comment until the following day. He said he would take the
same course; and, since it was certain that the Rothermere and
Beaverbrook organs would not explode, I felt pretty confident
now that the whole London press was safe.

Next day – Wednesday 2 December – there was a curious incident at
the Wyndham Club. Dawson was kept in touch with the situation principally through Baldwin. But Barrington-Ward was in touch with the
King indirectly through Walter Monckton. While giving lunch to a
friend, Barrington-Ward saw Monckton come into the room, and had
a few private words with him. He was on his way to the King: 'Thinks
it will be all right.'

Monckton then left, but shortly after telephoned him from the King's
room, asking him to remain at the club until he could get back to see
him. This Barrington-Ward did. On arrival, Monckton, who had been
sent back at the King's instruction, explained that His Majesty was
convinced that the comments in the *Yorkshire Post* and other northern
papers had been organized by Baldwin, Dawson and the Archbishop.
He also thought that *The Times* was going to publish a full life of Mrs
Simpson in the next day's paper. Barrington-Ward denied both allegations. Monckton told him that the King was very angry, which augured
ill for the interview fixed with Baldwin for that night. Mrs Simpson was
to leave England the next day. The King was anxious over his finances,
if and when he were to go, and he [Monckton] had been compelled to
abandon his private practice in order to seek a settlement.

That morning, as we have seen, *The Times* and other London papers
had published no comment on the King's affairs – although *The Times*
had contained a leading article laudatory of the Duke and Duchess of
York, who had been visiting Edinburgh. Now, on Wednesday, the Editor
pulled out from his drawer the notes which he had been drafting and
put together a comparatively mild leading article familiarizing readers
with the campaign in the American press and explaining the reasons for
the silence of the British newspapers. It went on to speak of 'a marriage
incompatible with the Throne' and called for a reassuring statement
from the monarch if the monarchy itself were not to be damaged.

That same Wednesday Dawson again saw the Prime Minister. The
latter was about to leave to tell the King the adverse replies of the
Dominion governments on the proposal for a morganatic marriage. 'He
had nothing much to tell me yet beyond reporting a solid front in the
Dominions and the House of Commons. He seemed indeed to be nearly
at the end of his tether and sat with his head in his hands on the table,
probably just glad to have someone with him till the time for his interview came.' (Dawson probably did not know that Baldwin, in August
had narrowly escaped a nervous breakdown.)

Then, in the late evening, the King made another attempt to approach *The Times*. The Prime Minister rang up – 'the only time, I think, that I ever heard his own voice on the telephone' – to say that the King was worrying him to find out, and if necessary stop, what was going to appear in *The Times*. He understood that there would be an attack on Mrs Simpson and instructed the Prime Minister to forbid it. Baldwin had explained that he had no control over *The Times* or over any other paper.

A little later the Prime Minister rang up again, to say that the King would now be satisfied, and would leave the Prime Minister alone, if the latter would read the leading article for him: 'Could I possibly let him see it for the sake of peace?' Dawson sent a proof down about midnight. Baldwin appears to have been asleep by the time it arrived. Neither *The Times* nor, with one or two exceptions, the other London newspapers made mention of Mrs Simpson by name that morning. The *News Chronicle*, alone, supported a morganatic marriage.

By now, matters were hastening to a close. On Saturday 5 December, the King informed Baldwin that he had decided to abdicate. *The Times* continued with a series of leaders, one, on Friday 4 December, clearly setting out the objection to the marriage on the grounds of Mrs Simpson's two divorces – 'The objection, conscientiously held by millions of the King's subjects, was not remediable by law.'

The next few days saw the movement for the organization of a 'King's Party', which caused Baldwin some anxiety. 'The mischief-makers,' as Dawson called them, were 'a curious alliance of Churchill, Rothermere and Beaverbrook with all their papers, the *News Chronicle* representing the Liberal intellectuals, and of couse Lady Houston and her *Saturday Review* . . . reinforced by Oswald Mosley's Fascists, who were organizing demonstrations in the streets.'

Although behind the scenes matters were progressing steadily in the direction of abdication, there were distractions. The King wished to broadcast to the people, but was prevented by the Prime Minister. There were threats of intervention by third parties with the King's Proctor, which might have had the effect of nullifying the decree *nisi* if the King abdicated. Dawson received warnings of these on two occasions. He passed the information on to Halifax, but they 'agreed it might only add to the Prime Minister's worries if we told him about it'.

On Tuesday 8 December *The Times* published a leader by Barrington-Ward once more demolishing the morganatic-marriage idea. It contained a phrase which gave offence: 'The Constitution,' he wrote, 'is to be amended in order that she [Mrs Simpson] may carry in solitary prominence the brand of unfitness for the Queen's Throne.' There were those who interpreted this as a hit at Mrs Simpson, but it is more likely that the writer intended it as a hit at Lord Rothermere and those who had proposed such a solution to the King's dilemma. Barrington-Ward in his diary for Monday, the day on which he composed the leader, merely notes: 'To the office. Wrote another leader to finish off Rothermere and the morganatic marriage. Dined with the 14th Div. at the Junior United Services Club.'

On that Monday, too, Mrs Simpson, who had hitherto remained silent, issued from Cannes her famous statement of renunciation:

> Mrs Simpson, throughout the last few weeks, has invariably wished to avoid any action or proposal which would hurt or damage His Majesty, or the Throne. Today her attitude is unchanged, and she is willing, if such action would solve the problem, to withdraw forthwith from a situation that has been rendered both unhappy and untenable.

The motivation of Mrs Simpson in issuing this statement, and indeed its exact interpretation, have remained a matter for some conjecture ever since. Issued a week earlier, it might have had considerable impact, but coming as it did after the King's decision to abdicate and the collapse of any popular movement in his favour, it was too late materially to influence events.

In the first edition *The Times* published Mrs Simpson's statement alongside a paragraph announcing that 'Thelma Viscountess Furness arrived at Southampton in the liner *Queen Mary* yesterday from New York'. Later in the evening this paragraph was moved to the column underneath the Court Circular. The paper was accused of malice, for it was through Lady Furness that the King and Mrs Simpson first met.

During Wednesday 9 December the constitutional papers necessary for the Act of Abdication were being prepared.

During the whole period of the crisis, a mass of letters had been received at *The Times* which would neither be published nor even acknowledged. It occurred to the Editor, during this period of lull, that a survey of these should be made and the results published, for the record, in a leader. Dermot Morrah, a senior home leader writer, was commissioned to undertake the task, and the result showed a gradual swing away from unquestioning loyalty to the King, through a period of doubt and criticism to a mood almost of hostility for putting private inclination before public duty. The survey confirms, if any valid inferences at all may be drawn from it, that press silence, which had been desired so keenly by both the King and Baldwin, worked in favour of the King and not the Prime Minister.

(iv) *The Final Act*
On Thursday 10 December the drama came to a close.

The scene in the House [wrote Dawson] – the Prime Minister's entry with the Royal Message and his subsequent speech – has been described so often that it need not figure in this narrative. I only record my personal impression of S.B.'s almost conversational manner, of the characteristic untidiness of his scraps of notes, of the skill with which he told the whole story without a word that could give offence, and of the simple sincerity of certain memorable phrases.

I came back to the office as soon as the House adjourned for an interval of reflection . . . I settled down in the end to the completion of my own contribution on 'King Edward's Choice'; and finished it just in time to send it to the printer before joining a great dinner party at Abe Bailey's – to be followed by a presentation from the Round Table.

King Edward [ran Dawson's leader in *The Times* next day] had most of the qualities that would have made a great Constitutional Monarch. He had shown himself brave, completely free from pompousness, chivalrous where his affections were engaged, conscientious in his everyday public duties, attractive to a crowd, genuinely interested in the condition of the poor as he went about among them. He was unfortunate, no doubt, in some of his intimates . . .

That, amid all his great qualities, there was also something lacking in himself is sufficiently shown by the unprecedented decision recorded this morning . . .

What seems almost incredible is that any man who was born and trained to such high responsibilities, who had clearly the capacity to undertake them, and who had in fact begun to exercise them with the complete good will of the nation, should sacrifice it all to a personal preference for another way of life. *Omnium consensu capax imperii nisi imperasset* – the well-worn quotation from Tacitus – is still irresistible.

And there [concludes Dawson in his narrative] the crisis was brought to an end so far as *The Times* was concerned . . . There were naturally comments in *The Times* on these events and on the smoothness and rapidity with which they had passed, but no further reference was ever made to the cause which had provoked them.

Dawson was afterwards accused of kicking a man when he was down by writing this leader. The charge scarcely seemed justified. As Editor of *The Times* he could not balk the issue of a final comment on so historical a constitutional struggle. His appraisal of the King was honest and dignified, and if anything went rather beyond his real feelings in giving credit where it belonged. Dawson did not dislike the King; but neither did he admire him. His attitude was *de haut en bas*, and faintly patronizing. Of the milieu that surrounded the King – and if one is looking for names some of them are to be found in the Court Circulars of the dinner parties already referred to – he frankly disapproved.

If further evidence of his view of King Edward VIII is sought it may be found in a letter written a year later to Sir Willmott Lewis, *The Times* Washington correspondent, giving him guidance on how to cover a visit by the Duke of Windsor, as he now was:

> No one here would like to see the Duke of Windsor received with anything but friendliness and hopefulness. At the same time this projected study of labour conditions is not, and cannot be, taken very seriously. The simple truth is that, while HRH has a naturally kind heart, and has always been sympathetic to distress when he sees it, he has never shown the slightest interest in the subject when away from his popular tours. There is little doubt that he has been incited in this outlet for his restless energy by people who would like to make use of him for their own purpose of fishing in troubled waters.

Dawson may have underestimated the Duke's abilities, which were greater than he allowed him, but he was not, as is sometimes alleged, activated by mere spite or malice. He was against the marriage, not the King. Delane in his day had deemed it his duty to criticize Queen Victoria when he thought that she was acting in a manner injurious to the monarchy. In the matter of the King's marriage Dawson could scarcely do less.

Of one indignity Dawson may certainly be acquitted. He did not 'weep crocodile tears' or try to 'collar the martyrdom', as the Archbishop and the Prime Minister were accused, not altogether unjustly, of doing. He stood four square and unemotional through it all. 'It was,' he concludes laconically on the final night, 'as may be supposed, a strenuous evening, and I went to bed pretty tired.'

The abdication was a crisis which the British came out of with credit. Both the winners and the losers understood instinctively the part they were expected to play in this Shakespearean dynastic drama.

Perhaps the greatest loss to Britain was the damage done to the political reputation of Churchill. He had been proved wrong on a domestic issue, at a time when it was most important that he should be trusted on a foreign one. What Ministers failed to recognize in the European tragedy about to be enacted was that when playing against the King they were matched against a man who played the game according to the rules, whereas when they were playing against Hitler they were not.

But the persons above all responsible for the fact that the abdication did no permanent damage to the British fabric were the Duke and

The vans of W. H. Smith collecting *The Times* at Printing House Square.

An artist's impression of Richard Pigott in the Witness Box.

TREMBLING ON THE BRINK

Nurse Sinister: "Now Master Charles don't be afraid; you'll find it nice and refreshing."

Bathing Woman: "Yes come to your Matha, come, come, come; you'll be quite a different boy when it's over."

Master Parnell: "Boo-hoo it's so cold, and I am afraid I shall be drowned."

By His Majefty's Royal Letters Patent.

LONDON, JUNE 25th, 1784.

M R. WALTER begs leave to inform the public, that, having obtained an affign-
ment of his MAJESTY's LETTERS PATENT, for the fole privilege of cafting,
and cementing for ufe or fale, Types of Words, &c. he has purchafed the King's
late Printing-Houfe, near Apothecaries-hall, which is now opened for carrying on
the printing bufinefs in general, upon an approved invention of compofing with
words entire, their roots, and terminations, inftead of fingle letters, from a fyftem of
arrangement, formed with the affiftance of the inventor, after a very laborious ftudy
and application.

It muft be obvious to the moft common underftanding, that when an arrangement
is formed, from which the Compofitor can with facility take up every word he wants,
without the fpace being fo far extended as to occafion delay, it muft have very
fuperior advantages to the prefent mode of printing. A treatife has been publifhed,
intitled, " An Introduction to Logography," in which a full account is given of the
propofed plan. It may, however, be neceffary to fuggeft, that a neatnefs and correctnefs has been experienced, much beyond the common method—it is far lefs liable to
literal errors—there can be no wrong fpelling, or letters inverted—no dirt can
adhere to make the letters at different diftances, and the errors of the prefs are very
trifling when a proof is taken. With thefe advantages, others arife of ftill greater
magnitude; the extraordinary expedition which will attend it, and the fhort time
required for the compofitor to learn his bufinefs, will tend when the heavy expences
already incurred are defrayed, to reduce the charge of printing.

An undertaking of fuch importance makes it effentially requifite that his friends
fhould intereft themfelves in the firft inftance to render him every fupport and affiftance till the merits of it are better known, as ftrangers cannot be expected to countenance it in prejudice to former connexions. The utility of fuch an improvement
muft be of great moment, and Mr. WALTER flatters himfelf, will call forth the
countenance and protection of a nation, famous for its improvement in the polite
arts; and they may be affured, neither affiduity nor expence fhall be wanting to render
it worthy their attention and encouragement.

N. B. Early next winter, A NEW DAILY PAPER will be publifhed, to be named THE
UNIVERSAL REGISTER, on a liberal plan, that fhall neither be devoted to
party invective or fulfome panegyric; and it is hoped the ufeful and neceffary
improvements to the method now adopted by moft of the prefent daily publications will meet general approbation. Of this paper a defcription will be given,
preparatory to its appearance.

Done at the LOGOGRAPHIC-OFFICE, Printing-houfe-Square, Blackfryars.

An early example of a publicity leaflet done at the Logographic Office,
Printing House Square.

Sir Denis Hamilton 1966–1967   Sir William Rees-Mogg 1967–1981

Harold Evans 1981–1982   Charles Douglas-Home 1982–

THE FOUR RECENT EDITORS

(OVERLEAF) The front page of the ill-fated April 30 1979, weekly edition of *The Times*, printed in Germany.

THE TIMES

Monday April 30 1979

No 60,471 A

Price fifteen pence

Threat to clear win in UK poll after 'scare campaign'

With the Conservatives' lead over Labour in the British election narrowing in the opinion polls, the possibility of an indecisive result for the third successive time could centre on whether the voters will heed Labour's warnings against a woman leader. Mrs Thatcher said on the issue: "I did not get here by being some strident female." Meanwhile a Tory spokesman has declared that a Liberal vote was a "dangerous" vote.

By Fred Emery
Political Editor

Would the Conservatives manage to throw away an almost certain victory in next Thursday's British election? That question hangs over the final hectic days of the campaign. And it raises again the possibility of an indecisive result in the third successive election.

It raises also a faint hope for Labour and the spectre for the Conservatives of having to rely on the Liberal Party for parliamentary support to form a government.

Towards the close, as the Conservatives' lead in the opinion polls began to falter, Mrs Margaret Thatcher and her colleagues sought to shake themselves out of the defensive posture they were continually being forced into by what they alleged was the Labour Government's scare campaigning.

Unexpectedly help came their way on the most unpredictable issue — whether British voters could, at the last, bring themselves to vote for their first woman leader for a party because the leader was a woman, Tory or Labour".

Sir Harold complained later that "he had been" the butt of misrepresentation", but he agreed that his wife Mary, was the sort of woman "more likely to vote for a party because the leader was a woman, Tory or Labour".

Sir Harold, although held in little regard these days by political

Some Labour ministers admit that in their constituencies people frequently complain that they should never have resigned in 1976. One likely result of his latest intervention was to bring the "woman" issue to the fore again.

It has been in the back of most minds all through. And the month-long recriminatory campaign has been fought largely on it as an unspoken premise, with Labour taking a perilous leap in the dark with a government led by a woman, and just as the right-wing Tory woman at that.

Mrs Thatcher, towards the close, has confronted the issue of her own identity head on. Living dangerously with her words, she told questioners in Glasgow: "I did not get here by being some strident female... I do not like strident females".

And she added, in a seeming invitation to all women to take a chance with her, that were she defeated, the chance might not return for a generation. "I could do a lot for women at the top, and indeed for women on the way to the top."

Until the final days of the campaign the Conservatives have tried to ride the wave of popular discontent stirred up in last winter's strikes while avoiding two things: mistakes, and specific detail in their promises.

Serious discussion was only sporadic as distinct from continual slanging — about what either party would do in government to revive Britain's industrial health.

The Prime Minister, who has enjoyed a successful personal campaign, put up Mrs Thatcher on her repeated accusation of

Callaghan challenge on new laws to curb union wreckers

Mr Callaghan gave warning that using the law to "get at them", as Mrs Thatcher wanted, was a sure recipe for confrontation and chaos in industry, worse even than that seen at the end of Mr Heath's term of office in 1974.

The apprehensions were taken up by Mr Len Murray, the TUC general secretary. In a notable speech at Scarborough he said: "We need industrial cooperation like we need a hole in the head".

In accusing the Tories of being two faced, he said: "It has been left to Mr Prior to make soothing noises about wanting to cooperate with the trade unions while Mrs Thatcher has been launching against the unions a series of unfair, inaccurate and irrelevant attacks".

Mr Prior, whose position as secretary of State for Employment would be crucial to a Conservative relations with the TUC, has repeatedly sought to blunt the offensive. Although originally he had no more favoured using the law on union reform than had Mr Callaghan, he insisted that strikers' abuses during the winter now made reform vital.

But equally he insisted that the legal reforms propposed were "limited", as well as enjoying the support of most "reasonable" people.

Mr Prior was one of several leading Tories towards the close of the campaign who chose to accentuate their apprehension of the Liberal vote.

Mr Norman St John-Stevas, who expects to be in a Conservative Cabinet, perhaps as Leader of the House of Commons, notably declared: "Beware of the

Mr Callaghan at his morning conference before going out to campaign.

a dangerous vote. They supported a socialism before, and given a chance they will do so again."

cent led over Labour: Conservatives 44 per cent; Labour 41 per cent; Liberal 12 per cent. Earlier in the week the poll had

Queen's visit to Africa complicates Tory policy

By Charles Douglas-Home

The Queen's visit to Africa in July and August has now become an important factor in future British policy towards Rhodesia, particularly if an incoming Tory Government responds favourably to the outcome of the Rhodesian election.

The Queen will visit Lusaka for the Commonwealth Prime Ministers Conference in August, but is due to pay state visits on the way, first in Tanzania and then in Malawi and Botswana. It is the Tanzanian visit which may present complications, for a Conservative Government, since President Nyerere has been one of the fiercest critics of the internal settlement in Rhodesia which has now, after the election, produced a government led by Bishop Muzorewa.

The Foreign Office hopes that a Conservative Government will postpone making any decision on Zimbabwe-Rhodesia as it will now be called by its first black-majority government, until Britain has met the full Commonwealth at Lusaka. Conservative leaders do not think they can wait until then, but intend to start immediate consultations with Washington, the Commonwealth and the EEC in which they will register their belief and hope that the Muzorewa Government should now be recognized.

If this action causes the Tanzanians to have second thoughts about the Queen's state visit, a Conservative Government would regret the fact, but find it difficult to mortgage its whole Rhodesian policy to this one visit.

Some hope is expressed in Whitehall that the Tanzanians will be preoccupied with their conquest of Uganda. There is also the fact President Nyerere and the Queen have a warm friendship and the President is known to have been particularly keen for the Queen to return his own state visit to London of 1975.

The Times weekly: voice that has earned a right to be heard

By Louis Heren

The international weekly edition of *The Times*, of which this is the first issue, is intended to maintain the title of the paper and serve our many overseas readers while daily publication of *The Times* remains suspended. It is written and prepared by our editorial staff in London and overseas, is printed by union labour, in western Europe, and will not be sold in Britain.

We cannot, unfortunately, provide our usual service with a weekly edition, the size of which is also limited by available printing capacity. Obviously, we cannot pour a gallon into a half-pint pot, but careful distillation will, we hope, maintain standards and provide an informative and readable newspaper.

Special emphasis has been given to home, foreign, business, sports and social news, and to leading articles and comment. Some of our features, reviews of arts and books, law reports, obituaries and of course the crossword are included.

Thomas Jefferson once said that if he had to make a choice between newspapers and government he would choose newspapers. He changed his mind when elected President of the United States, but neither democratic government nor the people they represent can flourish without the free exchange of news and opinion.

That is one reason why we are publishing this weekly edition, despite the opposition of unions in Britain. We also believe that newspapers can help to improve understanding between peoples, and if we cannot publish in Britain we can at least hope to serve our overseas readers, whose interest and support have made *The Times* a world newspaper.

We have long treasured this relationship with Commonwealth, European, American and Arab-world readers, not for financial gain, which is in fact slight, but because it has helped to give a global dimension to our contents.

The Times is also a voice of

1785, without interruption until recent years, and is regarded at home and abroad as a British institution.

We are grateful for such public esteem, but we prefer to regard ourselves as a newspaper: an independent newspaper, deeply involved in the concerns of the present but conscious of the lessons of the past and aware of our responsibility to the future.

We also know that a newspaper is more than the sum of its parts. A rich man can buy a printing plant and recruit journalists and production workers, but he will not necessarily create a newspaper.

At least, not a newspaper such as *The Times*. Tradition is one of the obvious reasons, but there are others.

The Times has always attracted honest reporters and good writers but has generally moulded them in its own image. And there has always been interaction between the journalists and the institution, each gaining from the other, but continuity has been vital to the development and progress of both.

That continuity cannot be broken for an indefinite period without damage to the newspaper and the men and women who write and edit it. We know that our readers and advertisers remain loyal to the paper and will return when we publish again, but we cannot put our journalists in cold storage.

It is the nature of journalists to respond to the events they report and comment upon. For most of them the story the reporting, the realization of what really happened, and the writing is as important as the event.

We can no longer put the future of *The Times*, which they corporately represent, at risk. For me, this is the decisive reason for launching this international weekly edition. It will help to keep alive the spirit and traditions of *The Times*.

The unions disagree, alas. They seem determined to use their

on future of Europe

By Our Foreign Staff

The United States is prepared to pay the price of increased competition from Europe in the interests of a stable international system, Mr Zbiginiew Brzezinski, the United States national security adviser, told correspondents of *Europa*, the economic monthly published by *The Times*, *Le Monde*, *Die Welt* and *La Stampa*.

Mr Brzezinski said that one of the inherent dilemmas of the American-European relationship was that Washington did not want a weak, pliant Europe and yet it recognized that as Europe became stronger and therefore more of a partner, Europe was also bound to contest the United States more.

"But that is a price we are prepared to pay because our historical perspective is one which involves a commitment to a world of diversity with a number of key players in it collectively contributing to world stability. For these players to be genuine players, they have to have the capacity and self-confidence from time to time to disagree with us.

"If the choice is between a passive and pliant Europe, or an allied, active but occasionally contesting Europe, it is the latter which is more in keeping with our image of a stable international system", Mr Brzezinski said.

Asked about European concerns that their security needs were not adequately met in Salt II, particularly on cruise missile technology transfer and theatre nuclear forces, Mr Brzezinski said that he felt there had been more frequent and more wide-ranging United States European consultations than on any other issue.

US swop spies for Mr Ginsberg

Five Soviet dissidents, including Mr Alexander Ginsberg, have been exchanged for two Russians jailed for spying in the United States.

The other four are Mark Dymshyts and Edward Kuznetsov jailed for an attempt to fly an aircraft to the West, Ukranian Velentyn Moroz, and the Baptist leader Georg Vins.

The two Russians arrived back in Moscow on Saturday. The exchange was the result of lengthy negotiations by Mr Brezezinski, the US national security adviser and the Soviet ambassador.

endanger Barre plan

The French steel industry exemplifies the cause and effect of the plan of M Raymond Barre, the Prime Minister, to restructure the French economy on a sound basis. The resulting unemployment and other troubles in the industry could also prove to be the undoing of the plan, Ian Murray writes from Paris. Page 6

Close study of manifestos

Party manifestos are not compulsive reading for most voters, but three important groups do study them closely. The Civil Service monitors them for possible changes in legislation; the House of Lords for important Labour policies that it judges it must not oppose; and party activists who use the documents as a moral yardstick to chastise a wayward leadership Page 2

Uganda's task

The civilian government in Uganda is faced with the daunting task of restoring the country's shattered economy after the damage done by the eight-year Amin regime. The problem of law and order also looms large as the retreating Ugandan army leaves a trail of chaos Page 7

M Chirac aims at presidential goal

M Jacques Chirac, the leader of France's Gaullist party, is set on a collision course with the Government over the European elections which he sees as a direct threat to national sovereignty. The motive behind his action is seen as a step towards his goal of the presidency. Page 6

Rich pickings in postal vote

The Conservative superiority in mobilizing the postal vote appears to be slowly eroding as the Labour Party becomes more aware of the rich electoral pickings to be gained. In past elections, the Conservative advantage, crucial in a close poll, has been estimated to be worth between five and 13 seats. Page 4

US budgets: California's Proposition 13 has started a bandwagon rolling in America for more prudent federal spending 15

Tennis: Leading women players returning in force to European circuit 12

Racing: Henry Cecil strongly represented in both Guineas races 13

International Edition

Pre-paid subscribers outside the United Kingdom and Eire receive this issue free of charge. A further announcement will be made in the next issue.

Overseas selling prices

Austria, Sch 18; Belgium, Bfr 28; Canaries, Pes 60; Denmark, Dkr 4.25; Finland, Fmk 3.50; France, Frs 3.50; Germany, Dmk 2.50; Greece, Dr 35; Holland, Dfl 2.00; Hongkong, HK$ 6.00; Italy, Lire 700; Luxembourg, Lf 23; Madeira, Esc 25.00; Malta, 13 c; Norway, K 4.50; Portugal, Esc 25; Spain, Pes 60; Sweden, Skr 4.50; Switzerland, Sfr 2.50; USA/Canada $1.00; Yugoslavia, Din 25.

Published weekly. 2nd class postage paid at New York, N.Y. 201 East 42nd St New York, N.Y. Tel 98 69 230

Leader page, 9
Letters: On money for the NHS from Sir Francis Avery Jones; and on *The Times*, from M. Jacques Fauvet and others.
Leading articles: General election; 'The Times;'; Foreign policy issues in the general election

Arts, page 11
John Percival interviews George Balanchine on a lifetime in ballet; William Mann on the Beecham legacy and legend; John Russell Taylor on painting in Paris and London; theatre and film surveys by Irving Wardle and David Robinson; Michael Radcliffe's Monday Book review

Sport, page 12 and 13
Football: Irony of inflated transfer fees; Rugby Union: Objective of England's Far East tour; Cricket: Need of rewards for good behaviour.

Business News, pages 14, 15
Tesco founder's shares; inflation accounting decision due; Ruhr financial aid; Times/Halifax house price index

Published by Michael Mander, and printed by Tercüman, Neu Isenburg/Zeppelinheim. Setting by Otto Gutfreund und Sohn, Darmstadt.
Responsible Editor: Michael Hamlyn, Darmstadt.

Home News	2,4	Court	10	Law Report	10
European News	6	Crossword	16	Letters	9
Overseas News	6,7	Diary	8	Obituary	10
Art	11	Engagements	10	Science	10
Business	14,15	Features	8	Sport	12,13

By Peter Hennessy

Mr Frederick Mulley, Secretary of State for Defence, has provoked a private but outspoken dispute with an all-party select committee of the Commons by his refusal to permit serving officers, civil servants and government scientists to give evidence about the options for a third-generation British nuclear deterrent to replace the Royal Navy's Polaris submarine squadron.

Feelings between the Ministry of Defence and the defence and external affairs sub-committee of the Select Committee on Expenditure have become progressively strained over recent months, with MPs and their advisers taking the view that the ministry has been niggardly in the provision of documents and witnesses across a range of inquiries.

Differences deepened into strongly worded exchanges about the constitutional rights of backbench committees when Mr Mulley made it clear that the only witness from the ministry on the deterrent issue would be himself.

The argument continued until Parliament was dissolved, with Mr Mulley determined to avoid widening, through public or private debate, the pronounced rift of opinion within the Labour Party about the desirability of a successor system to Polaris and the committee increasingly jealous of its rights.

A meeting was arranged for March 27 between the committee's chairman, Sir Harwood Harrison, then Conservative MP for Eye, its clerk, Mr Matthew Cooper, Mr Mulley and Sir Frank Cooper, permanent secretary to the ministry, to air the committee's accumulated grievances.

The meeting was postponed, however, because of the confidence debate in the Commons the next day. Mr Mulley replied to the committee's criticisms by letter instead. Sir Harwood's last letter to Mr Mulley, drafted by Mr Cooper in blunt terms, caused offence inside the ministry, which feels the committee has exhibited faults of its own in its approach to the deterrent inquiry.

Mr Mulley's reply reaffirmed his view that the Secretary of State must decide who appears before the committee on behalf of the ministry.

Among the officers and officials debarred by Mr Mulley from attending the committee's private hearings were Marshal of the Royal Air Force Sir Neil Cameron, Chief of the Defence Staff, Rear-Admiral Sir David Scott, Chief of the Polaris Executive, Rear-Admiral Ronald Squires, Flag Officer Submarines, Admiral Sir Henry Leach, Commander-in-Chief Fleet, and Mr David Cardwell, Director of the Atomic Weapons Research Establishment.

Continued on page 16, col 3

Trade hopes in Giscard Moscow trip

From Michael Binyon
Moscow

The Russians have always had a soft spot for France, and President Giscard d'Estaing's state visit comes at a time when Moscow appears eager to revive a special relationship that in recent years has been in danger of losing some of its warmth.

The meeting was not expected to lead to any important new political initiatives. But the Russians are anxious for reassurance that France retains some vestige of de Gaulle's vision of Europe from "the Atlantic to the Urals", and that President Giscard is not about to draw any closer to the Americans and Nato.

The French in turn hope the visit will reinforce their privileged trading position with the Russians.

Such an exchange of good political relations for increased trade has led to resentment from other West European countries.

The meeting in many ways was a test for President Brezhnev, whose uncertain health has been a topic of considerable speculation in the West. At the summit in Bonn last May there were reports that he was not able to depart easily from his negotiating brief or keep up intensive discussion for long.

UN force facing long stay in Lebanon

From Robert Fisk
Tibnin southern Lebanon

You only have to sit on the hills above the village of Houle just east of here to understand why last week's truce in southern Lebanon is likely to go the way of all ceasefires in this country.

Every few hours, a cloud of grey smoke will rise from the wadi to the north and then– far along the horizon near Metullah – artillery explosions will obscure the local Israeli observation post on the border.

The curiously innocent "popping" sound that the exchange of fire makes at this distance has a special meaning for the United Nations peacekeeping troops down here. It is not just one more truce violation – another unexplained artillery duel which will provoke their two-way radios to crackle with questions– but also a reminder that the United Nations Interim Force in Lebanon (Unifil) is no longer "interim" at all.

For what was intended to be a small-scale peacekeeping role is fast becoming a permanent and large-scale military operation that could conceivably go on for years.

The events of the last week in southern Lebanon only confirm the suspicion of United Nations officers here that the Security Council's desire to see Lebanese sovereignty extended over the entire country is a pipe-dream. They do not say so in those words, but there is no mistaking the new and graver tones in which they talk of their duties in the wild and mountainous countryside around Tibnin.

Colonel Vincent Savino, commander of the United Nations Irish 44 Infantry Battalion and a veteran of the Congo campaign, says that the shelling which his men underwent last week was "a very traumatic experience" and he is clearly under no illusions about the new truce.

"For me personally, the Congo was a very cut and dried operation," he says, with a soldier's interest in tactics rather than history. "I knew what was doing there. I knew what the mission was and I knew the mission could be fulfilled. Here in Lebanon, the mission cannot be fulfilled at the present moment...

In the Congo, although we lost a lot of men, we had a good idea of what was happening. Here we are in a vacuum in which various factions mill around, and from time to time we are completely lost."

It is not difficult to see why. The Irish – like their Norwegian, Dutch, Nigerian and other colleagues in Unifil – find it difficult to understand why the Israelis also want to shell them.

Officially, they say they do not know who fires the shells which land around their posts, but

Continued on Page 16, col 3

doubt about that; the suspended publication of *The Times* is but one example of the dissension that has plagued this once tolerant and pragmatic country for so many years.

A new internal balance will be achieved, if not by the new government then by the next. Until that happy day arrives, only impartial news reporting and fair and considered views and opinions can help readers towards an understanding.

We must also declare an intensely personal interest. *The Times* has been published since members. That is their right, but another right is at stake – the freedom of the press: in this instance, the freedom of *The Times* to print good newspapers without fear or favour from governments, proprietors, advertisers and trade unions.

The Times has fought for this right for nearly 200 years, and the new international weekly edition is but another skirmish in the long battle. Let us hope that it will become a thriving supplement to the paper when *The Times* returns, restored and with renewed robustness.

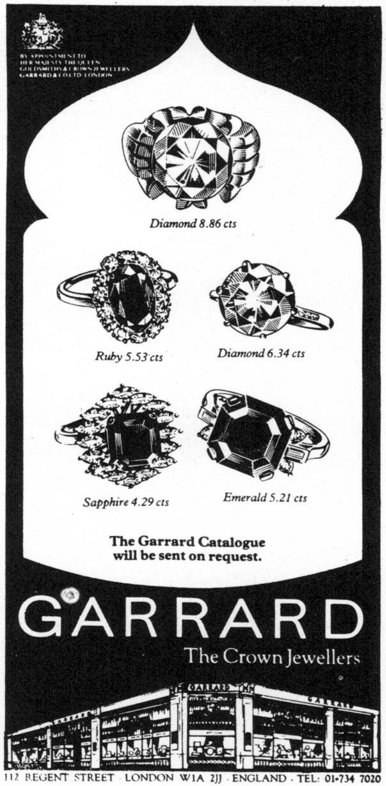

Rupert Murdoch, who bought *The Times* from the Thomson Organisation in 1981.

Duchess of York. The conventional view that George VI was a successful King because he represented a return to the era of George V is mistaken. George VI was more suited to the mood of the forties than Edward VIII would have been. King Edward was essentially a product of the 1914–18 war and the 'roaring twenties'. His brother assumed his responsibilities with just that mixture of humour, seriousness and modest courage with which thousands of his countrymen were to go to war in three years' time: 'If the worst comes to the worst, and I have to take over' – this *cri de coeur* uttered by him during the crisis well illustrates the semi-deprecatory approach which was intelligible to the new King's contemporaries. The new Queen exercised, and continued to exercise, a hold on the imagination of the British people such as has rarely been surpassed or equalled by a royal personage. Thus the abdication passed off as an episode, but not a catastrophe, in British constitutional history.

23 APPEASEMENT

(i) The Roots of Policy

On four occasions in history *The Times* has had to decide whether or not the nation should be advised to go to war. On two of these occasions Geoffrey Dawson was the Editor responsible for making the ultimate decision.

The paper's support for the Crimean War had been hesitant. *The Times* only committed itself to advocacy of hostilities against Russia after Delane became convinced that the state of public opinion had made war inevitable. Forty years later, in South Africa, the situation was different. *The Times*, under the influence of Moberly Bell if not of Buckle, was an active promoter of hostilities against the South African Republic. Nor, in the approach to the First World War, was the position of the paper ever open to question. Although the staff were never unanimous, those principally concerned in writing on and formulating policy were not in doubt from 1908 onwards as to the reality of the German menace, the necessity for rearmament, and the rightness of honouring the country's obligation to defend Belgium. In the event it was Northcliffe as much as Dawson who took the final decision.

The approach of *The Times* to the Second World War was entirely different. Those responsible for the direction of policy in Printing House Square emerged in the late 1930s as leading advocates of the policy of 'appeasement'. They hoped, by conceding peacefully what they judged to be Germany's just demands, to arrest the outbreak, or resumption, of war with Germany. Much has been written on the subject of *The Times* and appeasement. *The Times* has published its own history, edited and largely written by Stanley Morison, which is strongly critical of the parts played by Geoffrey Dawson and by the Deputy Editor, Barrington-Ward. To this there have been ripostes. Sir Evelyn Wrench, in his biography, has provided the apologia for Dawson, and more recently Donald McLachlan has done the same for Barrington-Ward.* Even though the events in question took place between thirty and forty years ago it is still difficult for contemporaries to write of them with the dispassionate impartiality required of an historian. But it is in this mood that the policy of *The Times* must be reviewed.

In Printing House Square appeasement was not a new concept adopted

* Donald McLachlan: *In the Chair*, Weidenfeld & Nicolson, 1971.

in a hurry under the threat of Hitler and the Munich crisis. Its roots reached back to Dawson's first editorship and the First World War. *The Times* then had always been clear that it would be impossible to make peace with Germany before the Allies were in a position to secure it on their own terms. Dawson had made this abundantly plain when he refused to publish the Lansdowne Letter advocating peace by negotiation in 1917. But in their attitude as to the nature of that peace when it came there was a sharp divergence of views between Dawson and Northcliffe.

The germ of their schism over the treatment of post-war Germany may be conveniently traced to an incident which occurred in October 1918. By that time, the rapid advances of the Allied armies had thrust upon the Government, and *The Times*, the necessity to discuss peace terms. Lord Milner, the War Minister – ever Geoffrey Dawson's mentor – gave an interview to the *Evening Standard* in which he advocated what later came to be known as 'a soft peace': 'Complete victory,' he said, was the 'destruction of Prussian militarism.' In comparison with this primary object other plans, such as the punishment of war criminals, reparations, and territorial readjustments were secondary. 'It is a serious mistake, Lord Milner thinks, to imagine that the German people are in love with militarism.'

There are a number of interesting points about this statement. On the day before delivering it Milner had lunched with the Prime Minister, other Cabinet Ministers, and Philip Kerr, Lloyd George's private secretary, a former member of the Milner Kindergarten – who, as Lord Lothian, was to become well known in the 1930s as one of the principal exponents of the policy of appeasement. On the following day Milner attended one of the regular dinners of the 'Ginger Group', where Geoffrey Dawson and Waldorf Astor as usual were present. Thus we may assume that his statement for the *Standard* had been cleared with both Lloyd George and Dawson.

The Times published it, after a week's delay, without editorial comment. But Lord Northcliffe, the paper's Proprietor, delivered an attack on it at an American officers' club in London in which he accused Milner – already suspect because of his German blood and education – of trying to 'let the Hun off' in order that he might be strong enough to deal with Bolshevism in Germany. This was, Northcliffe said, the surest way to create Bolshevism in England. The speech, curiously enough, was written for him by Wickham Steed, then Foreign Editor of *The Times* but also a member of Northcliffe's staff on the British War Mission. Thus the Editor had, by his silence, implied approval of Milner's peace aims, whereas the Chief Proprietor had clearly indicated his disagreement.

The Germans got the peace that Northcliffe wanted, not the one that

Milner had pleaded for. Lloyd George personally was favourable to a
'just' peace, but he was pressurized by his French allies and by the
British electorate, whipped up by the Northcliffe press, into agreeing
to a harsh treaty. 'Hang the Kaiser' and 'squeeze Germany till the pips
squeak' had been the slogans which won the day. In 1919 Geoffrey
Dawson had resigned from *The Times* and been replaced by Wickham
Steed.

Thus when Dawson returned to the Chair in 1922 he was already
committed to the revision of a treaty which, in defiance of the principle
of self-determination on which it was based, placed large German-
speaking minorities under the domination of Slav governments. To
reinforce him there was added to his staff a Deputy Editor, Barrington-
Ward, who had come by a different road to adopt the same beliefs.
Barrington-Ward's long and searing experience as a front-line soldier
had made it an article of faith with him that such a war must never
be fought again and that the only method of preventing it was to concede
justice to the vanquished.

These opinions were, during the 1920s, both relevant and respectable,
and probably commanded the support of a majority of Englishmen. But
from the German viewpoint, British opinion cut little ice in comparison
with that of the French who at that time were more effective in making
their views prevail, by force if necessary, as in the Ruhr in 1923. The
result was that the Germans were given the shadow of rehabilitation,
through admission to the League of Nations and inclusion in the system
of European pacts, particularly that of Locarno. But when it came to
what most Germans felt to be the substance – territorial changes, an
easing of reparations, and the right to rearm – little or no progress was
to be seen.

This was the position when Hitler came to power in 1933. Neither
Dawson nor Barrington-Ward saw any reason why the arrival on the
scene of this brutal and hectoring nationalist leader should make them
alter their opinions. On the contrary, they held, with some reason, that
it was the very refusal of the Allies to grant justice to reasonable
Germans that had produced this situation. But they went on to conclude,
erroneously, that to continue in the path of justice, even in the face of
provocation and broken pledges, was the only way to tame the tiger.
To condemn this as a tragic and disastrous error is easier now, with
hindsight, than it was then, when the truth was a matter of some
speculation.

(ii) Norman Ebbutt

Both Dawson and Barrington-Ward have been accused of having little
first-hand knowledge of Europe, and particularly of Germany. Dawson
was not an entire stranger to Europe, but his main interests lay in the

Dominions, and in different circumstances these would have stood to his credit. He was concerned with the development of what would now be called the 'Third World'. That he should have been called upon, during the last decade of his editorship, to deal almost exclusively with Germany, a country largely outside the scope of his experience, was unfortunate.

Barrington-Ward understood Germany much better. His first contact with the Germans had been as a soldier fighting them in war: in peace he had made it his business to visit Germany and study the country's problems. Moreover he numbered among his friends Germans, such as Kurt Hahn, the founder of Gordonstoun School, and Count Bernsdorff, the diplomat who was later murdered by the Nazis.

But even if the Editor himself lacked instinctive understanding of Germany it cannot be said that he was not well informed. In Norman Ebbutt, its Berlin correspondent, *The Times* possessed one of the foremost journalists of all time. Ebbutt was a rotund, stocky little man, a persistent pipe-puffer, with thick, rimless glasses. On leaving his office in Unter den Linden he would preside each evening in the Taverne public house at his special *Stammtisch*. Here would foregather other British and American journalists, or anybody else whom Ebbutt might honour with an invitation, to exchange and mull over the day's news. This routine formed part of Ebbutt's calculated policy. In his view it was more important to him, as *The Times* correspondent, to ensure that no piece of news ever eluded him than to preserve the exclusivity of some 'scoop' which he had succeeded in obtaining – especially in the very difficult conditions in which journalists were working in Germany. He worked on the principle of exchanging his findings with his colleagues in the evening, on the understanding that they would do the same.

In a letter dated 24 February 1927, the Foreign Editor, Harold Williams, wrote to Ebbutt:

> We have been unable as yet to make arrangements for filling the post of Chief Correspondent in Berlin, but we are looking to you to carry on in the meantime. On several occasions you have done very good work during Daniels' absence and we feel sure that you will be able to keep the service going in the interval until definite arrangements can be made. Although, as far as we can see, startling events are unlikely in Germany for some time to come, difficult situations may occasionally arise.

They did indeed. The Foreign Editor's limit of vision was evidently about three years. By then the temporary appointment had become a permanency.

The running stories during the early days of the Nazi régime were mostly domestic, but none the less dangerous for that. They included 'the night of the long knives' – 30 July 1934, when Hitler's men shot his associate, Roehm, and other Storm Troop leaders; the persecution of the Jews; and the campaign against the Churches. In gathering information on all these subjects Ebbutt had to be circumspect. Over-eager correspondents were being expelled from the country regularly, and their informants, if caught, were liable to be thrown into concentration camps.

Although as an ex-naval man Ebbutt was well posted on the construction of the pocket battleships, he was always careful to avoid any inquiries which might render him liable to charges of military espionage, nor did the Nazis ever accuse him of such. His information was particularly full and regular on Church matters. According to Donald McLachlan his principal informant on this subject may have been under the protection of Admiral Canaris, the head of the armed forces' intelligence organization, who was later hanged by the Nazis. Both the Lutherans and the Catholics put up stout resistance to Hitler. Motivated by fervent idealism, with a membership that had strong connexions with the Prussian and Bavarian 'Establishments', they were not easily brought to heel, and of all the Nazis' activities the campaign against the Protestants in Germany was the most damaging to their image in Britain. It struck home with men like Halifax and Dawson, who were sincere Churchmen, and Ebbutt's relentless pursuit of this sensitive topic was the chief cause of his expulsion in 1937.

The Times has been accused of suppressing Ebbutt's dispatches. To what extent was this true? Unlike the Government, who replaced an ambassador, Sir Eric Phipps, who was well informed and no dupe of the Nazis, with another, Sir Nevile Henderson, who only learnt the truth about the Nazis the hard way – when it was too late – *The Times* never attempted to shift its representative in Germany. On the question of suppression, there is Dawson's well-known and self-damaging admission in a letter dated 23 May 1937. It was written to Daniels, formerly *The Times* Chief Correspondent in Berlin and now transferred to Paris, who was on his way to Berlin to act as a stand-in while Ebbutt was away.

> ... But it really would interest me to know precisely what it is in *The Times* that has produced this new antagonism in Germany. I do my utmost night after night to keep out of the paper anything that might hurt their susceptibilities. I can really think of nothing that has been printed now for many months past to which they could possibly take exception as unfair comment ...
> I shall be more grateful than I can say for any explanation and guidance, for I have always been convinced that the peace of the

world depends more than anything else upon our getting into reasonable relations with Germany.

Dawson, as *The Times* historian noted in another context, was given to over-emphasis, and no doubt he was employing it when he wrote this letter. The key to it is that he was referring to 'comment,' not news. The evidence of his colleagues is that, although Ebbutt was a prolix and pernickety correspondent, requiring a good deal of pruning in the normal way, he was not subject to any form of cutting which would not have been applied to any other correspondent.

The letter is strange in another way, for it refers to the recent bombing of the Basque village of Guernica by German pilots. Dawson, one would have thought, must have realized that the reporting of this story by George Lothair Steer, *The Times* correspondent in Spain, would have infuriated the Germans more than any of Ebbutt's dispatches. *The Times*, like Ebbutt himself, had to exercise some discretion if it were to remain in business at all in a country dominated by the Gestapo. In 1934 Ralph Deakin, the Foreign News Editor, commissioned Simpson, the Munich 'stringer', to write a series of articles on the notorious concentration camp at Dachau. Simpson took infinite trouble over this painful assignment. He had to collect information from men released from Dachau who were determined never to go back there again, and from the widows of those who had been murdered by the SS guards. The work was not only painful, it was also dangerous. When he succeeded in obtaining a plan of the camp he hid it inside the frame of a picture on the wall of his flat. An assistant, who was taking it out of the country, was compelled to flush it down a lavatory when the SS started to search the train. Although Simpson received a cheque for his efforts, he remained disappointed that the article never appeared in print.

Germany was not the only country where *The Times* sometimes enjoined discretion upon its correspondents. A letter dated 5 April 1939 was addressed to Urch, *The Times* Riga correspondent, who used to cover Russia from that centre by perusing the Russian newspapers and interpreting them in the light of his previous knowledge of the country – a feat which Peter Fleming once compared to reporting a boxing match in the Albert Hall from the steps of the Albert Memorial.

> The Editor [ran the letter, signed by a member of the Imperial and Foreign Department] wishes me to say how pleased the office is with your recent messages, but to add a hint that we should like our references to Russia to be couched as far as possible in terms unlikely to offend. It is not, of course, a question of disguising the facts, but merely of expressing them in a diplomatic way.

Against all this must be set Dawson's unwavering loyalty in backing his correspondents. When finally asked to recall Ebbutt, the Editor refused. *The Times* expressed itself in dignified terms. The case against *The Times* correspondent 'was frankly based on dissatisfaction with his published record of affairs in Germany', ran a leader dated 17 August 1937. A German press campaign against *The Times* was being conducted

> with a volume of abuse which can hardly be realized in more stable communities. It is permissible, perhaps, to remind these well-drilled German newspapers that *The Times* has stood rather conspicuously for an attitude towards their country which is by no means universal in England. The distinction which it has always drawn is between the internal affairs of Germany (which are her own concern) and those national activities – due to some extent, no doubt, to the character of her rulers – which may threaten the peace and security of other countries, or strike at the world-wide freedom of religious belief. There is too much reason to believe that Mr Ebbutt's main offence has been his repeated exposure of these persecutions of religion which are the worst feature of the Nazi régime and which are bound to be a permanent stumbling block in the path of international friendship.

In spite of these arguments Norman Ebbutt was served with an expulsion order by the Berlin police two days later, and compelled to leave the country.

(iii) *Two Kinds of Appeasers*

With the help of personal diaries and official documents, we are now able to obtain a bird's-eye view of the Nazis and the appeasers, operating on each side of the hill. They appear as two groups of men moving in parallel lines which will never meet. Hitler did not want appeasement. He wanted aggrandizement, and to achieve it he was ready to use force. The appeasers included a large proportion of rational people in positions of authority. But there were two kinds of appeasers. The first were the supporters of appeasement *faute de mieux*, who thought it the only policy available, having regard to the international power situation and the state of domestic opinion; they hoped that, if the policy failed, the power balance and public opinion would by then have altered sufficiently to make resistance to Nazi aggression possible. The second group saw appeasement as a positive policy. These believed that, no matter the colour of the government in Berlin, the makers of the Versailles Treaty owed justice to Germany and that only on the basis of that justice could the structure of a stable peace be built. Both groups had this in common – they were prepared to go a long way in order to prevent a second world war.

Neville Chamberlain belonged to the second group after he became Prime Minister, and he was backed from the start by Barrington-Ward, who wrote most of the important first leaders on the subject of Anglo–German relations. He brought to the cause the fervour of moral earnestness. 'We must try and do in the discouraging circumstances of 1938 what we failed to do in 1919 and take the lead,' he noted during the Munich crisis. 'Be just to those to whom we do not wish to be just.'

Dawson's attitude is less easy to define. In part it dated back to his own policies at the end of the First World War, and to the views absorbed from Lord Milner and, after his death, from Lord Lothian and other members of the Round Table group. But it was also pragmatic. 'Personally', he wrote to Daniels in a letter dated 11 May 1937, 'I am, and always have been, most anxious that we should "explore every avenue" in the search for a reasonable understanding with Germany.' Yet he preserved a certain aloof scepticism, and there was always a hint that the avenue might prove a *cul de sac*. Besides, his imperial preoccupations made him particularly sensitive to imperial susceptibilities. On no account must the country drift into war without the support of the Dominions: 'Let me add that in my opinion the worst possible way to an understanding is to clamour for the retrocession out of hand of all the former German colonies'. But in spite of the nuances Barrington-Ward constantly emphasized in his diary that he and Dawson saw 'eye to eye'.

The first years of the Nazi régime were devoted to domestic, rather than foreign, conquests. Germany left the Disarmament Conference and the League of Nations, neither of which withdrawals could be represented as an act of belligerence. The Saar plebiscite of January 1935 returned a German population to Germany by legitimate means. In March of that year, following the issue by the British Government of their moderate White Paper on defence, Hitler denounced the demilitarization clauses of the Treaty of Versailles, at the same time admitting the existence of a German Air Force, which was soon to be double the first-line strength of the RAF, and introducing conscription, with the declared intention of raising an army of no less than thirty-six divisions.

In accordance with its policy of support for revision of the relevant clauses in the Versailles Treaty. *The Times* commented on 25 March 1935, that 'it becomes the part of statesmanship and common sense to arrange for their formal disappearance under the best conditions possible'. On the same basis, the signature of the Anglo–German Naval Treaty in June was welcomed in a leading article:

Although in principle it involves a tacit disregard of the Treaty

of Versailles, yet, inasmuch as it will substitute a new agreement
for a section of the disarmament clauses of the Treaty, it will
constitute an important advance in the process of getting peace
established upon the firm ground of agreements freely concluded.

The treaty allowed, of course, the building by Germany of surface
craft and submarines which could be required, in the long run, mainly
for use against Britain. Barrington-Ward preferred, however, to empha-
size the opportunity which he felt it offered as the jumping-off ground
for a new and healthier relationship with Germany. He was, indeed,
positively elated at the signature of the treaty. On 7 March 1936,
exactly a year after reintroducing conscription, Germany reoccupied
the demilitarized Rhineland, denounced the Locarno Treaty and offered
a new settlement. 'Wrote, and enjoyed writing', noted Barrington-Ward
in his diary, 'difficult leader trying to ensure, while condemning the
breach of her treaty, that her [Germany's] offer to negotiate a full
settlement should not be rejected'. The leader was telegraphed to Lit-
vinoff, in Moscow, at his request, at midnight, 'which shows how
anxiously Russia is watching British opinion and what [sic] finger
they now have in the European pie'.

To counterbalance the element of aggression in the German action,
Barrington-Ward put up his own constructive suggestion: the offer of
a complete British guarantee for the French and Belgian frontiers
which might compensate and reassure the French. Eden, consulted
through a civil servant, did not turn it down but thought it did not meet
the need of 'some moral re-establishment of the confidence in treaties
now shattered by Germany'. Nothing came of the suggestion. The
British Government was opposed to taking on any new commitments
in Europe.

But the denunciation of Locarno was in a different category from
breaches of the Versailles Treaty. It was the breaking of an 'agreement
freely concluded' by Germany and her former enemies. Many felt that
this was the first occasion on which Hitler offered a clear-cut pretext
for military intervention, and the last on which Britain and France
would have been able to undertake such an operation with a reasonable
chance of success. *The Times* made no such suggestion. Dawson and
Barrington-Ward had both been deeply impressed by the failure of
Britain, France and the League to impose effective sanctions on Italy
when she invaded Abyssinia. They were more concerned with the positive aspects of making the reoccupation of the Rhineland a starting-
point for fresh Anglo–German agreements. They concluded also, and
rightly, that British public opinion was strongly opposed to intervention.
It aroused memories of the occupation of the Ruhr by the French,
which had done more than anything else to rouse British sympathy for
Germany after the war.

The ability of the French army to conduct an offensive operation was also in question. Massive on paper, it lacked air support, its tactical doctrine was reactionary, its reserves ill-trained, and its morale suspect. 'Tanks and aircraft', preached its training manual, 'can never play a decisive role in modern warfare.'

(iv) Defenceless Britain

Defence was also the crux of the matter in Britain. The phrase 'negotiating from strength' had not yet been invented, but it was the inability to do so which was the root-cause of Britain's failure to deal with the German situation. To a nation in the defenceless state of Britain in the 1930s it mattered little if her policy was appeasement, collective security, or bilateral agreements to resist aggression. All were likely to fail because of lack of confidence that Britain was in a position to carry out her obligations.

The rate of rearmament, unlike the antics of Hitler, was, however, a matter subject in theory to the control of the British Government. But the leaders, to some extent, and the public, to an even greater extent, were in no mood to rearm. The British politicians of the 1930s, with few exceptions, placed exaggerated emphasis on the moral aspects of foreign policy, and The Times shared in this over-emphasis. Barrington-Ward was concerned with being just 'even to those to whom we do not wish to be just'. Douglas Reed, The Times Vienna correspondent and one of the most fervent opponents of appeasement, could write: 'In 1933 I would have been for putting our former German colonies into a common pool of appeasement. Only on that basis would we have had the moral right to demand the sacrifice of territory from Czechoslovakia.'

The Ministers who composed the so-called National Government were not all violently opposed to a measure of rearmament as such. Some of them were in favour of it. But they were all, with some reason, afraid of public opinion, and they knew that any alternative government was likely still further to reduce such defence forces as Britain had. Unfortunately Chamberlain, then Chancellor of the Exchequer, was the most persistent opponent of any increase in expenditure on arms, on grounds of economy – and he was also far more decisive than most of his colleagues.

The state of public opinion was held, both by Baldwin and The Times, to preclude heavy taxation for military purposes. Conscription, the only step which might have convinced Hitler that Britain meant business, was unthinkable. In April 1936 Baldwin gave a pledge not to introduce it in peacetime. The prospect of turning industry over to the production of arms on a significant scale horrified Ministers.

It has been questioned whether Baldwin and Dawson were right in

their assessment of public opinion. There were in those days no accepted
techniques of mass observation such as public-opinion polls. The Duke
of Windsor once complained that Baldwin, during the abdication crisis,
acted as a one-man Gallup Poll. For testing public opinion reliance had
to be placed on by-elections, such as that lost by the Conservatives at
East Fulham, irrelevant incidents such as the Oxford Union's vote
against fighting 'for King and Country', and the massive Peace Ballot
organized by a committed body, the League of Nations Union, which
showed that little over a half of those interviewed were in favour of
military action, even in support of the League, while the overwhelming
majority were in favour of disarmament. The Peace Ballot must have
been one of the most enormous exercises in wishful thinking ever
mounted in history. Moreover, hostility to Hitler varied in inverse
proportion to willingness to arm.

The Times made its own efforts to check on public opinion by
sending round the countryside a reporter highly experienced in such
matters, Lewis Northend. Even today, reporters of this stamp are
probably more reliable in testing public opinion than any other method,
though their deployment is slow and costly. In November 1934 Northend fully confirmed the view that the National Government was so
shaky that an election would provide the Labour Party with a landslide
victory. This was due in part to the prevalence of unemployment, but
even more to the conviction that the Government was 'war-mongering'.
Arthur Baker, another *Times* reporter, who had been asked to make a
confidential report on the East Fulham election by Conservative Central
Office, concluded that it had been lost purely on the pacifist issue.

In these circumstances the Government, alarmed by reports from
Germany, began to rearm almost by stealth. 'When you think of the
defence of England,' Baldwin cryptically stated in July 1934, 'you no
longer think of the chalk cliffs of Dover, you think of the Rhine.' The
Government began to put in hand the first instalment of a defence
programme which ultimately enabled the RAF to win the Battle of
Britain in 1940 by a narrow margin, though only after the army had
suffered a nearly catastrophic defeat on the Continent. The appointment
of Lord Swinton as Secretary for Air in June 1935 was a turning-point.
He at least was whole-hearted in his determination to provide the
country with an effective air arm.

The Times had the opportunity to supply the country with the
leadership which the Government was failing to provide, but it
sounded no clarion call. Instead, Dawson supported Baldwin almost
apologetically:

There is – so Mr Baldwin insisted – no cause whatever for panic
and no immediate risk of peace being broken: but the future is

uncertain. It will take not months but years to make good the
deficiencies, and the task can no longer be postponed. The steps
the Government propose to take should not jeopardize peace,
but rather should help to ensure it.

Why did *The Times* not come out more strongly? Unlike the Government, the paper had nothing to lose by so doing, and a policy of appeasement backed by a persistent, informed drive for rearmament would
have provided a more coherent policy than one in which the emphasis
was so heavily on appeasement alone. One answer lay in the scope
of Dawson's interests. Defence lay outside them; frankly, the subject
bored him. He possessed an almost Chinese contempt for the military
art and regarded those of his friends whose enthusiasm drove them
into any form of military service with an amused tolerance. Unfortunately Colonel Repington, the celebrated *Times* Military Correspondent during the First World War, was a confirmed intriguer and
self-advertiser. Because Dawson had found Repington so antipathetic
he failed to appoint a successor to him. Behind these attitudes was the
influence of the Milner Kindergarten, whose members had been opposed
to military entanglements in Europe – of which Repington was such a
keen advocate. Britain, in their view, was by tradition an imperial and
a sea power; deviation from this concept in the 1914–18 war was, they
believed, in part responsible for her decline.

With Barrington-Ward the case was different. He had had a successful
military career by any standards, and thoroughly understood defence
problems. But he was not a militarist. On the contrary, war filled him
with loathing. Furthermore, he was inhibited by his fear of advocating
too strongly a policy which might be branded in Berlin as 'anti-
German'. He was also sensitive to liberal opinion. A thoroughgoing
campaign to repair the gaps in the defence services would have been
branded as war-mongering. One aspect of defence he did espouse –
Civil Defence and ARP – which could not reasonably be objected to
on any of the above grounds.

Barrington-Ward at least took active measures to repair the gap in
The Times's own defence service. In 1934 he urged that it was time to
fill the gap left by Repington's departure. Unfortunately, the solution
he proposed was not a happy one for *The Times*. He secured the
appointment of one who was without doubt the most brilliant military
writer in the country – Basil Liddell Hart, then working as Military
Correspondent of the *Daily Telegraph*. But for a number of reasons
this appointment, which looked so promising, did not work out as
planned. In spite of his great gifts – some would say genius – Liddell
Hart never settled down on *The Times*, which would have done better
with a more humdrum Defence Correspondent. For Liddell Hart was

first and foremost a military theorist, lacking judgment when he tried to relate his theories to practical contemporary issues. Like Barrington-Ward, he had been lastingly disturbed by his experiences on the Western Front during the First World War. But the effect they had upon him was different. He set himself the task of devising means of war which would avoid the horrible bloodshed of the trenches. In this search he had come to advocate the use of small armoured élite formations, instead of large masses of infantry, and adoption of the theory of indirect approach rather than direct confrontation. Thus, although an opponent of appeasement and an advocate of modernization, his theories led him to oppose the dispatch of a conventionally armed expeditionary force to the Continent as had been done in 1914. If the object was to dissuade Hitler from overrunning Europe the policy of *The Times* Defence Correspondent, prominently proclaimed in its columns, was hardly likely to be of much help.

Two turnover articles, headed 'An Army across the Channel' expanding on these theories and favouring 'limited' rather than 'unlimited' warfare of the 1914–18 kind appeared in *The Times* on 7 and 8 February 1939; the second one was accompanied by a leading article entitled 'The Defence of the West' and gave qualified support to their views; this was written by Barrington-Ward. Their publication coincided with Chamberlain's statement that in the event of war, 'all the forces of Great Britain would be at the disposal of France', a coincidence not foreseen when the articles were prepared in December 1938. The effect was such that Chamberlain was forced to repeat his pledge three days later, and when the Secretary for War (Hore-Belisha) introduced his estimates on 8 March he specifically repudiated 'any theory of limited liability'.

Liddell Hart was a crusader, a controversialist, and a military thinker who reversed the maxim of Clausewitz by regarding diplomacy as the extension of strategy. He tried to interfere in the politics of the paper, particularly over non-intervention in Spain. He believed – wrongly, as it turned out – that Franco would ally himself with Hitler in a world war. This quickly brought him into conflict with Dawson over a major policy issue.

Finally, Liddell Hart was supremely unfitted to work as a member of a college, which *The Times* continued to be. He was an individual thinker, who wanted to use *The Times* as a pulpit for his theories. Not only did he fall foul of Dawson, deservedly earning the Editor's most damning appellation of being 'viewy', but even Barrington-Ward, most charitable of men, began to avoid his presence. He deluged these two busy men with long memoranda and before-breakfast telephone calls. The result was that many of his writings did not get into the paper. When the time came for parting, Barrington-Ward wrote: 'He has been drawing a large salary and doing almost nothing for it . . . He is a mono-lith of egotism and vanity.'

Liddell Hart came to exercise his influence more as the *éminence grise* of Hore-Belisha, and less and less as a journalist in *The Times*. It was another of the tragedies of the 1930s that *The Times* failed to reap the full benefits of having this first-class mind at its disposal.

(v) *The March on Austria*

German foreign policy reached the point of no return on 5 November 1937. On this day Hitler announced to a secret meeting his plans for the *Drang nach Osten*. These involved, as a preliminary, the absorption of Austria, Czechoslovakia, and Poland, by force, if necessary. Hitler's announcement came as a shock to his leaders. Some raised objections strongly enough to provoke their removal from office a few months later. Even Goering questioned the programme on practical grounds. But the British Government did not know about this meeting, the holding of which was only revealed at the Nuremberg trials after the war.

Ironically, it was but a fortnight later that Lord Halifax visited Hitler at Berchtesgaden in the vain belief that personal contact might serve to improve Anglo–German relations. The visit, if anything, did harm. Halifax failed to take the measure of Hitler, and probably unwittingly encouraged him to proceed with his plans for aggression in the East, the first step being the *Anschluss* with Austria nearly four months later. The bullying of Schuschnigg, the Austrian Chancellor, and the annexa-tion of his country, outraged Dawson and Barrington-Ward, but did not shift their policy on the main issue. 'I returned to the office and wrote a leader on the big Nazi advance in Austria – for such it evidently is', wrote Barrington-Ward in his diary, on 16 February. 'Deeply sorry for the Austrians, but Allied impolicy in the past has brought this upon us and them, and there is nothing we can do about it.'

When, on 20 February, Eden resigned, Barrington-Ward's comment was: 'Sorry on personal but not on public grounds. He really has no heart for any kind of direct talks with the dictatorial powers. This policy restricts diplomacy to a gamble on their collapse or to waiting for the next war.'

Dawson took over, and wrote the main leader on 14 March, after the Germans had marched in:

> Herr Hitler has enjoyed two days of triumphal progress from the Austrian frontier. Our correspondent leaves no room for doubt about the public jubilation with which he and his army were greeted everywhere . . . But the higher the value that is placed on their demonstrations, the more extraordinary it must seem that it

was thought necessary to surround so spontaneous a welcome with all the paraphernalia of tanks and bombers and marching infantry. There must be many thousands of thoughtful Germans who are reflecting even now that these are the methods that brought them to grief in the past . . . A preliminary order to the Austrian Nazis to refrain from voting [in the plebiscite which Schuschnigg had announced in an effort to save Austria from the Nazis] was followed on Friday by one ultimatum after another . . . and finally though all their humiliating demands had been conceded, by the invasion of German troops and the arrival of Herr Hitler's deputy in Vienna.

The moral drawn was the need to support the Government's unprecedented estimates for the defence services. 'There will also be fresh support for the movement for a more rapid, effective, and even compulsory organization of the people for civilian service of the type demanded by modern dangers, particularly of a panic caused by sudden air raids.'

By the standards of the day, these were fighting words. Private advice from *The Times* correspondents abroad brought no comfort. From Austria the Vienna correspondent, Douglas Reed, wrote on 16 March:

In my wildest nightmares I had not foreseen anything so perfectly organized, so ruthless, so strong. When this machine goes into action it will blight everything it encounters like a swarm of locusts. The destruction and the loss of life will make the World War look like the Boer War . . . Their real hatred is for England.

And on 18 March, from Prague, a special correspondent who had just seen Eduard Beneš, the Prime Minister, reported:

I am convinced that Nazi Germany has a long-term programme which she is determined to carry out – however peaceful her declarations are between bursts of action – and that she means both to break up this country [Czechoslovakia] and to challenge the British Empire . . . At what point are we going to cry 'halt'?

No doubt rumours of Hitler's Guy Fawkes Day meeting had by then percolated to Prague.

(vi) The Czechoslovak Crisis

The time was now fast approaching when Hitler would present the British Government with the reckoning for past years of neglect – neglect to secure just peace terms for Germany when it was still a democracy, and, what was now more relevant, neglect to maintain military forces adequate to make Britain's will respected.

At no time in its history has *The Times* incurred more odium than over its handling of the Czechoslovak crisis. But to understand the reasons that led Dawson to publish the leader of 7 September 1937 suggesting cession of the Sudetenland to Germany, it is necessary to go back to the period immediately following the *Anschluss*.

Dawson and Barrington-Ward were quite clear in their minds that Britain ought not to go to war on behalf of Czechoslovakia in the circumstances that then existed. They based their conclusion on a number of compelling arguments. In the first place, Britain held no treaty obligations with that country. Secondly, the Sudeten Germans had been included inside the frontiers of Czechoslovakia in blatant disregard of the very principle which had been invoked at the Versailles Conference as a reason for freeing the Czechs themselves from Austrian domination – namely, self-determination. This seemed to them totally unjust. Thirdly, they foresaw that if a war were fought to preserve Czechoslovakia, the situation of the Czechs at the end of that war was likely to be no better, and might well be worse, than it would be if some peaceable arrangement could be reached with Germany now to improve the political status of the Sudetenlanders. Fourthly – and this weighed particularly heavily with Dawson – the British Dominions would not at this stage consent to being dragged into a war to support Britain over a Central European frontier dispute. The South Africans had actually informed Hitler of their attitude. Finally, they did not believe that Britain could do anything to defend Czechoslovakia even if she wished.

Barrington-Ward put up a constructive plan to meet the situation. Czechoslovakia was a multi-racial state consisting of Czechs, Slovaks, Germans, Hungarians and some Poles. It had defensive alliances with Russia and France, as he noted in his diary;

> I drafted out and put to G.D. a possible scheme for an internationally guaranteed neutralization of Czechoslovakia. C-S to give up Soviet and French alliances and to grant federal status to her minorities. France, Britain, Germany, Italy and (?) Poland to guarantee C-S. C-S independence no longer to depend upon the French 'encirclement system'. Everybody would get something out of it. Put it to G.D. who thought rather well of it.

This was a copy-book solution which would have provided a good case to argue at the Peace Conference. In the power struggle now developing in Central Europe, with not only Germany, but Poland and Hungary already impatient to dismember Czechoslovakia, it had no real chance of acceptance, especially if put forward by a power which few people now credited with the will to fight. Not even the British Government showed interest in Barrington-Ward's scheme. Chamberlain, the Prime Minister, and Halifax, the Foreign Secretary, were both opposed to any measure which involved a guarantee to Czechoslovakia.

On 28 May Hitler issued secret orders to smash Czechoslovakia by military action in the near future. *The Times*, which was naturally ignorant of this decision, published a leader a few days later advocating the secession of the Sudetenland to Germany:

> For the rectification of an injustice left by the Treaty of Versailles the Sudeten Germans have an undoubted case . . . It is easily intelligible that the Czech Government might not willingly agree to a plebiscite likely to result in a demand for the transfer of the Sudetens and the loss of their territory for the Republic. Nevertheless, if they could see their way to it, and to granting a similar choice to the other minorities, Hungarian and Polish, the rulers of Czechoslovakia might in the long run be the gainers in having a homogeneous and contented people . . .

The Foreign Office, which had received reports of German troop movements in the neighbourhood of the Czechoslovak frontier, was afraid that the Czechs would regard the article as kite-flying on behalf of the British Government. It sent a message to the British Minister in Prague authorizing him to disown *The Times* leader. As *The Times History* points out, there is no evidence of collusion. The views expressed in the leader were merely a long-standing article of faith so far as Barrington-Ward was concerned.

The leader aroused some indignation among a section of *Times* readers. John Walter IV, still Co-Chief Proprietor, went so far as to write a letter of protest to Geoffrey Dawson:

> I feel that our leader on Czechoslovakia yesterday must have come as a shock to many readers . . . In contemplating the dismemberment of Czechoslovakia as a measure of justice to the Sudeten Germans, our leader writer made no allusion to the flood of injustice and cruelty that would certainly overwhelm the minorities thus handed over to the tender mercies of Messrs Hitler, Goering and Goebbels.

In his reply, Dawson upheld the leader. 'My own experience is that neither Hitler nor Henlein, the Sudeten leader, wants a revision of frontiers.' This view was confirmed to Barrington-Ward by the son-in-law of Dr Schacht, Hitler's Finance Minister, a few days later. No doubt he thought it was true.

During a large part of the summer both Dawson and Barrington-Ward were out of the office. In Barrington-Ward's case this was partly the result of an overdue operation on his knee which kept him in hospital and afterwards convalescing from 18 June to 15 July. Two weeks later he went on holiday from 30 July to 22 August – and again from 2 to 12 September. Dawson was on holiday from 8 August to 6 September, and again from 15 to 19 September. During the critical period 2 to 6 September both were away from Printing House Square, with disastrous results for the reputation of the paper.

These absences must be viewed in the light of the social habits of the period. Both Dawson and Barrington-Ward were hardworking men who had devoted their lives to the paper. The political crisis in those days appeared chronic rather than spasmodic. Barrington-Ward was undoubtedly overworking and in indifferent health. But the Editor and the Deputy Editor ought not to have been absent from the office simultaneously during this time, since they had kept the direction of policy exclusively in their own hands and had failed to find a third executive on whom they felt they could rely. This situation dated back to the late 1920s, when Dawson had decided to do without a Foreign Editor. In 1934 the Editor realized that the experiment had not been a success and instructed Barrington-Ward to look out for a foreign leader writer who could eventually be promoted into this post.

Of the Assistant Editors, C. W. Brodribb was a proof-reading functionary, unversed in foreign affairs. Greatly beloved in the office as a Pickwickian relic of a past age, he was hardly the choice for the Chair when Hitler was mobilizing armies on the Czech frontier. W. F. Casey, the Assistant Editor on the foreign side, was neutralized because he was a declared opponent of the paper's official line on Germany, And Leo Kennedy, the principal foreign leader writer, who was a personal friend of Dawson, was ambivalent in his attitude. Barrington-Ward described him as 'always impulsive and not a good or sensitive judge of a situation'. As for the young men, 'they are', said Barrington-Ward, when discussing these matters with Campbell Stuart, 'good, but just a bit too young'.

During August the war of nerves against Czechoslovakia reached a climax, Hitler, who had secretly fixed 1 October as 'D' Day for the invasion, was openly instructing Henlein, the Sudeten leader, in his negotiations with the Czech Government. A violent press campaign was conducted accompanied by troop movements and military manoeuvres. The resemblance to the pattern preceding the Austrian invasion was all too plain.

One of the objects of these partial mobilizations by Hitler was to force other countries to follow suit and thereby disclose their mobilization plans and the state of training of their reserves. The conclusions drawn by the German General Staff from observation of the French army on these occasions was that they would be incapable of launching a surprise crossing of the Rhine or advancing into southern Germany. This knowledge no doubt gave the Germans confidence that they could attack Czechoslovakia without danger of themselves being attacked

from the West. What impressed them most about the French (as about
the Poles) was the incompetence of the command and staff in handling
large bodies of troops in a war of movement.

Although Henlein's demands at this stage did not go beyond the
granting of an autonomous status for the Sudetenland within the Czechoslovak state, *The Times* continued to publish an occasional leader – on
13 June and 14 July, for instance – suggesting secession: 'No solution
should be too drastic'.

On 25 July the British Government sent Lord Runciman, a sixty-
seven-year-old Liberal who had been Asquith's President of the Board
of Trade but who had little or no knowledge of foreign affairs or of
foreigners, to Czechoslovakia as a mediator and adviser. The appointment dismayed the French and came as a surprise to the Germans. On
arrival, he was surrounded by Sudeten German cheer-gangs chanting:

> 'Liebe Runciman, mach uns frei
> Von der Tscheckosloakei'.

Runciman strove to the best of his capabilities for an impartial solution,
but passions and politics were overtaking his efforts.

On 29 August the French manned the Maginot Line and on 4 September Beneš, convinced that he would get no support from France and
Britain, summoned the Sudeten leaders to the Hradschin Palace and
offered them a settlement which conceded almost all their demands
including full autonomy within Czechoslovakia. They were flabber-
gasted. Beneš, now President, was well aware that his offer was unlikely
to satisfy Hitler. This was the position when *The Times* published its
famous leader of 7 September, once more putting forward secession as
a possible solution.

Neither the Editor nor the Deputy Editor had been in the office during
the middle days of August, but Barrington-Ward saw Halifax on 25
August for twenty minutes. It was, in fact, the morning after a crucial
Cabinet meeting in which the British attitude had slightly stiffened.
Barrington-Ward found the Foreign Secretary with a

> good commonsensible grasp of things but without any touch of
> cynicism.
>   . . . He is more impressed than formerly, though not wholly
> convinced by reports (chiefly coming through Van [Sir Robert
> Vansittart, Chief Diplomatic Adviser to the Government] it
> appears!) that the Germans mean to settle the Czechoslovakian
> question shortly and by force if necessary. Time for us (without
> encouraging Czech intransigence) to put what weight we can
> against these threats.

Should Britain, Halifax asked, give a 'precise guarantee'? Barrington-

Ward thought not. 'We agreed that wishful thinking was an error'. Barrington-Ward did not see Halifax again during the crisis, although he put in a request to do so some days later.

His assumption that Halifax's reports came from Vansittart was correct, though the implicit suggestion that they were prejudiced is unjustified. British intelligence about Germany in the 1930s was incomplete and ill-organized, but on this occasion Vansittart was in touch with an exceptionally good informant. Most of the staff at the German Embassy were anti-Nazi, the Ambassador was away, and at least one senior official there was supplying him with high-level top-secret information.

The following day Barrington-Ward lunched with Lady Colefax where he met Jan Masaryk, the Czechoslovak Minister in London, 'very cheerful in himself and not too gloomy about possibilities in Prague. Says Czechs will certainly fight, if required, though it would be a "massacre".' This conversation can only have served to strengthen Barrington-Ward's views.

At this point *The Times* policy received endorsement from an unexpected quarter. Kingsley Martin, Editor of the left-wing *New Statesman*, had come independently to the view that 'things had gone so far that to plan armed resistance to the dictators was now useless'. On 27 August the *New Statesman*, in a leader, declared that 'the strategical value of the Bohemian frontier should not be made the occasion of a world war'.

(vii) *The September Leader*

On Saturday, 3 September 1938, Barrington-Ward set out on the second instalment of his holiday. Dawson was not due back till Tuesday. It was not without qualms, and after consultations with Dawson, that he packed his guns and left for a shooting party in Scotland. The decision was the most momentous of his life. Barrington-Ward was nothing if not a cautious man. If he had decided otherwise, he would at least have been in a position to prevent, and might well have prevented, an error of judgment second only in the history of *The Times* to the purchase of the Parnell letters.

During the weekend A. L. Kennedy did some preparations for a leader on Czechoslovakia. Geoffrey Dawson came south on Tuesday, 6 September, arriving in Printing House Square by 3 p m. Did he see Lord Halifax en route? The suggestion is made in Lord Butler's autobiography that he did, but it does not appear physically possible. According to his own diary Dawson was in the train from 9.21 a m until 2.15 p m.

So to the office for an extremely arduous afternoon and evening.

Leo Kennedy was then rather reluctantly prepared to write on the Czech crisis which was obviously coming to a head and produced an article which I had to get him to re-write at the last minute. Even so it ventilated rather crudely the idea which we had often reviewed before, of a secession of the Sudeten fringe in Germany and there was a lot of hurried revision to be done at midnight. I dined in an interval at the Beefsteak . . . and went to bed deadbeat with a heavy cold moreover.

Dermot Morrah has described being summoned to Dawson's room at 4.30 and hearing him say to Kennedy 'We must have a leader, but I don't want you to commit us too far because I'm out of touch with the situation. Edward Halifax is lunching with me tomorrow, and after that I shall be able to see the way ahead more clearly.' That Dawson was uneasy about the leader is attested by others, including Casey, whose opinion he invited.

In its final version, the paragraph in *The Times* of 7 September 1938 which caused such devastating repercussions ran as follows:

No Central Government would still deserve its title if it did not reserve in its own hands Defence, Foreign Policy, and Finance. There does not appear to be any dispute about this principle in the minds of the Government or of Herr Henlein; and if the Sudetens now ask for more than the Czech Government are apparently ready to give in their latest set of proposals, it can only be inferred that the Germans are going beyond the mere removal of disabilities and do not find themselves at ease within the Czechoslovak Republic. In that case it might be worth while for the Czechoslovak Government to consider whether *they should exclude altogether the project, which has found* (a solution should not be sought on some clearly different lines) *favour in some quarters, of making Czechoslovakia a more homogeneous* (which would make Czechoslovakia an entirely homogeneous state) *state*, by the secession of that fringe of alien populations who are contiguous to the nation with which they are united by race. In any case the wishes of the population concerned would seem to be a decisively important element in any solution that can hope to be regarded as permanent, and the advantages to Czechoslovakia of becoming a homogeneous state might *conceivably* outweigh the obvious disadvantages *of losing the Sudeten German districts of the borderland.**

* The passages in italics appeared in the later editions only. The passages in parentheses show how the leader ran in the first editions. The correction to proofs are in Dawson's own handwriting.

In making these corrections, the Editor seems genuinely to have believed that he was toning the article down. But this was not the effect that the alterations produced in the minds of readers. The phrase 'which has found favour in some quarters' seemed to point directly to inspiration from the British Government. The whole story is a warning against the dangers of coming back from a holiday and plunging too suddenly into the intricacies of an extremely delicate situation.

'There was a hubbub, as I fully expected, over the morning's leader', wrote Dawson in his diary the next day, Wednesday 7 September. 'Hubbub' was an understatement. First repercussions came from the Foreign Office, which issued a statement – a public one this time – the same afternoon:

> A suggestion appearing in *The Times* this morning to the effect that the Czechoslovak Government might consider as an alternative to their present proposals the secession of the fringe of alien populations in their territory in no way represents the view of His Majesty's Government.

Runciman, still praying that Henlein would accept Beneš's proposals, wired from Prague,

> Leading article in today's *Times* has added to our difficulties . . .
> It would be useful to caution them again adventurous speculation at a time when we are hoping to make some progress. The last paragraph of the article is a recommendation to an *Anschluss*.

At 11 a m he told Iverach McDonald, *The Times* Special Correspondent in Prague, 'This is a black day for us.' By this time Henlein had shown that he would reject the generous Beneš offer.

Dawson duly had his lunch with Halifax at the Travellers' Club: 'Foreign Office went up through the roof – not so, however, the Foreign Secretary. . .He is as much in the dark as everyone else, as to what is likely to happen next.' Later Dawson told Barrington-Ward: 'Halifax does not dissent, privately, from the suggestion that any solution, even the secession of the German minority, should be brought into free negotiation at Prague, though the Foreign Office is in a high state of indignation about it.' Halifax, however, took the opposite line with Maisky, the Russian Ambassador, the next day. He agreed with him that the article had had 'the worst possible effect'.

Barrington-Ward heard the news on the wireless in Scotland. Later, after a talk with the Editor, he criticized the timing:

> It seems that G.D. was a little rushed into this leader. It was on the day on which he came back from Yorkshire. Before he [and

Kennedy] came back I had been putting to them the idea of the
Czechs letting their Germans go . . . He [Dawson] would have
presented it differently himself. So should I. It was abrupt and a
little naif in its timing. But essentially the thing is right and it
helps to prevent our having to fight on a false issue . . . That
is the simple story of what happened.

Wild indeed were the rumours that circulated. Claud Cockburn, who
had served on *The Times* and who now edited the news sheet *The Week*,
accused *The Times* of having submitted the article for approval to the
German Embassy. Cockburn had invented the term 'The Cliveden Set'
to describe Dawson, Lothian and others of the appeasers who regularly
visited the Waldorf Astors either at Cliveden or at their London house
in St James's Square.

The proposal was not . . . submitted to or approved by Lord
Halifax [wrote Cockburn]. The plan had been in process of
being cooked up in Printing House Square for more than a week.
It appears (though this is not quite certain) that it was submitted
for the supreme approval of the German Embassy . . . Before
the proposal was actually published Mr Dawson returned from
Yorkshire. The article itself was actually written by Mr Aubrey
Leo Kennedy. He acted apparently on direct instructions from
Mr Dawson to launch the proposal in the course of the article.

Dawson, in a letter to a correspondent, described the item in *The
Week* as 'a tissue of fabrication from beginning to end'. Barrington-
Ward more correctly called it 'a large garbling of a few accurate
details'. It is, in fact, a remarkably close account of the actual course
of events. Barrington-Ward suspects some 'innocent chatterbox' in
Printing House Square. It is more likely that the leak was deliberate.
Some members of the staff felt bitterly opposed to the policy of the
paper. Cockburn had more than one source from which he might have
picked up the information.

Amidst the 'hubbub' *The Times* stood its ground. In a leader published on Friday 9 September, Dawson personally wrote (the adjective
'grotesque' is a hallmark of his handiwork):

It is really grotesque that so much righteous indignation should
be expelled on the mere suggestion, which has frequently been
made in these columns before, that a revision of boundaries
should not be excluded entirely from the list of possible
approaches to a settlement. It is not a solution for which anyone
is likely to feel enthusiasm.

For *The Times*, the leading article of 7 September was the climax of the crisis. The paper had stated its articles of faith and from now until the outbreak of war it could do little more to influence events. When Neville Chamberlain flew to Berchtesgaden on 15 September Hitler immediately demanded secession, not autonomy, for the Sudetenland, and it was on this basis that the Munich Agreement was concluded. Chamberlain conceived the Munich Agreement as a positive contribution to peace. Those who supported appeasement *faute de mieux* accepted it because they could see no alternative.

The annexation of Czechoslovakia at last provided the revulsion of feeling necessary to end the policy of appeasement. The Government, finally faced with the necessity to call a halt to Hitler's aggrandizement, gave to Poland the guarantee of support against aggression which had been denied the Czechs. On 3 September 1939, the nation went to war. Barrington-Ward wrote in his diary:

> What folly, folly, folly, this is. We shall have to fight until Hitler is put out, but that means, again, taking some sort of responsibility for the next German Government. We didn't make much of a show of it last time. An unforced evolution *in* Germany is what Europe needs.

Against this Wagnerian backdrop of history, just how important was *The Times* leader of 7 September 1938? So far as the available evidence shows, Geoffrey Dawson inserted this leader without knowledge or adequate consideration of two important factors. One was that Beneš had just offered Henlein more or less full satisfaction of all his avowed demands on behalf of the Sudeten Germans. The other was that the British Government had exceptionally good information that Hitler intended, if necessary, to invade Czechoslovakia. Undeniably, the timing of the article queered the pitch of the negotiators. But it is extremely unlikely that in the long term the effect of its publication had anything more than tactical significance. Whether the Sudetenland obtained autonomy or secession was all one to Hitler. He was interested in nothing less than the annexation of the whole of Czechoslovakia. Indeed, the Munich negotiations were to him but 'the waltz of the flies'.

Dawson, in retrospect, appears to have sensed something of this. Casey once said that he could never quite make up his mind whether he had been responsible for a master stroke of policy, in easing the way to a peaceful solution, or whether, like a naughty boy with a catapult, he had shot the cat while aiming at the tree.

However that may be, the 7 September leader was an unmitigated disaster for *The Times*. Munich was but the outcome of a long period during which the British had tried to opt out of their international responsibilities by refusing to make the sacrifices necessary if they were to shoulder them. The leaders, the opposition and the electorate all bore their share of the blame, but in retrospect the leaders very naturally became the scapegoats. The British, if they had been guilt-ridden over Versailles, were certainly even more guilt-ridden over Munich. By the publication of this article *The Times* identified itself in the most dramatic way with the 'guilty' leaders in the eyes of contemporaries and posterity. It was the stooge of government, the creature of the 'Cliveden Set'. The image of *The Times* as the arch-appeaser was carried into the post-war era and proved impossible to cast off. *The Times History*, published in 1952, put on sackcloth for its sins. All this was a very heavy extra burden to carry for a paper which was to be launched into the merciless newspaper competition of the 1950s and 1960s and explains to some extent the severity of its struggle for survival.

(i) Emergency Plans

Once the Second World War had begun, *The Times* was faced with a struggle of a new kind. In the early days of its existence John Walter II had fought for independence against the Government and the theatre managers. Later, after the pecuniary losses incurred by the Parnell Commission, there came the struggle for financial survival. Now for the first time there was to be the struggle for sheer physical existence in face of the threat from the King's enemies.

That *The Times* was able to survive and maintain uninterrupted production throughout the war was due to two main causes. First, the decision by the Chairman, Major J. J. Astor, to proceed with the first stage of rebuilding, that of the machine room, enabled the whole production of the paper, editorial as well as mechanical, to be carried on in emergency underground. Second, early and thorough measures taken to train staff for Civil Defence and ARP duties provided Printing House Square with the most efficient organization for self-defence possessed by any firm in the City of London.

As a further insurance against interruption, standby arrangements for printing the paper both in and, if necessary, outside London were organized by the management. In spite of severe bombing, including one direct hit by high explosive, these facilities were never called upon. On the occasion of the direct hit, presses were stopped for only eighteen minutes. One's admiration goes out to the courage of the printers, publishers and journalists of those days who were determined to keep the presses rolling.

A department dealing with Air Raid Precautions was first established at the Home Office in 1935, but *The Times* did not become involved until 1937, when three members of the staff volunteered for first-aid work. In December of that year an ARP committee was set up, with the aims of training a minimum of 45 per cent of the staff, of setting up refuge rooms against gas in the basements, and making the telephone room bombproof and gasproof.

Arrangements were also made for maintaining production should the building be so severely damaged that *The Times* could not be brought out on its own premises. The main standby was the *Evening Standard*, where a sixteen-page issue of *The Times* could be printed. To cope with longer-term interruptions to production at Printing House Square, such as large-scale immobilization of all transport in London at night for long periods, additional standby arrangements were made with the Northamptonshire Printing and Publishing Company Limited at Kettering, where emergency eight-page issues of *The Times* and a sixteen-page issue (with cover) of the Weekly Edition could be produced. By the beginning of 1939 the preparations made by *The Times* had put them in advance of any other newspaper as far as self-help in an emergency was concerned.

Air Raid Precautions were not of course the only problem which faced *The Times* in the changeover from peace to war. There were problems of manpower, supply and public services.

Manpower problems were smaller than might have been supposed, being lightened by the need to limit the size of the paper to sixteen pages in the interests of husbanding newsprint supplies. Thus the calls for National Service in the Armed Forces, ARP and newspaper production about balanced out. In February 1939 the management issued a statement in which they declared that, although the Government had already announced that newspaper production was work of urgent national importance, 'every possible facility will be given to members of the staff who desire to volunteer for other forms of National Service in time of War'. In fact, out of a total staff of 1,570 at the outbreak of war, 584 joined the armed forces during its course. Financial help was given to members of staff with dependants whose income was cut when they joined up.

(ii) War Correspondents

From the first day of the war several members of the staff had to adapt themselves to a new but not uncongenial role – that of war correspondent. They were drawn from a wide variety of departments. Philip Ure and W. J. Prince had been on the parliamentary staff and also general reporters; Arthur Narracott was another ex-Gallery reporter and Deputy Lobby Correspondent; Eric Phillips had been Deputy Night News Editor; R. W. Cooper and R. C. Lyle in the Sporting Room (Tennis and Racing Correspondents); Gerald Norman a Foreign Sub-Editor. Only Christopher Lumby and R. O. G. Urch (the Riga Correspondent who covered the Russo-Finnish War of 1939) had practical experience of foreign correspondence. All acquitted themselves well.

By 1939 the position of war correspondents had greatly changed from the days of Russell, let alone from those of Crabb Robinson. They were now accredited persons, wore uniforms, drew rations, and were shepherded in their own transport by conducting officers of the service to which they were attached. In these relatively controlled conditions the correspondent could find the bounds within which he was confined irksome, but whenever the fighting opened up there was scope for individual enterprise and achievement. The anonymity rule of *The Times* kept these achievements largely unknown to the general public – not that any newspaper correspondents became household names as did, for the first time, some of the reporters for the BBC.

During the 'phoney war' winter of 1939–40 Cooper was correspondent with the French armies and H. A. R. Philby, who had reported the Spanish Civil War for *The Times* from the royalist side, was with the BEF. Both – particularly Cooper – found censorship inept and exasperating. Back in England after Dunkirk Cooper wrote a turnover in which he blamed 'Maginot folly' for the defeat of the French: 'Probably the greatest blunder of all was the absurd belief fostered in the public mind that the Maginot Line extended from the Channel to the Mediterranean, and here a rigid censorship was at fault.' With an insight that history was to justify he mentioned two names only of French generals who, to his certain knowledge, had distinguished themselves in the fighting – General Giraud, 'the Kitchener of France from his stature and remarkable resemblance', and General de Lattre, whose 14th Division had shown 'unexampled bravery'.

Philby, revealing an uncharacteristic and undetected glint of ideology, wrote on 22 June 1940 of the groups of French soldiers who were reported to be still harassing the Germans: 'In some respects these gallant bands recall the People's Army raised by General Chanzy after the disaster of Sedan in 1870, which succeeded in prolonging the war for many months.' This comparison proved unjustified. Philby soon moved to the other fields of action, but Cooper continued to report the war for *The Times* from India, Arakan, the Middle East, and the Normandy landings. He was early into Paris after its liberation, handing over the political story there to Gerald Norman, and following the Allied armies to Arnhem and Berlin.

Censorship takes many forms, and is not the only obstacle, in peace or war, that prevents a good story from getting into a newspaper. Years later, when the Anglo-French argument about membership of the Common Market was at its height, Norman recalled a forgotten incident from the days when he was *Times* correspondent in Algiers:

In March 1944 General de Gaulle delivered an address to the Provisional Assembly. One passage in this, inspired, it is believed, by Jean Monnet, sketched the outlines of what was ultimately to be the Common Market of the Six. The words de Gaulle used expressly stated that its frontiers were to be the Channel (or the North Sea), thus pointedly excluding Britain. The majority of de Gaulle's 'Ministers' and of the representatives in the Assembly were very strongly Anglophile, and this exclusion of Britain provoked a furore. For once de Gaulle yielded to pressure, and it was announced that he had misread his notes. The speech was amended, to allow the possible inclusion of the UK, and was published in the *Journal Officiel* in this amended form. This being the official version de Gaulle had no option but to use it when he came to publish his memoirs, but I was told at the time that his exclusion of Britain had been intentional. I sent a full message, giving both the original wording and the amended wording of de Gaulle's speech and the reasons which had prompted both versions. *The Times* published not a word of this despatch – only a straightforward agency message, which gave only the amended version.

After the fall of France the focus of interest for war correspondents shifted to the air (Narracott), the sea (Lyle), and the Middle East, where Christopher Lumby was resident correspondent in Cairo. Lumby's knowledge of Italy and an almost reckless devotion to duty were responsible for giving him the sort of story which all journalists dream of. It was April 1945, and the Fifth Army was held up before Milan. Lumby was at Mantua, and collecting a young colleague (Stephen Barber of the *News Chronicle*), a jeep and a driver he drove through the fluid Allied front line and across two hundred miles of German-held territory towards Milan, where he had friends. Several times it was only his determination and his mastery of German and Italian which got them out of extremely awkward situations. When they got to Milan they found the city in the hands of the partisans, and were given a rapturous welcome. During the night he and Barber were roused by some of the partisans who said that Mussolini and his mistress, Clara Petacci, had been captured and executed in a village near Como. Would they come and identify the bodies? (Lumby had known Mussolini when he was *Times* correspondent in Rome from 1937 to 1939. Mussolini had ordered, and then countermanded, his expulsion from Rome in May 1939). They were driven to the working-class Lereto quarter, and as the lead story in *The Times* of 30 April 'From Our Special Correspondent in Milan' reported: 'There were the bodies heaped together with ghastly promiscuity in the open square under the same fence against which one year ago 15 partisans had been shot by their own countrymen, Italian Fascists. Mussolini's body lay across that of Petacci. In his dead hand had been placed the brass ensign of the Fascist Arditi.' This dispatch was in fact filed from Army Headquarters, where Lumby returned to inform an incredulous American general that the city which they were encompassing had already fallen.

(*iii*) *The Home Front*

In Printing House Square the war provoked different problems. The air raid siren had sounded in the City of London for the first time in 'hot blood' on 25 June 1940, and for some time before the night operations of the Battle of London opened in September lone raiders reconnoitred the sky on 'nuisance raids'. On the night of the first alarm all work was stopped, in accordance with an agreement with the unions, and the staff went to shelter for three hours. Distribution of the paper by the railways was much impeded.

The lesson of the nuisance raids was that total stoppage of work at every air raid alarm was unjustified. The management had worked out a scheme by which all essential production, including sub-editing and news processing, could be carried out underground in the spacious Jobbing Department which had been provided in the new buildings. At a Board meeting on 5 September 1940, just two days before the real assault on London began, C. S. Kent, the Manager, reported that the trade unions had now agreed to men working during raids provided observers were posted on the roof to give warning of the approach of raiders. When this happened, all work would stop and shelter be taken till the raiders had passed. In return, a benevolent fund was set up by the Newspaper Proprietors' Association to pay compensation to men killed or injured on duty.

Conditions inside Printing House Square were graphically described by Tom Scott, of the Night Editor's staff:

> The basement was, of course, the permanent home of the big presses, and the foundry was also there, but the editorial and the printing department were now on 'foreign soil' and had to make, particularly the editorial night staff, the best of most unusual and uncomfortable surroundings. No provision whatever had been made at that time for sleeping, and the sub-editors and others on the night editorial staff had to make the best of lying down anywhere, on anything, on the floor or on the benches. It was safe to attempt to go home only when the 'all clear' was sounded, and that was about dawn.
>
> It was truly remarkable how few men, soon after we had taken up our abode in the basement, left their work to take shelter, even when the bombers were directly overhead. No one was demonstrating how brave he was; he probably felt that anything was better than the depressing atmosphere of that shelter. The men who were really brave, and were not given full credit for the distribution of *The Times*, were the van drivers who night after night drove their vehicles to the railway termini during heavy air raids.

Living underground with the minimum of comfort was taking a heavy toll of Geoffrey Dawson's health. He was no longer young; he was no longer middle-aged. Night after night he tried to sleep in a very tiny room. What this 'bedroom' was originally used for I have no idea. Nevertheless, it was a cubby-hole that was much envied by other members of the editorial staff whose makeshift beds were on the basement floor. I suppose that Dawson could have gone home each night before the bombing began, but for reasons best known to himself he chose to stay on with us. But the conditions were obviously too much for him. Ultimately he could not suffer even lying awake on his bed in the cubby-hole; he would come out into the comparative wide expanse of the basement, his cloak – a kind of opera cloak – draped round his stooping shoulders, look around at the editorial bodies lying on the floor, many of them in most inelegant attitudes, and then make his way slowly to the small bench that I used as a desk. At that time in the mornings I was the only one of the editorial staff who was officially on duty. Dawson would sit opposite me and open the conversation with the same remark each night, or rather morning, 'Anything of importance happening?' He never at any time mentioned the bombing that was going on. I would give him a summary of the news that had come in since the first edition of the paper, which he had already read. He would listen closely, his bottom lip drooping as it usually did when he was listening to every word spoken to him.

I learnt a great deal [continues Scott], from Dawson's conversation during those early morning visits when he could not sleep in his cubby-hole.

I knew very little about Dawson before war broke out, except that he was the Editor and that I did not agree with a great deal of his policy regarding Nazi Germany. I grew to like him very much, first as a fine man and, second, as a first-class journalist who was assisting a younger newspaperman enormously. It saddened me a lot to read after the war some estimates of this much-maligned Editor.

C. S. Kent, the Manager, was disconcerted by some of the activities of the Americans in the office, who shared with *The Times* staff the dangers and discomforts of the Blitz.

The Times Publishing Company was at that time printing and publishing the *Stars and Stripes*, the United States Services newspaper which had its editorial staff at Printing House Square. This newspaper was a source of anxiety to the Manager, Mr C. S. Kent, not because we were unable to cope with the printing demands of the American journalists. On the contrary, a fairly large number of our compositors was devoted exclusively to the printing of the *Stars and Stripes*. Mr Kent's worry was that too many pictures chosen by the Americans for publication in their paper – pictures of girls in the very nearly nude – were in his opinion too near the knuckle.

On the evening of Wednesday, 24 September 1940, the air raid alarm sounded at 8.22 pm and the All Clear was not given until 5.36 in the morning. Those in the Control Room maintain that they had that night a sense of foreboding.

At 1.50 am a spotter on the roof at No. 1 Post, W. J. Rayner, reported to the Control Room that he 'did not like the sound of a plane coming in from the south west'. Then he and two others with him heard the whistle of bombs 'as close as breathing' and ducked. In a matter of seconds they knew that the building had been heavily hit. There were three hundred people on the premises at the time. Down in the Control Room, on the ground floor, Patrick Bishop, Assistant Manager, was on duty.

> Mr Cutler [he wrote in the *House Journal*], was there at the desk, and in the outer room were several of our volunteer firemen standing by . . . There is no truth in the statement that you do not hear the bomb which is coming your way. You hear it very well, and for a long time . . . I am not quite sure what we did, but I have an impression that Cutler was no longer in the chair, but in the corner, and that I was rather foolishly holding him by the arm. Then the crash, and darkness, and dust, and glass.
>
> In the corridor outside the Control Room our professional fireman is rallying his squad. With torches and hurricane lamps – what a miracle of foresight those lamps were – we advance to find out what has happened . . .
>
> And here is the Chairman [Major Astor]. He was asleep in the Board Room, and must have had a nasty shaking. But he shows no sign of it, and is most insistent to know about the safety of the staff . . . 'Every one accounted for? Good.'

In fact, barring one or two cases of shock, and some cuts and bruises, there were no casualties. Dawson, too, had been asleep on the premises. So loud was the explosion that he thought not one but two bombs had fallen.

> A very noisy night [he recorded in his diary]. Retiring to my camp bed below about midnight. Two hours later there was a

terrific and very near bang and a general buzz of excitement. I
came up to find that two bombs had struck the front of the
office . . . my own room was deep in glass and debris but otherwise intact. It was impossible to do much in the dark. Kent
arrived to see to salvage and John [Astor] and I went home to
sleep.

The bomb had fallen at a slant on the old building completed by
John Walter III in 1874, which fronted on Queen Victoria Street. This
was fully occupied in the daytime by editorial and managerial staff,
but of course there was nobody in it at night except one or two individuals who chose to sleep there on sofas and camp beds.

Underground the production staff carried on. Only 80,000 copies out
of a print of 189,000 had been run off. There was a smell of gas and the
lights had gone out, but the engineers saw to that, and within eighteen
minutes the presses were turning over again. The real problems revealed
themselves in the morning. The main building was uninhabitable and
all the Advertisement Department's records and the Editorial Department's files were scattered about the floors and streets. The bomb had
passed straight through John Maywood's Intelligence Department and
Library, where he was accustomed to sleep on a camp bed. This was
probably the department which suffered most.

Damage to communications was severe. *The Times* was on the special
list for warning by telephone of an impending air raid. So the management had installed an alternative telephone exchange underground and
within the day the news agencies were round putting in new tape
machines, which enabled the Home and Foreign News Departments to
carry on.

On the day after the bomb fell, John Walter IV visited Maywood in
the wreck of his Information Department. 'A sad day for Printing House
Square,' he said. 'But thank God for Bear Wood bricks,' replied
Maywood, for it may be remembered that the Walter Bear Wood
estates provided all the building material for the new offices of *The
Times* in the 1870s.

German reactions were interesting. The bomb had struck in the small
hours of Thursday 25 September but no announcement was allowed in
the British press until 12 October. On Saturday 27 September the
German News Agency announced that *The Times* office had been hit
and that the paper was being published 'in the provinces'. On the
Sunday the Germans were changing the story:

One of the workshops for the distortion of the truth in London
nearly disappeared from the surface of the globe. It is learned,
in fact, that the administrative and editorial offices, as well as
several storeys of the building occupied by *The Times*, have been

heavily damaged by a bomb of large calibre. Other printing
offices in the City undertook the production of the paper.

From 10 Downing Street Churchill wrote:

My dear Astor,
Congratulations on the remarkable way in which *The Times* has
carried on in face of all the damage and discomfort caused by
the bombing of Printing House Square.
     None of your readers could discover from the paper that your
editorial and management departments have been destroyed.
     The resourcefulness and adaptability of your staff are beyond
praise.

The 'Night of the Bomb' was the highlight of the Blitz for the
inmates of Printing House Square. But many other threats and afflictions
lay ahead. In December 1940 and May 1941 the buildings were peppered
with firebombs during the great fire-raising raids. In February 1941 the
Government informed newspapers that they should carry on publication
in case of invasion, and plans were made for members of the staff to
sleep on the premises if and when the Germans landed. In July there
were heavy downpours of rain and the condition of the building,
battered as it was by bombing, was such that it failed to keep out the
water and there was extensive flooding. Another threat came, as it had
in the general strike of 1926, from officialdom. Air Raid Precautions
in Printing House Square had been organized early, and efficiently, on
a voluntary basis. But many other firms in the City, and throughout
the country, had not been as energetic and public-spirited. Inevitably,
towards the latter half of 1941, compulsory measures had to be introduced for fire watching and *The Times* then became involved in a
'paper war' with the authorities, the purpose of which was to defend
The Times's organization from being disrupted by government interference. Eventually Printing House Square was given official recognition as an independent ARP zone with autonomous control of its own
operations, so that the threat from officialdom, like the threat from the
Luftwaffe, was successfully met and surmounted.
     John Astor, the Chairman, played a key role in the military defence
of the City of London. Side by side with the ARP volunteers worked
The Times company of the Home Guard, whose official title was 'A'
Company, 5th City of London (Press) Battalion, Home Guard. Major
Astor – now promoted Lieutenant-Colonel – was the Commanding
Officer of the battalion, with Patrick Bishop as his second-in-command.
     The Press Battalion was one of the most efficient units in the Home
Guard. Formed originally for local defence of its own newspaper offices,
it was raised in 1941 to the status of a General Service Battalion – the

only one in the City at that time – and it formed the nucleus of the local defences of the City. Colonel Astor was therefore asked to assume operational responsibility for the City Defences Command co-ordinating the various static units there, together with stray elements of other battalions whose headquarters happened to be in the City. Had invasion come that year the Press Battalion, under Colonel Astor, would have borne the brunt of any attempt to drop parachutists or to otherwise assault the City of London. Conscious of the importance of its role, the unit ran its own Weapon Training School and incorporated intelligence, signals and medical sections, together with an armoured car driven by 'Nobby' Clarke, one of the editorial chauffeurs, and a mobile canteen presented by the citizens of Guelph, Ontario. Hugh Astor recalls that the armoured car was constructed out of Colonel Astor's peacetime Rolls, painted in his racing colours – pale blue with black radiator. Now, with an improved armoured superstructure, it was used to patrol the streets of London.

(iv) Newsprint Shortage

Next to the bombing, the greatest threat to production was the shortage of newsprint. During the worst period of the war consumption was cut to one-fifth of peacetime volume.

The newspaper industry was indeed in the most vulnerable situation, since all its principal raw material, newsprint, was imported by sea, whether in a wholly manufactured form or as wood pulp to be processed in British mills. As soon as the war began the Government set up machinery for rationing, the principle being that so far as possible the industry should undertake the ordering of its own affairs. Consumption was cut to 60 per cent, bringing *The Times* down to about fourteen pages. But this comparatively easy state of affairs did not last long. Two-thirds of British newsprint supplies, including practically all the pulp for the home mills, came from Norway, Sweden and Finland. There-fore, when the Germans invaded Norway, Britain was cut off overnight from all sources of raw material except those in Canada. At the time, there were stocks for only twenty-seven weeks' production in the country.

As an immediate reaction, consumption was cut to 30 per cent, bringing *The Times* down to twelve pages and the penny press to eight. Both paging and circulation were pegged, and that familiar feature of the street corner, the contents bill, was banished, never to return in its full prewar glory. Only a few months later, in July, *The Times* was further cut to ten pages and the penny papers to six. Circulation for *The Times* was pegged at 181,900 copies against an average sale of about 200,000 before the war.

Meanwhile, in May, the newspaper industry had embarked on a

remarkable co-operative effort in setting up the Newsprint Supply Company, a venture so successful that it was to outlast the war. This was a private limited company, organized rather on the lines of the great news agencies, in which all the papers had a stake. Colonel Astor, on behalf of *The Times*, was a director. The Newsprint Supply Company undertook the acquiring, pooling, importing, rationing and distribution – through the British mills – of all newsprint for the British press. The Company even acquired its own fleet of eleven ships, seven of which went to the bottom of the ocean during the course of the war. This fine example of co-operative enterprise on the part of an industry was fully approved by government and worked in consultation with the Ministry of Supply, which however left all the mechanics of the operation to the company to organize.

The Times had certain special problems. Ever since the beginning of the war, the Ministry of Information had been acquiring copies to send abroad to the press attachés in British embassies and especially for propaganda purposes in neutral countries. Nearly 2,000 copies were utilized in this way, and later, in August 1944, when the Air Edition was started, the number rose to 2,500. In February 1941 *The Times* made representations that these copies should not be printed out of their quota stock of newsprint and it was agreed that a special allocation should be made for copies supplied to the Ministry.

Then, in March 1941, the Board of *The Times* took a major decision. By now it was clear that further cuts in tonnage were on the way. The Board agreed that the paper could not fall below a size of ten pages without materially damaging its capacity to fulfil its role in the national society. They therefore chose to cut circulation rather than further decrease the number of pages. It was a decision in line with the philosophy of John Walter III when he decided at the time of the repeal of the stamp duties that *The Times* should remain a quality newspaper of limited circulation.

The decision involved consequential measures. If the circulation should drop below 150,000 the price would have to be increased from 2d to 3d. This in fact was done in April 1941 without loss of sales. A group to suffer were those who received the paper at a reduced price. Some 15,000 civil servants, bank and insurance employees lost their concession, as did over 7,000 clergymen.

At the beginning of 1942, the amount of space allowed in papers for advertising was restricted to 40 per cent – not surely an unreasonable restriction, although *The Times* protested at the interference. By the end of the war rationing and other restrictions were still in operation and were only slightly relaxed for the general election of 1945. But, rather to the surprise of those involved, the paper prospered under these restrictions. The circulation had been at 203,000 in 1938. Because of rationing, it was forced down to 157,000 in 1942. But by 1945 sales were back to 203,000 and continuing to climb. In terms of profits, the year 1940 was a black one. It was the first year in the history of the paper when it recorded a dead loss – £13,000. But it quickly picked up. In the following year the profit was £45,000, and it continued to climb:

1942	£96,000
1943	£131,000
1944	£132,000
1945	£141,000

The Times, and Fleet Street as a whole, were beginning to learn the dangerous lesson that rationing ruled out competition and was good for business. Restricted print orders saved costs on newsprint and small papers meant small staffs. And no matter what was the price charged, the public had to pay it, especially when there was a war on and it was hungry for news. For once in their lives the newspapers were enjoying the effects of what was virtually a monopoly situation. The experience tended to blind some managements about what was likely to happen when rationing was abolished and they had once more to face the cold winds of competition.

The second half of the war had brought not only economic and physical but political and social challenges to *The Times*. The publication of the Beveridge Report at home and the complete *volte-face* in international relations brought about by Hitler's invasion of Russia forced Barrington-Ward, who succeeded to the Chair on the retirement of Dawson in October 1941, to make a new assessment of the paper's position. It was agreed that post-war Britain must be a different and a better place. That was the mood of the country, and of the new Editor. But what was *The Times* to say?

The responsibility rested on Barrington-Ward; its execution to a great extent on E. H. Carr, an assistant editor and chief foreign leader writer. But the Editor was a cautious pragmatist, Carr a committed 'progressive'. As Barrington-Ward's biographer, Donald McLachlan, wrote: 'Reservations in the minds of both men made it likely that the partnership could not survive the national crisis...In the event it lasted over five years, long enough to see the war out and a Labour Government in.'

25 THE POST-WAR CHALLENGE

(i) Unanswered Questions

The Times emerged from the Second World War in a position of commercial strength but faced with a fundamental problem. This was the place of *The Times* in the changed society that the war had brought. The hallmarks of this change, from a newspaper point of view, were the fragmentation of society at the top and the spread of secondary and university education. For *The Times* particularly it struck at the roots of its traditional function. Barrington-Ward had foreseen this development when he began to shift the policy of the paper left of centre, but there were powerful influences at work in Printing House Square which failed to respond to the signs of the times. Within the paper there developed an almost unspoken conflict of views between those who wanted to maintain the élite character of *The Times* and those who favoured broadening its base. And there were some who recognized that, in spite of the satisfactory profits recorded during most of the war years, there were battles still to be fought.

One of those who saw problems ahead was Frank Waters, the new Assistant Manager who had been brought in when Patrick Bishop left to run the Newsprint Supply Company. In a memorandum delivered to the Board in March 1948, putting forward a scheme for air deliveries to Scotland, Waters wrote:

> The question whether or not to embark upon air transport depends to a great extent upon long-term policy. What does the future hold for *The Times*? How are trends in the newspaper industry to be interpreted? What are the conditions likely to be met with over the next five or ten years? Is there to be an expansion of circulation to meet the needs of the growing better-educated public? Is there to be a widening of the influence of Printing House Square, not only throughout the British Isles but all over the world – a development that can only take place provided the paper is as good as it can be made, provided the element of time-lag can be overcome, and cost of delivery to the reader established on an equitable basis. These are questions for decision on the highest level.

These were indeed questions that needed answering in 1946. Waters's

327

scheme for air deliveries was turned down as uneconomic, yet the problem remained. About nine-tenths of *The Times*'s sales lay within 175 miles of London. Nearly all the other national dailies printed in Manchester as well as London, with the result that they were able to supply northern readers with more up-to-date news than *The Times*, which could not afford to print outside London.

Waters's concern about the future was shared by some, but not all, of his colleagues. While circulation had remained steady there was a continuous decline in the share of the national readership by *The Times*. The size of this share in 1915 had been 5.56 per cent. By 1940 it had dropped to 1.82 per cent and by 1948 to 1.62 per cent. Nor was the trouble to end there.

In the next decade the total circulation of the four 'quality' news-papers (*The Times*, *Daily Telegraph*, *Manchester Guardian* and *Financial Times*) when added together showed an increase of 10 per cent. But whereas the circulation of the other three had gone up that of *The Times* was comparatively static. In other words as the potential of educated readership for quality newspapers increased, *The Times*'s relative share of it decreased. In the long term the situation was ominous.

The long-term prospects, however, were not the main consideration of those responsible for the management of the paper in the years immediately after the war. Judging by contemporary diaries, minutes of meetings and the recollection of those concerned, the main pre-occupations at this time were the finding of a new Manager and, more quickly than had been expected, of a new Editor.

When conditions of peace were restored C. S. Kent, the Manager, was sixty-three, with two years to go to retirement. The assumption had been that he would be succeeded by Frank Waters, but Kent had not taken kindly to the introduction of a potential successor. He avoided the devolution of responsibility to his new Assistant Manager, and when information about Waters's proposals for the delivery of *The Times* by air reached the Chairman by an informal route, and before they had been presented to him by the Manager, Kent made an issue of the impropriety and Waters left, subsequently to become Managing Director of the *News Chronicle* and *Star*. The directors had to think of someone else to take over the management.

After three or four candidates had been considered Stanley Morison suggested the name of Francis Mathew, the Manager of St Clement's Press, who had, Morison suggested, 'all the abilities required for the management without any temptation to meddle with the editorial part, great as his sympathy would be with it'.

Francis Mathew was appointed Manager from 1 July 1949. He was forty-one at the time of his appointment, and during the next sixteen

years he was, with Sir William Haley, one of the two great formative
influences at *The Times* in the years after the war. Most managers have
some specialist background. Kent had been an accountant. Mathew was
first and foremost a printer, though his years as managing director of a
prominent printing firm had given him a wider experience of running a
business. A broad-shouldered man of medium height, with heavy horn-
rimmed glasses, he was a forceful personality able to inspire personal
loyalty. There was in his make-up something of the buccaneer.

Even before the succession to the management had been settled the
Chief Proprietors, Colonel John Astor and Mr John Walter, were compelled, at short notice, to appoint a new Editor. Barrington-Ward,
exhausted by the strains of the war years and by his capacity for taking
pains, which often kept him at his desk for fourteen hours a day, died
in 1948 while on a health cruise round Africa. No long-term disposition
for the succession had been prepared. The three Assistant Editors were
W. F. Casey, who took the editorial chair when Barrington-Ward was
away but who had already intimated his readiness to retire, Donald
Tyerman, who had joined the paper from *The Economist* in 1944, and
A. P. Ryan, who had been Editor of the BBC News Services throughout
the war and who had just agreed to join *The Times*. E. H. Carr had left
the paper in 1946.

Throughout the pages of his diary Barrington-Ward makes it clear
that he wished Tyerman to be his successor. But his sudden death
plunged all into confusion. With their usual predilection for outside
talent members of the Board had been sounding Geoffrey Crowther on
the possibility of the succession, should Barrington-Ward's health com-
pel him to resign, but Crowther had just agreed a long-term contract as
Editor of *The Economist*. Two senior members of the editorial staff
were Casey and Tyerman. After some hesitation the Chief Proprietors,
having consulted the Board, decided in favour of the older man. The
appointment was conceived of as a temporary one, but like many
temporary arrangements it lasted longer than originally intended. Casey
held the chair from March 1948 until the autumn of 1952.

The editorship of Casey, like that of Chenery, was really an interregnum. The new Editor had never aspired to the chair, but on attaining
it he seemed to those around him to take on a new lease of life. His high
professional competence and wide range of knowledge, particularly of
foreign affairs and the arts, were an asset to the paper. His original love
had been the theatre, and he had written plays in his youth for the
Abbey Theatre in Dublin. For some years he had served *The Times* as
a Paris correspondent. He edited efficiently and without fuss, and got
the best out of his staff. If he began to leave the office earlier in the
evening than his predecessors had been wont, it was perhaps only the
due of one who had spent so much of his life deputizing for others in

the evening, and in Donald Tyerman he possessed an ideal *de facto* managing editor.

Yet the interregnum was almost certainly one of the factors which contributed to the future troubles of *The Times*. The period was crucial for editorial development, requiring the energies of a younger man capable of aggressive innovation. During these four years other newspapers were reading the Fleet Street map and pre-empting positions from which *The Times* was unable later to drive them.

(ii) Haley Takes the Chair

With the appointment of Casey the search for an Editor from outside Printing House Square did not cease, and one of those on whom the Chief Proprietors cast their eyes was Sir William Haley, who had been Director-General of the BBC since 1944, and who had started his journalistic career as a foreign telephonist on *The Times*. Haley had later joined the *Manchester Evening News*, the sister paper of the *Manchester Guardian*, where he had risen to be Managing Editor, and later joint Managing Director of the two papers. Not only did he have the professional qualifications for the job in the fullest sense, but he could hardly be described as an outsider since Printing House Square had been his cradle as a newspaperman. When first asked Haley, like Sir Oliver Franks, the British Ambassador in Washington, who had also been informally approached, turned down the offer. He felt at the time that his commitment to the BBC was too strong, and publication of the Beveridge Report on the future of broadcasting policy was then imminent. A year later he changed his mind, and became Editor in October 1952.

The choice of Haley for the Chair broke another *Times* precedent. Barnes, Delane, Dawson and Barrington-Ward had all been marked out as potential editors and brought into Printing House Square at a comparatively early age with the succession in mind. Chenery, Wickham Steed and Casey had been precipitated into the Chair, after long service with the paper, because of a vacancy occurring when the Proprietors had no candidate ready whom they had consciously prepared for the appointment.

With Haley the proprietors were for the first time introducing to the Chair from outside the office a man who had already achieved the status of a national figure, and one who approached the editorship of *The Times* as the crowning achievement in a brilliant career. The appointment was a compliment both to the individual and the paper.

What sort of a man was it who strolled unobtrusively into the room in October 1952 and started turning over the supplements while Casey still sat in the Chair? Seemingly unconcerned, did he study his future colleagues out of the corner of his eye as they came in and out on their daily business? They certainly studied him, for his reputation had run before him. They saw a man whose spare figure, fine profile and air of aloof authority made him appear taller than average height.

The outward man was certainly forbidding. A quiet but rasping voice, iron-grey wiry hair, a hard mouth and unsmiling eyes were the first impressions of a public figure who was essentially a private man. Those who encountered Haley in his official capacities saw only the professional who, having graduated in a hard school, was contemptuous of all but professionals. For those who possessed this quality, even if their views might conflict with his own, he had respect. But this was only one aspect of a complex man, and those who did not know him could have no measure of the depth and warmth which lay beneath the somewhat awesome exterior. His professionalism and also his enthusiastic appreciation of good work in others were to prove stimuli to his colleagues. As they were to discover, the private man could prove a congenial, relaxed companion. Haley's eyes could change in such a manner as to alter the whole personality of the man. When with companions who shared his interests in books, poetry and music, and with whom he felt no barriers, his eyes seemed to have an almost poetic gentleness and understanding which could change to an agate hardness towards those for whom he felt an antagonism or indifference.

Haley was born in Jersey in 1901, but his father was a Yorkshireman. His mother's forebears were Jersey-French. After his brief service as a telephonist with *The Times* he joined the *Manchester Evening News* and, after three years, in 1925, at the age of twenty-four, rose to be Chief Sub-Editor. From then on, in various roles, he became the effective controller of the paper, which he built up from an old-fashioned provincial evening daily into a successful modern newspaper. In 1939 he became joint managing director of the Manchester Guardian group. By then he had become a legend of ruthless and single-minded dedication to the job. But it was a Manchester legend, not yet a national one. He began to achieve a national reputation when he joined the boards of the Press Association and Reuters. In 1943 he was appointed Editor-in-Chief of the BBC, and in the following year he became Director-General. The successor of Lord Reith, in more senses than one, he restored to the BBC direction and a sense of purpose. Haley believed passionately in the education of the common man, and he tried to use the BBC to that end. But it was his position as the head of the most influential of the communications media during a crucial period of the war which gave him his public position, and his standing as a member, though always a critical and sometimes a rebellious member, of the Establishment.

At the time of his arrival in Printing House Square Haley was not apprehensive that *The Times* was approaching a time of dire crisis.

He made no immediate drastic changes. His influence was rather to be felt in an all-pervasive change of style in editing. There was a quickening of tempo. 'The fact is,' remarked one special writer, 'and I don't think one can altogether quarrel with him over this, that the new Editor expects us all to work much harder.'

He certainly did, but none worked harder than Haley himself. He was more of a writing editor than any of his predecessors save Barnes and Wickham Steed. He not only wrote leaders for great occasions but also on subjects that particularly interested him, and he was not above writing a leader to help out, if the leader-writing staff was a little depleted over a weekend or during a holiday period. He also introduced, and wrote himself under the name of Oliver Edwards, a weekly article on books. He read everything that went into *The Times*, and frequently commented on it, seldom failing to praise a piece of good writing or a well-judged report from home or foreign correspondents. He was equally quick to draw attention to lapses, particularly when other newspapers had stories that *The Times* did not. And he had a good nose for news. His chosen method of getting things moving was to dictate, from home early each morning, short memoranda to the heads of his editorial departments which would be waiting for them when they arrived at their desks. These memoranda, which would have a range of subjects as wide as those covered by *The Times* itself and might deal with anything from an instruction on the space to be given to a particular story to comment on a reporter's over-stretched simile or misplaced comma, served not only as a spur to action. They were also a daily reminder to the staff that there was at the top a man who expected much of them, and who also had a clear idea of what was required of *The Times*.

Haley's fundamental objective as Editor was to broaden the paper's editorial scope. He believed that the days when *The Times* could be satisfied with addressing a small national élite were gone. The paper had to appeal to intelligent readers of all ages and in every walk of life, and that meant that it should be eager to explore change, without losing its perspective. *The Times* was to include more regular reports, on science and medicine, education and sociology, sport and the arts, as well as the regular fare of politics, finance, commerce and industry, and all had to be written in language that was simple enough to be understood by the intelligent non-specialist in any of those subjects. He did not believe that this broadening of the base affected the role of *The Times*, which he once described, in a rare interview (Haley did not think editors should be public figures), as being first, to be a journal of record, secondly, to be an organ of information and opinion about matters of importance 'to everybody from Prime Ministers to parish clerks', and thirdly to cover as much of life in general as possible.

He summed this up, in the same interview, by declaring that the paper's purpose was 'to try to help educate its readers, or more exactly, help them to educate themselves'.*

Less than a year after Haley's arrival *The Times* pulled off one of the biggest journalistic coups in its history. This was the exclusive coverage by James Morris of the conquest of Mount Everest by John Hunt and his party of climbers on the eve of the Coronation in 1953.

James Morris had done his national service as a cavalry officer in the 9th Lancers, and was an undergraduate at Christ Church when he offered himself as a holiday trainee in the foreign sub-editors' room. In 1952 *The Times* special correspondent in the Canal Zone, Colonel F. G. Macaskie, died at a time of major political and military crisis. No experienced member of the staff was available to replace him and Morris was sent off as a promising stand-in. Arrived in the Canal Zone, he quickly found the key to the problem that had challenged all military correspondents since William Howard Russell, that of sending home plenty of operational reports while at the same time keeping the confidence of the military authorities. A dark-haired Welshman, as sensitive as an exposed nerve, he was already a stylish writer. He was twenty-seven when he received the assignment to cover the Everest expedition. His reports were to make him internationally known overnight. What added to their panache was the fact that he, a completely untrained and amateur mountaineer, was able to accompany the climbers as far as Camp IV, beyond the ice-fall at the head of the Western Cwm, 22,000 feet up. Few newspaper correspondents since H. M. Stanley can have had a more rewarding moment than Morris when, with the other members of the expedition, he first caught sight of the returning assault party:

> I rushed to the door of the tent, and there emerging from a little gully, not more than five hundred yards away, were four worn figures in windproof clothing. As a man we leapt out of the camp and up the slope, our boots sinking and skidding in the soft snow. Hunt wearing big dark snow-goggles, Gregory with the bobble on the top of his cap jiggling as he ran, Bourdillon with braces outside his shirt, Evans with the rim of his hat turned up in front like an American stevedore's. Wildly we ran and slithered up the snow, and the Sherpas, emerging excitedly from their tents, ran after us.
>
> I could not see the returning climbers very clearly, for the exertion of running had steamed up my goggles, so that I looked ahead through a thick mist. But I watched them approaching dimly, with never a sign of success or failure, like drugged men.

* *The Observer*, 8 May 1966: interview with Kenneth Harris.

Down they tramped, mechanically, and we raced, trembling with expectation. Soon I could not see a thing for the steam, so I pushed the goggles up from my eyes: and just as I recovered from the sudden dazzle of the snow I caught sight of George Lowe, leading the party down the hill. He was raising his arm and waving as he walked! It was thumbs up! Everest was climbed! Hilary brandishing his ice-axe in weary triumph, Tenzing slipped suddenly sideways, recovered and shot us a brilliant white smile; and they were among us, back from the summit, with men pumping their hands and embracing them, laughing, smiling, crying, taking photographs, laughing again, crying again, till the noise and the delight of it all ran down the Cwm and set the Sherpas, following us up the hill, laughing in anticipation.

Morris's own part in getting the news back so that it was in time for Coronation morning was not the least remarkable achievement of the Hunt expedition. In a Sherpa hamlet where he had spent the night he turned on his radio next morning:

A moment of fumbling; a few crackles and hisses; and then the voice of an Englishman. Everest had been climbed, he said. Queen Elizabeth had been given the news on the eve of her Coronation. This news (said that good man in London) had been first announced in a copyright dispatch in *The Times*.*

At home Haley meanwhile had attended to the urgent problem of restoring a unified Foreign Department. For five years Iverach McDonald had been an Assistant Editor with a special mandate to supervise foreign affairs. The proud title of Foreign Editor was now resurrected in his favour, and a foreign department was organized under him, with all the centralized responsibility and external status enjoyed by Sir Donald Mackenzie Wallace in the days of Moberly Bell. It was a simple, necessary and obvious measure of reform. Three Editors in turn had hovered over it, and it was typical of Haley's direct approach, and habit of reducing problems to their essentials, that he wasted no time in grasping this particular nettle.

In 1955 Donald Tyerman, who had been effectively Deputy Editor under three Editors and who had provided much of the stability needed during these years of transition as well as contributing significantly to the shaping of the paper's domestic policy after the war, left *The Times* to become Editor of *The Economist*. Maurice Green, who was later to become Editor of the *Daily Telegraph*, was brought over from the City Office to become Assistant Editor in general charge of home affairs.

* James Morris: *Coronation Everest*, Faber & Faber, 1958.

The first real test of the new team came in the following year, when on 26 July President Nasser announced the nationalization of the Suez Canal company. As it happened Haley was at that time sailing on the Astor yacht and out of contact with the office, so McDonald and his deputy, Oliver Woods, had to bear the brunt of formulating *The Times*'s initial response to this crisis. The paper had a tough leading article that night, and on the following day McDonald went to 10 Downing Street for a private talk with the Prime Minister, Sir Anthony Eden:

> Eden was quite calm. I asked what the Government planned to do. According to my memorandum, dictated immediately afterwards, he replied that ministers and the chiefs of staff had met during the morning and had agreed that Nasser's action could not be accepted. 'If need be, we should go into the Canal area, and we had the power to do it.' At the time he stressed – it is useful to recall his first reactions in view of what came later in the year – that he wanted to go forward in full agreement with France and the United States and with the Commonwealth countries.*

On August 1, before the first debate in Parliament, *The Times* commented in its leading article:

> When the Commons takes up Suez tomorrow there is one thing they can be sure of. It must be their guiding thought. If Nasser is allowed to get away with his *coup* all the British and other western interests in the Middle East will crumble. The modern world has suffered many acts, like Hitler's march into the Rhineland or the Stalinist overthrow of freedom in Czechoslovakia, which were claimed to be assertions of domestic sovereignty. They were, in fact, hinges of history. Nasser's seizure of the canal company is another such turning point. Quibbling over whether or not he was 'legally entitled' to make the grab will delight the finicky and comfort the fainthearted, but entirely misses the real issues.
>
> The first is quite simple. Freedom of passage through the Suez Canal, in peace or war, is a prime western interest. That freedom can be assured only if the canal is in friendly and trustworthy hands. Nasser's grab and his accompanying speeches give final proof that he is both unfriendly and untrustworthy. The second issue is no less obvious. The great oil works and fields of the Middle East are one of the main foundations of Britain's and Western Europe's industry and security. Anyone who thinks that

* Iverach McDonald: *A Man of The Times*, Hamish Hamilton, 1976.

a victory for Nasser would not encourage other extremist demands against the oil fields – and against strategic bases – should confine himself to tiddleywinks or blind man's bluff. The third issue is wider still. There can be no stability and confidence in the world so long as agreements can be scrapped with impunity.

When Haley returned he endorsed the firm line *The Times* had embarked upon, but already events had begun to shift, and as they did so did the view of *The Times*, as indeed did the opinion of the Opposition in Parliament, and perhaps also of the country. Though recognizing that force might have to be used in the last resort, the paper emphasized that Britain must also take care not to be seen as an aggressor. The wisdom of the decision to intervene, when it finally came, was questioned, and not just because of the suspicion of collusion with Israel. The paper was particularly concerned at the lack of candour between Britain and the United States and Commonwealth countries, and at the fact that the free world had been bitterly divided over the venture, with a large majority of the United Nations ranging themselves against Britain and France. 'The censure of the United Nations could be tolerated,' the paper declared, 'if the Anglo-French action had been manifestly sound and right.' The implication clearly must be that in *The Times*'s view the action was manifestly neither sound nor right, though the paper did not actually say so, adding simply that 'from the first there was a contradiction in the declared objectives'. Like the country at large, opinion within *The Times* office was divided about the Suez crisis, and this was sometimes reflected in the elliptical judgments published in the paper's leading articles.

The Editor had no hesitation in giving a firm lead when the Conservative Government of Mr Harold Macmillan ran into what came to be known as the Profumo crisis of 1963. Mr John Profumo was Secretary of State of War in Mr Macmillan's Cabinet, and for some time before the crisis broke in March public rumours had been rife that he had been sleeping with a woman named Christine Keeler, who had also been sharing her bed at times with the assistant Russian naval attaché in London, Captain Eugene Ivanov. If true, it was held that there might be some risk to national security. Questioned on the subject of the rumours by the Prime Minister's private secretary, Mr Profumo denied that there had been any impropriety in his acquaintanceship with Miss Keeler, and he later repeated the denial in a personal statement to the House of Commons, made on 22 March. Some six weeks later it became clear to him that this deception could no longer be sustained, and on 5 June he resigned from office, acknowledging that he had lied in saying that there had been no impropriety in his relations with Miss Keeler.

The news broke during the Whitsun recess, when the Prime Minister and many of his colleagues were out of London, but it was evident that they would face a debate in the House as soon as Parliament reassembled. The Leader of the Opposition, Mr Harold Wilson, had announced that his party's concern would be about security, not about morals, but *The Times*, in a celebrated leader published on 11 June, took a different view:

> Everyone has been so busy in assuring the public that the affair is not one of morals, that it is time to assert that it is. Morals have been discounted too long. A judge may be justified in reminding a jury 'This is not a court of morals'. The same exception cannot be allowed public opinion, without rot setting in and all standards suffering in the long run. The British are not by and large an immoral nation but through their pathetic fear of being called smug they make themselves out to be one.

The leader was given the heading 'It *Is* a Moral Issue'. It was a title, as Iverach McDonald observed, that could have been given to many leaders during Haley's editorship.

Haley's commanding influence over the character of the paper, his deliberate broadening of its content and his insistence on the highest standards in both news-gathering and writing, reassured both staff and readers that *The Times* was a newspaper and not just a journal of record, and had satisfactory results in circulation. From a low of 221,000 in 1956 the paper climbed steadily to a circulation comfortably above 250,000, at which level it remained for the first half of the 1960s. Suez started the rise – the Manager reckoned that the paper's circulation rose by 20,000 out of this episode – and its continued increase thereafter was attributed partly to the introduction of the 'Top People Take *The Times*' advertising campaign, though the slogan's suggestion of exclusivity tended to work against the Editor's ambition of attracting readers from outside the traditional establishment. Later, when *The Times* was trying to reach a more catholic audience, the Top People image proved hard to obliterate, and it was noticed that much of the increase in circulation brought about by the campaign had been among students, who enjoyed concessionary rates of subscription, and among people living overseas, who were costly to serve and who were, like students, of little interest to advertisers.

(iii) *The Battle for Paper*

In common with all newspapers in the post-war period *The Times* was harrassed by rising costs. The largest single factor in the cost of producing the paper was newsprint – the paper on which the newspaper was printed. The problem of newsprint was one which affected *The*

Times in a special way and to which it was to find a special, and controversial, solution. Newsprint prices rose steadily during the war, from £11 5s a ton in 1939 to nearly £40 a ton in 1947, but the severity of these price increases was muted because there was little newsprint available for any newspapers to buy, and it was severely rationed. By the end of the war popular papers were reduced to four pages, *The Times* to six.

After the war the Board of *The Times*, the management and successive editors were united in their struggle to shake off the shackles of paper rationing. It could hardly have been foreseen that this would last for eleven years after the conclusion of hostilities and that, in 1956, newsprint would be the last commodity to be taken off the ration. *The Times* played a leading part in ending the ration, but it paid a high price for it.

The majority of the press was not so strongly opposed to rationing, which kept newsprint costs down and forced advertising rates up, and many newspapers benefited from the system which allowed unlimited growth of circulation but restricted the paging. For *The Times* the system of rationing reduced the amount of space available for publishing both news and advertising, and it also imposed a limitation on the freedom of the press, as the paper pointed out in a leading article on 24 March 1954:

> The Government's hesitation implies that they are in doubt whether it may be reasonable or not to sacrifice the freedom of the Press to publish as much as it wants for the sake of 0.4 per cent of annual dollar expenditure. Such hesitation is unworthy – and the doubt unintelligible. The Press should have been at the head of the list for freedom, not at the tail, and it will be to the Government's lasting shame if control of the newspapers becomes the sole *raison d'être* of the Minister of Materials. It is time for the Government to show that they no longer rate the service of public opinion so far behind the enjoyment of tobacco, sweets and Hollywood films.

But *The Times* had other means than exhortation for forcing its will on government. As long ago as the 1930s Lints Smith and Kent had held discussions with a British paper mill called Townsend Hook, which as well as newsprint also manufactured paper not classified as newsprint and not rationed. After the war negotiations were reopened and on Mathew's appointment as Manager he was authorized to continue them. In these negotiations *The Times* was largely influenced by the possibility of using a superior quality paper to escape newsprint rationing.

On 1 December 1949 an agreement was signed by which *The Times* Publishing Company bound itself to use Townsend Hook paper exclusively so long as it was available in sufficient quantities to meet the needs of *The Times*. Townsend Hook for their part bound themselves to increase their capacity until they could meet this need. The agreement was binding for twenty-five years, renewable after twenty.

Townsend Hook paper had one big drawback – it was costly. Under the terms of the contract the price of the paper would be not more than 5 per cent higher than the London price of newsprint, but extra freight charges, due to the greater weight of the mechanical printing paper, as it was called, sent costs up some 15 per cent higher. This extra cost, the Manager claimed, was in part justified by the quality of the paper. 'Quality of print means more to *The Times* than to any other newspaper,' he wrote, 'and we rely to a large extent on prestige advertising. The surest way of increasing our advertising would be to improve the quality of print.'

One source of worry for the Board was how to ensure that Townsend Hook would continue to deliver the goods. They began therefore to acquire shares in the company and gradually established a controlling interest. The position was not unlike that by which Walter in earlier days paid the printing works out of the printing of *The Times*. Townsend Hook proved a sound investment.

Having signed the contract Mathew was able to persuade the Government to classify its supplements as periodicals, and print them on Townsend Hook paper. Three new quarterlies were started up, the *British Colonies Review* and the *Science Review* in 1951 and the *Agricultural Review* in 1952. The use of Townsend Hook paper released newsprint hitherto consumed by other supplements for use in the production of *The Times* itself, which was thereby able slightly to increase its paging.

In 1955 Townsend Hook was able to produce sufficent paper to print *The Times* itself. The company therefore proposed that it should be allowed to print exclusively on Townsend Hook paper, resigning its share of rationed newsprint to the Newsprint Supply Company's pool, and be permitted unrestricted size and circulation. The logic of *The Times*'s case was hard to refute, but it was at this point that the Government abolished newsprint rationing.

For *The Times* it was a moral victory, but in commercial terms it was a pyrrhic one. Just at the moment when free competition was restored to the newspaper industry the paper found itself obliged to pay for twenty years some 20 per cent more for its paper than any other newspaper.

(iv) Rebuilding Printing House Square
The most costly venture undertaken by the post-war Board was the rebuilding of Printing House Square. The question of rebuilding had a

long history. When in 1922 Astor purchased from the Northcliffe estate, through John Walter, the majority holding in *The Times* Publishing Company, the assets of the company were the newspaper and the mechanical plant only. The Walter family had retained ownership of the freehold of the building, and of miscellaneous leaseholds adjoining. In 1930 John Walter, having bought out the shares held by other members of the Walter family, finally sold the buildings to the company for £300,000 'without', as the Board Minutes of 3 July recorded, 'imposing any conditions.' The object of the purchase was to enable the company to rebuild, and at the October meeting of the Board the decision was taken to proceed at an estimated gross expenditure of £1,200,000, spread over three years. Certain other adjacent buildings, such as the Lamb and Lark public house, were to be acquired in order to facilitate a comprehensive redevelopment of the area.

At the meeting Lord Brand expressed a note of caution. He warned about the possible loss of dividends; he emphasized that editorial standards must not be lowered to pay for the building, and pointed out that the country was suffering from a general economic depression. Against this it was argued that building costs were at their lowest since the war and were likely to rise. The Board agreed that the decision should be left to the two Chief Proprietors and, on their initiative, it was decided to proceed. By 1939 the first phase had been completed, so that the printing presses had been safely lodged underground when the bombing began, making it possible for *The Times* to remain in production at Printing House Square throughout the war.

By 1954 the resumption of rebuilding was again under discussion, and Lord Brand was again urging caution. The Manager quoted an estimate of £1,900,000. Lord Brand expressed fears, only too well-founded, that costs would escalate. Nonetheless the decision was made to rebuild on site, the cost to be met out of current revenue assisted, if necessary, by a bank overdraft. Mr Richard Llewelyn Davies (later Lord Llewelyn Davies) was commissioned as consultant architect, and the rebuilding began in 1960. It was completed in 1965. To meet the cost it had been necessary for the company to realize gross annual profits of £500,000 over a period of five years. As the building proceeded profits began, in 1962, to fall below this figure, and it was necessary to call on Barclays Bank for overdraft facilities. But in 1964 Francis Mathew sold *The Times* shareholding in Townsend Hook (which had cost about £10 million) to the *News of the World* at a profit of £1,114,000, enabling the building costs, which finally totalled more than £4,500,000, to be met.

It was without doubt an astonishing five years' achievement. The staff had continued to produce the paper while the building came crashing about their ears. On one occasion the Foreign News Editor,

John Buist, complained that two bricks came through the glass roof of the room to which his department had been temporarily relegated. Nerves of steel were required to carry on production under these conditions, and some of the older members of the staff undoubtedly suffered from the strain. But they stood it, as did the finances.

This is not to say that there was not a price to pay of a different kind. The money that went into bricks and mortar over those five years was money that did not go into editorial and other development, and without doubt editorial standards were affected. *The Times* was forced to curtail foreign assignments at a time when its rivals were extending theirs, and had to meet the demands of reporting home news with a complement of reporters in London and the provinces which was less than half that of the *Daily Telegraph*.

(v) The Cooper Report

Between November 1957 and February 1958 a comprehensive inquiry into the organization, administration, and financial position of *The Times* Publishing Company was carried out by Cooper Bros, a firm of chartered accountants. This inquiry, the first of its kind in Printing House Square, had important repercussions. So secretly was it conducted, and so effective was what a *Times* leader writer, John Pringle, once described as the 'silken curtain' between management and editorial, that few of the latter were conscious of the extent to which this report called their activities and policies into question.

The idea of calling in outside consultants to appraise the management of *The Times* was put to the Board by Gavin Astor, who was anxious about the situation he might find himself called on to face when he eventually became Chairman. He was also concerned at the extent to which Mathew, the Manager, kept control in his own hands without consulting the Board. Mathew made no secret of his view that the Board, being part-time and in the main ignorant of the newspaper industry, should be a rubber-stamp. Gavin Astor, therefore, was not alone among his fellow directors in advocating some form of inquiry by outside management consultants.

The decision to proceed was stimulated by the fact that the company's steady record of profit had been broken in 1957. The financial year 1957–8 was a bad one for *The Times* because advertising dropped due to the adverse effects on industry caused by the Suez crisis. It was one of the few years in its history when both the paper and the company made a loss.

The picture over the past five or ten years, which the Cooper report would have to examine, was not encouraging. Circulation of the paper had dropped 8 per cent from 1949 to 1956, when it began to recover because the Suez crisis, as is always the case with such emergencies, increased the demand for newspapers. Meanwhile the circulation of its main competitors were going up – the *Daily Telegraph* (12½ per cent), the *Manchester Guardian* (25½ per cent) and the *Financial Times* (40 per cent).

During the same period profits were unsteady. From £388,000 in 1948 they had fallen to £118,000 in 1952, thereafter recovering to £323,000 in 1956, the year before the 1957 loss. Paging had been increasing at a steady rate from an average of nine pages in 1948 to eighteen pages in 1957. As a result gross advertising revenue had more than doubled, from £950,000 in 1949, to £2,250,000 in 1957. On the other hand, production costs were rising at an almost identical rate, from £1,500,000 in 1953 to £2,100,000 in 1957. The only difference between the two figures was that, whereas the rise in the revenue was halted by Suez, the rise in costs continued on its upward way. It is scarcely surprising that the future Chairman was alarmed.

The Cooper Report proved to be comprehensive and wide-ranging. It criticized the whole system of management which dated from the 1922 agreement, including the non-executive, part-time Board. Too much power, it implied, was concentrated in the person of the Manager. The compilers were struck by the lack of internal communication between departments – which, indeed, dated back to the days of the Crimea, if not before, but which some in Printing House Square chose to ignore. The accountants' department they found well staffed, but concentrated on producing meticulous detail rather than projection into the future. There was little interpretation or statistical analysis and there was no system of budgetary control. There was an ignorance of the principles of newspaper finance among the staff, and little comprehension of the relationship of the size of the paper, the cost of production, and the proportion of advertising needed to produce each day a profitable issue of *The Times*.

The inquirers did some sums which were disquieting. They found that in the decade after the war the Company had indeed averaged a profit of £250,000, but during this period *The Times* had not been using Townsend Hook paper, as it was now bound to do at an extra cost of about £150,000 a year. Nor had any promotional advertising been undertaken in this period, as was now being done at the cost of another £100,000 to £125,000 a year. If these two types of expenditure had been provided for the post-war profits would have been converted into losses or at best into very small profits. Furthermore, the air mail and overseas distribution of *The Times*, which was kept up for prestige reasons and for its indirect benefit to the advertising revenue, was run at a loss of another £70,000 a year. Although revenue had doubled in the decade this increase had to be set against a 50 per cent decrease in the value of the pound sterling over the period.

The report made some illuminating comparisons with other news-papers:

> Further light on the reasons for the recent lack of financial success of *The Times* is given by the comparison with the *Daily Telegraph*. The two papers had an almost identical number of total columns in their make-up [in the year ending 31 December 1957]. *The Times* had, however, nearly 1,100 fewer colunms of advertising and correspondingly more editorial columns...If therefore *The Times* had obtained as many columns of adver-tising as the *Daily Telegraph* and had correspondingly reduced its editorial space, it would have earned about £155,000 more profit...

The proportion of advertising to size of paper, the Report noted, was 40.2 per cent in the case of the *Daily Telegraph*, as against 37.2 per cent only for *The Times*. During the previous five years the proportion of display advertising in *The Times* had increased, whereas that of financial and classified had decreased. The *Financial Times*, the Report considered, was offering severe competition in the field of financial advertising, while the *Daily Telegraph* had 'established a reputation for classified advertisements for appointments which were previously pub-lished in *The Times*'.

Circulation targets were discussed:

> The Editor has in view a circulation of 500,000 to be attained over a period of perhaps fifteen years. The Manager has in view a circulation of 300,000 over a shorter term but does not think that this figure is likely to be materially exceeded so long as the paper is presented in its existing form. Some of the other officials were doubtful if 300,000 could be reached and named even lower targets. In view of the experience of other newspapers...we think that it is urgent to formulate a plan to recover the circula-tion lost by *The Times* in relation to that gained by its com-petitors and to change the outlook of those officials who are pessimistic about circulation.

The Cooper Report suggested a target circulation of not less than 400,000 within five years, and 600,000 within ten.

Under the section dealing with circulation the Report then introduced half a dozen paragraphs in which it advocated editorial reforms of the most sweeping kind. Among possible changes listed were a less ponderous style of writing; more emphasis on trade and industry; more, and shorter, news items; alteration of the types of news items; reduction of space allotted to leaders; increase in special features; relaxation of the rule of anonymity; a political cartoon; changes to attract more young readers; and alterations in heading, form and layout to make the paper livelier.

The Report singled out for particular criticism Home News and photographs. It advocated switching news to the front page as 'a form of continuous daily publicity, without cost'.

This section ended by recommending that a joint editorial-management committee should be formed to consider 'what changes will attract new readers without estranging the old'.

These criticisms trespassed into editorial territory, but some of the weaknesses adduced were already well recognized in Printing House Square. Of eighteen suggestions put forward seventeen were in fact implemented over the next ten years, some by Sir William Haley, the other after the merger with the *Sunday Times*, although the new Proprietors were never, it appears, shown a copy of the Report. Nor, it should be added, were all the Cooper suggestions a success.

Criticisms of the Cooper Report came from several quarters. The traditionalist viewpoint was pungently expressed in an anonymous memorandum of thirty-nine pages, labelled 'To the Chief Proprietors only'. A copy sent to the Manager carries the date 7 April 1958, in Stanley Morison's handwriting, and is worth quoting as an extreme statement of the convictions underlying much of *Times* policy:

> Since 1922, they [the Chief Proprietors] had known that the prime responsibility of the Chief Proprietorship is to organize the office so that the tradition, authority and leadership of the paper are maintained in the present, and safeguarded for the future. The national interest clearly demands it. It is difficult for any outside critic to deny this. Obviously Great Britain cannot function without a strong, educated, efficient, informed governing class. *The Times* is the organ of that class. It remains and, for all we can see to the contrary under a non-capitalist economy, must remain absolutely necessary to that class. As long as free political discussion is the necessary pre-requisite of legislation this is obvious. Secondly, the due discussion of the country's affairs cannot be adequately conducted in Parliament alone so long as it is elected quinquennially and sits only for a few months in the year.
>
> The existence of a competent governing class is rightly said to be absolutely dependent upon *The Times* because no other newspaper attempts to rival it in self-respect, impartiality, independence, range of significant news, capacity to reason upon the matter printed. No other newspaper possesses the space in which adequately to discuss in leading articles and letters to the Editor the topical and national problems of today and tomorrow. This

was true a hundred years ago and it is true today. A country like Great Britain depends for its administrative efficiency upon its politically intelligent and professional men; these in turn depend upon *The Times* for the material upon which to reflect, and, ultimately, act.

The Manager, Francis Mathew, who regarded much of the Report as an attack on his position, picked up Morison's argument in a memorandum dated 3 June 1958:

When Lord Camrose brought the *Morning Post* in 1937 he foresaw that the *Daily Telegraph* and *Morning Post* could not assail the position held by *The Times* in the nation's affairs. He chose instead to develop a section of the whole market – the Conservative middle and lower-middle classes – as his newspaper's preserve. In that, he was eminently successful. His vision has a lesson for *The Times*. There is a special market for *The Times*: there is a special market for the *Daily Telegraph*. Neither impinges on the other, nor on the mass market as a whole. If either steps out of its defined market it will go under in the dog fight for circulations.

No changes would be justified, Mathew concluded, if they involved a deliberately forced extension beyond the special market for which *The Times* was published. 'Such an extension of the market automatically compels a lowering of the standards of *The Times* to meet the needs of the Reading Public as opposed to the governing class.' It was, however, probable, he admitted, that the size of the market for *The Times* would grow in a technological age and with increased university and higher education.

To take the heat out of the discussion over the Cooper Report the Board decided that a sub-committee should be formed 'to discuss Cooper Brothers' Report with the Manager and make recommendations to the Board under the following headings: Organisation of Management; Advertising Revenue; Circulation and Publicity'. (At a later date the Townsend Hook contract was also included.) It was not until 5 February 1959, when the sub-committee reported, that Sir William Haley responded to an invitation from the Board to tell them 'how the Editor sees it'. His reply constituted a major statement of principle on the conduct of the newspaper.

The Editor began by setting forth the three purposes for which, in his view, *The Times* was produced. These were to be a 'journal of record', a daily paper which plays a useful part in the running of the country, and a 'balanced, interesting, and entertaining paper for intelligent readers of all ages and classes'. He thus gave a new definition to *Times* readership which differed both from the 'reading public' of the Cooper Report and the 'governing class' of Morison's memorandum. Haley's definition was closer to Morison's, in that he still appeared to aim at a relatively élite audience, but it was of a much less restricted composition than Morison's concept. The running of the country, Haley continued, did not merely mean 'Westminster and Whitehall'. It comprised, as well, local government, banking, industry, the professions, science and 'all activities which go to make our national life'.

These purposes of *The Times* which the Editor had listed were achieved by people, by money, and by space. He would begin by discussing space, because 'if we could only be clear about the part space must play in the combined purpose of *The Times*, then we shall at all events see what our fundamental problem is'.

> The Committee [he went on] speak of the 'continued existence of *The Times* as the greatest newspaper in the world'. I think in the privacy of this room we must ask ourselves whether the phrase represents a fact or whether we are merely making an empty noise. Can you be the greatest newspaper in the world when you are fourteen pages; with perhaps only six columns for home news and six for foreign news?

He then gave the size of the élite newspapers in other countries, such as the *New York Times* and the *Neuer Zurcher Zeitung*. *The Times*, he considered, needed a minimum eighteen and a regular twenty-page paper to do the job.

The Times had in the past five years introduced something like twenty regular features. These were necessary, but 'the trouble with features is that they are only effective if they are regular'. Haley stressed the need for more advertising to achieve larger papers. He added that larger papers 'would also do more than anything else to make every issue of *The Times* profitable, for the larger the paper gets the higher can be the proportion of advertising.'

Turning to money and people, the Editor wrote:

> If you were to ask me whether the Editorial feel 'financially restricted at present', I would answer 'not unduly'. We must naturally be sensible about this...We could do with more people. It would be better if they could travel more...*The Times* is not really in the hunt with the *New York Times* when it comes to having its own men out and about covering the world...
> There is also a need to be stronger at home. For instance, the *Daily Telegraph* has 40 general reporters in London, *The Times* 13. The *Daily Telegraph* has 20 staff men in the Provinces, *The Times* 3...the discrepancy should not be so great.

The present editorial budget, Haley pointed out, was £694,000 a year.

> If the Board suddenly found they could double it, I think I should ask them to put some of the money into buying the Editorial some space...I view the proposal in the Cooper Brothers' report that when papers are small the Editorial's share should be cut down in order to maintain a fixed ratio of advertising with very great alarm. *The Times* just could not fulfil its three purposes were that to happen.

The Editor went on to warn against too rapid change. There had, he noted, been a deliberate change of emphasis from politics and matters of interest for the professions to science, technology, industry and generally to 'the new generation's new interests'.

'There is still a need for some changes, there always will be, but there is an art in changing *The Times*. It must be done slowly. Readers of *The Times* tend to dislike change...we have to proceed with careful judgment.' But, he maintained, it was wrong to fear that *The Times* had an ageing readership. The IPA Readership Survey for 1957–8 showed that it had the largest proportion of readers in the sixteen-to-twenty-four age group of any national daily except the two tabloids, the *Daily Mirror* and the *Sketch*.

He was worried about the failure to break into certain markets. 'Why,' he asked, 'does almost all the women's advertising of our class go into the serious Sunday papers?' He was worried too about the perennial problem of the Saturday paper and its small volume of advertising. But, 'for the next four years, we cannot afford to gamble. The project for a greatly enlarged Saturday paper will have to be examined in this light'.

The next four years, Haley concluded, would be strenuous and trying but he was convinced that they could succeed if '(a) We get our priorities right, (b) We can get on with the job...Can we now therefore begin a post-Cooper era and concentrate on our task.'

The fate of the Cooper Report was similar to that of many others of its kind. The sub-committee drew up a list of recommendations for action on the Report's proposals. Few of these were carried out immediately or in the exact form expressed. Nevertheless the Report did have impact in the long run. Many of its suggestions were elementary common sense. It let in fresh ideas to a company which had become somewhat set in its ways and in large areas out of date. Opinions which would have seemed alarmingly unorthodox a few years earlier became topics for normal discussion and debate and in the end many of the proposals were adopted.

(*vi*) *Front Page News*

The Editor was not slow to follow up on the opportunities provided by the Board's concern. Allocated a special sum for editorial development he decided to spend most of it on improvements to Home News, the section of the paper which had been picked out for particular criticism in the Cooper Report, and following Maurice Green's departure to edit the *Daily Telegraph* he appointed Oliver Woods, the Deputy Foreign Editor, to take charge of the operation as an Assistant Editor. John Grant, the Defence Correspondent, took over the key appointment of Home News Editor, and a hitherto unknown lieutenant-colonel in the 'A' Branch of the War Office, Alun Gwynne-Jones (who was later, as Lord Chalfont, to join Harold Wilson's Government), succeeded Grant as Defence Correspondent. The additional funds were used to increase the number of staff reporters and to pay for extensive features, such as 'The Pulse of Britain', dealing with contemporary opinion throughout the country, and 'The Dark Million', describing the life of the immigrant population. On the foreign side the news service was strengthened by the appointment of David Holden as roving correspondent and by the creation of an additional staff post in America.

Such improvements were not of themselves sufficient to get the circulation moving to the level that was now seen to be required. In October 1964 a committee was set up to study the 'modernisation, development and expansion' of the paper. The chairman was Sir William Haley, who had proposed it, and the other members were Francis Mathew, now styled 'General Manager', his deputy, Mr (later Sir) George Pope, and a recently appointed Assistant General Manager, Mr Tom Cauter. The Manager noted with satisfaction that only one member of the editorial staff was a member of the committee, which would, he thought, enable greater freedom of discussion. The Chairman defined the committee's functions as:

> ensuring the closest thinking, planning and co-operation between the Editorial and Management side of *The Times* to meet so far as is reasonably practicable, in the presentation of the paper, the tasks and requirements of our existing and prospective readers in the late twentieth century. Our aim is a circulation increase to 350,000 at a very early date.

The committee reported in April 1965. Having had the issue constantly under discussion for six months, it recommended that 'news be put on the front page', and emphasized that the effect of this change was needed at once.

The argument over putting news on the front page had raged backwards and forwards for several years. The reasons against were part commercial, part psychological. The advertising staff were naturally concerned at the loss of revenue which might be incurred by moving the personal column and other classified advertising away from the most easily read page in the paper. Others argued that the traditional front page was the hallmark of *The Times*, comparable to the distinctive bonnet of the Rolls-Royce car. By jettisoning it, one director remarked, 'we should be losing the only gimmick we have'. Those who favoured the change pointed out that it had been successful in raising the circulation of almost every other paper which had adopted it, including the *Daily Telegraph* in 1939 and the *Guardian* in 1952. News was the most important content of the paper and ought to occupy the best position. Moreover, readership was falling and nothing short of this drastic and dramatic step would bring it back.

The idea that *The Times* had never before carried news on the front page was itself a myth. News and comment had appeared there on thirty-two occasions. Most of these were in the eighteenth and early nineteenth centuries, including the account of the Battle of Trafalgar on 7 November 1805, and during the First World War special Sunday editions of the paper had featured front page news.

Other major improvements were introduced by the Editor as part of the scheme which later became known as 'Operation Breakthrough'. One was the creation of a Features Department under James Bishop, recently brought back from New York as Foreign News Editor, who was among other things to be responsible for building up a larger Saturday paper by instituting a regular feature page and for introducing a daily woman's page, whose first editor was to be Susanne Puddefoot. Other innovations were the introduction of a diary, or gossip column, and of a political cartoon.

Haley's plan was to introduce the minor changes progressively. The big change, to news on the front page, was scheduled originally for January 1966, but the sub-committee, under Iverach McDonald, set up to plan the consequential changes discovered problems of greater complexity than the simple decision, and the changeover did not finally take place until 3 May that year. It was a dramatic occasion, reflected by the fact that *The Times* was itself that day featured on the front pages of newspapers in many parts of the world. In a leading article, headed 'Modern Times', the paper was at pains to reassure its readers that there was no intention of altering the essential character of *The Times*:

> The same people have produced today's issue as did yesterday's. They will produce tomorrow's. They will continue to have the same sense of responsibility and the same standards. They will at the same time use all their professional skill to make *The Times* more comprehensive, more interesting, more explicit, more lucid.

The Times aims at being a paper for intelligent readers of all ages and all classes. The more it can have of them the better. Some people have expressed the dark suspicion that one of the reasons *The Times* is modernising itself is to get more readers. Of course it is. And we shall go on trying to get more readers for as long as we believe in our purpose.

The effect on circulation was certainly spectacular. By the end of the first six months it had risen to 300,000, an increase of 20 per cent. Thus *The Times* took a big step away from the concept of a small élite readership and towards the newer, better-educated democracy which Haley had seen as the paper's main target, and to which his editorship had been largely dedicated. But success in these terms had other significant consequences which were not foreseen by many of those responsible, and which were to prove fatal both to Haley's tenure of the Chair and to the Astor proprietorship.

26 CHANGES OF OWNERSHIP

(i) Seeking a Partner

The rapid rise in circulation after 3 May 1966 greatly increased the run-on cost of producing *The Times*, and thus the paper's losses. The theory of newspaper economics is that such losses are met by additional advertisement revenue, since the charge for advertisements can be increased as the circulation rises. Profits result from the preservation of a careful balance between the two prime sources of revenue – the sale of copies and the sale of advertisements – so that the total received from both more than meets the total cost of producing the newspaper. Popular mass-circulation papers generally rely on copy sales to provide about three-quarters of their revenue. In the case of *The Times* the traditional ratio was at the other extreme: only about 25 per cent of revenue came from copy sales, and 75 per cent from advertising. As the price paid per copy in 1966 (sixpence) only met about one quarter of what it cost to produce, and as advertisement rates could not be put up until a new circulation level had been reached and held for a reasonable time, and proved by retrospective audit, there had to be an interval during which the losses mounted. For Gavin Astor, the Co-Chief Proprietor, Chairman, and owner of virtually 100 per cent of the equity of *The Times* Publishing Company, the cost became unendurable.

Gavin Astor had long been concerned about the financial weakness of the company and its dependence on the family fortune, which was itself vulnerable to estate duty. His father, who was created Baron Astor of Hever in 1956, had transferred his 90 per cent controlling share of the company in 1954 and five years later relinquished the chairmanship, which he had held for more than 36 years. It was at Gavin's insistence that the Board had agreed to the setting up of the Cooper inquiry, but his efforts to diversify the company's interests were not supported, and his early warnings of the financial perils facing the paper seemed to fall on deaf ears. In 1962 the Selwyn Lloyd Budget forced his father to emigrate to France in order to protect the Astor inheritance from death duties, and in the following year Gavin was appointed Co-Chief Proprietor with his father and John Walter IV, who like Lord Astor had made over most of his shares in *The Times* to his son.

When his father left England Gavin Astor took over the estate at Hever with no new capital or income. He thus had responsibility for two large but unremunerative assets. The assumption by the staff of *The Times*, the general public, and even some members of the Board, had long been that come what might the Astor millions would always safe-guard the paper. Gavin had great difficulty in getting it generally realized that with modern taxation and death duties they were no longer in a position to do so. His friends said that every morning when he set out for the office he used to wonder what would happen to the indepen-dence of *The Times* if he stepped under a bus.

Some astute outsiders had recognized *The Times*'s problems with greater clarity than many of its staff. One of these was the newspaper proprietor Lord Thomson of Fleet, who was looking for a daily paper to run in conjunction with the *Sunday Times*, which he had bought from Lord Kemsley in 1959. Lord Thomson made a tentative approach to Lord Astor when he called at the Astors' home in the South of France in 1963, but was rebuffed. He met with no more success when, in the presence of the Manager, Francis Mathew, he made John Walter Junior a substantial offer for his 10 per cent stake in the equity. John Walter did not take up the offer, but the Manager told Gavin Astor of the approach, with the result that Gavin himself purchased the shares for £250,000. To do so he had to borrow from the bank, paying the interest on the loan from his own pocket. The transaction gave him virtually 100 per cent of the shares in the company, but added to his financial burdens. He regarded it, as he explained to his fellow directors, as a bridging operation, until either the assets of the company had been reorganized or until a new partner or partners could be found.

During this period there was a general reorganization of the Board. Older members either died, or were asked to resign. Sir Campbell Stuart, Sir Harold Hartley and Lord Brand, all of whom had been active directors in all the affairs of *The Times* for many years, left the scene. New directors appointed in 1962 were Lord Rupert Nevill, a member of the Stock Exchange, Mr Seymour Egerton, a banker, Captain Iain Tennant, Chairman of a whisky company, and Mr Vincent Fairfax, an Australian newspaper proprietor. Later they were joined by Mr Kenneth Keith, a chartered accountant and Gavin Astor's financial adviser, and Lord Sherfield, Chairman of the United Kingdom Atomic Energy Authority and former British Ambassador in the United States.

The new Board was more receptive to Gavin Astor's warnings about the financial plight of *The Times*, and with his demands that the paper should be made profitable. He spelt out his concern in a strongly-worded memorandum to the directors, and in more measured terms in a statement published in *The Times House Journal* in 1965. 'Like any other business *The Times* must operate profitably,' he wrote. 'But the measure of its success ought not to be purely commercial. It is a peculiar property, in that service to what it believes are the best interests of the nation is placed before the personal and financial gains of its Proprietors.

'With only these qualifications, voluntarily imposed by the Proprietors themselves, are the Board and Management of the Publishing Company restricted in their efforts to make profits.

'One of the great strengths of *The Times* today is that the Editor is known beyond all doubt to have absolute independence in the control of all editorial content and editorial policy in the paper and is answerable only to the Chief Proprietors of *The Times* who alone are responsible for his appointment. Thus the Proprietors have the influence without the power, while the Editor has the power without the security.'

Many valuable years had been lost by *The Times* while the debate went on within the company about how best the paper might assure its future, years during which other quality newspapers gained ground at its expense. And when finally the decision to put news on the front page was taken it was already evident that the cost could not be met by the Astor proprietorship on its own. The search for a partner continued even while preparations for the editorial changes were under way. It increased in intensity as 'Operation Breakthrough' began to put up the circulation, but as full realization of the cost of the operation sank home in Printing House Square the search became one not for a new partner but a new owner.

The field was limited. The problem was that outside money was unlikely to be attracted to *The Times* in its unprofitable state without strings being attached, and such strings would probably involve some participation in policy-making – by which most men with money would mean having a say in editorial policy. This was an idea calculated to raise the most sensitive hackles among the paper's editorial staff, who not only learnt the horror stories of the Northcliffe era as part of their induction training but had been living happily for years under the benign regime of the Astors, who had respected the Editor's right to propound policies with which they did not always agree. It rapidly became evident that the only realistic opportunities available for partnership, merger or transfer of ownership likely to prove satisfactory from *The Times*'s point of view were in the newspaper field. There were at that time six other quality newspapers in the country – three Sundays and three dailies. Of these two – the *Daily Telegraph* and the *Sunday Telegraph* – could be ruled out. They belonged to a rival stable and a merger with them would mean virtual extinction for *The Times*. That left the *Guardian*, the *Financial Times*, the *Observer*, and the *Sunday Times*.

Another consideration had to be borne in mind. Logically, the partners in a merger should be complementary rather than identical. There were obvious advantages in combining a Sunday with a daily, or a specialist with a non-specialist paper. Obviously, too, the new partner should be a profitable concern. With *The Times* likely to find making a profit difficult there would be little benefit for it from combining with another paper in the same predicament. In fact two of these possible partners were in this depressed state. Nonetheless discussions took place with all four of them.

Before they became urgent the General Manager, Francis Mathew, died suddenly at the age of fifty-seven. He had been a staunch upholder of a high-priced *Times* aimed at a small but influential readership, but as a member of the modernization committee that proposed putting news on the front page he seems to have accepted the change as inevitable. His death, at a time when so much change was taking place, necessitated a radical reorganization of top management. Sir William Haley became Chief Executive, with a seat on the Board. George (later Sir George) Pope became General Manager. Haley retained the editorship, but was not now able to give all his time to editing. Iverach McDonald, the Foreign Editor, was therefore appointed Managing Editor, with Oliver Woods as Deputy Managing Editor. It was an emergency organization to meet an emergency situation, and it put much of the burden of searching for a partner for *The Times* on Haley and Pope.

Of the four possibilities a merger with the *Guardian* was the least logical. Like *The Times*, the *Guardian* was a non-specialist newspaper and a merger, however presented, would lead to the demise of one or the other. As they stood for different political traditions and had different readerships this could hardly have been seen as being in the best interests of either, or of the newspaper-reading public. The *Guardian*, moreover, was in a financial position not unlike that of *The Times*. The group to which it belonged was showing a profit, but the paper was not. Haley and Pope did in fact hold discussions with Laurence Scott, Chairman of the *Manchester Guardian* and *Evening News* Ltd, and the man who had increased the *Manchester Guardian's* circulation so dramatically by putting news on the front page, dropping Manchester from the title and finally transferring its headquarters to London (a move which challenged *The Times* in its own territory). There it lodged with the *Sunday Times*, being printed and edited in Gray's Inn Road, in much the same way as the *Observer* was lodged at Printing House Square. The talks between *The Times* and the *Guardian* may fairly be described as no more than exploratory.

The *Observer* negotiation was in a different category. The two papers had been moving closer together over the past decade. The *Observer* was now housed and printed by *The Times*, and made use of a number of common services. The Editor, David Astor, was the cousin of the Chairman of *The Times*. There was thus a family, and, more remotely, a financial connexion. Of all the proposals for a merger, this was the one most strongly favoured by Haley.

Possible schemes for closer association had been discussed, on and off, for some time. There were difficulties. The *Observer* was owned by a trust, which would need to be modified for a link-up with *The Times*, though this was not an insuperable objection. A much stronger one was that the *Observer* trust itself was making a loss, and was in need of a large capital sum for development. The combined organization, it was felt, could not raise capital any more readily than the papers could on their own, and *The Times* would find it easier to face its difficulties alone rather than in conjunction with the *Observer*.

In May 1966 another serious negotiation was begun. This was for a merger with the *Financial Times*. The basis of this proposal was that a single paper should be produced, the business section of which should be the equivalent of the *Financial Times* and the rest the equivalent of *The Times*, less its business pages. As a journalistic proposition there was much to be said for the proposal. Haley was to be Chairman of the new company, with a position equivalent to that of the publisher of an American newspaper. Mr Gordon Newton, Editor of the *Financial Times*, would be the Editor of the combined paper. Lord Cowdray, the owner of the *Financial Times*, would have the predominant interest in the new company.

Kenneth Keith was instructed to negotiate the financial terms on behalf of *The Times* Publishing Company, and Lord Poole of Lazards represented the *Financial Times*. Although agreement was reached on the method of operation of the papers the Cowdray financial offer was not acceptable – derisory was the word used by some of those involved – and the attempt to unite the two papers was abandoned in September 1966.

It was at this point, with *The Times* estimating that it would need a capital injection of some four million pounds to meet its development costs and establish the paper on its new footing, that a merger with the fourth possible partner, the *Sunday Times*, became virtually inevitable. Lord Thomson had the money, had already expressed his interest, and was not a man to be put off or upset by the decidedly cool response to his early approaches. He recognized, as he noted without rancour in his autobiography,* that one of the obstacles was himself, and accordingly instructed Denis Hamilton, the Editor of the *Sunday Times* and a highly successful and respected journalist, to keep in touch with Astor and Haley and to offer, if the opportunity arose, a deal which would safeguard the editorial independence and integrity of *The Times*. The essence of the proposal was that a new company should be formed of

* Lord Thomson of Fleet: *After I was Sixty*, Hamish Hamilton, 1975.

The Times and the *Sunday Times*, with a Board which would include a number of public men, appointed in equal numbers by Thomson and Astor, to form a 'blocking third', and from which Lord Thomson reluctantly agreed to exclude himself. On 30 September 1966 it was announced that the new company, Times Newspapers Limited, had been formed to own and publish *The Times* and the *Sunday Times*. Gavin Astor was to be Life President, Sir William Haley Chairman, Kenneth Thomson (Lord Thomson's son) Vice-Chairman, and Denis Hamilton as Editor-in-Chief and Chairman of the Executive Committee. Other directors would comprise three nominated by the Thomson Organization, two by Gavin Astor, four independent national figures (two nominated by the Thomson Organisation and approved by Astor, and two nominated by Astor and approved by the Thomson Organisation), and the General Manager of the new company, who was to be Geoffrey Rowett. In addition George Pope was to be on the Board for the first year. It was agreed that Haley would relinquish the chairmanship to Kenneth Thomson after three years, but in the event Haley left the company in 1968 to work with the *Encyclopaedia Britannica*.

The financial arrangements included immediate payment of £1 million by Lord Thomson to Gavin Astor for the title of *The Times* and for the plant and buildings at Printing House Square. A further £1 million was to be paid in ten years, and in the meantime Astor was to receive the interest on that million. In return for surrendering his shares in *The Times* Astor also received a 15 per cent holding in the new company, though the Thomson Organisation, as holder of the 'A' shares in the new company, would receive each year the first £1 million of pre-tax net profit.

There was some criticism about the price paid for the Printing House Square site and freehold, which certainly seemed on the low side. But the real value was difficult to assess. The office building was modern and stood on a valuable site, but it was purpose-built as a newspaper office and the planning permission was restricted to that purpose. Gavin Astor got substantially more than he was offered by the *Financial Times*, and he said afterwards that he felt that Lord Thomson would need some extra money to develop the paper, which certainly proved to be so. In any case he regarded speculation on the price which Printing House Square might fetch as a building as idle. In a personal message to each member of the staff at the end of 1966 he said that to have rendered *The Times* homeless by sale of the building would have destroyed the paper. He regarded the building as an essential part of the dowry, without which the marriage necessary to save *The Times* would not have been possible.

He also explained his view that to be the private owner of a 'National Institution', whose Editor was answerable to non-executive Proprietors and whose General Manager was answerable to a non-executive Chairman and Board, and which was inhibited in its commercial enterprise by voluntary and statutory restrictions, was an anachronism. 'I have come to realize,' he wrote, 'that to carry the entire financial risk as Proprietor no less than the full legal responsibility as Chairman for the success or failure of the Company, without also carrying executive power, is not a satisfactory situation. So now the merger of *The Times* and the *Sunday Times* into a new company called Times Newspapers Ltd will concentrate responsibility and the power where it should be – with the Board.'

The new Board thus differed from the old in that most of its members were executive officers of the company, or of the Thomson Organisation. The first four national directors were Sir Eric Roll and Lord Robens (appointed by the Thomson Organisation) and Lord Shawcross and Sir Donald Anderson (appointed by Gavin Astor). Their purpose was primarily to represent the public interest by ensuring that the 'National Institution' traditions of *The Times* were not betrayed. They were, in this sense, the successors of the *ex-officio* trustees set up under the 1922 settlement – the Lord Chief Justice, the Warden of All Souls College, Oxford, the President of the Royal Society, the President of the Institute of Chartered Accountants, and the Governor of the Bank of England. These trustees, whose existence had become something of a legend, were informed individually of the merger plan, although the terms of the Articles of Association did not give them any official standing in the matter. They were informed as a matter of courtesy, as was the Prime Minister, Mr Harold Wilson, who gave the union his blessing.

The agreement of 30 September still had an important hurdle to clear before Times Newspapers could come into being. The negotiators now had to appear before the Monopolies Commission, which had to decide whether the merger would operate against public interest. Evidence was submitted by both parties, as well as by outside organizations. Lord Thomson and Denis Hamilton gave assurances on the independence of the two Editors and on the preservation of the independent character of the two papers. In addition Lord Thomson gave assurances of his determination to maintain and develop *The Times*, and told the Commission that he expected to lose over £1 million in the first year and perhaps spend £5 million before *The Times* could be put into a position of viability. His appearances before the Monopolies Commission, he wrote in his autobiography, were like being on trial:

> Not once but many times I told them that I was only taking on *The Times* because I reckoned its rescue and restoration to health would be a worthy object and perhaps a fitting object for a man who had made a fortune out of newspapers. I knew, I said,

that I was going to lose a lot of money before *The Times* became viable again, and if it ever did become a profitable concern, it would very likely never repay the big sums, the millions, we would have to invest in it. We knew that, my son and I, yet we were prepared to devote a large amount of our private fortune to this end...It would be our money that would be lost, I assured them, not anybody else's. The financial arrangement was that in the first place *The Times* losses would be shouldered by the *Sunday Times*. If the *Sunday Times* were to make too little profit in any one year to cover those losses, then my son and I would forego enough of the dividends which would be due to us on our 78 per cent of Thomson Organisation shares. This would leave the outside shareholders of the organization untouched. To make this a fool-proof arrangement, Thomson Scottish Associates, a company which derived its income wholly from the Thomson Organisation and from which my son and I got our private fortune in Britain, gave an official company guarantee to cover *The Times* losses.

The Monopolies Commission gave its approval of the merger on 22 December 1966. On 1 January 1967 the new company took over.

(ii) *The Times on the Move*

The Board of Times Newspapers Ltd met for the first time on 12 January 1967, when it appointed as Editor William Rees-Mogg, who had been Deputy Editor of the *Sunday Times* since 1964. Iverach McDonald, who as Managing Editor of *The Times* had been holding the fort during the changeover, was appointed Associate Editor, and the former Deputy Managing Editor, Oliver Woods, became Chief Assistant to Denis Hamilton, the Editor-in-Chief. The smooth transition of editorial responsibility in the ensuing months owed much to these two men, both of whom were gifted writers and loyal and long-serving members of *The Times* editorial staff, and were young enough still to have had hopes of succeeding to the chair. Those in Printing House Square who had been concerned at the sale of the paper were at first made more apprehensive by the appointment of a man from the *Sunday Times* as Editor in preference to favoured candidates from within *The Times*, and perhaps even more so by what they saw as an invasion of marketing men and other executives from the Thomson Organisation whose presence was, in the words of one old *Times* man, 'more obvious than their function'. But many such fears were allayed by the continued presence of McDonald and Woods in senior and influential positions on the paper, and by the recognition among other senior editorial and management men of *The Times* (whose calibre, as he later admitted, took the new Editor by surprise) that the paper needed new ideas and new blood as well as greater financial resources.

They also knew that Rees-Mogg had, at the age of thirty-eight, many of the qualities required in an Editor of *The Times*. Educated at Charterhouse and Balliol, he had been President of the Union and had subsequently acquired the education in practical politics that standing as a parliamentary candidate can bring (he twice unsuccessfully contested Chester-le-Street as a Conservative). He began his journalistic career on the *Financial Times*, where he was chief leader-writer and later an Assistant Editor. He joined the *Sunday Times* as City Editor, then in 1961 became Political and Economic Editor, and finally Deputy Editor three years later. A reserved and sometimes shy man of scholarly interests and an enthusiasm for academic discussion which led him naturally to give particular attention to the editorial judgments of the paper as expressed in its leader columns, Rees-Mogg nonetheless did not lack the determination and toughness necessary to establish his editorial control. He took his first editorial conference on the day after his appointment was announced, and wrote his first leader the same night.

Within the next few days he made a decisive change to the style of *The Times* by abolishing the tradition of anonymity. Reporters, foreign correspondents and specialist staff wrote their major pieces, from 16 January on, under their own names instead of under such traditional labels as 'From Our Own Correspondent' and 'From Our Special Correspondent'. There was no discernible decline in the authority of the reporting or the standard of writing (as in the past it had been feared there might be) from the revelation to the reader that, for example, the consistently brilliant dispatches from Washington were filed by Louis Heren, or that the well-informed political correspondence came from the pen of David Wood, or that some of the most elegant prose in the paper was written by a home reporter named Philip Howard.

Other changes were on the way. The home and foreign news coverage was strengthened, more and better features were introduced (including regular columns by, among others, Ian Trethowan, Leonard Beaton, Auberon Waugh and Bernard Levin), and additional space was found for the arts and sport. The rearrangement of the order of the paper that accompanied the introduction of news on the front page in 1966 had left the Personal Column and other classified advertisements uneasily housed on page two. On 11 April 1967 these were moved to the back of the paper and home news was brought forward, so that an orderly sequence of news followed the front page as it does today. Pages were re-styled and the number of type-columns increased. At the same time a daily Business News section, separate from the main paper, was introduced. Later in the year a Saturday Review, also separated from the main paper, was created to meet the growing interest in leisure activities. Pre-print colour was introduced in 1968, allowing the paper to publish a company report in full colour, the first of its kind in any newspaper, as well as a memorable colour souvenir of man's landing on the moon.

The editorial innovations were accompanied by ambitious promotion and advertisement sales campaigns, and there was no doubting the success of these combined initiatives in terms of copy sales. A circulation of 301,000 at the end of 1966 climbed to 364,000 in 1967, to 415,286 by the end of 1968 and to a peak of 451,000 in March 1969. Advertisement volume was increased by some 70 per cent during the same period. But such successes came too quickly, and the cost was too high. The greatly increased print runs and issue sizes stretched production and distribution facilities to the limit and sometimes beyond it. Trains were missed, edition changes had to be limited, the paper had to go to press too early, and an amazing number of literals began to appear in a paper that had always prided itself on its accuracy, there no longer being time for it to be properly 'read' and corrected. It proved difficult to win union agreement to some of the changes that rapid growth made necessary, such as a speeding-up of the presses. And all the while *The Times* was losing money.

The cost to Lord Thomson of his first three years of ownership – years of expansion when he once commented that the men in Printing House Square were spending money like drunken sailors – was reckoned at not less than £5 million. The money was provided, as Lord Thomson had promised it would be. The new proprietor meticulously observed all the guarantees he had given to the Monopolies Commission, and he proved as scrupulous as the Astors had been in respecting the independence of the Editor. Though there were times when he disagreed with and was plainly baffled by the editorial views and policies expressed in his paper he never suggested to the Editor that they might be changed. Rees-Mogg had no complaints on this score. He had, he told a BBC interviewer in 1968, 'complete freedom in the sphere of what I put in the paper, whether it is news or opinion, with not the faintest indication of what anyone might even prefer', and he had in addition 'quite remarkable freedom to shape the editorial character of the paper in the way that I thought fit, even in terms of broad strategy'. There was no doubt that the paper Rees-Mogg and his editorial team were producing was attracting a larger public than *The Times* had had for many years, but the cost, both in financial terms and in the strain on production capacity, was becoming prohibitive.

The original objective of securing a circulation of 500,000 by increasing the size and editorial coverage of the paper while holding the price at sixpence now began to be questioned. In October 1969 the price of *The Times*, which had remained at sixpence for five years, was raised to eightpence, and was increased by a further penny in June of the following year and by another threepence in November 1970. At the same time costs, particularly of newsprint, continued to rise, and in spite of the boosts to revenue from the cover price increases the losses on *The Times* continued to run at well over £1 million a year. To relieve the Thomson Organisation of this burden Lord Thomson assumed personal financial responsibility for the paper through the parent company, Thomson Scottish Associates, as he had undertaken he would do to the Monopolies Commission. By an agreement made in June 1970 Times Newspapers Ltd, while continuing to own *The Times*, licensed Thomson Scottish Associates to publish it, any profits or losses accruing to the parent company. At the same time Lord Thomson emphasized that there was no question of *The Times* running the risk of disappearing – a public reassurance that had become necessary in order to still speculation that the future of the paper was again in doubt.

During 1970 the financial situation of all Fleet Street papers became increasingly precarious, and the total profitability of all the morning, evening and Sunday papers at that time was estimated to be no more than £2 million. On *The Times* there was a re-think about the original objectives. Denis Hamilton felt that there had been too much pressure on the accelerator. Some mistakes had been made: the introduction of Business News, for example, had been too hurried, with the result that it was not authoritative enough and failed to carry conviction with the business community at whom it was aimed. It was concluded that circulation growth should no longer override all other considerations, a decision that was dramatically demonstrated by the doubling of the cover price within little more than a year. Denis Hamilton succeeded Kenneth Thomson (now Co-Life President) as Chairman (while remaining Editor-in-Chief), and in 1971 he brought in Marmaduke Hussey, who had been Managing Director of Harmsworth Publications since 1967, was brought in as Chief Executive and Managing Director. Duke Hussey saw as his first task the restoration of confidence, both within the paper, particularly on the management side, and outside it. He set about forming a new management team as dedicated as he was to the aim of making *The Times* viable. Michael Mander, who had previously been with Associated Newspapers, joined the company as Advertisement and Marketing Director, and Harvey Thompson was brought in from the *Guardian* as Director of Production.

Visible signs that the paper was drawing in its horns soon appeared. The issue sizes became smaller. Business News and the Saturday Review were brought back into the main paper instead of being separate sections. The quality of the paper on which *The Times* was printed was reduced, following cancellation of the contract with Townsend Hook, and, perhaps most noticeable of all so far as the readers were concerned,

Stanley Morison's Times Roman type was abandoned and replaced by Times Europa. The justification for this change, as a leading article declared, was that Times Roman was not satisfactory in the smaller 8-point typeface on the thinner newsprint that *The Times* was now using, and a smaller face was needed in order to 'pack as much news and analysis as possible into the available space every day.'

Space-saving and cost-cutting did not stifle initiative. In October 1971 *The Times* launched a *Higher Educational Supplement*, which quickly established a place for itself alongside its formidably successful parent, *The Times Educational Supplement*. The profitable special reports spread themselves into many new areas, including a series on European subjects launched jointly with *Le Monde, Die Welt* and *La Stampa* in 1972, containing identical editorial and advertisements in four languages. These supplements developed, in October 1973, into a monthly survey called *Europa. The Times* also began publishing reports of the European Parliament and regular European law reports and, following Lord Thomson's visit to China in 1972, appointed David Bonavia as correspondent in Peking, the first British newspaper correspondent to be established there.

In 1973 the measures taken to make *The Times* viable began to show results. Had it not been for a bad final month, caused by the national industrial troubles leading up to the imposition of the three-day week, the paper would have recorded a profit for the year as a whole. As it was it showed a loss of £187,000, which was more than £1 million less than in 1972.

For the men and women who worked on *The Times* a greater convulsion was still to come. The economics of production made it seem inevitable, from the moment of the merger of *The Times* and the *Sunday Times*, that the two papers should at some time be physically brought together so that they could be printed on the same machines instead of on separate presses in two buildings, one in Blackfriars and the other in Gray's Inn Road. The facilities in Printing House Square were not sufficient to accommodate both, so logic dictated that *The Times* should be the one to move. The building and freehold at Blackfriars were sold and a site for New Printing House Square acquired alongside the *Sunday Times* building, and on Saturday 22 June 1974 *The Times* published its last issue from the site where the first issue of the *Daily Universal Register* was printed 189 years before. The issue of Monday 24 June was published from Gray's Inn Road. The new offices were far from finished, indeed barely operable, for the first ten days, and passersby could only stand and gape at the state of the building from which Britain's leading national daily newspaper was being published at that time. There were hold-ups in publications during the first week, and it was some months before efficient production was achieved, but the move itself went with remarkable precision and nothing vital to the production process, human or mechanical, was found to have been left behind. Inevitably there was sadness among members of the staff at leaving the historic Blackfriars site, but the break with the past was perhaps no greater than that of the early 1960s, when the private house of the Walter family and the old Victorian offices of *The Times* gave way to a modern block, and the physical discomfort and inconvenience of the move was borne, as the annual report put it, with 'tolerant fortitude' by most of the staff.

(iii) In Search of Peace

The two papers which had been brought together by the creation of Times Newspapers Ltd, and which were now to live alongside each other, sharing some services though occupying separate buildings connected by a make-shift bridge at first-floor level, were in spite of their similar titles papers of different histories and traditions. The *Sunday Times* was founded in 1822 by Henry White, who adopted the title in the hope of benefiting from the success of the daily paper after he had failed to make any progress with a weekly paper sold under other titles. The paper had an unsettled existence under a variety of proprietors until it was bought by the Berry brothers during the First World War, and it was from the brother who took over the *Sunday Times*, Lord Kemsley, that Lord Thomson bought it in 1959. Editorially it was more casual, adventurous and sensational than *The Times*, as was to be expected from a Sunday paper that did not have to concern itself with the daily record, and as the papers continued to have separate editorial staffs and editors, with their independence assured, the physical link did not produce any substantial new problems. The same was not true of the printing and production side, where the traditions were equally different but, given the need to use the same presses, neither so easy nor so desirable to keep apart.

Until 1961 the *Sunday Times* had been printed under contract by the *Daily Telegraph*, formerly owned by the other Berry brother, Lord Camrose, and latterly by his son, Michael Berry, later Lord Hartwell. Soon after his purchase of the paper Lord Thomson was given notice of the termination of the contract to print the *Sunday Times* in the Fleet Street offices of the *Daily Telegraph*. The original notice was six months, but this was extended to twelve when it was discovered that this was the minimum permissible notice period under the terms of the contract. One year was nonetheless an almost impossibly short time in which to plan, order and install new presses, a composing room and a distribution line in Gray's Inn Road, and to find the staffs to run them. The result was a fight against time which the paper just managed to win, but at the cost of some teething troubles with the new machinery, as the normal proofing period had had to be dispensed with, and reliance on a scratch staff of mainly casual workers.

The Times, on the other hand, was staffed in the production and printing departments by men who proudly described themselves as a Companionship. Many had worked on the paper all their lives, and often their fathers before them. There was a strong tradition of loyalty to the paper, and pride in its achievements, not least in the record of unbroken publication which survived, through wars and the General Strike, until 1955, when together with other national newspapers publication of *The Times* was halted for 26 days by a strike of engineers and electrical workers. The tradition broken, other occasional stoppages followed, particularly after 1966 when the pressure to produce more copies became intense. Nonetheless until the 1970s *The Times* record in industrial relations was substantially better than that of most Fleet Street offices. The deterioration that then set in had many causes and was common to all national newspapers, but in the case of *The Times* the move to Gray's Inn Road was undoubtedly one of the contributary factors. Not only was it unsettling, but it gave staff the opportunity on a day-to-day basis to make comparisons with those alongside whom they now found themselves working. The comparisons created discontent, which in turn led to claims for more money or different working conditions and, on an increasing number of occasions, to disruptive action in support of such claims. In normal times these problems might have been more easily resolved, but for Fleet Street the 1970s were not normal times.

Every newspaper during this period suffered from labour disputes leading to the loss of copies or of complete issues, sometimes for days or weeks on end. Often disputes seemed minor, involving only a small proportion of the employees of the afflicted paper, but because of the protective nature of the labour structure within newspapers a handful of men in almost any department could bring production to a halt on almost any pretext.

The protective organizations of print-workers – known as chapels – have been a part of the printing trade almost from its beginnings, when Caxton set up his wooden press in Westminster in 1476. The origin of the word chapel in the printing trade is unknown, but its structure was based on the association and apprenticeship systems, and evidence that the chapels had established an order of demarcation within the trade at an early date is provided by Benjamin Franklin, who worked briefly in a London printing house in 1725 and found to his wrath that as he moved from one job to another he was required by his fellow workers to pay five shillings as entry to the chapel governing that particular function in the printing house. The prime purpose of the chapel was to protect entry into what was already a well-paid and desirable occupation, so that not too many new recruits came in to dilute the advantages or challenge the security of those already in. But as competition between printing houses grew, and regulation of the industry disintegrated, print workers found that they were no longer satisfactorily protected by chapels within single printing houses. They therefore established links between chapels in different houses, and by the end of the eighteenth century these unions had begun to make deals with employers governing the pay and conditions of their members, as they do today.

The loyalty of the print worker to his union is immensely strong. To it he owes his entry into the trade, his apprenticeship, his job, his rate of pay and his conditions of work. The union will also provide him with opportunities for part-time casual work, on lucrative Saturday shifts for Sunday newspapers for example, and some protection if he is out of work or in dispute. In a modern newspaper office the principal descendants of the old craft unions are the National Graphical Association (NGA), who are most strongly represented in the composing room and the foundry, and the Society of Lithographic Artists, Designers and Engravers (SLADE), a smaller group who make blocks for illustrations. The printing room and clerical workers are mostly made up of members of the National Society of Operative Printers, Graphical and Media Personnel (Natsopa), and the paper handlers and distribution staff are generally members of the Society of Graphical and Allied Trades (SOGAT). Journalists may belong to the National Union of Journalists (NUJ) or to the Institute of Journalists (IOJ) or, in the case of Times Newspapers which is not a closed shop in this area, to no union at all. In addition to these a newspaper office will also need engineers, electricians, carpenters and others who are members of other unions.

The complexity of the labour structure within newspapers is aggravated by the continued existence of many small subordinate chapels within the unions, sometimes comprising no more than a dozen men, dedicated to the preservation of the traditional tasks and financial status of their members, and each forming an individual negotiating unit headed by a father (the printing trade's word for a shop steward). In almost every case the men represented by these chapels carry out some task which forms a vital link in the chain of production and distribution of the newspaper; if any one chapel found itself in dispute, either with management or with another chapel, and refused to carry out its task, the chain would be broken and copies would be lost.

At Times Newspapers in the 1970s there were eight unions and sixty-five chapels operating within the company. *The Times* and *Sunday Times* had been instructed to abide by the Government's pay restrictions by their parent company, the Thomson Organisation, which was vulnerable, because of its oil and travel interests, to Government retaliation if the pay limits were exceeded. The combination of these restraints and the management efforts to cut costs sparked a growing number of stoppages. Other newspapers were known to be breaking the pay restrictions which meant, as the fathers of the chapel were not slow to point out, that their members' wage rates had fallen behind those of their colleagues.

Due to the immensely complicated structure of payments in Fleet Street it is not easy to establish exactly how much printing workers are being paid. Some are paid piece rates, others by time, and in addition there are extra payments for a wide variety of processes – for more pages, extra editions, for the number of tasks that are not carried out but which might have been had they not already been done elsewhere (as for example with advertisements, which are often now prepared by outside printers or processors), and for casual labour that does not always report for duty though the pay packets are made out and shared by those who have been working. Such 'old Spanish customs', as they are called, makes it difficult for management to assess the real rates of pay of some of their staff.

But there is little doubt that by 1978 the pay of the staff of *The Times* and *Sunday Times* was near the bottom of the Fleet Street league. The result was a growing incidence of disruption at Times Newspapers which came to a head in the early part of 1978. During the first three months of the year *The Times* had failed to publish at all on four days and had not completed the full print run of copies on twenty-one nights, while production of its weekly supplements had been disrupted on seven occasions and of the *Sunday Times* on nine. All the disputes had been unofficial, often involving no more than a handful of the total workforce of some 4,300 people. The cost, in terms of lost copy sales and advertisement revenue, was estimated at £2 million. To a paper in *The Times*'s condition, which had only just edged its way back to break-even point, such losses were clearly unendurable.

The Managing Director, Duke Hussey, wrote to all members of the staff on 10 April to explain the problems the papers had been encountering, and he promised action. He also arranged a meeting between the general secretaries of the unions and some of the executive directors of the company, including Dugal Nisbet-Smith, who had become general manager following the death of Harvey Thompson at the beginning of the year, Michael Mander, and the two editors. At this meeting the deteriorating position of the company was explained in considerable detail, and subsequently Hussey sent the union leaders a letter in which he listed the company's objectives for putting things right. These included the securing of uninterrupted production, the establishment of a disputes procedure that would be adhered to and thus eliminate unofficial stoppages, the reduction of manning levels, and the introduction of modern printing techniques and operating methods. As these arrangements would, if achieved, improve efficiency and productivity it would then be possible, under the Government's pay policy, to increase wage levels. Hussey concluded his letter by warning that if agreement on all these proposals had not been reached by 30 November the company would suspend publication of *The Times* and the *Sunday Times* and lay off the staff.

At this stage the management's objectives seemed to have the support, or at least the sympathy of, the union leaders, who had problems of their own in dealing with the indiscipline of their members, but as time went on it became evident that it was not just the national leaders who had to be persuaded, but the individual chapels and their fathers, who had not been consulted in the early stages, and who resented both that and the long interval that followed the imposition of a deadline and the revelation of the company's detailed plans. The delay in the presentation of these plans, which were known as the New Agreement Proposals, was partly caused by difficulty in arranging further meetings with the national union leaders, and by the fact that some of them, notably the NGA, now flatly rejected Hussey's April letter – though the reply from that union was not received until July. A further meeting with the general secretaries was not finally arranged until 18 September, and it was then that the full New Agreement Proposals were presented.

The most sensitive of the proposals concerned the introduction of new technology. An electronic computer-based typesetting system had already been purchased from the Systems Development Corporation in California, and installed ready for use on *The Times*. Among the facilities that the system offered was direct access to typesetting by journalists and the tele-sales staff who typed out classified advertisements, which thus by-passed the Linotype operators in the composing room. The system was already in common use in the United States, but had not been introduced in its fully-developed form in any British national newspaper, and in America it had been brought in by stages. The first step had been to feed the Linotype machines with punched tape; next the Linotype and hot metal were abandoned in favour of what is called 'cold type'; finally, with the introduction of the computer, separate operators were dispensed with and journalists were able to write their stories and set them in type on the same machine with a single keystroke. It was this single keystroke operation which became the main area of conflict in the Times Newspapers dispute. The company regarded it as an essential feature of the New Agreement Proposals. The NGA, who represented the compositors, refused to concede the principle that others should have access to the typesetting process, and accused the company of trying to jump overnight from Caxton to the computer. Although the company agreed, in the course of negotiations, that it would guarantee for a number of years to keep all its NGA men on the payroll, and the NGA agreed to accept a move to cold type, the issue of single keystroking became one on which neither side was prepared to give way. And while this dispute was continuing other unions and chapels were not disposed to hurry into negotiation on the New Agreement Proposals that concerned their particular operations. By 30 November 1978 only nineteen of the sixty-five chapels had reached agreement, and on that day *The Times* published its last issue for forty-eight weeks.

(iv) Times Out

When publication was suspended opinion was divided, both within the company and the unions, about its likely length, but no one imagined that it would last for nearly a year. Even as the papers ceased publication there was hope that they might be back within a week or two. An emergency debate in the House of Commons on 30 November, during which many speakers took up the unions' complaint that there had not been sufficient time to reach agreement, was followed by a decision by the company to postpone for two weeks the sending out of dismissal notices, to provide further time for negotiation after the newspapers had been closed down. But the interval produced little more than further argument about time, and when the two weeks were up dismissal notices were sent to the staff of those chapels which had not settled.

To most of the staff of Times Newspapers the suspension was a shock. One journalist on the *Sunday Times*, Eric Jacobs, an experienced writer on industrial and trades union affairs, and who was subsequently to publish a vivid and detailed account of the dispute, described it as an outrage. The journalists on the papers, he wrote, 'had no quarrel with anybody; our careers were shortened by a year; it was a gross offence against the idea of a free press, since total silence is the severest form of censorship. For others of the staff it was also an outrage, though perhaps of a different kind. Many had been with the newspapers all their working lives. They thought of themselves as *Times* men and women, and the experience of being dismissed seemed likely to leave permanent scars. They would never feel the same about their company again.'*

The Times, in the last days before it was closed, revealed the extent of the damage that had been caused by unofficial disputes during the eleven months of the year. More than fourteen million copies of the papers had been lost; *The Times* had failed to be published at all on nine days and the *Sunday Times* on two; the loss in revenue amounted to nearly four million pounds, which represented a loss in profit of £2,700,000. In a signed article on 29 November William Rees-Mogg

* Eric Jacobs: *Stop Press*, Andre Deutsch, 1980.

said he believed it was the first duty of an Editor of *The Times* not to be the last one, but he nonetheless believed that the policy now being pursued was the right one. 'In 1978 we have given our readers on *The Times* the least reliable service in the history of the paper; all the hard work of ninety per cent of the staff has repeatedly been destroyed by the unofficial and irresponsible action of small groups.' The leading article on the last day of publication was headed 'There will be an interval.'

During that interval almost continuous attempts were made to make progress on the necessary agreements, but once the deadline had been passed there was less cause for urgency on the union side. All the dismissed staff continued to receive pay during their notice periods, and once these had expired most seemed able to find a fair amount of casual work, in part because other Fleet Street newspapers began printing more copies to replace the missing issues of *The Times* and *Sunday Times*, which meant employing more labour recruited for them by their unions. During this period also some other newspapers made arrangements to introduce new technology to their printing processes, though leaving keystroking in the hands of the NGA. Such measures inevitably strengthened the determination of some unions to resist Times Newspapers' New Agreement Proposals. In spite of this attempts to resolve the dispute continued, and in the spring of 1980 the Secretary of State for Employment, Albert Booth, stepped in with proposals that seemed likely to bring about a settlement. But although a target date, 17 April, was agreed for the resumption of publication the day passed without *The Times* appearing. The peace initiative foundered again on the issue of single keystroking.

After five months it had become clear that the policy of trying to resolve all *The Times*'s problems – unofficial stoppages, overmanning, and the introduction of new technology – in one move, a policy known within the papers as the 'big bang', was not working. Following the collapse of the Booth peace plan something new seemed to be needed, something dramatic to break the mould that had hardened round the disputing parties like plaster of Paris. To achieve this effect the company decided to try to publish an international edition of *The Times*. It was felt that producing the newspaper even in the limited form of a weekly edition would be good for the morale of the remaining staff, would remind the world of the paper's existence by providing the paper with an opportunity to report and comment on the forthcoming general election in Britain, and might, if it could be successfully produced in defiance of the unions, persuade them to return to the negotiating table in a more conciliatory frame of mind. With these aims in view *The Times* began to search for a printing house in Europe capable of and willing to produce 80,000 copies of a sixteen-page weekly edition.

In so doing the paper embarked on an adventure that at times combined elements of farce with some of the swashbuckling spirit of *The Times*'s early days and a strong undercurrent of intrigue and violence reminiscent of a novel by John Le Carré. Certainly Smiley's people would have felt more at home than Hussey's as they moved into Europe and found themselves at times having to wear disguises, lay false trails and adopt other furtive activities to try to conceal their intentions from those who had set out to stop them.

The search for a suitable printing works was carried out by Michael Mander. He eventually settled on a company in Frankfurt, a subsidiary of the Turkish daily newspaper *Tercüman* which printed an edition for circulation among Turkish émigrés in Europe, with typesetting to be done by another company, Otto Gutfreund and Sohn, in Darmstadt, about thirty miles away. In conditions of great secrecy preparations began. Journalists were told that they would not have to work on the European edition if they had conscientious objections to it, but on a majority vote the NUJ chapel decided to go ahead. Other unions strongly objected, and the NGA urged its opposite numbers in Europe to find out where publication was to take place and prevent it. Mander himself, like other executives of *The Times* known to be involved in the project, became a marked man and had to resort to wearing dark glasses, a cap and other non-executive clothing to try to avoid being identified on the way to and from Frankfurt.

The cover did not last long, and three days before printing of the first edition was due it was common knowledge that Frankfurt was to be the location and that Gutfreund and *Tercüman* were the printers. The bulk of the printing was to be done on the Saturday night, 21 April, and pickets had begun to gather outside the *Tercüman* building that morning. They grew in number throughout the day and became more aggressive as night fell. Shortly before the presses were due to start petrol-impregnated rags were found stuffed in the machinery, evidently designed to start a fire when the presses rolled. In view of the danger printing was abandoned that night. On the following day the *Tercüman* plant was provided with much stronger police protection, but as it became evident that the start of the printing was likely to set off a riot, it was again decided not to print. The pickets dispersed when this was announced, but after they had gone about 10,000 copies of the new international edition of *The Times* were printed and sold in European cities and in the United States – though not in Britain.

Though the actual production process had been remarkably easy and trouble free, a fact that did not go unnoticed by those who had been putting the paper together, the opposition of the pickets persuaded *The Times* that the adventure was not worth repeating. Perhaps, had the project succeeded, it would have had the desired effect of speeding the process of settlement. As it was three union secretaries did get in touch with *The Times* management shortly after the Frankfurt adventure, and it did demonstrate, as one senior editorial man said, that the paper after five months had not lost the art of creating a newspaper.

Two months later the company tried a new initiative. It was suggested that the issue of keystroking should be set aside, to be settled within twelve months of a resumption of publication, and by agreement not just between the company and the NGA, but with the NUJ and Natsopa as well. And it was decided that the initiative should come from the owners rather than the management of *The Times*. Hitherto the second Lord Thomson, Kenneth, who had succeeded his father as proprietor when Roy Thomson died in 1976, had remained in the background. Kenneth Thomson, who fully accepted his father's commitment to *The Times*, lived in Toronto, where the ultimate holding company of his organization, the International Thomson Organisation, was based, but through the company in Britain, now known as Thomson British Holdings, he supported the efforts of *The Times* to put its house in order. It was the Chief Executive of the organization, Gordon Brunton, who had insisted early in 1978 that Times Newspapers should take some action to resolve the newspapers' problems. In May of that year the financial responsibility for *The Times* had been handed back from the Thomson family to the organization, which was fortunately well placed financially because its revenues from North Sea oil were amounting to some £2 million a month. It was a price Thomson was prepared to pay if, at the end of the day, Times Newspapers could be assured of a secure and profitable future. However to avoid confusion about where ultimate power lay, and in pursuance of the Thomson policy of letting the managers of each company run their own business, the Thomson Organisation did not involve itself directly either in the fashioning of Times Newspapers' strategy or in negotiation with the unions.

After seven months' shutdown and faced with the prospect of continuing stalemate the management of Times Newspapers decided that it might now be beneficial to bring in Lord Thomson and Gordon Brunton. Thomson met union leaders on 29 June at 4 Stratford Place, part of an elegant Adam-style terrace that houses the London headquarters of the Thomson Organisation, and agreement was quickly reached on the formula for setting aside the keystroking issue. But once again the proposed settlement was bogged down among some of the chapels, all of whom were required to endorse the agreement before publication could be resumed. The Natsopa chapels found much to disagree with, and when they had eventually accepted it was on terms which the NGA regarded as upsetting to their traditional differentials. Once again settlement was delayed while negotiations resumed with the

NGA chapels. Finally this apparently endless ping-pong of negotiation was terminated by the gathering in London of the directors of the boards of Times Newspapers and Thomson British Holdings for meetings at which it was believed a decision to close the papers permanently would be taken. Brunton gave the unions a few days' grace and declared that the NGA could have until 4 pm on Sunday 21 October to reach agreement with the company. The final ultimatum had its effect. After a frenzied series of meetings in New Printing House Square agreement was reached with only minutes to spare that Sunday afternoon. On 12 November *The Times* resumed publication.

(v) Up for sale

The shutdown and the final settlement that brought it to an end cost about £40 million. As the company did not achieve all its objectives it was easy to see after the event that the policy of the big bang had been a costly mistake, although some significant gains were made on the production side. There was agreement that the total staff of Times Newspapers should be reduced by some 15 per cent, that larger issues of the *Sunday Times* could be produced, that the presses could run faster, and that some new machinery could be worked, including the transition from hot metal to cold type. The management estimated that, overall, productivity should have been increased by some 30 per cent. Unfortunately even these agreements did not stick. There was victimization by their union of some of the overseers who had stayed at work during the closure to maintain the machines. The new technology did not come into operation, even in the limited way that had been agreed. And both *The Times* and the *Sunday Times* again began to lose copies as one chapel after another found cause for discontent. Once more the company was forced into trying to seek agreements to avoid disputes and losses of production and to allow the working of new technology, as it had been two years earlier and almost as if nothing had happened in the meantime. However there were important differences. There was a new management team. Duke Hussey had become Deputy Chairman to Denis Hamilton, and had been succeeded as Chief Executive by James Evans, a director of Thomson British Holdings. Michael Mander had left to become Managing Director of Thomson Magazines Ltd. Dugal Nisbet-Smith had been appointed Managing Director. Following the experience of the shutdown there was less expectation that the problems could be resolved, and as the recession of 1980 deepened the losses of *The Times* grew more heavy. Even the *Sunday Times*, because of the failure to meet its print runs on so many occasions, began to seem vulnerable, and by the middle of the year Times Newspapers, facing an expected loss of some £12 million, was dependent on Thomson British Holdings for money to keep it going. Once again the money was provided, but it was becoming increasingly clear that the parent organization no longer viewed its commitment as unlimited.

Having invested so much money for so little return it seemed unlikely that the organization would now be prepared to lose the small gains that had been achieved, and as *The Times* and the *Sunday Times* slipped back towards the old routine of disruption it was not long before the papers were again plunged into crisis. The moment came in August, 1980, when the journalists on *The Times* went on strike.

The immediate cause was the rejection by the management of an arbitrator's recommendation that journalists' pay should be increased by 21 per cent. In July the company had proposed an increase of 18 per cent, with a total increase of 27 per cent over eighteen months. This was rejected by the NUJ chapel, and as the company refused to pay more, the issue was put to arbitration, though neither side was prepared to agree in advance that the decision should be binding. The arbitrator took the view that the ability of the company to pay wage increases was not the concern of the employees, and recommended an immediate increase of 21 per cent. This the company refused to accept. On the morning of 22 August, while Denis Hamilton, who had been asked to return from holiday in Italy to talk to the journalists, was still in an aircraft en route to London, the NUJ chapel met and voted to strike. Although the number voting represented a minority of the total editorial staff, not all of whom were members of the NUJ, and although there was a sufficient number of editorial staff willing to go on working and well able to produce the paper, it was believed that the NGA would not co-operate with any attempt to continue publication. So *The Times* once more was brought to a halt.

The strike only lasted a week, and it was settled virtually on the terms offered by the company in July. But its effect was fatal to the Thomson ownership. Roy Thomson had always said that so long as he had the support of the journalists he would continue to fund *The Times*, and his son repeated that pledge. The editorial staff had been paid and had their jobs protected throughout the previous year's stoppage, and on resumption of publication they had had a 45 per cent settlement to catch up on the lean years. To Kenneth Thomson the decision of the journalists to strike seemed like a betrayal. He was bewildered by it, and concluded that if the paper had lost the loyalty of its journalists then he could fairly be absolved from his own commitment to it.

After a series of meetings in the weeks following the journalists' strike the board of Thomson British Holdings decided that there was no alternative but to put the papers up for sale. On 22 October 1980 Gordon Brunton announced that the organization had decided to withdraw from publishing *The Times*, the *Sunday Times* and the supplements, and to try to sell the papers. He added that if a suitable buyer could not be found the papers would be closed down in March 1981.

In his public statement Brunton made clear that the main reason for the board's decision was the continuing industrial disruption following the resumption of publication in November 1979. He also revealed that since the formation of Times Newspapers in 1967 more than £70 million had been advanced to the company from Thomson sources, and that in the current year a pre-tax loss of some £15 million was expected, with further borrowings of £22 million from Thomson British Holdings. On the same day Lord Thomson said that the decision had been reached with great regret. 'My father and I have repeatedly made it clear that our continued support for Times Newspapers was conditional on the overall co-operation of the newspaper employees, and I have sadly concluded that this co-operation will not be forthcoming under our ownership,' he said. 'It grieves me greatly that in spite of the millions of pounds which have been provided to Times Neswapers over the years to enable these newspapers to survive, and in spite of the efforts of many loyal employees who have built the papers to their present eminence, and to whom I express my deep gratitude, we have been unable to secure the co-operation of important sections of the workforce on a reliable and consistent basis. I believe that a change of ownership could provide Times Newspapers with the opportunity to create a new and constructive relationship with its staff.'

The task of finding a new owner was not going to be easy. The troubles of Times Newspapers had been well publicized, and though the prestige of owning *The Times* was still attractive the experience of the two Lord Thomsons, and of Lord Astor before them, suggested that the cost of ownership was likely to be high. Nor, though Thomsons naturally wanted to recover some of its losses, was price the sole, or even the main, criterion. Gordon Brunton made it clear that in seeking a new owner the national interest, as well as the interests of the share-holders, staff, advertisers and readers, would be taken into account. To ensure that this was so the national directors of Times Newspapers were brought in to act as assessors together with Denis Hamilton, the two Editors, William Rees-Mogg and Harold Evans, and Lord Astor of Hever. The four national directors were Lord Dacre (Regius Professor of History at Oxford, better known as Hugh Trevor-Roper), Lord Greene (formerly Sid Greene of the National Union of Railwaymen), Lord Robens (former Labour Cabinet Minister and Chairman of the Coal Board) and Lord Roll (Chancellor of Southampton University and a Director of the Bank of England). They were given four guidelines by which to examine possible purchasers. The first of these was their commercial and managerial record, particularly in the newspaper business (it was assumed that the most likely candidates would already be involved in newspaper publishing). Second was their acceptability to

Parliament, staff and trade unions, and the assurances they gave about preserving the editorial independence of the papers. Third was their will and determination. And fourthly was the question of their financial resources.

To ensure that genuine offers came in before the March deadline for closure Thomsons ruled that prospective bidders must lodge their offer by 31 December 1980. By the time this first deadline arrived bids had been received from a surprising number of organizations, both within the United Kingdom and from overseas. Only three of them were ultimately treated as serious contenders. They were Lord Rothermere of Associated Newspapers, 'Tiny' Rowlands of Lonrho, and Rupert Murdoch of News International. The three were reduced to two when Lonrho asked for a second extension of the deadline, a request which Thomsons refused, having already agreed to one. Of these Associated Newspapers put in the higher offer – £25 million, plus payment of redundancies and the year's losses. News International's offer was £12 million, plus coverage of redundancies and losses. But Thomsons saw problems about selling to Associated Newspapers. Publishers of the *Daily Mail*, it was known that they were keen on acquiring a Sunday newspaper, and clearly the *Sunday Times* would admirably satisfy this desire. The question was, did they want *The Times*? Thomsons did not receive assurances adequate enough to persuade them that the future of *The Times* was guaranteed – in fact they were told that no such assurances could be given. The offer of News International was therefore accepted, and on 22 January Gordon Brunton announced that conditional agreement had been reached for the transfer of ownership of all the titles.

The agreement was conditional for two reasons. First, Rupert Murdoch had to complete negotiations with the unions representing the staff of Times Newspapers. Secondly, there was the question of whether the sale to Murdoch, who already owned the daily paper with the largest circulation in Britain, the *Sun*, and the paper with the biggest Sunday circulation, the *News of the World*, of two additional national newspapers was against the public interest. There was no doubt that the arrangement would bring about a greater concentration of ownership of national newspapers than had yet been experienced in this country, and there were many who believed that the deal should be referred to the Monopolies Commission, under the provisions of the Fair Trading Act of 1973, as had the Thomson purchase in 1966. However it was also recognized that the offer would probably fall through if the arrangements were delayed for the amount of time it would take for the Commission to conduct its hearings. The Act did not require reference to the Commission if the businesses concerned were uneconomic, and as the Department of Trade concluded in this case that Times Newspapers was not a going concern the Secretary of State, Mr John Biffen, decided to agree to the transfer of ownership, and after an emergency debate on 27 January the House of Commons supported him with a majority of 42.

The Minister gave his consent subject to a number of conditions which Murdoch readily agreed to, and which were in fact in line with undertakings he had already given to the Thomson vetting committee. These were that the system of independent national directors would be preserved and their number increased, that the independence and authority of the Editors were guaranteed, each being free to make his own decision on matters of opinion and news, that Editors would be appointed or removed only by the agreement of the majority of the independent national directors, that the Editors would not be subject to instruction from either the Proprietor or the management on the selection and balance of news and opinion, that they had the right to refuse to publish any advertisement, and that they would make all appointments to the journalist staff. It was also agreed that any future sale of any of the papers would require the agreement of a majority of the independent national directors. These safeguards were to be incorporated in the company's articles of association, and any change would require ministerial consent.

The completion of the sale now only required the conclusion of agreements with the unions on manning levels and work practices. After three weeks of tough bargaining these were agreed on 12 February. A voluntary redundancy scheme was accepted for some 563 full-time staff, representing a reduction of about 20 per cent of the workforce, and a move to electronic photo-composition was agreed by the NGA chapels The three supplements were henceforth to be printed outside London. With the completion of these negotiations, during which both sides made concessions, the new proprietor, the fifth in the history of *The Times*, was ready to take command.

Rupert Murdoch, an Australian whose father, Sir Keith Murdoch, was a distinguished journalist and newspaper owner, was forty-nine when he became owner of *The Times*. He was educated at Geelong Grammar School and Oxford University and learnt his journalism on a number of papers in England before returning to Australia to begin his career as a newspaper proprietor. He made his early reputation as an aggressive publisher of popular newspapers, but he also founded *The Australian*, a serious national quality newspaper. He came back to Britain in 1969 to acquire control of the *News of the World* and the *Sun*, and in the 1970s moved into the American newspaper business to buy the *New York Post*, *New York Magazine* and the *Village Voice*. By the time he acquired *The Times* and *Sunday Times* he had thus established sizable business operations in three continents. His decision to take on *The Times* when two wealthy proprietors had had to give it up was, as the paper itself noted, an act of considerable courage. But it was also the act of a determined man who, as a shrewd entrepreneur and a newspaperman of great experience, had every reason to know what he was doing. After operating and launching newspapers all over the world, he said, he regarded this new undertaking as the most exciting challenge of his life.

At the first meeting of the new board of Times Newspaper Holdings Sir Denis Hamilton was appointed as an independent national director, and agreed to remain as Chairman for a limited period, to ensure continuity. He handed over the chairmanship to Rupert Murdoch and resigned from the board before the end of the year. Others who joined the board at its inception were Sir Edward Pickering, Vice-Chairman of the Press Council and a former Editor of the *Daily Express*, Lord Astor of Hever, Lord Drogheda, former Chairman and Managing Director of the *Financial Times*, Lord Catto, Chairman of the merchant bankers Morgan Grenfell, and Richard Searby Q.C., a director of The News Corporation of Australia, the ultimate parent company. Two journalist directors were also appointed – Louis Heren, Deputy Editor of *The Times*, and Peter Roberts, Managing Editor of the *Sunday Times*. As William Rees-Mogg had already indicated that he did not wish to continue his editorship one of the board's first duties was to decide on a new Editor for *The Times*. From within the organization the favoured candidates were Louis Heren and Charles Douglas-Home, the Foreign Editor, and Harold Evans, Editor of the *Sunday Times*. The choice fell on Evans, who took over the chair at the beginning of March 1981.

The new Editor had already earned a high reputation for his work on the *Sunday Times* and before that as Editor of the *Northern Echo* in Darlington. Born in Manchester in 1928, the son of an engine driver, Harry Evans became Editor of the *Sunday Times* in 1967. He was already well-known as a thoroughly professional journalist and a tireless campaigner, and he employed both these gifts to the full in making his mark on the Sunday paper, which throughout his term conducted a series of spectacular investigations and exposés, including the Savundra car insurance fraud, sanctions busting in Rhodesia, and the thalidomide case, the details of which the *Sunday Times* was only able to publish after the case had been taken to the European Commission for Human Rights. At *The Times* Evans began at once to make his presence felt. Radical changes were made to the make-up of the paper and many new features introduced, including the spread of news to the back page and the creation of a daily 'Information Service'.

These editorial changes were made in spite of continuing disruption to production of the paper. During 1981 copies of *The Times* were lost on several occasions, and threatened stoppages were frequent. The rumbling crisis came to a head in February 1982 when Rupert Murdoch announced to the staff of *The Times* and the *Sunday Times* that both papers would be closed down unless a further six hundred redundancies were agreed within days. In a letter to all members of the permanent staff he said that he had had no meaningful response to a request to the chapels in November for further staff reductions, with the result that the company faced a loss of £15 million in the current year. 'As Times Newspapers Limited stands today,' he wrote, 'we are literally bleeding to death.' After a month of negotiations it was agreed that a total of 430 full-time jobs would go, and these, together with some productivity agreements and the introduction of photo-composition, would save the company an estimated £8 million during the year. It was, the Chairman said, a base on which to build for the future, and he lifted the threat to close *The Times*.

The easing of this crisis was rapidly followed by a convulsion on the editorial side of the paper. The costly changes introduced by the Editor had been accompanied by a substantial number of new senior editorial appointments. Not all of these were welcomed by the existing editorial staff, whose responsibilities sometimes seemed to be in conflict with those of the new appointments. The result was confusion and a divergence of loyalties within the editorial team that went well beyond the creative tension normally to be found in newspaper offices. Matters came to a head early in 1982 when both the Deputy Editor, Charles Douglas-Home, and the Managing Editor, John Grant, tendered their resignations. The Chairman refused to accept them, and instead asked Evans for his resignation and appointed Douglas-Home to succeed him. After a few days of disorder on the editorial floor, when Evans declared that he was not resigning and continued to occupy the Chair, it was finally confirmed on 15 March that he had indeed resigned at the Chairman's request and that the independent national directors had been asked to approve the appointment of Douglas-Home. The board confirmed the appointment of the new Editor, the twelfth in the history of *The Times*, two days later.

The change restored a semblance of dignity and stability to the editorial department. Charles Douglas-Home had been on the paper for seventeen years, first as defence correspondent and then in a number of senior positions, including Features Editor, Home Editor, Foreign Editor and Deputy Editor. He was thus experienced in all the main editorial departments of the paper, and had earned the respect of his colleagues during many difficult years. Born in 1937, he was educated at Eton and first entered journalism as a general reporter on the *Scottish Daily Express*. Speaking to the staff after his appointment was announced Douglas-Home made clear that there would be no going back on the changes his immediate predecessor had made to the paper. 'My style will be slightly more stable, more mechanical,' he said. 'I hope that the machinery of the paper will be well oiled and will function; that there will be a routine and a rhythm about things which I am trying to get established on a daily, weekly and monthly basis.'

After the alarms of the previous five years no one was inclined to dispute the need for a period of tranquillity for *The Times*. Neither tranquillity nor stability are qualities normally associated with newspapers, which thrive on the turmoil of events and tend to reflect the same characteristic in reporting them. As has been seen *The Times* during its long and often turbulent history has always seemed at its strongest, and in greatest demand, when events were critical. On such occasions its authority and accuracy have served the nation well. Its reputation may have suffered during the traumas of the 1970s and early 1980s, when so much of its thunder was directed upon itself, but it survived, and retained its unique character, forged from many historic struggles and from the ideals of so many men and women of courage and integrity. While such people exist and continue to work for *The Times*, its story should have no end.

INDEX

THE
Universal
Printed Logographically

LONDON
TUESDAY
MAY 3 1966

ROYAL EDITION

The   Tim

N°. 46,253

LONDON, SATURDAY, OCTOBER 1; 1932

ROYAL EDITION

THE

No. 46,254